How are children's social lives at sch achieve and how do motivational and s children's adjustment at school? This volume, featuring work by leading researchers in educational and developmental psychology, provides new perspectives on how and why children tend to thrive or fail at school. The individual chapters examine the unique roles of peers and teachers in communicating and reinforcing school-related attitudes, expectations, and definitions of self. Relations of children's school adjustment to school motivation, interpersonal functioning, and social skillfulness are also explored.

The developmental and social perspectives on motivation and achievement presented in this volume provide new insights into the complex processes contributing to school success. This book will be vital reading for educators and developmental psychologists interested in the contextual as well as intrapersonal processes that contribute to social and academic competence.

Social motivation

Understanding children's school adjustment

Cambridge Studies in Social and Emotional Development

General Editor: Martin L. Hoffman, New York University

Advisory Board: Robert N. Emde, Willard W. Hartup, Robert A. Hinde, Lois W. Hoffman, Carroll E. Izard, Nicholas Blurton Jones, Jerome Kagan, Franz J. Mönks, Paul Mussen, Ross D. Parke, and Michael Rutter

Social motivation

Social motivation

Understanding children's school adjustment

Edited by

Jaana Juvonen
University of California at Los Angeles

Kathryn R. Wentzel
University of Maryland

Published by the Press Syndicate of the University of Cambridge
The Pitt Building, Trumpington Street, Cambridge CB2 1RP
40 West 20th Street, New York, NY 10011-4211, USA
10 Stamford Road, Oakleigh, Melbourne 3166, Australia

First published 1996

Printed in the United States of America

Library of Congress Cataloging-in-Publication Data

Social motivation : understanding children's school adjustment / Jaana
  Juvonen & Kathryn R. Wentzel, eds.
       p.   cm.
    Includes bibliographical references and indexes.
    ISBN 0-521-47324-1 (hc). — ISBN 0-521-56442-5 (pb)
       1. Achievement motivation in children.   2. Achievement motivation
  in adolescence.   3. Student adjustment.   4. Social desirability in
  children.   5. Social desirability in adolescence.   6. Peer pressure
  in children.   7. Peer pressure in adolescence.   8. Motivation in
  education.   I. Juvonen, Jaana.   II. Wentzel, Kathryn R.
  BF723.M56S63   1996
  155.42'438—dc20   95-47456
                                                                  CIP

A catalog record for this book is available from the British Library

ISBN 0-521-47324-1 (hc)
ISBN 0-521-56442-5 (pb)

To our parents,
Ulla-Maija and Jaakko Juvonen,
Ruth and Herman Wentzel

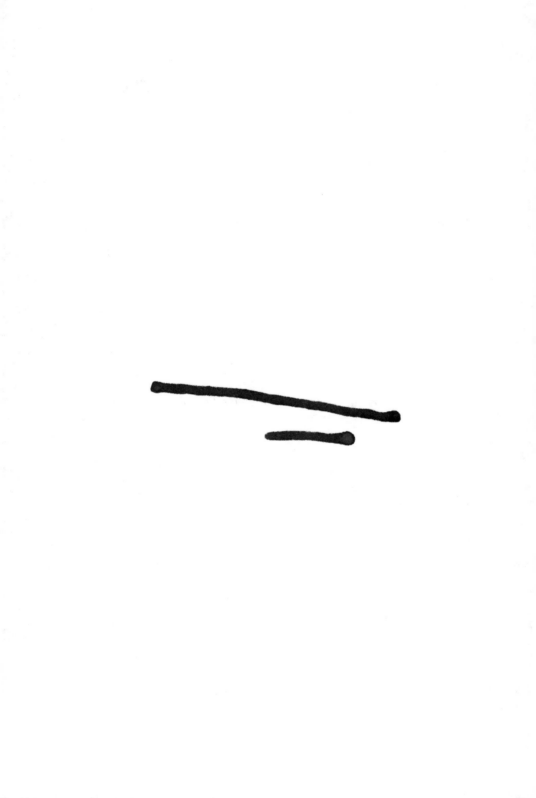

Contents

Contributors

Thomas J. Berndt
Department of Psychological Sciences
Purdue University
West Lafayette, IN 47907

Sondra H. Birch
Department of Educational Psychology
University of Illinois
1310 S Sixth Street
Champaign, IL 61820

Kathy S. Buchele
Department of Psychology, CB#3270
University of North Carolina
Chapel Hill, NC 27599

Colin Comfort
Faculty of Education
University of British Columbia
2125 Main Mall
Vancouver BC, Canada 6VT 1Z4

Carol S. Dweck
Department of Psychology
Columbia University
119th St. and Amsterdam Ave.
New York, NY 10027

Cynthia A. Erdley
Department of Psychology
University of Maine
Orono, ME 04469

Martin E. Ford
Graduate School of Education
George Mason University
4400 University Drive
Fairfax, VA 22030

Ellsworth Gibson, Jr.
Department of Psychology
Portland State University
P.O. Box 751
Portland, OR 97207

Sandra Graham
Graduate School of Education
UCLA
405 Hilgard Ave.
Los Angeles, CA 90095

Susan Harter
Department of Psychology
University of Denver
2155 South Race St.
Denver, CO 80208

Shelly Hymel
Faculty of Education
University of British Columbia
2125 Main Mall
Vancouver BC, Canada
6VT 1Z4

Jaana Juvonen
Department of Psychology
UCLA
405 Hilgard Ave.
Los Angeles, CA 90095

Keunho Keefe
Reiss-Davis Child Study Center
3200 Motor Ave.
Los Angeles, CA 90034

Thomas A. Kindermann
Department of Psychology
Portland State University
P.O. Box 751
Portland, OR 97207

Janis B. Kupersmidt
Department of Psychology, CB#3270
University of North Carolina
Chapel Hill, NC 27599

Gary W. Ladd
Department of Educational
    Psychology
University of Illinois
1310 S Sixth Street
Champaign, IL 61820

Tanya L. McCollam
Department of Psychology
Portland State University
P.O. Box 751
Portland, OR 97207

Patricia McDougall
Faculty of Education
University of British Columbia
2125 Main Mall
Vancouver BC, Canada 6VT 1Z4

Kimberly Schonert-Reichl
Faculty of Education
University of British Columbia
2125 Main Mall
Vancouver BC, Canada 6VT 1Z4

Dale H. Schunk
1446 LAEB Room 5108
School of Education
Purdue University
West Lafayette, IN 47907

Constantine Sedikides
Department of Psychology, CB#3270
University of North Carolina
Chapel Hill, NC 27599

Mary Ellen Voegler
Department of Psychology, CB#3270
University of North Carolina
Chapel Hill, NC 27599-3270

Bernard Weiner
Department of Psychology
UCLA
405 Hilgard Ave.
Los Angeles, CA 90095

Kathryn R. Wentzel
Department of Human
    Development
University of Maryland
College Park, MD 20742

Barry J. Zimmerman
Graduate School
City University of New York
23 West 42nd Street
New York 10036

Preface

The idea for this book developed over the last few years, when we found ourselves at the same conferences, assigned to the same sessions, presenting research on children's and adolescents' social relationships in school. We felt that it was time to pool our efforts and invite others to join us to write about achievement motivation and social functioning, not as two distinct topics, but as interrelated aspects of school adjustment. We both believed that students' acclimation to school is colored by their social experiences – an aspect that had often been neglected, especially in educational research. Furthermore, motivational approaches open up new ways to interpret interpersonal interactions and relationships in the classroom – an observation that has not been widely acknowledged in research on social development.

While editing this book, there was an increase in interest in social influences in the school setting. We want to especially thank all our contributors for their enthusiasm. The authors were at different phases of their social-motivational thinking; some were at the planning stage, while others were in the process of compiling further data and extending their prior findings. We welcomed this variability in conceptualizations that quite accurately reflected the current state of research in this area. Throughout the editing process, we appreciated the encouragement and support from our friends at the University of Delaware and the University of Maryland. Also, we want to acknowledge the support for our own research from the National Academy of Education Spencer Fellowship Program and the Office of Educational Research and Improvement Fellows Program. Finally, thanks are extended to Bernard Weiner for his encouragement and support as well as to Khanh-Van Bui for her assistance.

Jaana Juvonen
Kathryn R. Wentzel

Foreword

Bernard Weiner

In the middle 1940s, David McClelland and his coworkers initiated what might be considered the first systematic experimental research pursuing issues in human motivation. An early goal they set for themselves was to develop a measure of human motives in order to identify individuals differing in motive strengths. A thermometer metaphor guided this work. It was reasoned that a "good" thermometer would register an increase when the heat was turned on. In a psychological context, the idea was to manipulate some antecedent that would produce an increase in motive strength under arousal conditions, as opposed to contexts in which there was no stimulating occurrence.

In achievement contexts, it was reasoned that failure would function to galvanize achievement needs. Thus, some individuals failed at an achievement task, whereas others succeeded or were given a nonachievement-related activity to perform. Then the thermometer was thrust into the mouth (or, in this case, in front of the eyes) of the individual to ascertain if increased motivation was registered. The measuring device selected was a projective instrument called the Thematic Apperception Test (TAT). Indeed, stories to TAT cards did contain more achievement imagery following failure than after success or some control experience. In this manner, it was deemed that an appropriate instrument to assess achievement desires had been developed. It therefore also followed that when persons respond to the TAT under neutral or nonaroused conditions, those with higher scores are "walking around" aroused; that is, they are more motivated to achieve than those exhibiting lower scores in this neutral context.

This conclusion led to hundreds of studies in the achievement domain, followed by many others that may not have used the TAT but nonetheless had the goal of illuminating our understanding of achievement strivings. Indeed, achievement has been the focus of research in human motivation, incorporating self-related affects and cognitions including pride, probability of success, ego-orientation, and the like.

This same line of reasoning was applied to the study of affiliative motivation. It was believed that if the TAT was a good thermometer to assess achievement needs, then it also should be able to register affiliative tendencies. The question then became what antecedent, what "source of heat," in the affiliative domain would be analogous to achievement failure; that is, what would arouse affiliative concerns. The procedure selected was to gather individuals from a fraternity and have them stand before others and be rated on their desirable and undesirable qualities. After doing this, the TAT was administered and the content was scored for affiliative motivation. This proved to be a source of great heat, and the TAT did register increased affiliative concerns after this experience. The heat was so intense, however, that persons being rated by others experienced severe stress and anxiety, some broke into tears, and the ethics as well as the efficacy of the procedure was called into question. Notice that this did not happen following an achievement failure – that was merely a small blaze, not a forest fire.

A number of long-lasting effects on the field of motivation resulted in part from this early history:

1. Researchers focused their efforts on the field of achievement motivation, partially because it lent itself to experimental manipulations.
2. Researchers drew away from affiliative motivation, partially because it was perceived as not lending itself to experimental study.
3. Achievement and affiliation were thought of as very distinct motivations: their interaction and interplay were not considered.

This book begins to redress this imbalance and counter misperceptions. Here we see that achievement and affiliation are intertwined. Feelings of rejection, lack of support, and dissatisfaction of affiliative needs affect achievement motivation and school performance. For example, students lonely and isolated in the classroom are likely to give up achievement strivings, and drop out of school. In addition, one's achievements influence with whom one will affiliate. For example, students with similar achievement strivings tend to form friendships and peer groups, and those whose behavior is consistent with the values of their instructors are approved by their teachers. Finally, peers provide students with models for appropriate academic as well as social conduct.

It also is apparent that experimental manipulations pertinent to the study of affiliation are quite possible. But even more evident is that procedures are available that can be used in field settings that enable the study of affiliation and social influences in real-life contexts.

I regard this book as a landmark volume that not only gives affiliative motivation its proper role and respect, but also should be of great benefit to researchers in the achievement field, where I believe new life-lines are necessary. Peer and other social influences cut across motivational domains, including achievement, aggression, and virtually all other motivational systems. Thus, there is potential for a general theory of motivation that has affiliation – the establishment and maintenance of social bonds – at its very core.

1 Introduction: New perspectives on motivation at school

Kathryn R. Wentzel

The social worlds of children are a pervasive and influential part of their lives at school. Each day in class, children work to maintain and establish interpersonal relationships, they strive to develop social identities and a sense of belongingness, they observe and model social skills and standards for performance displayed by others, and they are rewarded for behaving in ways that are valued by teachers and peers. We also know that children who display socially competent behavior in elementary school are more likely to excel academically throughout their middle and high school years than those who do not (see Wentzel, 1991).

Our purpose in bringing together the authors for this volume was to enrich this portrayal of how children's social and academic development are intertwined. We asked the contributors to focus on specific ways in which children are influenced by and motivated to achieve things social as well as academic when they are at school. In response, the authors provided us with a diverse set of unique perspectives on social aspects of motivation. Collectively, however, the various perspectives bring to the forefront the range of social outcomes that children strive to achieve at school and consider ways in which these outcomes contribute to and in fact represent valued aspects of school adjustment. In doing so, many of the authors emphasize the important role of social goals, self-referent beliefs, and social cognitions in explanations of school-related competence. In addition, the social motivational perspectives presented in this volume draw attention to the need for models of school success that consider not only intrapersonal processes as motivators of behavior but the critical role of interpersonal relationships and social concerns as well.

In general, research has paid little attention to the possibility that children's social development is related to classroom motivation and school adjustment. Indeed, much of the recent work on motivation at school portrays children as striving to achieve primarily intellectual outcomes in response to academically-related aspects of curriculum and instruction (see,

1

e.g., Ames & Ames, 1989). The empirical work presented in this volume, however, attests to the fact that children are motivated to achieve social as well as academic goals at school and that indeed, school children often behave in direct response to their social environments. We hope, therefore, that the work presented in this volume will provide inspiration and a challenge to continue research and theory development on social motivational perspectives and in doing so, further understanding of children's lives at school.

Themes of the volume

The social motivational perspectives presented in this volume reflect several broad themes. At the outset, the authors remind us that children must be socially as well as intellectually adept if they are to be successful students. The chapters provide multiple definitions of school adjustment, ranging from academically-related outcomes such as attitudes, values, and motivational orientations towards school (Berndt and Keefe; Birch and Ladd; Harter), task engagement (Kindermann, McCollam, and Gibson), self-regulation (Schunk and Zimmerman), grades and test scores (Wentzel), and dropping out (Hymel, Comfort, Schonert, and McDougall), to social and personal outcomes such as the quality of interpersonal relationships with peers (Kupersmidt, Buchele, Voeller, and Sedikes), prosocial and antisocial behavior (Erdley; Ford; Wentzel), self-esteem (Harter), and public presentations of the self (Juvonen).

In addition, ways in which students' social goals and related psychological functioning can either facilitate or hinder school adjustment are examined. In particular, the authors highlight the social goals and motives that underlie school adjustment, including needs for belongingness and relatedness (Birch and Ladd; Hymel et al.), needs for social approval (Juvonen), in addition to needs for admiration, self-enhancement, and verification (Berndt and Keefe), goals to achieve prosocial and socially responsible outcomes (Erdle; Ford; Wentzel), and orientations toward intrinsic and extrinsic rewards (Harter).

Several authors also discuss how needs and goals can vary as a function of levels of difficulty and proximity (Schunk and Zimmerman), aspects of social integration (Ford), and the importance and type of relationship children have with their peers (Kupersmidt et al.). Other aspects of intrapsychological functioning that facilitate goal pursuit also are considered. Self-efficacy and self-regulatory skills (Erdley; Schunk and Zimmerman), attributions (Erdley; Juvonen), agency beliefs, emotions (Ford), self perceptions (Harter), and social cognitions (Erdley; Juvonen; Schunk and Zimmerman; Wentzel) are presented as processes that are central to the successful accomplishment of goals and the realization of personal needs.

Finally, interpersonal relationships with teachers and peers are described as potentially powerful social contexts that motivate student behavior. Although social relationships are considered to be the central motivational forces underlying socialization and social development (Baumeister & Leary, 1995; Hartup, 1989; Maccoby, 1992), their role in motivating school success (or failure) has not been studied in systematic fashion (see work by Eccles (1993) and Epstein (1989) for noteworthy exceptions). Therefore, in addition to focusing on intrapersonal influences such as social goals and social cognitions, the authors also focus on interpersonal relationships with teachers and peers as motivatiors of school success.

The chapters in this volume present several ways in which social relationships provide school-aged children with motivational contexts for development. Several authors explore the motivational impact of group membership by focusing on ways that peer groups and classroom teachers communicate and reinforce specific values and attitudes toward school, behavior, and even definitions of the self (Berndt and Keefe; Harter; Juvonen; Kindermann et al.; Kupersmidt et al.; Schunk and Zimmerman). Dyadic relationships are also discussed, with specific mention of ways that friendships with peers and teacher-student relationships influence social goal pursuit (Kupersmidt et al.; Wentzel), satisfy social needs (Berndt and Keefe; Birch and Ladd), and promote healthy social-emotional and intellectual functioning (Berndt and Keefe; Birch and Ladd; Hymel et al.; Kupersmidt et al.; Wentzel).

Finally, several chapters in this volume illustrate how social relationships influence or motivate student behavior, depending on the specific functions they serve. For example, they provide students with emotional support and nurturance (Birch and Ladd; Hymel et al.; Kupersmidt et al.; Wentzel). Relationships are also portrayed as sources of information – about the self, about the expectations and values of others, and about how to accomplish specific tasks (Berndt and Keefe; Harter; Juvonen; Kindermann et al.; Schunk and Zimmermann).

Challenges to the field

The notion that social concerns and influences are relevant for understanding motivation and academic performance is certainly not new. In the early 60s, the need for Affiliation, identified by McClelland (1987) as a central motive in people's lives, was linked to academic performance independent of need for Achievement (McKeachie, 1961). Crandall's work (1963) related classroom achievement to children's need for social approval, and Veroff (1969) proposed that social comparison was an integral part of motivation to achieve in school-aged children.

More recently, theory and research has focused on motivational factors embedded in learning contexts. Research on classroom reward structures (Ames, 1984; deCharms, 1984), organizational culture and climate (Maehr and Midgley, 1991), and person-environment fit (Eccles and Midgley, 1989) has greatly expanded our understanding of how the social environments within which learning takes place can motivate children to learn and behave in very specific ways. Theories of motivation once again recognize social and affiliative concerns as basic goals and needs that underlie student achievement (Connell & Wellborn, 1991). We believe that the perspectives presented in this volume contribute to and extend this work by focusing on the motivational significance of *social*-psychological functioning and the more proximal contexts of interpersonal relationships.

We hope that the perspectives introduced in this volume provide the field with new questions and challenges for understanding motivation and adjustment at school. For instance, can models of motivation traditionally used to understand skill and task-related performance be used to understand the development of social competence? Juvonen's extension of attribution theory to the domain of social information processing and social behavior provides one example of how this can be accomplished. Berndt and Keefe's use of expectancy-value theory to understand the role of friendships in school adjustment provides another. Ford's Motivational Systems Theory illustrates how general principles of motivation can be applied to the social domain of caring.

We might also ask how theories of socialization and social development can inform models of motivation and school adjustment. Work described in chapters by Harter and Schunk and Zimmerman illustrates how social role expectations and modeling can be powerful socializers of self processes that motivate academic behavior. Chapters by Birch and Ladd, and Wentzel suggest how family socialization processes known to promote healthy social and emotional development might also reflect mechanisms by which teachers and peers motivate social competence as well as academic excellence in the classroom.

A consideration of interpersonal relationships as motivational contexts clearly introduces additional levels of complexity to models of motivation. Using theories of social cognition and identity development, several authors suggest that the degree to which relationships are influential depends in part on the unique perspectives and belief systems of the individual (Harter), and the degree to which the individual can identify with socialization agents (whether they are teachers or peers) along certain dimensions (Juvonen; Schunk and Zimmerman). Other authors suggest that when relationships do form, they operate as systems that have qualities separate from those of the individuals that form the relationship (Berndt and Keefe; Birch and Ladd).

When considered as a whole, the perspectives presented in this volume suggest that further exploration of social-cognitive and other social psychological factors, and identification of variables that capture the quality of relationships and social contexts, must take place before the nature of "social" motivation can be understood fully. Commentaries by Dweck and Graham suggest that perhaps even more elaborate models of motivation might be necessary to accomplish this task. Carol Dweck provides us with a complex and dynamic model of psychological processes that underlie accomplishments in both social and academic domains of functioning. Using an attributional perspective, Sandra Graham highlights the role of emotions in describing the mechanisms that link interpersonal relationships to social cognitions and student behavior. Both Dweck and Graham remind us that the search for specific mechanisms and processes that can explain social influences on motivation and behavior is still in its inception and remains a challenge for the field. We hope that the chapters in this volume will provide the impetus for continued efforts in this regard.

Overview of the chapters

Although there was considerable overlap in themes and perspectives across the eleven chapters, we divided the book into two sections. The first set of chapters focuses primarily on intrapsychological processes that motivate school adjustment.

Susan Harter provides a developmental perspective on three aspects of school adjustment, intrinsic/extrinsic dimensions of motivation, self-esteem, and students' "voice." In her discussion of these outcomes, Harter draws particular attention to the need to study change over time, individual differences in student's perceptions of and reactions to change, and the role of teachers and peers in the social construction of the self.

Jaana Juvonen discusses school adjustment in terms of children's understanding of implicit norms for social conduct. Drawing on attribution

2 Teacher and classmate influences on scholastic motivation, self-esteem, and level of voice in adolescents

Susan Harter

The classroom setting represents not only an educational arena but a powerful social context in which the psychological adjustment of children and adolesents can be affected. This chapter will focus specifically on the role played by teachers and classmates. Teachers not only instruct, but serve to represent and communicate a particualr educational philosophy, including the standards by which students will be evaluated. They not only provide feedback regarding students' academic performance, but have a major impact on students' motivation to learn. Not only do they convey specific approval or disapproval for scholastic achievement, but teachers communicate their more general approval or disapproval for the child as a person (see Birch & Ladd; Wentzel, this volume). Classmates serve as potential companions and friends, meeting important social needs of the developing child. However, they also represent a very salient social reference group that invites intense social comparison. In addition, the approval or disapproval that classmates display can have a major effect on a child's or adolescent's sense of self (see also Berndt & Keefe; Kindermann, et al. this volume).

In this chapter, I will examine the impact of teachers and classmates on three constructs that represent different indices of adjustment within the school context. These include: (a) intrinsic and extrinsic motivation for classroom learning, (b) self-esteem, and (c) level of "voice," namely the ability to express one's opinions in the classroom. Specific attention will be given to the antecedents and mediators of the constructs, leading to an emphasis on individual differences. Such an approach forces one to question the reality of certain generalizations that have dominated the literature, for example, that most students lose their intrinsic motivation as they move through the school system, that self-esteem suffers in early adolescence, particularly for girls, and that at this same developmental juncture, girls' voices go underground. A consideration of the determinants of these

11

constructs will enhance our understanding of individual differences and highlight the need to exercise caution in promoting or accepting such generalizations.

Intrinsic/extrinsic motivation

The distinction between intrinsic and extrinsic motivation has proved viable not only as a framework for predicting and interpreting behavior, in general (deCharms, 1968; Deci, 1975; Deci & Ryan, 1985; Lepper, Greene, & Nisbett, 1973) but for understanding children's behavior within the educational setting, in particular (deCharms, 1976; Condry & Koslowski, 1979; Connell & Ryan, 1984; Eccles & Midgley, 1988, 1990; Eccles, Midgley, & Adler, 1984; Harter, 1981, 1992; Harter & Connell, 1984). With regard to the classroom context, investigators have posed the question of whether a given child's motivation to learn is driven by an intrinsic interest in the subject material, by curiosity and preference for challenge, or by an extrinsic orientation in which one is motivated by the desire to obtain grades, to win teacher approval, to avoid censure, namely, to meet the external demands of the school system.

In our own work, we were initially interested in the developmental course of these motivational constructs. The instrument that we first developed to tap intrinsic versus extrinsic orientation in the classroom (Harter, 1981), pitting these orientations against one another in the following manner. We first identified three components: (a) preference for challenge versus preference for easy work assigned, (b) curiosity or intrinsic interest versus getting grades/pleasing the teacher, and (c) independent mastery versus dependence on the teacher. Thus, we were interested in (a) does the child like hard, challenging work *or* does the child like the easier assignments and school subjects, (b) does the child work to satisy his/her own interest and curiosity *or* does the child do schoolwork in order to merely satisfy the teacher and obtain the desired grades, and (c) does the child prefer to figure out problems or difficult assignments on his/her own *or* does the child rely on the teacher for help and guidance, particularly when it comes to figuring out challenging problems or assignments.

The particular question format we developed for this instrument directly pits these orientations against one another, as alternative choices. Thus, children are presented with a two-part statement that reads: If a school subject is hard to understand, some kids want the teacher to explain it to them BUT Other kids would like to understnd it for themselves. The respondent is first asked to decide which of the two alternative children described in each part of the item are most like him/her, and then asked to indicate whether that statement is "Really true for me" or just "Sort of true for me." Items are scored on a four-point scale, where 4 is the most intrinsic and 1 is the most extrinsic. It should be noted that the question content is not specific to any particular school subject matter or context, since it was our intent to assess a child's *general* orientation to classroom learning.

With regard to developmental differences, our own work (Harter, 1981) has demonstrated a systematic, grade-related shift from a predominantly intrinsic motivational orientation in third grade to a more extrinsic motivational orientation by ninth grade. Scores in third grade ($M = 3.10$) reveal that children are intrinsically motivated. However, scores systematically decline over the grade school years, such that in junior high school, scores hover around 2.25, revealing an extrinsic orientation. The biggest drop is between sixth grade ($M = 2.60$) and 7th grade ($M = 2.30$).

Other cross-sectional developmental data document a similar pattern of decreasing intrinsic interest in learning as a function of grade level, particularly with the shift to junior high school (Brush, 1980; Eccles & Midgley, 1988, 1990; Eccles et al., 1984; Harter, 1981; Simmons & Blyth, 1987; Simmons, Blyth, & Carleton-Ford, 1982; Simmons, Rosenberg, & Rosenberg, 1973). Gottfried (1981) has documented such a decline in intrinsic motivation at seventh grade for specific school subjects, namely reading, science, math, and social studies.

Several psychological analyses of the causes of such shifts have now emerged. In our own work, we initially speculated that students face the demands of a school culture that increasingly reinforces ans external motivational orientation, especially through grading practices (Harter, 1981). Thus, as the educational focus gradually shifts to the products of one's learning, evaluated through grades, children adapt to this reward system, and their interest in the learning process itself declines.

Eccles and her colleagues (Eccles & Midgley, 1988, 1990; Eccles et al., 1984) have provided a much more complete analysis of the possible reasons why children's attitudes toward school learning and achievement become increasingly negative as they progress through the school system, identifying specific changes in the school environment as critical. Their earlier reviews suggested that with the transition to junior high school, the school environment becomes more impersonal, more formal, more evaluative, and more competitive than in the elementary grades. It is primarily the teachers who communicate these changing values and standards. There is also increasing emphasis on social comparison as students come to be graded in terms of their relative performance on standardized tests and assignments and as information about individuals' performance levels becomes more public. Moreover, teachers are perceived as having increasing control over evaluative outcomes. Nicholls (1979) specifically highlights the implications of such changes for the self, suggesting that they lead students to focus on the assessment of their *ability*, rather than on the learning task itself. He argues that this change in focus, in turn, has a negative impact on children's motivation to learn.

More recently, Eccles and her colleagues (Eccles & Midgley, 1988, 1990) have elaborated on their analysis in the form of a model of person-environment *fit*. They suggest that the *lack* of fit between the junior high school environment and the needs of young adolescents contributes to the documented shift toward more negative self-evaluations and attitudes toward school learning. They note that teachers become more controlling, just at the point that adolescents are seeking more autonomy. In addition, the teacher-student relationship is becoming more impersonal at the same time that students, in their bid for autonomy, increasingly need the personal support of adults other than their parents. Finally, various forms of social comparison are increasingly promoted, just as adolescents are entering a period of heightened self-consciousness.

Although these analyses provide a general framework for understanding grade-related changes in motivational orientation, they do not speak to (a) the longitudianl study of actual change over time within the same individuals, to (b) possible individual differences in students' reactions to educational transitions, or to (c) students' perceptions of the postulated changes in the academic environment. In our most recent work, we have begun to address each of these concerns.

Patterns of change upon entrance to junior high school

Employing a seven-month longitudinal design, we first examined the motivational orientation of 6th grade elementary school children in the spring of the academic year, before their transition to junior high school. We then retested them in December of the following school year, several months after the shift to the new school environment. Based on preliminary findings, we questioned whether all students would react to such a transition with declines in intrinsic motivation, as the literature had implied. Rather, we suspected that individual children would react differently to the environmental changes accompanying school transitions. More specifically, we anticipated that three groups of students would emerge: those whose intrinsic motivation would *decrease*, those whose intrinsic motivation would actually *increase*, and those who would report *no change* in motivational orientation. This is precisely the pattern that the data revealed (Harter, 1992; Harter, Whitesell, & Kowalski, 1992).

With regard to the factors that may cause or produce stability or instability in motivational orientation over time, we have focused on how educational transitions initially impact *perceived scholastic competence*, which in turn influences motivation. Our studies have consistently revealed that motivational orientation and perceived scholastic competence are very highly related (Harter, 1981a; 1981b; Harter & Connell, 1984; Harter & Jackson, 1992). Thus, students who evaluate their competence positively will typically report that they are intrinsically motivated, whereas those with negative perceptions of their competence will invariably report that they are extrinsically motivated.

With regard to factors that impact students' perceptions of their competence as a function of the transition to junior high school, our model identifies the influences of both teachers and peers. Specifically, we anticipated that with the transition to junior high school, particular teacher and classmate factors would serve to cause scholastic competence to become more *salient* as well as susceptible to change. With regard to the impact of teachers, our analysis draws upon the observations of Eccles and her colleagues, cited earlier (Eccles et al., 1984; Eccles & Midgley, 1988, 1990). Thus, we anticipated that hypothesized grade-related change in educational practices, namely, teachers' greater emphasis on grades, their greater focus on competition and on control, which leads to heightened external evaluation of performance, coupled with teachers' decreasing personal interest in students, should lead students to reevaluate their sense of competence.

Classmate influences should also contribute to such reevaluation. Typically, there are several elementary feeder schools from which junior high school students are drawn. A significant portion of the seventh grade junior high school class, therefore, will be students whom one did not previously know. Thus, the social reference group is widely expanded, requiring that students reassess their competence in relationship to members of this new social comparison group. This increasing emphasis on social comparison within the junior high school environment also serves to foster a reevaluation of one's scholastic competence, relative to the abilities of the new cohort of classmates. These comparisons can have devastating psychological effects for a large number of students who conclude that they are relatively incompetent, compared to those at the top. This general model is presented in Figure 2.1.

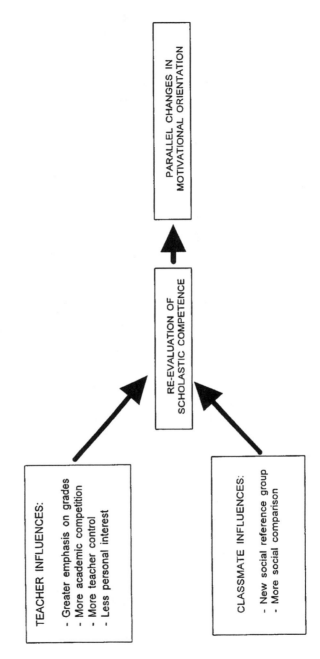

Figure 2.1. Model of teacher and classmate influences on perceived scholastic competence and motivational orientation.

In our longitudinal study we anticipated, therefore, that a certain percentage of students facing this school transition would alter their perceptions of competence, some feeling more competent in the new environment and some feeling less competent. We also expected that there would be a subgroup of students who would maintain stable perceptions of competence. Our findings supported these predictions in that approximately 50 percent of the students reported either substantial increases or decreases in their perceptions of competence, whereas the remaining 50 percent maintained relatively stable estimates of their academic abilities.

The hypothesis that change in perceptions of competence should predict parallel changes in motivational orientation, was also supported by our findings, as can be seen in Figure 2.2. Increases in perceived competence were associated with increases in intrinsic motivation, decreases in perceived competence predicted declines in intrinsic motivation, and students reporting no change in perceived competence manifested negligible changes in motivational orientation. One could certainly argue that the causal factors on our model, namely teacher and classmate influences, also have a *direct* impact on motivational orientation, undermining intrinsic motivation for many, but by no means all, students. However, that the mediational role assigned to perceived competence would seem to best explain the *individual differences* in motivational orientation that we have obtained.

Student's awareness of changes in the educational environment

Our interpretation of transition-related changes in children's academic self-concepts and motivational orentation rests heavily on the assumption that changing educational practices instituted by teachers caused the evaluation of one's ability to become more salient, particularly in the face of a new social reference group to whom one's performance can be compared. However, do students actually *experience* the types of alterations in the academic environment that Eccles and her colleagues have identified? Since students are the direct recipients of the educational practices that have been interpreted as changing, it seemed essential to examine students' perceptions directly.

To address this issue, we conducted a follow-up study in which we asked middle school students to compare their school environment in the current year to that of the previous year (Harter, Whitesell, & Kowalski, 1992). Students rated a number of dimensions, including importance of grades, level of competition, teachers' emphasis on the products of learn-

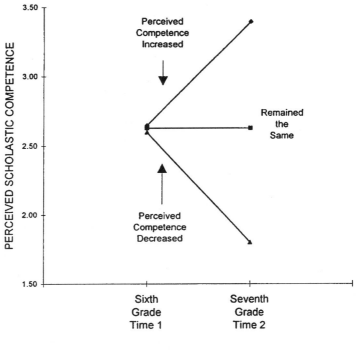

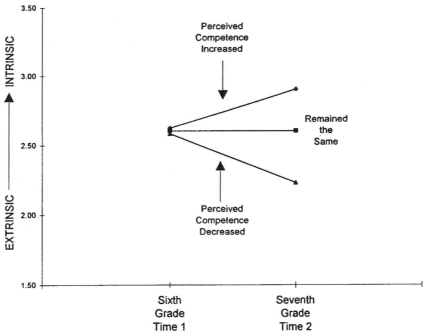

Figure 2.2. Relationship between changes in perceived competence and changes in motivational orientation.

ing (i.e., knowing the correct answer), teacher control, preoccupation with ability, and social comparison. They provided two sets of ratings, one for their current educational environment, and one for the previous school year.

The findings revealed that the vast majority of middle school adolescents reported the types of changes observed by Eccles and her colleagues. In comparing educational practices in their current school environment to those in the previous school year, these students perceived a definite increase in competition, focus on grades, external evaluation, teacher control, and concern with their academic ability. These subscales, which formed one factor, were rated 3.23 (on a four-point scale) for students' current school year compared with 2.83 for the previous school year. Moreover, the absolute values of these scores are also noteworthy, since they document students' perceptions of considerable emphasis on external evaluation.

Less dramatic, although significant, increases in social comparison were reported (2.88 for the current school year compared with 2.60 for the previous school year). We suspect, however, that social desirability response tendencies restrain students from admitting that they use social comparison information. Ruble (1983) has reported that while social comparison increases as students move up the academic ladder, students' willingness to admit that they are engaging in it decreases. In previous studies, we have also found that students acknowledge only modest use of social comparison information. However, when we have asked young adolescents to give specific examples of classmates at six different levels of scholastic competence, they have no trouble identifying the academic level of every student in their class! Thus, if is clear that they are well aware of differences in the scholastic ability of their peers, and where they stand by comparison.

In general, therefore, it would appear that students recognize that the educational climate shifts as they move up the acadimic ladder. They report their awareness of a constellation of changing teacher behaviors that undermine perceptions of competence and intrisic motivation as well and increased use of social comparison. These perceived changes would appear to provide sufficient impetus for students to reexamine, and possibly alter, their perceptions of competence, thus producing the pattern of individual differences to school transitions that were reported above.

We have, most recently, refined our measure of students' perceptions of the educational climate that is fostered by teachers and classmates, in order to further investigate these issues. We were particularly interested in students' perceptions of why students lose their intrinsic motivation. Thus, we asked them to respond to a number of reasons why they felt that students get turned off to schoolwork, why they may not be interested in learning, why they wouldn't be curious, and why they might not want to figure things out on their own. This most recent instrument contains seven subscales, and places more direct emphasis on the role of teachers as the conveyers of educational values and standards. Four of the subscales define one factor that concerns dimensions of external evaluation. These were (a) *Grades* ("The teachers put too much emphasis on grades"; "Teachers seem more concerned about the grades students get than about what they are learning"); (b) *Competition* ("Teachers expect students to compete too much with their classmates"; "Students have to compete with each other to get good grades"); (c) *Control/choice* ("The teachers don't give students enough say or choice in the schoolwork they do"; "Teachers don't let students decide what work they want to do"); (d) *Lack of personal interest* ("Teachers don't really care that much about the students and their feelings"; "Teachers don't seem that personally interested in students as people").

A separate subscale tapped *social comparison* ("The teachers let students know how well everyone in the class is doing"; "Teachers make students' grades too public by letting others know how they have done on tests and assignments"). In addition, we added two new subscales. One tapped the extent to which students were turned off to schoolwork because it was deemed *boring* or *irrelevant* ("Most of the schoolwork is pretty boring"; "Schoolwork just isn't that important or relevant to students' lives"). Another directly tapped the perception that feeling *stupid* was a motive for becoming turned off to schoolwork ("The students are not doing that well and it makes them feel stupid"; "Students feel like they are dumb because they don't do well at their schoolwork").

We examined these components in a large middle school population (6th, 7th, 8th grades) drawing from lower-middle and middle-class families. Figure 2.3 reveals systematic grade differences for all four components, where the differences between sixth and seventh grades are somewhat bigger than between seventh and eighth grades. With increasing grade level, students perceive teachers to be more evaluative. In addition, students report increasing emphasis on classmate social comparison. Interestingly, the higher the grade level, the more students feel that schoolwork is boring and irrelevant. Finally, the higher the grade level, the more students endorsed "feeling stupid" as a motive causing one to be turned off to schoolwork. Of further interest was the finding that the more stu-

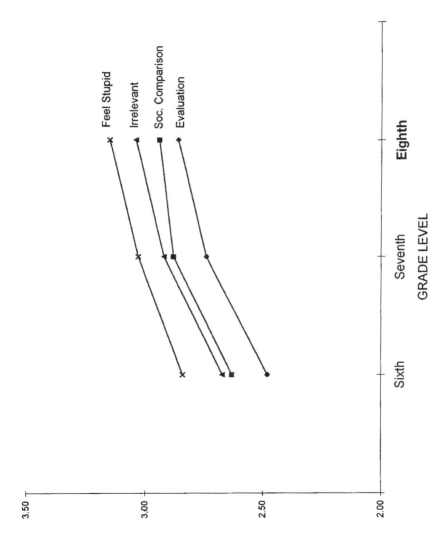

Figure 2.3. Relationship between changes in perceived competence and changes in motivational orientation.

dents felt that teachers emphasized the components of external evaluation, the more they reported feeling stupid as a motive undermining intrinsic interest ($r = .48$). Thus, the pattern supports the contention that students are aware of the dimensions that have been hypothesized to undermine perceptions of both scholastic competence and intrinsic motivation, and feel thay they increase in intensity across the middle school years.

In this study we also asked *teachers* to rate these same items, ratings which we could compare to students' perceptions. Not surprisingly, perhaps, teachers ($M = 2.07$) did not feel that they were emphasizing the external evaluation components nearly as much as did students ($M = 2.69$). Nor did teachers ($M = 2.22$) feel that they were making social comparison as salient as did students ($M = 2.81$). Teachers ($M = 2.91$) did agree with the perceptions that students feel that schoolwork is boring and irrelevant ($M = 2.87$). In so doing, teachers would appear to be placing the onus for lack of interest in learning on students who fail to see the importance of schoolwork. Finally, teachers ($M = 2.86$) and students ($M = 2.90$) agreed that if students felt stupid, it would undermine their intrinsic interest in schoolwork. However, there was no evidence that teachers felt that their educational practices might contribute to students' experience of stupidity.

In this same study, we were interested in whether there was a relationship between students' perceptions of their educational environment and their own self-reported motivational orientation. We hypothesized that students low in intrinsic motivation (and high in extrinsic motivation) would be more likely to report negative environmental influences than would students high in intrinsic motivation (and low in extrinsic motivation). That is, those low in intrinsic motivation (and high in extrinsic motivation) would be more likely to report that teachers' focus on external evaluation (for the combination of emphasis on grades and competition, lack of student choice and personal interest in students), that social comparison is more salient, that schoolwork is irrelevant or boring, and that feeling stupid will undermine one's interest in school learning. Our predictions were based on the assumption that students who perceived their environment to stifle intrinsic interest in learning would be less likely to display such interest.

As Figure 2.4 reveals, this is precisely the pattern we obtained. All comparisons revealed marked differences that were highly significant ($p < .001$). Moreover, the general finding that lowered perceptions of scholastic competence are associated with a more extrinsic orientation ($M = 2.63$) was replicated. Intrinsically-oriented students reported considerably higher levels of competence ($M = 3.38$). With regard to the focus of this chap-

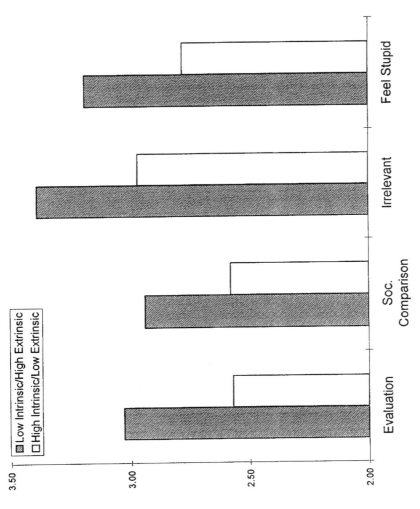

Figure 2.4. Perceptions of the social/educational environment as a function of motivational orientation.

more highly). Thus, in order to obtain classmate approval, one must be good looking, likeable, and athletically talented. Our more comprehensive causal modeling efforts further confirm this conclusion in that perceived adequacy in these three domains is highly predictive of classmate support (Harter, Whitesell, & Marold, 1991). However, as noted in the discussion of perceived scholastic competence, there may be natural limitations to one's ability to improve in these areas, preventing them from garnering the classmate approval that is so critical to self-esteem. (See other chapters in this volume by Erdley, Juvonen, Kindermann et al., Kupersmidt et al., and Ladd & Birch, which offer additional models for children's lack of peer support).

Within the school context, it is classmate support that is most critical to self-esteem; however, the impact of teacher support is not trivial. The correlations between teacher approval and self-esteem may actually underestimate the influence of a given teacher in a child's life, since our questions asked them about support from teachers in general. Anecdotal evidence makes it clear that among middle school and junior high school students, who have different teachers for different school subjects, some teachers may be perceived as far more supportive than others. Our procedure did not allow us to make this discrimination, however. Thus, in the future it would be instructive to have separate ratings on different teachers in order to determine whether some have a greater influence on self-esteem than others.

Evidence from our laboratory further reveals that teacher support may serve to compensate for low parent support. Thus, students who reported both low parent and low teacher support had self-esteem scores of 2.57. However, students with low parent support who reported high teacher support had self-esteem scores of 2.80, a significant difference. The additive nature of parent and teacher support could be observed at moderate and high levels of parent support, where higher teacher support resulted in higher levels of self-esteem.

The directionality of the link between classmate approval and self-esteem

Although the correlation between approval from various sources and self-esteem would seem to support the symbolic interactionist position in which the opinions of others are presumed to impact one's self-evaluation, one can also raise the issue of whether one's self-evaluation impacts one's perceptions of the opinions of others. Felson (1993) addresses this very issue. He observes that it may well be that, in contrast to the looking glass formulation in which the opinions of others are internalized and therefore dictate one's level of self-esteem, that one's level of self-esteem may be driving what one perceives to be the opinions of others. He reports a series of studies revealing that children who like themselves assume that their parents' and peers' reactions to them are favorable, leading to an alternative interpretation which he terms the "false consensus effect." That is, one falsely, perhaps, assumes that others share your own view of the self. Although the label "false" seems a bit pejorative, it is highly likely that both effects, internalization of others' opinions as well as assumptions that if one likes the self, others in turn will manifest their approval, are operative.

We became particularly interested in this issue with regard to the "generalized other," operationalized as classmates in our studies. We have discovered that there are *individual differences* in the directionality of the link between classmate approval and self-esteem, differences which have a predictable pattern of correlates (Harter, Stocker, & Robinson, in press). We first became intrigued with the issue of whether adolescents consciously endorse a looking glass self metatheory, meaning that they acknowledge that they need to have other people evaluate them positively in order to like themselves as a person (our definition of self-esteem). The competing metatheory is that if one likes oneself as a person, then others will necessarily like or support the self, as well. Thus, with regard to the directionality of effects, in the first case, approval precedes self-esteem whereas in the second, self-esteem precedes approval.

We initially demonstrated that there are adolescents who endorse each of these metatheories about the directionality of the causal links between approval and self-esteem. Moreover, a third group emerged, namely adolescents who reported that there was no relationship between the approval of others and how much one liked oneself as a person. Important to these distinctions were adolescents' open-ended verbal descriptions, which converged with their directionality choice. Looking-glass self subjects generated explanations such as: "If other kids approve of me and say good things about me, then I look at myself and think I'm not so bad, and I start liking myself"; "By having other people approve of you it gives you self-confidence and so you like yourself"; "If other people don't like me as a person, then I wonder if I am a good person, I care about what people say about me"; "If nobody liked you, you probably wouldn't like yourself very much." It is of interest that this group appears to couch their descriptions in the language of the "generalized other," making reference to people, kids, and to others in general, rather than particular people.

Those reporting that their self-esteem precedes approval from others provided such descriptions as: "If I like myself as a person, then I know that the other kids will feel pretty much the same"; "You have to appreciate yourself first, as a person, if you wait for other people to make you feel good, you could be waiting a long time!"; "The way I figure it, if you can't like the person you are first, then how do you expect other people to like you?"; "If you like yourself, and feel good about yourself, other kids will like you more."

The third group denied that there was any link between approval from others and self-esteem. Sample descriptions were: "If someone doesn't like me, they can't make me feel bad if I'm confident enough about myself, what they think doesn't matter"; "I really don't care if someone doesn't like me because its their problem"; "It doesn't matter what other people think of me, it doesn't have anything to do with how much I like myself."

Having established the meaningfulness of these three groups of adolescents, each of whom had very different metatheories about the link between approval and self-esteem, we next sought evidence for a predicted pattern of correlates. We specifically hypothesized that there would be certain liabilities associated with the endorsement of a looking-glass perspective, at this particular developmental level. The pattern of findings supported our predictions. First, those endorsing the Approval to Self-esteem directionality (the looking-glass self subjects) reported significantly greater preoccupation with peer approval than the Self-esteem to Approval group, with the No Connection group reporting the least preoccupation.

The findings also revealed that the looking-glass self subjects reported greater *fluctuations* in perceived peer approval and self-esteem, compared to either of the other two groups. While adolescence, as a general developmental period, tends to usher in volatility in the self-concept (Harter, 1986; Harter & Monsour, 1992; Rosenberg, 1986) those basing their self-esteem on peer approval would appear to be particularly vulnerable to changes in self-esteem. Given that they are basing their self-esteem on what they perceive to be fluctuating peer approval, it is understandable why their self-esteem should fluctuate, in tandem.

Of further interest was the finding that looking-glass self adolescents also reported a lower *level* of peer approval than those in the Self-esteem to Approval group. Given this pattern, we also hypothesized that the level of *self-esteem* should be lower for the looking-glass self subjects, given that by definition, they are basing it on peer approval. Finally, the liabilities of a looking-glass self orientation extend beyond mere perceptions, in that teachers observed behavioral ramifications in the classroom. Teachers' ratings revealed that the looking-glass self students were more likely to be socially distracted from their scholastic activities, which may be due to their preoccupation with peer approval. (The No Connection group were the least distracted.)

The pattern reveals that there are clear liabilities associated with the endorsement of a looking-glass self model in adolescence. It is important to point out that *developmentally*, a looking-glass self model represents an important mechanism through which opinions of others come to impact the self. However, the healthiest developmental course would appear to be one in which the standards and opinions of others are eventually internalized, such that truly *self*-evaluations become the standards that guide behavior. When or if one reaches this stage, one endorses a directionality orientation in which how one evaluates the self will impact others' opinions of the self.

What is it that might prevent individuals who endorse a looking-glass self model in adolescents from pursuing the path to internalization? At this time, we can only speculate. The developmental history of such individuals may have been characterized by more parental disapproval, inconsistent or fluctuating approval, or support that was *conditional* upon meeting the demands of others. Such a history could lead to preoccupation and concern over support, perceptions of lower and fluctuating support, which in turn would lead to lower and fluctuating self-esteem. There would also appear to be some parallels between the looking-glass self group and the "preoccupied" or anxious ambivalent attachment style, as well as between the Self-esteem Precedes Approval group and the securely attached style. Moreover, many of the No Connection style subjects who indicated that they did not *care* about the opinions of others suggests a defensive posture reminiscent of the "dismissing avoidant" attachment style (Bartholomew, 1990). Thus, future research may do well to focus on those child rearing antecedents identified by attachment theorists, given their view that early relationships with caregivers provide working models of self and others that children carry into relationships with peers.

Suppression of voice

The third construct to be examined is students' ability to express their opinions. Our interest in this topic emerged in the course of our research on the emergence of "false self behavior" during adolescence (Harter, Marold, Whitesell, & Cobbs, in press). False self behavior involves acting in ways that do not reflect one's true self as a person, the "real me." In their open-ended descriptions, adolescents frequently describe false self behavior as "not saying what you think," "expressing things you don't really believe or feel," "not stating your true opinion," "saying what you think other people want to hear." These observations converge with what Gilligan and her colleagues (Gilligan, 1982; Gilligan, Lyons, & Hanmer, 1989) have referred to as "loss of voice," namely the suppression of one's thoughts and opinions. Gilligan finds loss of voice to be particularly problematic for *females*, beginning in adolescence.

Gilligan observes that before adolescence, girls seem to be clear about what they know and most are able to express their opinions forcefully. However, with the onset of adolescence, many cover over what they knew as children, suppressing their voice, diminishing themselves, and hiding their feelings in a "cartography of lies." For Gilligan, there are several compelling motives leading females, beginning in adolescence, to silence their voices. During this developmental transition, adolescent girls begin to identify with the role of "woman" in the culture. They quickly perceive that the desirable stereotype of the "good woman" involves being nice, polite, pleasing to others, and quiet if not shy. In what is still largely a patriarchal society, they observe that women's opinions are not sought after, not valued, not supported. Therefore, their own voice begins to go underground. Moreover, many girls observe these behaviors in their own mothers, who serve as role models for how women in this culture should act. Thus, they identify with their mothers, whom they observe to be suppressing their own opinions; they accept their role as women, and eventually come not only to not *speak* their minds but to not *know* their own minds. Thus, they no longer even have an opinion.

Gilligan also describes another constellation of proximal motives that derive from the relational impasse in which adolescent girls find themselves. Given the importance of connectedness to others for females, in particular, behaviors that threaten relationships are to be avoided at all costs. Thus, beginning in adolescence, females compromise their authenticity, they take themselves out of "true relationship," in order to preserve connectedness in some lesser form. If they were to speak their mind, express their true voice, it may well cause tension in the relationship, make the other person angry, hurt others' feelings, and, at worst, lead others to abandon them altogether. Thus, they opt not to take the risk of rejection or relationship dissolution.

Gilligan's analysis is quite provocative, and her observations, including interviews and dialogues with adolescent girls, clearly reveal that for many female adolescents, suppression of voice becomes the only path through which they can preserve relationships. However, Gilligan's efforts have not resulted in any systematic analysis of the prevalence of loss of voice among females, nor has she chosen to address these issues in adolescent males. To what extent are their individual differences in the expression of voice, and what factors might be predictive of such differences, in males as well as females?

We have recently begun to address these issues in our own research. In our initial study, we included young adolescent females and males, ages 12 through 15, in grades 6,7, and 8 of a middle school (Harter, Waters, & Gonzales, 1994). We were particularly interested in level of voice in three different relational contexts, namely, with close friends, with peers (people of the same age who were not close friends), and with teachers in the classroom. A sample item tapping level of voice with peers was as follows: "Some kids usually don't say what's on their mind or what they're thinking to people their age *BUT* Other kids *do* say what's on their mind or what they're thinking to people their age." Subjects first select the kind of kids that they are most like, and then indicate whether that choice is "Really True for Me" or "Sort of True for Me." Items are scored on a four point scale where 1 equals the lowest level of voice and 4 the highest. (The content of the items was identical for close friends and teachers.)

In order to begin to explore the potential causes of individual differences in level of voice, we speculated that endorsement of gender role stereotypes in the form of femininity, masculinity, and androgyny may well be an important predictor. We hypothesized that for females, in particular, individual differences in level of voice would be related to their sex-role orientation. Specifically, those endorsing a feminine orientation (and eschewing the masculine role model) should report greater loss of voice than those endorsing either an androgenous (high femininity, high masculinity) or a masculine-only orientation. We reasoned that those with a feminine orientation would be most likely to adopt the relational values of the "good female" in our society, which in turn would dictate suppression of voice.

Feminine sex-role items adapted from Boldizar (1991) included "I care about what happens to others," "It makes me feel bad when someone else is feeling bad," "I am a gentle person," "I'm good at understanding other people's problems," "I like small babies and children a lot," "I am a kind and caring person." Masculine items included "When I play games, I like to win," "I can control the other kids in my class," "I make a strong impression on most people I meet," "I am sure of my abilities," "I am a leader among my friends."

With regard to level of voice across the three different relationships, the findings revealed that overall, young adolescents are most outspoken with their close friends ($M = 3.11$), followed by peers ($M = 2.75$), and then teachers (2.63). As Gilligan has observed, it is within one's relationship with closest friends that voice should most likely be expressed, consistent with our findings. Levels of voice were virtually identical for boys and girls in their relationships with close friends and peers. Thus, in these contexts there is no evidence, as Gilligan implies, that loss of voice is a particular problem for females. However, with regard to voice with teachers, the adolescent females did report significantly less voice ($M = 2.49$) than did males (2.77). Just why female students, in particular, are reluctant to express their opinions to teachers is an interesting topic to which we shall return.

Of greatest interest were the findings related to sex-role orientation, particular with regard to voice with peers. As hypothesized, those females who were high on femininity and low on masculinity reported significantly lower levels of voice ($M = 2.49$) than those who were androgenous ($M = 2.86$). The small number of females reporting only a masculine orientation reported even higher levels of voice ($M = 3.06$). Thus, it definitely appears that gender role orientation is a powerful factor determining individual differences in voice among female adolescents. For adolescent males, the pattern was somewhat comparable in that the small number of boys who endorsed a feminine orientation reported lower levels of voice ($M = 2.73$) than those endorsing either the androgenous ($M = 2.93$) or the masculine ($M = 2.97$) orientation.

The findings suggest, therefore, that gender role *orientation*, rather than gender, per se, appears to be a major factor contributing to level of voice among young adolescent males and females. Those of either gender who adopt feminine sex-role stereotyped behaviors are at greater risk for lower levels of voice. Whether those who suppress their voice in adolescence have actually *lost* their voice is an interesting question for further study. That is, at what point in development might such a relationship emerge? Might it be that we would find individual differences related to gender role orientation during mid to late childhood, such that at even earlier stages of development the adoption of a feminine sex-role stereotype (for females and males) puts one at risk for the expression of one's opinions? These are intriguing questions that we plan to address in our future work.

Lack of voice in the classroom

Given the focus of this volume, our findings on voice in the classroom, around both teachers and classmates, seem particularly pertinent. As noted above, in a middle school sample, voice with teacher was lower than voice with peers and close friends, and this effect was more marked for females. In a more recent sample of adolescent girls in an all-female high school, Johnson (1994) found that voice with teacher was lower than voice with close friends, parents, or classmates. The only group Johnson noted with whom voice was lower than with teachers was boys in social situations.

These findings are very timely, given observations from the AAUW report (1992) and the work of the Sadkers (Sadker & Sadker, 1994) demontrating that girls are shortchanged in our school system. According to these reports, girls receive less attention, less encouragement, less opportunity to develop their ideas, and less support for their abilities from teachers in the classroom, compared to boys. From our perspective, one logical outcome would be loss of voice around one's teachers, given the hypothesized lack of support or validation.

However, one needs to be cautious in making generalizations about a given gender. Our own findings reveal tremendous individual differences within gender. As noted above, gender role orientation is a more powerful predictor than gender per se. In Johnson's dissertation, it was hypothesized that perceived *support* for voice would also predict self-reported level of voice. Support for voice was operationalized by items stating that others were interested in what they had to say and encouraged them to express their opinions. In order to examine the combined effects of gender orientation and support for voice, we first identified two groups within our all-girls high school sample, those who could be categorized as *feminine* and as *androgynous*. (The masculine group was too small to include in these analyses.) We divided subjects within each of these two groups into three levels of support for voice, low, medium, and high support. For the purposes of this chapter, we will report the findings for voice with teachers and voice with classmates (although the patterns are quite similar across the other relationships, namely males in social situations, parents, and close friends).

The patterns for voice with teachers and with classmates are presented in Figure 2.5. The additive effects of gender orientation and level of support are quite clear. As in our middle school study, we find that the feminine girls report considerabley lower levels of voice than do the androgynous girls. Moreover, within each of these gender orientation groups, the effects of support for voice are systematic and quite striking. Low perceived support for voice results in lower levels of voice than does moderate support, which in turn results in lower levels of voice than does high support. The differences between the extreme groups are also very dra-

(Jordan, 1991; Jordan, Kaplan, Miller, Stiver, & Surrey, 1991; Stiver & Miller, 1988) also refer to the lack of zest and related depressive symptoms that accompany the suppression of one's authentic self. This constellation in turn, limits one's ability to achieve one's potential, to make meaningful contributions to society, and to be productive in one's chosen areas of endeavor. Thus, identifying those factors that lead both females and males to suppress their true selves is an important step in hopefully preventing loss and lack of voice in children, adolescents, and adults. The school context is a particularly powerful arena warranting intervention with children and adolescents.

Conclusions

I began with an exploration of those factors that may serve to attenuate students' intrinsic interest in learning, focusing on both teacher and classmate variables. It would appear that a constellation of factors identified by Eccles and her colleagues are responsible for attenuating intrinsic motivation in some, but not all, students. Teachers' increased emphasis on grades, competition, and control of students, coupled with a decreasing personal interest in students, as well as increases in classmate social comparison, were specifically examined. Support was offered for a model in which these environmental factors heighten the salience of one's academic ability. During educational transitions, such factors also serve to cause students to reevaluate their scholastic competence, relative to other students. Those students who report that their competence had decreased as a function of the transition show parallel decreases in intrinsic motivation. Conversely, those who feel more academically competent in the new setting report increases in intrinsic motivation. Those reporting no change in their level of competence also report no change in their level of intrinsic motivation. Further evidence reveals that students are aware of the hypothesized shifts in the educational philosophy espoused by teachers as well as of increases in social comparison. The students low in intrinsic motivation report that the school environment is more debilitating than do those high in intrinsic motivation.

The effects of perceived scholastic competence, as well as classmate and teacher approval on self-esteem, as another index of adjustment were also examined. Findings reveal that perceptions of competence are substantial predictors of self-esteem. With regard to the opinions of significant others, both classmate support and teacher approval are predictive of self-esteem. Findings indicate that it is the support of classmates, namely peers in the "public" arena, which can be construed as approval from the "generalized other," that is particularly relevant, more than the support of close friends. Of further interest are findings revealing that those adolescents who consciously endorse a looking-glass self model, asserting that their self-esteem derives from the opinions of classmates, fare worse in terms of greater preoccupation with approval, greater fluctuations in perceived approval, greater fluctuations in self-esteem, lower levels of both approval and self-esteem, as well as distractibility in the classroom.

Although teacher approval is somewhat less predictive than classmate support, it is nevertheless another critical determinant. Of particular interest is the finding that among students who report low parent support, the presence of teacher support serves to increase students' level of self-esteem, suggesting a compensatory process. The overall pattern, with regard to parent and teacher support, reflects an additive model in which the highest levels of self-esteem are displayed by students reporting high parent and teacher support, whereas the lowest levels of self-esteem are found in students with both low parent and low teacher support.

Finally, factors that cause adolescents to display one form of false self behavior, namely, suppression of their voice, were examined, as another index of adjustment. According to Gilligan, females are particularly at risk as they move into adolescence, when they suppress their opinions in order to conform to societal expectations and to preserve relationships by compromising the self. Our own findings reveal that it is those adolescent females (as well as males) who endorse feminine sex-role stereotypes that are most likely to exhibit loss of voice. Moreover, suppression of voice is also strongly predicted by perceived support for voice. Thus, our findings caution against generalizations that loss of voice is primarily gender related. Our process analysis reveals that both gender orientation and perceived support for voice are highly predictive of level of voice. Level of voice is particularly relevant to psychological adjustment since it is also related to self-esteem, hopelessness, and depression. Our analysis of the antecedents of the three constructs in question, motivational orientation, self-esteem, and level of voice not only caution against generalizations but identify those variables that may be critical targets for intervention.

Acknowledgments

The research reported in this chapter was supported by a grant from NIH. The author would like to thank Steve Cohen, principal as well as the teachers and students of Flood Middle School for their cooperation in making these studies possible.

References

American Association for University Women's (AAUW) Report. (1992). How schools shortchange girls. American Association of University Women Educational Foundation.

Bartholomew, K. (1990). Avoidance of intimacy: An attachment perspective. *Journal of Social and Personal Relationships, 7,* 147–178.

Boldizar, J. P. (1991). Assessing sex-typing and androgeny in children: The children's sex-role inventory. *Developmental Psychology, 27,* 505–515.

Brush, L. (1980). *Encouraging girls in mathematics: The problem and the solution.* Cambridge, MA: Abt Books.

Condry, J., & Koslowski, B. (1979). Can education be made "intrinsically interesting" to children? In L. Katz (Ed.), *Current topics in early childhood education,* (vol. II). Norwood, NJ: Ablex.

Connell, J. P., & Ryan, R. M. (1984). A developmental theory of motivation in the classroom. *Teacher Education Quarterly, 11,* 64–77.

Cooley, C. H. (1902). *Human nature and the social order.* NY: Charles Scribner's Sons.

de Charms, R. (1968). *Personal causation.* New York: Academic Press.

deCharms, R. (1976). *Enhancing motivation in the classroom.* New York: Irvington, Halsted-Wiley.

Deci, E. L. (1975). *Intrinsic motivation.* New York: Plenum.

Deci, E. L., & Ryan, R. M. (1985). *Intrinsic motivation and self-determination in human behavior.* New York: Plenum Press.

Eccles, J., & Midgley, C. (1988). Stage-environment fit: Developmentally appropriate classrooms for young adolescents. In R. E. Ames & C. Ames (Eds.), *Research on Motivation in education, goals and cognitions* (vol.3 pp. 139–186). New York: Academic Press.

Eccles, J. S., & Midgley, C. (1990). Changes in academic motivation and self-perceptions during early adolescence. In R. Montemayor, G. R. Adams, & T. P. Gullotta (Eds.), *Advances in adolescent development: From childhood to adolescence* (vol. 2, pp. 134–155). Newbury Park, CA: Sage.

Eccles (Parsons), J., Midgley, C., & Adler, T. F. (1984). Grade-related changes in the school environment: Effects on achievement motivation. In J. G. Nicholls (Ed.), *The development of achievement motivation.* Greenwich, CT: JAI Press.

Felson, R. B. (1993). The (somewhat) social self: How others affect self-appraisals. In J. Suls (Ed.), *Psychological perspectives on the self* (vol. 4). Hillsdale, NJ: Lawrence Erlbaum Associates.

Gilligan, C. (1982). *In a different voice.* Cambridge, MA: Harvard University Press.

Gilligan, C., Lyons, N., & Hanmer, T. J. (1989). *Making connections.* Cambridge, MA: Harvard University Press.

Gottfried, E. (1981). *Grade, sex, and race differences in academic intrinsic motivation.* Paper presented at the Annual Meeting of the American Educational Research Association, Los Angeles.

Harter, S. (1981). A new self-report scale of intrinsic versus extrinsic orientation in the classroom: Motivational and informational components. *Developmental Psychology, 17,* 300–312.

Harter, S. (1986). Processes underlying the construction, maintenance, and enhancement of the self-concept in children. In J. Suls & A. G. Greenwald (Eds.), *Psychological perspectives on the self* (vol. 3, pp. 137–181). Hillsdale, NJ: Erlbaum.

Harter, S. (1990). Causes, correlates and the functional role of global self-worth: A life-span perspective. In J. Kolligian & R. Sternberg (Eds.), *Perceptions of competence and incompetence across the life-span* (pp. 67–98). New Haven, CT: Yale University Press.

Harter, S. (1992). The relationship between perceived competence, affect, and motivational orientation within the classroom: Process and patterns of change. In A. K. Boggiano & T. Pittman (Eds.), *Achievement and motivation: A social-developmental perspective.* New York: Cambridge University Press.

Harter, S. (1993). Causes and consequences of low self-esteem in children and adolescents. In R. F. Baumeister (Ed.), *Self-esteem: The puzzle of low self-regard.* New York: Plenum.

Harter, S., & Connell, J. P. (1984). A comparison of alternative models of the relationships between academic achievement and children's perceptions of competence, control, and motivational orientation. In J. Nicholls (Ed.), *The development of achievement-related cognitions and behaviors.* Greenwich, CT: JAI Press.

Harter, S., & Jackson, B. J. (1992). Trait vs. nontrait conceptualizations of intrinsic/extrinsic motivational orientation, *Motivation and Emotion, 16,* 209–230.

Harter, S., Whitesell, N. R., & Kowalski, P. (1992). Individual differences in the effects of educational transitions of young adolescents' perceptions of competence and motivational orientation.

Harter, S., Marold, D. B., & Whitesell, N. R. (1991). A model of psychosocial risk factors leading to suicidal ideation in young adolescents. *Development and Psychopathology, 4,* 167–188.

Harter, S., Marold, D. B., Whitesell, N. R., & Cobbs, G. (In press). A model of the effects of parent and peer support on adolescent false self behavior. *Child Development.*

Harter, S., & Monsour, A. (1992). Developmental analysis of opposing self-attributes in the adolescent self-portrait. *Developmental Psychology, 28,* 251–260.

Harter, S., Stocker, C., & Robinson, N. (in press). The perceived directionality of

sive reactions from others, children learn to manipulate others' responses by altering their causal explanations for events that could potentially elicit anger, blame, and disapproval (Darby & Schlenker, 1989). Thus, in the face of potential conflict situations, youngsters can deflect personal responsibility by using excuses that reveal the cause of the transgression was unintentional or uncontrollable by them (e.g., "I was late because my Mom forgot to wake me up"). In contrast, students should not readily admit that they were late on purpose or because of some controllable reason (e.g., "I just didn't feel like getting up") given that this does not reduce personal responsibility.

To investigate developmental differences in children's understanding of the social consequences of "good" and "bad" excuses, Weiner and Handel (1985) had American 5–12 year-old children listen to short stories describing a broken social contract (e.g., "You promised to go to your friend's house to finish up a school project but never showed up"). The children were then given four explanations that portrayed the transgressor as responsible (e.g., "You didn't feel like going") and four accounts that conveyed lack of responsibility or intentionality (e.g., "Your bike got a flat tire on the way to your friend's house") for why they did not show up. They indicated how likely it was that they would reveal or withhold each of these eight explanations. After each account, children also predicted how angry their friend would be. The results documented that children in all age groups (5–7, 8–9, and 10–12) preferred explanations that convey lack of responsibility. Also, children perceived that such accounts elicit less anger than do the ones that depict the person as responsible for breaking the social contract. These findings suggest that by 5–7 years of age, children recognize both the principles and functions of excuse-giving.

In a similar experiment, I asked a group of second-grade Finnish students (8-year-olds) to role play a scenario in which they had, contrary to a prior aggreement, failed to help either their classmate (with homework because the friend had been absent from class) or their teacher (with setting up a class exhibit after school) (Juvonen, 1995). Rather than asking them to respond to a set of good and bad excuses, they were to produce explanations that "would not make the teacher/classmate mad." The children spontaneously provided accounts that clearly conveyed lack of intentionality. The most used cause was memory (e.g., "I forgot!"/"Didn't remember") when dealing with their teachers, whereas with friends they were equally likely to implicate their forgetfulness and other commitments (e.g., "I had to visit Grandma"). It is interesting to note that children do not necessarily externalize the reason, as Snyder and Higgins (1988) have proposed, but rather manipulate the perceived intentionality of the act (such as blaming their memory).

How children's understanding and repertoire of excuses expands and becomes more sophisticated are interesting questions to examine further. Based on some preliminary findings, I expect that there are at least three overlapping levels or phases that capture the development of excuse-making:

1. Denial of the act (i.e., "I didn't do it").
2. Denial of intent (i.e., "I didn't mean to do it").
3. More sophisticated methods to reduce personal responsibility. This can be achieved, for example, by conveying a reason that is uncontrollable by the account giver or by presenting a mitigating circumstance.

Besides examining the types of explanations that children are likely to communicate, it is equally important to study students' understanding of the affective and social consequences of excuses. In another experiment with Finnish children, I asked sixth-grade students to predict the reactions of the victims to classmates' explanations of their transgressions. They reported that when a classmate explains to her peer that she did not show up at the movies because of some personally controllable reason (e.g., "I didn't feel like it"), the victim is more likely to be angry, less likely to trust them, and the peer and the classmate are less likely to get along with one another than when an uncontrollable reason is communicated (e.g., "Mom wouldn't let me go"). Similarly, they predicted that when students tell their teacher that they did not complete the homework assignments because they were out playing with friends all night, the teacher is more angry and less likely to get along with the student than if an uncontrollable explanation was communicated (e.g., "I was sick"). Thus, the students seemed to realize that bad excuses have not only short-term negative affective consequences but that they can also have undesirable long term effects on one's relationships.

What happens then when a child is not aware of excuse-making tactics or when a child is not concerned about the reactions of others? In a recent study, Graham, Weiner, and Benesh-Weiner (1995) documented that one group of children who have rather serious social adjustment problems at school, that is, aggressive males, were less sophisticated in reasoning about excuses and more likely to use "bad" excuses (i.e., controllable explanations) than their nonaggressive peers. These findings may in part explain the reputation and the social difficulties of aggressive youngsters. By attributing violations of norms and obligations to causes that are controllable by them, they are likely to be perceived as insensitive, rude, and defiant by their peers as well as by instructors. Furthermore, once they acquire such reputations, their actions are likely to be interpreted in a negative light; that is, they are more likely to be blamed for negative encounters and less likely to be credited for prosocial actions or intentions (cf. Hymel, 1986; Hymel, Wagner, & Butler, 1990). Hence, children who do not understand the relationship-maintaining function of excuses or who do not care about maintaining positive interactions with others are likely to be confronted with more frequent conflict situations than other children. They therefore become entrapped in a cycle of maladaptive behaviors that exacerbate poor interpersonal relationships (cf. Dodge, 1993; see also Erdley, this volume).

In future research, it would be important to disentangle whether motivational or social-cognitive deficits (or a combination of the two) account for social problems of aggressive children and youngsters who for some other reason are rejected by their peers. By doing that, appropriate intervention tactics could be identified. Interventions that involve training in excuse giving might sound somewhat questionable, yet the principles underlying successful social functioning appear to be captured by this very phenomenon. After all, effective excuse giving presumes prosocial goals (i.e., to reduce anger, to promote positive relations) as well as rather sophisticated social skills to come up with appropriate strategies to accomplish these goals. Apparently, there is a fine line that most children learn to recognize between "healthy" excuse-making and pathological lying. Although socially skillful excuse-makers are likely to be accepted, chronic liars tend to elicit strong negative reactions from others.

How effective excuse-giving relates to moral development is another interesting issue to explore. For example, it may be that children at some point are guided more by moral rules (i.e., understanding of right and wrong) than by attributional principles. Thus, they may consider honesty to be the primary goal and expect "telling the truth" to best facilitate positive relationships. Thus, it would be informative to compare children's views of the social consequences of excuses and confessions.

Excuse giving thus represents only one form of impression management. Excuses pertain to situations in which a social contract or an agreement with another person is violated (cf. Scott & Lyman, 1968), and involve a manipulation of the communicated reason. But what about the self-presentational process in situations that do not involve such a social violation? For example, what is communicated to others about the causes of personal academic failures and successes? How can students "impress" their teachers and peers in achievement situations? I will turn to these issues next.

Personal achievement outcomes: The function of public accounts

Starting the first day at school, students are likely to be preoccupied by social concerns, such as: "Does my teacher like me?", "What do the other kids think of me?". Furthermore, students try to "fit in" and act according to the expectations and norms of a desirable peer group or of a person they desire to befriend. To master impression management strategies that facilitate the approval of others, children must (a) be aware of what the other values or expects, and (b) present themselves in a manner that is consistent with the other's values or expectations (cf. Baumeister, 1982; Goffman, 1959; Leary & Kowalski, 1990).

Research on impression management has demonstrated that there are a host of such strategies that people can use to gain acceptance from others (e.g., Jones, 1964; Jones & Pittmam, 1982). Consider, for instance, conformity: Adolescents modify their physical appearance to match that of popular ("cool") peers, they engage in behaviors (e.g., smoking, drug-use) that are perceived to be highly valued by the socially powerful others, and they adopt interests (e.g., listening to certain types of rock music) compatible with those they admire (Berndt, 1979; Eckert,1989).

Rather than analyzing overt strategies to conform, I again focus on attributional self-presentation tactics that are used in everyday discourse (cf. Cody & Braaten, 1992; Turnbull, 1982). By altering causal explanations of events, the account giver can influence others' impressions of oneself and thus manipulate their reactions (Weary & Arkin 1981; Weiner, 1992; Weiner et al. 1987; Weiner et al., 1991). As Turnbull writes:

> "Consider, for example, a student who does much better than anyone else on a very difficult examination. When asked by a classmates, "How come you did so well?" the student could answer, "It's simple. I'm smarter than the rest of you," or "I dunno. Somehow I was just able to figure out what the questions were likely to be, and so I was well prepared." The first explanation is likely to lead to the perception that the speaker is smug and insensitive; whereas, in contrast, by playing down

the superior performance, the second explanation both attests to the speaker's modesty and protects others' competence. Clearly the only student in a class who is able to infer the questions that are on the examination is a superior student. But the two ways of expressing the same information have very different interpersonal effects." (Turnbull, 1992, 107).

Although true for all types of impression management tactics, it is especially clear that verbal accounts are audience-specific (Jones & Pittman, 1982; Jones & Worthman, 1973; Leary & Kowalski, 1990; Schlenker & Leary, 1982). That is, an adolescent may want to portray herself as lucky or "good at guessing" when confronted with classmates, but the same explanation is not likely to be communicated to a teacher. Instead, a student may tell the teacher that she succeeded because she studied hard, given that teachers are known to value diligence (e.g., Weiner & Peter, 1973).

To examine students' understanding of the social function of achievement accounts, Tamera Murdock and I conducted a series of experiments that examined students' perceptions of hypothetical others and their self-presentational preferences in negative and positive achievement situations. In the first experiment (Juvonen & Murdock, 1993), we examined whether early adolescents are aware of the social implications of achievement attributions. We asked American eighth-grade (Caucasian, upper-middle to middle class) students to evaluate teachers' and peers' approval of imaginary students who varied in terms of their achievement level as well a their level of ability and effort (cf. Weiner & Kukla, 1970). We expected students to understand that the social responses of others vary not only as function of how successful one is in school, but also depend on *why* one does well or poorly. Furthermore, we presumed that early adolescents realize that people's reactions depend also on their values and expectations (e.g., whether they regard diligence as desirable or not).

The results revealed that the eighth graders believed that regardless of the achievement level, teachers prefer diligent pupils over lazy ones (cf. Weiner & Kukla, 1970; Weiner & Peter, 1973). Whereas instructors were perceived to most like the high achievers who are smart and diligent, these individuals were believed to be least popular among their peers. Thus, early adolescents appeared to be well aware of the *different* impact of effort and ability ascriptions on the approval of teachers versus classmates.

In the second experiment, the same eighth grade students responded to scenarios in which they themselves were to explain to their teachers, classmates, and parents why they had failed or succeeded on an important exam. We expected that their understanding of the social consequences of effort and ability attributions would mirror their own self-presentational preferences. For instance, we predicted that the eighth-graders would portray themselves to their instructors and parents as more diligent than to their peers. In addition to rating the likelihood of communicating effort and ability accounts, two other typical achievement explanations, namely, test fairness and luck, were also included. To control for the social motive across the three audiences (i.e., their motivation to get along with each), the participants were asked to respond in ways that would facilitate social approval.

The results showed that the eighth-graders were more willing to convey to the two adult audiences than to their classmates that they did well because they studied hard (see Figure 3.1). By the same token, in the failure situation they were less likely to tell their teachers and parents than their peers thay they failed because they did not study, as shown in Figure 3.1. Thus, adolescents recognized that parents as well as teachers value

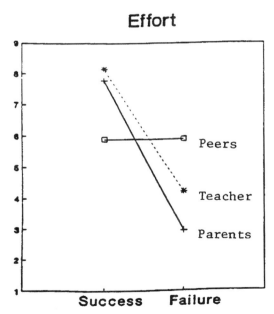

Figure 3.1. Likelihood of communicating effort accounts as the reasons for exam success and failure to teachers, parents, and peers. Data from Juvonen & Murdock (1993).

diligence and thus, they wanted to portray themselves as hard workers to elicit the adults' approval. With peers, on the other hand, they desired to portray a different perception of themselves. They wanted to convey to their classmates that they did not exert effort.

When dealing with parents and teachers, as opposed to classmates, adolescents were also more likely to ascribe their positive achievement outcomes to their competence and less inclined to attribute their success to good luck. The high endorsement of ability and effort explanations versus low endorsement of luck accounts suggests that early adolescents believe that personal (i.e., internal) attributions increase adults' approval. These findings are consistent with the self-presentation tactics of adults, who tend to take credit for positive outcomes in the presence of their superiors, but not when dealing with their co-workers (Pandey, 1981). Thus, it appears that modesty rather than self-enhancement is a tactic that elicits approval of peers, whether co-workers or classmates.

A somewhat surprising finding was obtained regarding students' preferred public accounts for failue. The early adolescents were more likely to convey to the adults than to their classmates that their poor grades were due to low ability. Furthermore, compared to the other accounts, the students were rather willing to use this explanation with both their parents and teachers. As pointed out earlier, failure due to low ability is known to elicit sympathy in others (Graham, 1984). It appears that students in this experiment realized they they could use this attribution-emotion link in their favor. By attributing their failure to low ability, they not only reduced their responsibility for the outcome (and thus decreased anger and disapproval of the adults) but perhaps hoped to elicit a sympathetic and nurturing response from their parents and teachers.

Although adolescents were generally more likely to convey similar reasons to the two adult groups than to their classmates, there was one exception: They were less willing to tell their instructors than parents (and peers) that their poor performance was due to the unfairness of the exam and more likely to admit to their teachers than parents (and peers) that they were successful because the test was fair. Attributing failure to the test appears to negatively impact a student-teacher relationship in that such an explanation is likely to be interpreted as an accusation. In contrast, by ascribing one's success to the exam, the student compliments the teacher and thus enhances the relationship with the instructor. In summary, the results of these experiments intimate that early adolescents are both sensitive and responsive to their audiences.

One of the most intriguing findings of the research just described was that early adolescents desired to portray themselves to their classmates as not putting forth effort in failure situations and downplayed the role of hard work in the face of success. Given that these self-presentational styles conflict with one of the fundamental values communicated at school (i.e., the importance of effort), we wanted to further examine students' understanding of the social meaning or value of diligence versus laziness. We were especially interested in comprehending the *development* of self-presentation tactics that might undermine one's achievement strivings.

Assuming that the audience-specificity of achievement accounts reflects the perceived values and expectations of authority figures versus peers, we hypothesized that there should be age-related changes in students' self-presentational use of effort ascriptions. Given that young children are more willing to accept the values and comply with the norms endorsed by authority figures (e.g., the importance of diligence) than are adolescents (Berndt, 1979; Steinberg & Silverberg, 1986; Youniss & Smollar, 1985), the values and norms of their peer culture are likely to be consistent with, or at least not oppositional to, those of adults. Hence, we predicted that the audience specificity of students' responses should increase by early adolescence. We also examined the preferences of youngsters to publicly attribute their failures and successes to ability because age-related changes in youngsters' preference to be diligent versus not hard-working have been associated with their developing understanding of the link between ability and effort (e.g., Harari & Covington, 1981; Nicholls, 1978; Nicholls, Patashnick, & Mettetal, 1986; Chapman & Skinner, 1989).

Adopting the methods from the earlier investigation, we instructed an American public school sample of 4th, 6th, and 8th grade students (1/3 African-American, mixed SES) to explain to their teachers and popular peers why they failed or succeeded in an important exam (Juvonen & Murdock, 1995). Teachers rather than parents were used as the adult audience because instructors and classmates are both present in the context where students' failures and successes take place. The peer group was defined as those who are considered popular because popular peers are typically perceived to be the ones that others look up to, wish to be like, and also elicit the most envy. The students were again asked to respond in ways that would facilitate their relationships with the teacher and peers. To examine youngsters' perceptions of the social value of the two attributions, we also included the experiment in which participants evaluate teachers' and peers' approval of imaginary students who vary in their achievement, ability, and effort levels. I will discuss the main findings of the two experiments jointly by focusing first on effort accounts.

Effort explanations

We found that by fourth-grade, students can vary their explanations of negative and positive achievement events in ways that they assume promote social approval. For example, fourth graders believed that both teachers and popular students like those who put forth effort more than those who are lazy. Accordingly, they wanted to portray themselves as diligent to their teachers as well as popular classmates. Although the eighth graders also perceived that instructors prefer effortful students to lazy ones, they believed that popular peers are more likely to accept high achieving classmates who do not exert effort (see dotted lines in Figure 3.2) than those who are diligent (see solid lines in Figure 3.2). (Note that the perceived peer status of the smart and diligent students dropped from the most popular at the fourth grade to the least popular at the eighth grade. In contrast, the low ability, lazy students were viewed as least popular at the fourth grade but among the most popular by the eighth grade.) Consistent with these beliefs, the eighth graders were less likely to convey to their peers than instructors that they had done well because of effort and more willing to tell peers than teachers that they failed because they did not study (see Figure 3.3).

Considering the results across the failure and success conditions, a clear grade-related difference was documented in student preferences to communicate effort accounts to their peers versus their teachers. Furthermore, the results of our study revealed that this shift in self-portrayal indeed paralleled grade-level differences in the perceived effects of diligence on peer popularity.

But why would early adolescents want their peers to believe that they did not study? Given that high effort implies that the task is important to the actor (Brown & Weiner, 1984), lack of effort could be believed to communicate lack of importance or indifference. Inasmuch as effortful achievement behavior is recognized as valued by teachers and parents, reports of lack of effort should indicate that the student does not agree or comply with such values. Defiance of adult norms and values, in turn, should appeal to peers, assuming that adolescents question authority and challenge traditional school norms (Coleman, 1961; see also Fordham & Ogbu, 1986).

Another interpretation of the willingness of adolescents to downplay

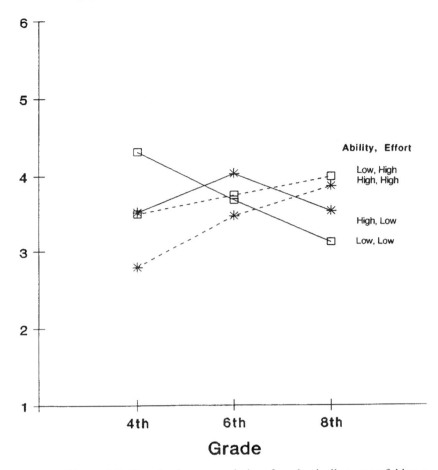

Figure 3.2. Perceived peer popularity of academically successful hypothetical students across the fouth, sixth, and eighth grades. Data from Juvonen & Murdock (1993).

the lack of effort is that this might protect the student from public humiliation and shame (Covington,1984). After all, unlike younger children, adolescents believe that the relation between effort and ability is compensatory (Nicholls, 1978). Hence, by claiming that their failure is due to lack of effort, they can protect their high ability perceptions (Covington,1984; Jagacinski & Nicholls, 1992). However, if this was the case, it is unclear why they would want to do this with their peers but not with their instructors. Also, the results regarding students' willingness to attribute their fail-

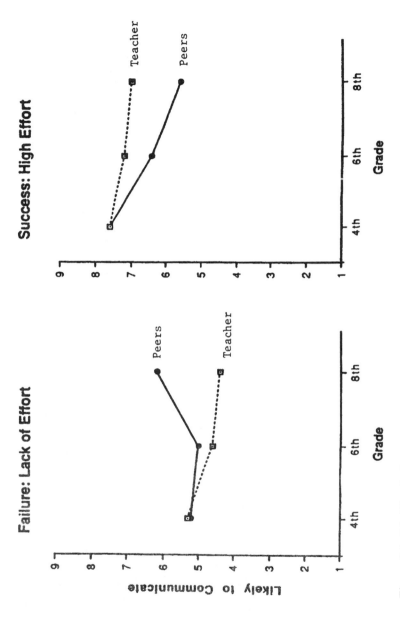

Figure 3.3. Likelihood of communicating effort accounts to teachers and peers as the reasons for exam failure and success across the fourth, sixth, and eight grades. Data from Juvonen & Murdock (1995).

ures to low ability (discussed below under "ability explanations") do not support this hypothesis.

Students' downplaying of effort is likely to be guided by their belief that effort expenditure is devalued by their popular peers. It may be that the perceptions of increased devaluing of effort in the peer group is influenced, in part, by differences in the educational environments between elementary and middle-schools. Certain alterations in structural features, educational policies, and instructional practices that create a poor match between the psychological needs of early adolescents and their educational environments are known to be detrimental to school adjustment (Eccles & Midgley, 1989; Simmons & Blyth, 1987). It seems likely that some of these changes (e.g., increased anonymity due to larger schools and compartmentalized classes, tracking according to performance level that promotes differences rather than similarities among students, and increasingly competitive grading practices) would cultivate peer norms and values, which promote beliefs that one should not try hard or at least not admit that one studies (Ames, 1992; Maehr & Midgley, 1991). For example, when normative grading practices are used, a smart student who works hard and "sets the curve" makes others look bad and is therefore likely to be ostracized. Thus, students may not wish to work hard to excel, or at least show that they do, because of a fear of peer rejection (cf. Brown, 1993). I will return to the educational implications of these findings after discussing the results on perceived social meaning of ability ascriptions.

Ability explanations

In the experiment in which the ability of hypothetical students was manipulated along with their effort and achievement levels, the ability was not perceived to independently impact teacher liking or peer popularity at any grade level. However, the eighth-graders were most likely to tell their teacher that their poor grades were due to low ability in the subject matter. These results replicate our earlier findings, yet they are inconsistent with much of self-presentation research suggesting that people do not want to portray themselves to others in ways that question their ability or competence, especially when seeking social approval (Covington & Omelich, 1979; Jagacinski & Nicholls, 1990; Snyder & Higgins, 1988). However, as I indicated earlier, the present results are sensible from an attributional perspective. Compared to young elementary school age children, adolescents are known to view ability as an uncontrollable cause (Nicholls, 1978). Uncontrollable causes elicit sympathy from others (Graham, Doubleday, & Guarino, 1984) which, in turn, facilitates prosocial behaviors and social acceptance (Graham & Barker, 1990; Juvonen, 1991b; Weiner, 1986). Thus, the present data intimate that in unsuccessful achievement situations, there may be social benefits in portraying oneself as incapable or low in ability in a particular subject or task. Students might believe that they can avoid punitive social responses and instead elicit approval, especially from their teachers. Using low ability as a self-presentation tactic requires rather sophisticated understanding of practices that favorably impact the reactions of others. This may also explain why only the oldest participants were likely to use low ability to account for their achievement failures.

In summary, the cross-sectional study showed that audience-specificity of presenting oneself to others as diligent or low in ability increased with advancing grade-level. These findings suggest that students recognize the different values and expectations of their audiences and can modify their public explanations of positive and negative events accordingly. Thus, in contrast to the rather simple principle of excuse giving (i.e., reducing responsibility to avoid anger and disapproval), the strategies for seeking social approval are more sophisticated. Based on these experiments, a few specific strategies that enhance the approval of significant adults and peers can be identified. For example, it appears that in positive achievement situations, middle school students (i.e., early adolescents) are able to facilitate social approval by (1) eliciting praise from those in the position of authority by portraying themselves as personally accountable (i.e., by using internal attributions) for their achievements, (2) complimenting their instructor by crediting her or him for their successful achievements, and (3) appearing modest to peers by downplaying the role of personal (cf. internal) achievement accounts. On the other hand, in the face of failure, early adolescents can earn social approval by: (1) Denying personal responsibility for achievement failures when dealing with superiors (e.g., teachers or parents); (2) eliciting sympathy from superiors by providing accounts that are personally uncontrollable; and (3) accepting responsibility for personal failures when dealing with others of similar or equal status (i.e., peers).

In a more recent set of experiments with Finnish students, I expanded the analyses of audience specificity of achievement explanations to include positive and negative relationships (Juvonen, 1994). That is, students were asked to respond to liked versus disliked teachers and liked versus disliked classmates. The results showed that preadolescents can use their knowledge of others' values and expectations in ways that communicate their negative sentiment toward another. For example, students were more likely to convey to the disliked teacher than the liked instructor that they failed because the exam was unfair. Thus, it seems that early adolescents realize the relational implications of public accounts. They can use achievement explanations not only to please people but also to aggravate those they dislike.

I am currently examining whether these attributional self-presentation tactics are related to the social status of students. One would expect that youth who do not vary their achievement accounts according to the values and expectations of their audiences are not socially adjusted. That is, students who continue to portray themselves as diligent to their instructors as well as to their classmates in middle-school might be considered as "nerdy" or labelled as "teachers' pets" and thus are unlikely to be accepted by the majority of their classmates. Feelings of lack of acceptance and support from peers, in turn, are likely to color these students' school experiences (see Birch and Ladd, in this volume; Kupersmidt, Buchele, Voegler, & Sedikides, in this volume). Those who are ridiculed or "put down" by others tend to feel lonely and experience lack of support (Cassidy & Asher, 1992; Juvonen, Murdock, Curran, & Gordon, 1994).

In additon to affecting social approval, one would expect that the productivity of the individual who is not accepted by her or his peers (cf. coworkers) suffers in such conditions. To investigate how self-presentation tactics in achievement situations may be related to actual achievement behavior is another area of research that we are beginning to explore. Although I do not have any data to present at this point, let me discuss possible implications of some of our findings on achievement.

Self-presentation tactics and achievement

Given that effort expenditure and diligence are considered important indices of achievement motivation, it is important to investigate ways in which public portrayals of lack of effort and laziness might affect one's actual achievement. First of all, youngsters (early adolescents) may be quite well aware of the function and meaning of self-presentational tactics, such as downplaying the role of effort when interacting with their peers. They may promote this public image of themselves, yet privately value the importance of effort and study diligently at home. In Harter's (1990; this volume) terms, these youth would be likely to ascribe this somewhat "schizophrenic" behavior to their "false self." In these cases, one would not expect to find any relation between students' social and academic status.

However, impression management research on adults indicates that public behaviors are more committing than private behaviors or thoughts because they force individuals to build a reputation by which they are known and treated (McKillop, Berzonsky, & Schlenker, 1992). As discussed in the context of excuses of aggressive youngsters, public images are difficult to revoke (Goffman, 1959; Hymel, et al., 1990; Tedeschi & Norman, 1985; McKillop, et al. 1992). For example, a "cool kid" who has a reputation of being uninvolved in school work cannot easily change his or her achievement behavior without it affecting his or her social status in the classroom. Thus, teachers and peers alike may treat such a student in ways that become self-fulfilling prophesies. Hence, in some cases, social success among peers may be gained at the expense of academic failure.

Also, some youngsters may not necessarily distinguish their own identity from their reflected appraisals (Harter, 1990, this volume). They may be primarily concerned about earning approval of their peers and, hence, adopt (and eventually internalize) values and behavior patterns that are consistent with those of their friends (Berndt & Keefe, 1992) or peers to whom they look up (Brown, 1993). In other words, students may not only claim that they do not study, but also reduce their actual achievement efforts in their search for peer approval. Indeed, it is during early adolescence when students' grades, interest in school work, and self-concept decline (see Eccles & Midgley, 1989; Simmons & Blyth, 1987 for reviews). It would therefore be important to investigate whether peer group norms can be altered in ways that promote effort expenditure. For example, decreased competition and endorsement of small group cooperation might change the social meaning of effort (cf. Ames, 1992; Elliott & Dweck, 1988). Instead of fostering negative interdependence, effort could be construed as a prosocial force that would unite peers with a common achievement goal.

Similarly to lack of effort, low ability accounts might have certain implications for students' actual academic performance. Although we found that only the oldest students were likely to communicate low ability accounts, I assume this may not necessarily capture an age-related phenomenon but rather a behavior that is promoted by certain experiences. Based on anecdotal evidence, I expect that compared to typical children, students who have confronted frequent failure situations are more likely to use low ability accounts to elicit sympathy and to lower the expectations of their instructors. In working with children with disabilities, I have noticed that they are quite clever in manipulating the social responses of others (especially of adults who do not know them well). They might tell a substitute teacher that their eyes hurt when asked to read a passage or that they cannot produce better handwriting because they are not able to properly hold their pencil. In other words, some children might use their disabilities to persuade the instructor to reduce demands or lower expectations. This type of self-handicapping behavior appears to be learned, and hence experience rather than age (or developmental stage) would explain the prevalence of it. Obviously, such self-presentational tactics might also affect students' actual performance, either through other communicated low expectations or via internalization of the public self.

Conclusion

As stated in the beginning of this chapter, my goal was to demonstrate that students' choices of excuses and publicly communicated achievement explanations show how their understanding of naive psychology (e.g., attribution-emotion-behavior links) enables them to effectively use public accounts to suit their social goals. This research also depicts the complexity of students' social life in school. Obviously, many more questions remain to be investigated. For example, which other type of self-presentation tactics are used by students? What happens when middle school students want to simultaneously please their instructor as well as a "cool" group of classmates? Or what do students opt to do when their own achievement values conflict with those of their friends? The multiple and complex social contexts that influence children's and adolescents' behavior in school provide rich data that researchers have just begun to explore.

Acknowledgment

This research was supported by the National Academy of Education Spencer Post-Doctoral Fellowship.

References

Ames, C. (1992). Classrooms: Goals, structures, and student motivation. *Journal of Educational Psychology, 84*, 261–271.

Baumeister, R. F. (1982). A self-presentational view of social phenomena. *Psychological Bulletin, 91*, 3–26.

Berndt, T. J. (1979). Developmental changes in conformity to peers and parents. *Developmental Psychology, 15*, 608–616.

Juvonen, J., (1995). *A developmental analysis of excuses as relationship maintaining strategies.* Unpublished manuscript.

Juvonen, J., & Murdock, T. B. (1993). How to promote social approval: The effects of audience and outcome on publicly communicated attributions. *Journal of Educational Psychology, 85,* 365–376.

Juvonen, J., & Murdock, T. B. (1995). Grade-level differences in the social value of effort: Implications for self-presentation tactics of early adolescents. *Child Development, 66,* 1694–1705.

Juvonen, J., Murdock, T. B., Curran, A., & Gordon, T. (1994). *Age-related changes in peer attitudes, perceived social support, and loneliness of bullies and victims.* Paper presented at the Annual Meeting of the American Educational Research Association, New Orleans, 1994.

Leary, M. R., & Kowalski, R. M. (1990). Impression management: A literature review and two-component model. *Psychological Bulletin, 107,* 34–47.

Maehr, M. L., & Midgley, C. (1991). Enhancing student motivation: A schoolwide approach. *Educational Psychologist, 26,* 399–426.

McKillop, K. J., Berzonsky, M. D., & Schlenker, B. R. (1992). The impact of self-presentations on self-beliefs: Effects of social identity and self-presentation. *Journal of Personality, 60,* 789–808.

Nicholls, J. G. (1978). The development of concepts of effort and ability, perceptions of own attainment, and the understanding that difficult tasks require more ability. *Child Development, 49,* 800–814.

Nicholls, J. G., Patashnick, M., & Mettetal, G. (1986). Conceptions of ability and intelligence. *Child Development, 57,* 636–645.

Pandey, J. (1981). A note on social power through ingratiation among workers. *Journal of Occupational Psychology, 54,* 65–67.

Schadler, M., & Ayers-Nachamkin, B. (1983). The development of excuse-making. In C. R. Snyder, R. L. Higgins & R. J. Stucky, *Excuses: Masquerades in search of grace.* New York: Wiley.

Schlenker, B. R., & Leary, M. R. (1982). Audiences' reactions to self-enhancing, self-denigrating, and accurate self-presentations. *Journal of Experimental Social Psychology, 18,* 89–104.

Scott, M., & Lyman, S. (1968). Accounts. *American Sociological Review, 23,* 46,62.

Simmons, R. G., & Blyth, D. A. (1987). *Moving into adolescence.* Hawthorne, NY: de Gruyter.

Snyder, C. R., & Higgins, R. L. (1988). Excuses: Their effective role in negotiation of reality. *Psychological Bulletin, 104,* 23–35.

Snyder, C. R., & Higgins, R. L., & Stucky, R. J. (1983). *Excuses: Masquerades in search of grace.* New York: Wiley.

Steinberg, L., & Silverberg, S. B. (1986). The vicissitudes of autonomy in early adolescence. *Child Development, 57,* 841–851.

Tedeschi, J. T., & Norman, N. (1985). Social power, self-presentation, and the self.

In B. R. Schlenker (Ed.), *The self and social life* (pp. 293–322). New York: Mc-Graw Hill.

Turnbull, W. (1992). A conversation approach to explanation, with emphasis on politeness and accounting. In M. L. McLaughlin, M. J. Cody, & S. J. Read (Eds.), *Explaining one's self to others: Reason-giving in a social context* (pp. 105–130). Hillsdale, NJ: Erlbaum.

Weary, G., & Arkin, R. M. (1981). Attributional self-presentation. In J. H. Harvey, W. J. Ickes, & R. I. Kidd (Eds.), *New directions in attribution research.* Hillsdale, NJ: Erlbaum.

Weiner, B. (1986). *An attributional theory of motivation.* New York: Springer-Verlag.

Weiner, B. (1992). Excuses in everyday interaction. In M. L. McLaughlin, M. J. Cody, & S. J. Read (Eds.), *Explaining one's self to others: Reason-giving in a social context* (pp. 131–146). Hillsdale, NJ: Erlbaum.

Weiner, B. (1994). Ability versus effort revisited: The moral determinants of achievement evaluation and achievement as a moral system. *Educational Psychologist, 29,* 163–172.

Weiner, B. (1995). *Judgments of responsibilty: A foundation for a theory of social conduct.* New York: Guilford.

Weiner, B., Amrikhan, J., Folkes, V. S., & Verette, J. (1987). An attributional analysis of excuse giving: Studies of naive theory of emotion. *Journal of Personality and Social Psychology, 52,* 316–324.

Weiner, B., Figuroa-Munoz, A. & Kakihara, C. (1991). The goals of excuses and communication strategies related to causal perceptions. *Personality and Social Psychology Bulletin, 17,* 4–13.

Weiner, B. & Handel, S. (1985). Anticipated emotional consequences of causal communications and reported communication strategy. *Developmental Psychology, 21,* 102–107.

Weiner, B. & Kukla, A. (1970). An attributional analysis of achievement motivations. *Journal of Personality and Social Psychology, 15,* 1–20.

Weiner, B., & Peter, N. (1973). A cognitive-developmental analysis of achievement and moral judgments. *Developmental Psychology, 9,* 290–309.

Wentzel, K. R. (1991). Social Competence at school: Relation between social responsibility and academic achievement. *Review of Educational Research, 61,* 1–24.

Youniss, J., & Smollar, J. (1985). *Adolescent relations with mothers, fathers, and friends.* Chicago: University of Chicago.

4   Social self-discrepancy: A theory relating peer relations problems and school maladjustment

Janis B. Kupersmidt, Kathy S. Buchele, Mary Ellen Voegler, and Constantine Sedikides

A growing body of literature indicates that problematic peer relations in childhood and adolescence are predictive of both academic and behavioral problems in school (see Kohlberg, LaCrosse, & Ricks, 1972; Kupersmidt, Coie, & Dodge, 1990; Parker & Asher, 1987, for reviews). The findings from this literature have been important for the development of criteria for defining, identifying, and screening children at risk for school maladjustment. Despite the fact that the relation between problematic peer relations and school maladjustment has been replicated across samples of children from different ethnic, geographic, and developmental groups, little is known about the mechanisms by which problematic peer relations may affect school maladjustment. The development and testing of such mechanisms has been slow, in part, because the transactional relations among social, behavioral, and academic functioning over time have been difficult to study due to methodological limitations and practical constraints. It is likely that there is a bidirectional influence between peer relations and school maladjustment; however, this chapter focuses only on one side of the equation, namely, the influence of problematic peer relations on school maladjustment. In this chapter, school maladjustment is defined in terms of behavioral, emotional, or academic difficulties that may interfere with adequate functioning in school.

One mechanism that has been proposed for understanding the impact that problematic peer relations have on children's school maladjustment suggests that poor peer relations are stressful for children due to both the experienced negative affect and the accompanying lack of social support that, in turn, increases children's vulnerability to other life stressors (Armacost, 1989; Colton & Gore, 1991; see also Birch & Ladd, this volume). In fact, children report that being disliked or picked on by peers is a major stressor (Jones & Fiore, 1991) and they rate negative changes in peer acceptance as equally stressful as other life events, such as failure of a year in school or hospitalization of a parent for a serious illness (Johnson, 1988). Children with poor peer relations may be socially isolated or ostracized and may, in turn, isolate themselves from peers by not attending school to avoid further exposure to stress. If the social isolation of children is associated with teasing or peer victimization, they may also develop heightened social anxiety and fear of public performances in school, such as reading aloud.

Although problematic peer relations can have negative consequences in terms of mental health and school maladjustment, these consequences do not necessarily generalize to all children. There may be children for whom problematic peer relations do not affect adjustment. For these children, the level of need for relatedness, affiliation, or peer status may be relatively low. For example, they may describe themselves as not caring what others think about them or not wanting or needing friends. Alternatively, these children may have other means of satisfying their social needs, such as a positive affiliation with a pet, parent, or sibling. Thus, we need to know a child's desired type, quality, and quantity of peer relations in order to be able to predict his or her reaction to different kinds of interpersonal stressors with peers.

In this chapter, we propose a model for understanding the differential impact of peer relations problems on children's school maladjustment. Specifically, we propose that individual differences in cognitions about the social self may account for this differential impact (see also Erdley, Juvonen, this volume). The aim of the present chapter is to begin to develop a framework for explaining individual differences in the impact of the type, quality, and quantity of chidren's peer relations problems on school maladjustment. We will develop a theory about the ways in which social self cognitions mediate the relation between problematic peer relations and school maladjustment. In addition, we will present the preliminary results of focus group discussions that are relevant to our theory.

In order to begin to examine the proposed model, we conducted focus group discussions with 3rd, 5th, 7th, 9th, and 11th grade students. Trained adult interviewers conducted separate groups with boys and girls. The older groups (7th, 9th, and 11th grades) consisted only of African-American, inner-city children, whereas the younger groups (3rd and 5th grades) consisted of both Caucasian and African-American children. We conducted all groups in school or a school-based summer camp during the day. The interviewers were trained to use a semi-structured interview and were guided by a standard script of questions used with each group of students. Children were asked to discuss five types of peer relations including social networks, best friends, boyfriends and girlfriends, popularity, and being disliked or rejected by peers. The results of these focus group discussions will be presented throughout the chapter to complement the existing empirical literature.

The specific organization of the chapter is as follows. In the next section, we will briefly discuss the importance of positive peer relations for normal development, and we will provide a brief review of the literature on the prediction of school maladjustment from different kinds of peer relations problems. In the following section, we will discuss the existing adult literature relevant to our theory. Because mediators of problematic peer relations on school maladjustment have not been directly examined in the child literature, we reviewed the adult literature for ideas about social cognitive mediators of interpersonal stess on maladjustment. This review provides the foundation for the remainder of the chapter, which begins with a discussion of the concept of social needs followed by sections on a working definition of social needs and the domains of social needs. We then review group and individual differences in social needs. Finally, we will introduce self-discrepancy theory as a potential framework for understanding the impact of interpersonal stress, more broadly, and peer relations problems, more specifically, on maladjustment. In the final section, we will discuss various mechanisms through which cognitions about the social self in the context of problematic peer relations may affect school maladjustment.

The importance of peer relations for school maladjustment

The importance of establishing and maintaining healthy peer relations in normal social development has been well-documented. Vandell and Mueller (1980) note that in the first six months of life, children begin to show evidence of interest in peers, such as touching, peer-directed smiling, and babbling. Social interactions increase in frequency during the preschool years (Rubin, Fein, & Vandenberg, 1983). The presence of reciprocated friendships provides the opportunity for modeling and corrective feedback in the social skill development of school-aged children (Hartup, 1989). Relationships with peers become increasingly important to children, and children report that the functions these relationships serve grow to equal or sometimes surpass relationships with other central network members (Furman & Buhrmester, 1985).

The following comments from focus group discussions suggest the importance of peer relations to children and adolescents: "I come to school to get the gossip." "[I like] the social life. Just to see people. That's why I like school." When asked what they like most about school, children's most common response was "coming to see my friends." Thus, not only are peer relations subjectively important to children, but they also appear to motivate them to attend school.

Most of the developmental psychopathology literature in the last 15–20 years that has examined the role of peer relations has focused upon children's relations with same-aged peers as the primary indicator of problematic peer relations. The following section discusses five types of peer problems that may be associated with increased risk for school maladjustment and how each type of problem relates to other types of peer problems. We will also discuss, when possible, individual variation in response to exposure to each particualr peer problem.

One way that peer problems have been operationalized is through the use of peer nomination methods to identify "rejected children," or children who are actively disliked by a substantial number of peers while simultaneously being most liked by few, if any, peers (Coie, Dodge, & Coppotelli, 1982). This dislike or negative affect directed towards certain peers has been found to be correlated with negative behavior being directed toward rejected children as well. Rejected children are often the targets of overt aggression (Coie & Kupersmidt, 1983; Dodge, Coie, & Brakke, 1982) as well as the victims of relational aggression (Crick & Grotpeter, 1994).

Rejected children have been found to be at heightened risk for a wide range of school-related problems including absenteeism, school dropout, low academic achievement, poor grades, and grade retention (Coie, Lochman, Terry, & Hyman, 1992; DeRosier, Kupersmidt, & Patterson, 1994; Kupersmidt & Coie, 1990; Ollendick, Weist, Borden, & Green, 1992; Wentzel, 1991; see also Hymel et al., this volume). In tests of the effects of the chronicity and proximity of peer rejection on behavioral and academic adjustment, even one experience of peer rejection was predictive of increases in school absenteeism, after controlling for prior levels of absenteeism in the model (DeRosier et al., 1994). Likewise, the interaction between the chronicity of peer rejection and prior levels of aggression was associated with heightened levels of aggression in school. The strength of the correlation between prior aggression and later aggression was directly related to the chronicity of peer rejection. The academic achievement of children in early elementary school was more negatively affected by chronic peer rejection than the achievement of children who experienced chronic peer rejection later in elementary school (DeRosier et al., 1994). In addition to the impact of peer rejection on behavioral and academic functioning, rejection has also been associate with internalizing problems including anxiety and depression (Asarnow, 1988; French & Waas, 1985; Waas, 1987).

In addition to these more recent findings on peer rejection and its consequences, an earlier literature on unpopularity also suggests an association with school-related problems (see Parker & Asher, 1987, for a review); however, the operational definition of unpopularity varied substantially across these earlier studies. Despite the consistent findings regarding negative outcomes associated with peer rejection, the specific form of negative outcome appears to vary across individuals, leading some to suggest that peer rejection may operate as a general stressor rather than a specific precursor to a specific disorder (Kupersmidt & Coie, 1990; Kupersmidt & Patterson, 1991). In addition, substantial individual differences in the response to peer rejection have been observed. For example, Kupersmidt and Coie (1990) reported that approximately 35% of rejected children dropped out of school.

More recently, interest in the *normal* development of dyadic peer relationships among children has emerged in the theoretical and empirical literature (Bukowski & Hoza, 1989; Parker & Asher, 1993). Based upon this line of research, a second way that having a peer relations problem has been operationalized is the absence of a best friendship using reciprocal peer nominations. Although group acceptance and friendship are considered to be distinct constructs, some empirical evidence has emerged that suggests that these constructs are related. For example, low status children (e.g., rejected or neglected) are less likely than other children to have a group of prosocial friends or a best friend and are more likely than other children to have low or average status friends (Kupersmidt, DeRosier, & Patterson, 1995; Kupersmidt, Griesler, & Patterson, 1994; Parker & Asher, 1993). Likewise, higher status popular or controversial children are more likely than other children to have friends and have higher status friends. However, it is noteworthy that some low status children do have both reciprocated friendships and best friends (Kupersmidt et al., 1995; Kupersmidt, Griesler, & Patterson, 1994; Parker & Asher, 1993). Nevertheless, low status children report less caring, instrumental aid, intimacy, and more conflict and betrayal in their reciprocated best friendships than higher accepted peers (Parker & Asher, 1993).

Although it has been shown that dyadic relationships, particularly best friendships, are important to children and adolescents (Furman & Buhrmester, 1985), little is known about the consequences for school behavior and performance of not having a friend. One exception is from a recent cross-sectional study by Parker and Asher (1993), in which they reported that not having a reciprocated best friend and low group acceptance made separate contributions to the prediction of loneliness. Thus, this finding presents new evidence to suggest an additive relation between two peer problems as independent risk factors.

A third peer relations problem has been defined through ratings or observations of the quality of the best friend relationship. Although many low-accepted children have friendships, they report less caring, instrumental aid, and intimacy, and more conflict and betrayal in their reciprocated best friendships than do higher-accepted children. Some have suggested that having a poor quality relationship with a best friend such as one characterized by frequent conflicts may have negative effets on children's development (Berndt, 1989; Rook, 1984). In particular, Berndt (1992) reported that adolescents with more supportive friendships were better adjusted to school than adolescents with less supportive friendships. In addition, Goodyer, Wright, and Altham (1989) reported that friendship difficulties were associated with both anxiety and depression. Finally, Parker and Asher (1993) reported that various friendship qualities made independent contributions to the prediction of loneliness, even after controlling for peer acceptance.

A fourth kind of peer relations problem concerns the lack of membership in a social network. The relations among low peer status, lack of a best friend, and lack of a social network have not been thoroughly investigated, so that the prevalence of the co-occurrence of these problems is not known. In addition, the short- and long-term consequences of this type of social isolation have not been well investigated.

A fifth kind of peer relations problem concerns the characteristics of the child's best friend or peer network members. Members of children's peer groups have been found to be similar with respect to their level of motivation in school (Kindermann, 1993; this volume) and although there is substantial turnover in the membership of groups, groups remain fairly stable in their motivational composition. In other words, according to Kindermann (1993) children who were very motivated in school tended to affiliate with one another, and those who were less motivated also tended to hang out together. Similarly, Tesser, Campbell, and Smith (1984) reported homogeneity among affiliated peers with respect to school performance and Cairns, Cairns, Neckerman, Gest, and Gariepy (1988) reported that aggressive children tend to associate with one another in antisocial networks. In addition, adolescents who are friends and, in particular, those who stay friends across time tend to become more similar to one another in behavior, attitudes, and school motivation (Berndt, Laychak, & Park, 1990; Epstein, 1983b; Kandel, 1978a, 1978b). Adolescents also report substantial peer group influence that affects many aspects of life including their appearance and illicit behaviors and cognitions (O'Brien & Bierman, 1988). Social affilation with an antisocial peer group is a powerful predictor of a range of school-related problems and antisocial behaviors (Dishion & Loeber, 1985; Elliot, Huizinga, & Ageton, 1985; Patterson & Dishion, 1985).

A recent longitudinal study examined developmental patterns of five indices of problematic peer relations including low group acceptance, not having a reciprocated best friend, low perceived social support from the best friend, high conflict with the best friend, and having aggressive friends as predictors of aggression and delinquency (Kupersmidt, Burchinal, & Patterson, 1995). Multiple peer relations problems were additively associated with the prediction of each outcome, suggesting that children with more problems were at higher risk than children with fewer problems. In this way, these findings are consistent with those reported earlier for the prediction of loneliness by Parker and Asher (1993), suggesting that the evaluation of social risk factors requires the assessment of multiple aspects of social functioning with peers. In addition, these findings provide additonal evidence for substantial individual differences in the impact of each peer relations problem on a variety of negative outcomes.

In summary, five different kinds of peer relations problems have been identified that are expected to be associated with heightened risk for school maladjustment, including being rejected, not having a best friend, having a poor quality friendship, lack of membership in a social network, and being a member of an antisocial network. Individual differences in the negative impact of these problems on school maladjustment were reported in thes studies. Additional research on each of these peer relations problems is needed in several areas. First, the prevalence and interrelations among different kinds of peer relations problems need to be studied across development. Second, the prediction of school maladjustment from both independent peer relations problems as well as from multiple peer relations problems needs to be examined. Most importantly, additional theory and research is needed on the mechanisms by which these processes operate.

Because mechanisms underlying the link between the various types of children's peer relations problems and school maladjustment have not been studied directly, we reviewed the literature on social self cognition factors that mediate the effects of interpersonal stress on adult adjustment. The next section provides a brief review of this adult literature and our conclusions about how these findings provided direction for the development of our theory of social self cognitions as mediators of the effects of children's peer relations problems on school maladjustment.

Social needs as a mediator of adult maladjustment

It has long been hypothesized that deficits in the formation of social relationships (Fromm-Reichmann, 1959; Sullivan, 1953) or the loss of social relationships (Bowlby, 1980) lead to negative outcomes. These ideas have been explored in the adult literature, with particular attention to loneliness and depression as outcome measures. The results of these studies have been mixed. Russell, Peplau, and Cutrona (1980) found that loneliness correlated positively with time spent alone, whereas others found no significant relation between number of friends reported and loneliness (Jones, 1982; Stokes, 1985; Williams & Solano, 1983). In the past decade, a great deal of research has been devoted to explaining individual differences in the extent to which the adequacy of adults' social relationships predicts loneliness or depression. The research in each of these areas has identified social needs as one of the mediating variables between actual social relationships and these specific negative outcomes for adults.

The adult loneliness literature has suggested that two types of loneliness exist and are related to different social needs (Weiss, 1973). Weiss (1973) proposed that emotional loneliness occurs when an intimate attachment is not present. He distinguished emotional loneliness from social isolation, which occurs when a network of social relationships is absent or inadequate (Weiss, 1973). Weiss' theory suggests that the presence of specific kinds of relationships is necessary for everyone, and that loneliness can be predicted by simply measuring all of the relationships that exist in a person's life. Later work has shown that the quality of relationships is more important than the quantity in making this prediction (Rook, 1987; Shaver & Buhrmester, 1983). Several researchers have theorized that the prediction of loneliness is dependent on the degree of discrepancy between an individual's desired and actual social relationships (Peplau & Perlman, 1982; Rook, 1988). From this perspective, loneliness is a function of the discrepancy between an individual's social needs and the individual's perception of his or her actual social relationships.

The adult depression literature had taken a similar approach, considering the interactions among an individual's social needs, actual social relationships, and psychological adjustment. Beck (1983) proposed that personality traits could be used to predict which individuals would become depressed when faced with certain kinds of life stressors. Specifically,he hypothesized that sociotropic individuals (individuals who are dependent on interpersonal relationships for safety, help, and gratification and highly dependent on feedback from others) will be prone to depression when rejection by or separation from others is experienced, whereas autonomous individuals (individuals who are dependent on meeting achievement-related internal standards and goals and are less dependent on feedback form others) will be relatively unaffected by these social stressors. In support of this theory, several researchers have found that depression in sociotropic adulsts is correlated with negative social events (Hammen, Ellicott, Gitlin, & Jamison, 1989; Robins & Block, 1988; Robins, 1990). From this perspective, then, depression is a function of an interaction between an individual's social needs (conceptualized as a personality trait) and negative changes in his or her actual social resources.

In both the loneliness model and the depression model, the discrepancy between social needs and perceived social relationships is thought to be a cognitive mediator between social relationships and psychological adjustment. Although this idea had been supported empirically for adults, it has not yet been extended to the study of children's social relationships. The adult psychiatric literature led us to consider the application of individual differences in social needs as underlying the negative impact of children's peer relations problems on school maladjustment.

The model we will propose differs from the adult models in several ways. First, in the adult literature, the social needs construct is conceptualized as a global personality variable (such as sociotropy or need for relatedness). In contrast, we are conceptualizing social needs as being domain-specific. In the case of children's social needs, domain-specificity refers to the type (e.g., group, dyadic), quality (e.g., conflict, support), and quantity of peer relations. We theorize that a child's social needs within each domain will be relatively independent of his or her social needs in other domains. Second, the adult literature guided us only in terms of developing theories related to the specific outcomes of depression and loneliness as a function of the discrepancy between social needs and actual social resources. Although both of these affective problems are associated with school performance and behavior, we were interested in developing a model that would help to explain a broader range of school outcomes including absenteeism, disruptive behavior, and aggression in school. Thus, we reviewed the social psychological literature on the social self. Finally, the adult literature presents a static model of how mental health may be affected by interpersonal stress exposure and stable individual differences in social needs. In contrast, our model is conceptualized from a developmental perspective, with the expectation that social needs will differ not only across individuals, but also across developmental periods.

Given that the adult literature guided us to examine social needs as a mediator of peer relations problems on school maladjustment, we began the development of our theory by defining the construct, thinking about the domains or features of social needs, and by examining any normative data on social needs in children of different ages. We were also interested in gender, cultural, and individual differences in reported social needs. The next section reviews these points.

Characteristics of social needs

Definition of social needs

The study of children's social needs has not been directly examined in the empirical literature on social development. The literature that comes closest to examining this construct focuses in the study of children's social goals (see also Ford, Berndt & Keefe, Erdley, Wentzel, this volume). A "social goal" is defined within a social information-processing model as a type of social cognition that may determine the choice of strategies used to solve a social problem. Social goals have been operationalized in terms of the proximal and immediate goals for specific social situations (e.g., Renshaw & Asher, 1983). Although this line of research has proven fruitful, the present chapter defines social needs in a broader context than the more behavioral or instrumental definitions used for the study of social goals. Social needs are thought to reflect cognitive structures representative of the social self. These structures are thought to be chronically accessible in memory and capable of influencing social goals and behavior in specific situations (Sedikides & Skowronski, 1990, 1991; see also Higgins, 1990).

In our model, a social need is defined as an individual's subjective evaluation of the importance of and desire for various types, qualities, and quantities of social and interpersonal relations. For example, a person for whom having a best friend is viewed as very important would be said to have a high level of need for that type of relationship. Likewise, a person to whom being popular is relatively unimportant would be said to have a low level of need for popularity. Thus, social needs may or may not be situationally specific and may influence, but do not refer to situationally specific goals.

Domains of social needs

We use three broad domains to organize our discussion of social needs. First, social needs may vary with regard to the *type* of social need; specifically, whether the type of desired peer relation is a dyadic or group affiliation or a particular status. In other words, some children may desire a best friend, others may want a group with which to hang out, and still others may want to be popular. There are at least two aspects of the type of peer relations that also are likely to vary across individuals. First, in addition to desiring a specific type of relationship, a child may *target* a paritcular person to fulfill that need. For example, a boy may want to have a girlfriend (a certain type of relationship) and may want a particular girl to be his girlfriend (a specific target). In addition, social needs may vary with regard to specific *characteristics* of the target of the relationship, such as gender. For example, a child may want to be friends with a group of boys. Another child may desire to have a best friend who is very popular with the peer group. In these examples, the characteristics of the targeted peer(s) are important components of the type of desired relationship.

Second, social needs may vary with regard to the *qualities* of the peer relationship or the functions provided by the relationship, such as admiration, acceptance, avoidance of rejection, companionship, intimacy, aid, safety, affection, enhancement of worth, trust, and resolution of conflict (see Furman & Buhrmester, 1985; Weiss, 1974, for a discussion of relationship qualities). For example, one child may have a need for companionship and not a need for intimacy, whereas another child may report a need for both qualities. In addition, the qualities or provisions of peer relationships desired by children may be experienced in varying *levels*. Children may have a high need for trust, a moderate need for companionship, and a low need for admiration.

Third, social needs may vary in terms of the *quantity* of relationships that a child desires. One child may have an extremely high level of need for a large quantity of best friends and be dissatisfied with less than five 'best friends.' Another child may also have a high need for best friend relationships, but desire and be satisfied with having one best friend.

In addition to social needs varying in terms of their domains or features, children may vary in terms of their *flexibility or rigidity* in meeting particular social needs. For example, a child may be satisfied only with a best friend relationship with a particular person (indicating low flexibility) and may ahve difficulty having this need fulfilled by this particular person. Rigidity in social needs may prove to be frustrating and problematic for children, because it may be more difficult for them to have their social needs met. Other children may be more flexible in having their social needs met and experience less discomfort as a result of their social relationships. In addition, social needs may vary in terms of their *complexity*. For example, one child may need a best friend, a boyfriend, and to be popular in order to feel fulfilled, whereas another child may feel fulfilled simply by having a best friend.

Perceptions of social needs may also vary in terms of their *developmental timing and appropriateness*. For example, nonnormative social needs such as a precocious need for a physically intimate relationship with a member of the opposite sex may present problems for children.

Finally, social needs related to peers may compete at a particular point in time or in a particular setting with *other needs* such as the need for achievement. For example, a child who wants friends more than good grades may choose to neglect his homework rather than jeopardize a friendship by being unavailable after school to play.

Group differences in social needs

Developmental differences in social needs. The specific social needs of children and adolescents as a function of development are not well understood due to a paucity of research on this topic. The examination of developmental trends in social needs has been limited to cross-sectional work with specific age groups and, for the most part, has examined self-reports of social goals or the relative importance of different kinds of relationships. Research on children's social networks suggests that children engage in different types of relationships at different ages and that relationships with different people are reported to be relatively more important across development (Furman & Buhrmester, 1985). Specifically, students' interest, dependency, and conformity to peers increases from childhood through adolescence as their reliance on parents decreases (Berndt, 1979; Costanzo, 1970; Steinberg & Silverberg, 1986). We might speculate, then, that the overall decline in achievement task values reported by Wigfield and Eccles (1992) may reflect a developmental shift to a higher valuation of tasks that meet social needs.

The relative importance of having a best friend increases across child-

Gender differences in social needs. Gender differences have also been identified as an important factor in examining the definition and development of children's social needs and goals. However, as was found in the literature on developmental differences on social needs, the influence of gender is not well understood. Research on the affiliation patterns of children as a function of gender suggest that upon entrance to elementary school, boys name more friends than do girls in the same class (Tuma & Hallinan, 1979). Eder and Hallinan (1978) found that girls tend to have more exclusive friendships than boys, and that boys report larger social networks than girls (Clark & Ayers, 1988; Maccoby & Jacklin, 1974); although no sex differences in the size of average friendship groups were reported in adolescence (Hansell, 1981). Sherman (1984) reported that girls evidence greater intimacy and sociability with same-sex friends than do boys. In addition, Clark and Ayers (1988) reported that friendships become increasingly reciprocal for girls as age increases. Boys report less intimacy, caring, instrumental aid, and more difficulty resolving conflicts with their best friend than do girls (Bukowski, Gauze, Hoza, & Newcomb, 1993; Parker & Asher, 1993). Males also report that popularity is more important to them than it is to females (Epstein, 1983a). Most of these studies do not address differences in social needs by gender; however, the findings suggest that girls possess stronger social needs for intimacy than do boys, whereas boys report greater need for popularity than do girls.

In our focus group discussions, gender differences emerged in discussions of boyfriend/girlfriend relationships and popularity. Older girls indicated that having sex was a necessary step to keep a boyfriend: "If you don't do it with 'em they think you're boring." "[If you don't have sex] they drop you right then." Boys, in contrast, did not identify sex as necessary to keep a girlfriend. Older children also saw popularity as different for boys and for girls. They reported that to be popular, girls "have sex," "play sports," and "get their hair fixed," whereas boys "go to a different crowd of people and change your friends . . . get with a different girl."

Research on social goals provides additional evidence for differential goals as a function of gender. Wentzel (1993) found that early adolescent girls reported higher academic and social responsibility goals than males. In contrast, Sewell et al. (1982) reported that within an all-African-American adolescent population, males demonstrated greater achievement motivation than females. These mixed findings may be attributed to the use of different measures in each study, as well as to possible interactions between gender and ethnicity. Overall, these findings provide important additional evidence regarding the presence of multiple and possibly conflicting goals in school in adolescence.

Ethnic or cultural differences in social needs. A final sociodemographic variable examined in the context of social needs and goals is ethnicity or culture. We were able to locate only a few studies that addressed the contribution of ethnicity or culture to social needs. Wentzel (1993) reported that early adolescent Caucasian children demonstrated higher social responsibility goals than non-Caucasian children. Sewell et al. (1982) studied an African-American sample of adolescents with regard to achievement goals, but did not compare this group to a non-African-American population. Although Wentzel's findings suggest that cultural factors affect social goals, they do not explain the development of these cultural differences nor the mechanisms by which ethnicity or culture influence children's and adolescents' social needs.

Research on differential friendship patterns as a function of ethnicity suggest that children tend to play or be friends with others from their same ethnic group (Kupersmidt, DeRosier, & Patterson, 1995). In addition, African-American youth report somewhat different qualities in their friendships compared to Caucasian youth. For example, African-American males and females reported greater intimacy and support from peers than did Caucasian males, and less than Caucasian females (DuBois & Hirsch, 1990). DuBois and Hirsch (1990) also found that African-American peer networks included more neighborhood relationships than did Caucasian networks, although the size of the in-school networks did not differ. Clark and Ayers (1988) reported that African-American students made more nonreciprocated friendship choices compared to Caucasian students. Again, these findings are limited in their applicability to the characterization of social needs in different ethnic groups, but the results offer some indication that African-American and Caucasian students may differ in their affiliation needs with African-American youth possessing a greater need for affiliation, support, and intimacy than Caucasian youth.

Individual differences in social needs

In order for social needs to be useful as an important mediator for explaining individual differences in response to peer relationship problems, evidence demonstrating individual differences in social needs would need to be observed. Individual differences in distress about one's social experiences could provide additional evidence in support of this hypothesis. We located several studies that provide initial support for each of these assumptions. For example, Crick and Ladd (1993) reported considerable within-social status variation in social distress (e.g., 16% of popular children and 44% of unpopular children reported high levels of social distress). In addition, Asendorpf (1993) has described three different types of children who may exhibit high rates of solitary behavior. He suggested that one type of child may prefer being alone to social activity and also prefer to play with toys or do school work (Asendorpf, 1991; Coplan, Rubin, Fox, Calkins, & Stewart, 1994). In contrast, another type of child may want to interact with his or her peers, but does not do so. Their social withdrawal is most obvious in novel settings where they fear negative evaluation of others (Asendorpf, 1991). A third group may consist of children who desire social interactions with others and do not try to isolate themselves, yet they may be isolated by peers due to their incompetent social behavior (Coie & Kupersmidt, 1983; Dodge, 1983; Rubin & Mills, 1988). Thus, taken together, these studies suggest that there are individual differences in levels of social needs and in the importance of different types of social interactions across individuals.

In addition, several studies have reported differences in children's social goals as a function of having different kinds of peer relations problems or behavior problems that are associated with peer relations problems. In conflict situations, unpopular or rejected children are more focussed on instrumental rather than relational outcomes (Crick & Ladd, 1990) and rank-order positive, social goals lower (Renshaw & Asher, 1983) than do more popular children. Likewise, very aggressive youth endorse goals that are hostile in nature (Slaby & Guerra, 1988) and place high value on dominance or control of peer victims (Boldizar, Perry, & Perry, 1989; Lochman, Wayland, & White, 1993) as compared to less aggressive youth. Taken together, these findings are consistent with theoretical work that suggests that less socially competent children have problems prioritizing goals and coordinating multiple goals as compared with socially competent youth, particularly in conflict situations (Dodge, Asher, & Park, 1989).

Social self-discrepancy theory, problematic peer relations, and school maladjustment

We conducted a review of the social psychological literature on self-cognitions to attemtpt to explain the mechanism by which the discrepancy between adults' social needs and their social resources produced loneliness or depression. Self-discrepancy theory, developed by Higgins and his colleagues (Higgins, 1987; Higgins, Bond, Klein, & Strauman, 1986; Strauman & Higgins, 1987), provides an excellent framework for understanding social needs as a mediator of the effects of problematic peer relations on school maladjustment. Self-discrepancy theory distinguishes between domains of the self and standpoints on the self. Two domains of the self were relevant to explaining the discrepancy of interest, namely, the actual self (representation of attributes actually possessed) and the ideal self (representation of attributes that might ideally be possessed). In addition, the theory emphasizes two standpoints on the self: own (representations that stem from a personal point of view) or other (representations that stem from the point of view of a significant other.)

There is an important difference between the original conceptualization of self-discrepancy theory, as described in the above paragraph, and our adaptation of the theory for the purposes of our research. The original proposal addressed self-discrepancies within the totality of self- representations, whereas we are concerned with self-discrepancies within the representations that are relevant to the social self. Specifically, we define the actual social self as children's actual social resources (e.g., the type, quality, and quantity of peer relations). We define the ideal social self as children's subjective accounts of their ideal social resources or their social needs (e.g., the desired type, quality, and quantity of peer relations). Consistent with the original theory, these subjective accounts of the actual social self can represent the standpoint of either the children themselves or significant others (e.g., peers, parents, teachers; see Hartup, 1989, and Higgins, 1991, for discussions of the important socializing roles of peers, parents, and teachers; see also Harter, this volume).

Studies with adults have found that discrepancies between the actual self and the ideal self are strongly associated with dejection-related emotions such as feeling sad, disappointed, or discouraged (Higgins et al., 1986; Higgins, Klein, & Strauman, 1985; Strauman & Higgins, 1987). In our case, then, a discrepancy between one's ideal social self (social needs) and one's actual social self would be expected to be associated with dejection-related affect. Although this discrepancy has not been studied directly among children, several studies have examined children's subjective experiences or reports of different types of desired peer relations. For example, the lack of best friendships, low peer acceptance, and poor quality friendships were all associated with loneliness when examined in the context of hierarchical regression models (Parker & Asher, 1993). This theory would speculate, then, that loneliness could be predicted from the discrepancy an ideal:actual social self-discrepancy were implied, namely, avoiding school and committing suicide. This example provides a clear illustration of how the ideal:actual social self-discrepancy can impact school malad-justment. These findings are consistent with the hypothesis suggested by Coie (1990) that a child who wants to be liked by members of his or her peer group, but who is rejected by them, may avoid peers to avoid further rejection and to decrease exposure to negative behaviors directed at them by peers.

In addition to the ideal and actual domains of the self, self-discrepancy theory introduces another self-cognition that is relevant to broadening the scope of our theory. This third domain is termed the ought self, and is de-fined as a representation of attributes that ought to be possessed. In our case, the ought domain would be defined as the norms or standards for so-cial development (e.g., the type, quantity, and quality of peer relations that a child of a particular age "should" possess). Higgins (1987) hypothesized that a discrepancy between the actual self and the ought self would be as-sociated with agitation-related problems such as feeling worried, nervous, or tense. Several adult studies have reported a relation between the actu-al:ought discrepancy and anxiety-related symptoms (Higgins et al., 1986; Higgins et al., 1985; Strauman & Higgins, 1987). In the social domain, a discrepancy between one's social standards and one's actual social ability or resources might be expected to produce social anxiety. In this case, for example, socially rejected children who think they should be well-liked (as opposed to ideally wanting or needing to be well-liked by peers) would be expected to be socially anxious if they perceived themselves to be dis-liked by peers.

Social anxiety could function as a motivator for either a change in cog-nitions or a change in behavior that would reduce the ideal-ought social self-discrepancy. A child with a social standard that isn't met might be flexible and change this standard. This change may result in a reduced dis-crepancy which may, in turn, reduce anxiety-related affect. In the school setting, social anxiety might lead to a refusal to speak or perform in front of others in class and a timidness in social situations that form the fabric of everyday life in school. Figure 4.2 shows a hypothetical example of one way in which the ought:actual social self-discrepancy could lead to behav-ior change with implications for school maladjustment. Figure 4.2 depicts one component of this pathway, in that the discrepancy is reduced by a change in the actual social self that is accomplished by a behavior change of not participating in class.

One example from our focus group discussions illustrates the

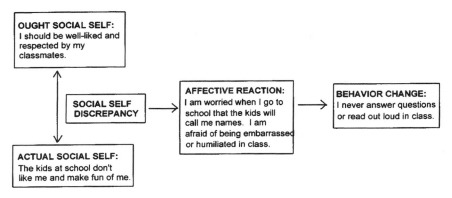

Figure 4.2. An example of a school-related behaivor change resulting from an ought:actual social self discrepancy.

actual:ought social self-discrepancy was "She may not try to answer a question that she really knows, because she's scared she'll get it wrong, and she don't want to be really, really disliked." Although there are no direct studies on this actual:ought social self-discrepancy hypothesis for children, some studies suggest support for this hypothesis. For example, Durlak (1992) found that anxiety-related affect was related to school refusal and school phobia, and that children with internalizing disorders demonstrated heightened test and performance anxiety. Also, submissive-rejected middle school students report more concern about the possibility of being rejected or humiliated after lunch and between classes than do average students (Parkhurst & Asher, 1992). Rejected children reported more anxiety of the form of greater concern about peer evaluations than did more accepted peers (La Greca, Dandes, Wick, Shaw, & Stone, 1988).

A final mechanism is based upon the work of Ogilvie (1987) who introduced the concept of the undesired self. This notion is consistent with Sullivan's (1953) ideas about the "good" me, the "bad" me, and the "not" me. Applying Sullivan's theory, the ideal self would be derived from the good me, whereas the undesired self would have images of the bad me and the not me. Ogilvie argues that the "not me" is the most dangerous and disowned image of the self, because these images are derived from memories of dreaded experiences, embarrassing situations, fearsome events, and unwanted emotions. He argues that a discrepancy between the ideal self and the not me or the undesired self may produce a strong negative affective reaction and perhaps would be even more motivating than the negative affect produced by other types of self-discrepancies.

A child who has developed an undesired social self, based on previous negative experiences at school, then, would have a strong motivation to reduce this discrepancy, either through changes in cognition or behavior. Figure 4.3 depicts a hypothetical example in which behavior change is motivated by negative affect associated with an undesired:ideal social self-discrepancy, with implications for school maladjustment. In figure 4.3, the discrepancy is reduced through avoidance of the undesired social self. This avoidance is accomplished by the behavior change of affiliating with an antisocial peer group rather than be friendless.

This modification to self-discrepancy theory provides an expanded motivational framework for explaining observations and theories in the peer relations literature, such as the "shopping" metaphor introduced by Patterson, Littman, & Bricker (1967) to describe the developmental process involved in the initiation and maintenance of friendships among antisocial peers. Children and adolescents highly value having a group of friends or being part of a peer cluster (Oetting & Beauvais, 1987). However, there are some children who are disliked, have poor social skills, and have difficulty developing friendships with peers. These individual differences provide the substrate or underlying conditions that may affect the likelihood that an individual child will associate with others who have problems with school, authority, and crime. Students who get into trouble in school tend to affiliate with one another as well as to get into trouble together and have a modest negative influence upon one another (Berndt,

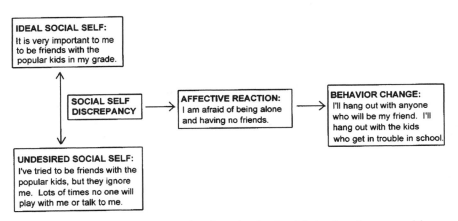

Figure 4.3. An example of a school-related behavior change resulting from an ideal:undesired social self discrepancy.

1992). In fact, a few longitudinal studies have demonstrated increases over time in friends' similarity on antisocial behaviors and attitudes (Epstein, 1983b; Kandel 1978a). The observed homophily among low status, low achieving, and antisocial students may be explainable as a reaction to the fear of being socially isolated and lack of access in establishing relationships with more desirable partners.

Self-discrepancy theory does not provide us with a means for explaining why social influence processes occur. We believe that the tenets of social learning theory as well as recent theoretical work by Berndt (1992) concerning mutual influence processes in friendships provide a better explanatory base for a discussion of influence processes. However, self-discrepancy theory provides a framework for understanding individual differences in the motivation behind the initiation of relationships with problematic peers, as well as individual differences in the susceptibility to peer influences on school misbehavior, school failure, and school dropout.

Conclusions

The model that we have proposed in this chapter represents an attempt to integrate previous research on self-cognitions with the peer relations literature, with an emphasis on school maladjustment as an outcome. We have attempted to go beyond description of the relations among different kinds of peer relations problems and school maladjustment and to focus on a possible mechanism that may underlie the observed relation between social and school functioning. We have proposed one broad framework within which these mechanisms may be understood and tested. In this chapter, we have argued that discrepancies among various aspects of the social self can be powerful elicitors of negative affect which, in turn, may motivate behavior.

In the present framework, our goal has been to focus on peer problems and their relation to school problems; however, self-discrepancy theory may also be applicable to explain the relation between social success and school competence. This approach is not incompatible with other research on motivation and social behavior. The social needs:social resources discrepancy undoubtedly operates within a network of other motivators to produce an affective outcome.

The ideas contained in this chapter outline a clear agenda for future sesearch as described below. The peer relations field has been richly developed over the past two decades, and has begun to describe the topography of social relations across different developmental periods. However, cognitions about social relationships across different developmental levels are less well known. We have proposed that one type of cognition, children's desire for various types, qualities, and quantities of peer relations may play an important role in the association between peer and school problems and warrants systematic investigation. We have also introduced two additonal social self-cognitions, including the ought and undesired selves, that have not been previously investigated in children and that also have potential explanatory power as mechanisms that may mediate the relation between peer and school problems. In addition to the study of individual differences in social as well as other needs, developmental, ethnic, and gender differences need to be examined. The use of a framework such as this will allow the field to move beyond the description of social relationships and their impact on youth to the development of explanatory models of the processes involved.

Acknowlegments

This research was supported in part by a William T. Grant Faculty Scholars Award and a University of North Carolina at Chapel Hill University Research Council Grant to the first author. The authors would like to thank the students and staff of the Durham Public School System for their help in conducting the study reported in this chapter.

References

Aronson, E. (1969). The theory of cognitive dissonance: A current perspective. In L. Berkowitz (Ed.), *Advances in experimental social psychology* (vol. 4, pp. 1–34). San Diego, CA: Academic Press.

Armacost, R. L. (1989). Perceptions of stressors by high school students. *Journal of Adolescent Research, 4,* 443–461.

Asarnow, J. R. (1988). Peer status and social competence in child psychiatric inpatients: A comparison of children with depressive, externalizing, and concurrent depressive and externalizing disorders. *Journal of Abnormal Child Psychology, 16,* 151–162.

Asendorpf, J. B. (1991). Development of inhibited children's coping with unfamiliarity. *Child Development, 62,* 1460–1474.

Asendorpf, J. B. (1993). Abnormal shyness in children. *Journal of Child Psychology, Psychiatry, and Allied Disciplines, 34,* 1069–1081.

Beck, A. T. (1983). Cognitive therapy of depression: New perspectives. In P. J. Clayton & J. E. Barrett (Eds.), *Treatment of depression: Old controversies and new approaches* (pp. 265–290). New York: Raven Press.

Berndt, T. J. (1979). Developmental changes in conformity to peers and parents. *Developmental Psychology, 15,* 608–616.

Berndt, T. J. (1989). Obtaining support from friends in childhood and adolescence. In D. Belle (Ed.), *Children's social networks and social supports* (pp. 308–331). New York: Wiley.

Berndt, T. J. (1992). Friendship and friends' influence in adolescence. *Current Directions in Psychological Science, 1,* 156–159.

Berndt, T. J., Laychak, A. E., & Park, K. (1990). Friends' influence on adolescents' academic achievement motivation: An experimental study. *Journal of Educational Psychology, 82,* 664–670.

Berndt, T. J., & Perry, T. (1986). Children's perceptions of friendships as supportive relationships. *Developmental Psychology, 22,* 640–648.

Boldizar, J. P., Perry, D. G., & Perry, L. C. (1989). Outcome values and aggression. *Child Development, 60,* 571–579.

Bowlby, J. (1980). *Attachment and loss. Vol. 3: Loss.* New York: Basic Books.

Brown, B. B., Eicher, S. A., & Petrie, S. (1986). The importance of peer group ("crowd") affiliation in adolescence. *Journal of Adolescence, 9,* 73–96.

Bukowski, W. M., & Hoza, B. (1989). Popularity and friendship: Issues in theory, measurement, and outcome. In T. J. Berndt & G. W. Ladd (Eds.), *Peer relationships in child development* (pp. 15–45). New York: Wiley.

Bukowski, W. M., Gauze, C., Hoza, B., & Newcomb, A. F. (1993). Differences and consistency between same-sex and other-sex peer relationships during early adolescence. *Developmental Psychology, 29,* 255–263.

Cairns, R. B., Cairns, B. D., Neckerman, H. J., Gest, S. D., & Gariepy, J. L. (1988). Social networks and aggressive behavior: Peer support or peer rejection? *Developmental Psychology, 24,* 815–823.

Clark, M. L., & Ayers, M. (1988). The role of reciprocity and proximity in junior high school friendships. *Journal of Youth and Adolescence, 17,* 403–411.

Coie, J. D. (1990). Toward a theory of peer rejection. In S. R. Asher & J. D. Coie (Eds.), *Peer rejection in childhood* (pp. 365–401). Cambridge, England: Cambridge University Press.

Coie, J. D., Dodge, K. A., & Coppotelli, H. (1982). Dimensions and types of social status: A cross-age perspective. *Developmental Psychology, 18,* 557–570.

Coie, J. D., & Kupersmidt, J. B. (1983). A behavioral analysis of emerging social status in boys' groups. *Child Development, 54,* 1400–1416.

Coie, J. D., Lochman, J. E., Terry, R., & Hyman, C. (1992). Predicting early adolescent disorder from childhood aggression and peer rejection. *Journal of Consulting and Clinical Psychology, 60,* 783–792.

Colton, M. E., & Gore, S. (Eds.) (1991). *Adolescent stress: Causes and consequences.* New York: Aldine de Gruyter.

Coplan, R. J., Rubin, K. H., Fox, N. A., Calkins, S. D., & Stewart, S. L. (1994). Being alone, playing alone, and acting alone: distinguishing among reticence and passive and active solitude in young children. *Child Development, 65,* 129–137.

Costanzo, P.R. (1970). Conformity development as a function of self-blame. *Journal of Personality and Social Psychology, 14,* 366–374.

Crick, N. R., & Grotperer, J. (1994). *Children's treatment by peers: Victims of relational and overt aggression.* Unpublished manuscript. University of Illinois at Urbana-Champaign.

Crick, N. R., & Ladd, G. W. (1990). Children's perceptions of the outcomes of social strategies: Do the ends justify being mean? *Developmental Psychology, 26,* 612–620.

Crick, N. R., & Ladd, G. W. (1993). Children's perceptions of their peer experiences: Attributions, loneliness, social anxiety, and social avoidance. *Developmental Psychology, 29,* 244–254.

DeRosier, M. E., Kupersmidt, J. B., & Patterson, C. J. (1994). Children's academic and behavioral adjustment as a function of the chronicity and proximity of peer rejection. *Child Development, 65,* 1799–1813.

Dishion, T. J., & Loeber, R. (1985). Adolescent marijuana and alcohol use: The role of parents and peers revisited. *American Journal of Drug and Alcohol Abuse, 11,* 11–25.

Dodge, K. A. (1983). Behavioral antecedents of peer social status. *Child Development, 54,* 1386–1399.

Dodge, K. A., Asher, S., & Parkhurst, J. T. (1989). Social life as a goal coordination task. In C. Ames & R. Ames (Eds.), *Research on motivations in education* (vol. 3). New York: Academic Press.

Dodge, K. A., Coie, J. D., & Brakke, N. P. (1982). Behavior patterns of socially rejected and neglected preadolescents: The roles of social approach and aggression. *Journal of Abnormal Child Psychology, 10,* 389–410.

DuBois, D. L., & Hirsch, B. J. (1990). School and neighborhood friendship patterns of blacks and whites in early adolescence. *Child Development, 61,* 524–536.

Durlak, J. A. (1992). School problems of children. In C. E. Walker & M. C. Roberts (Eds.), *Handbook of clinical child psychology (2nd ed.). Wiley series on personality processes* (pp. 497–510). New York: Wiley.

Eder, D., & Hallinan, M. T. (1978). Sex differences in children's friendships. *American Sociological Review, 43,* 237–250.

Elliot, D. S., Huizinga, D., & Ageton, S. S. (1985). *Explaining delinquency and drug use.* Beverly Hills, CA: Sage Publications.

Epstein, J. L. (1983a). Examining theories of adolescent friendships in J. L. Epstein & N. Karweit (Eds.), *Friends in school: Patterns of selection and influence in secondary schools* (pp. 39–61). New York: Academic Press.

Epstein, J. L. (1983b). The influence of friends on achievement and affective outcomes. In J. L. Epstein & N. Karweit (Eds.), *Friends in school: Patterns of selection and influence in secondary schools* (pp. 177–200). New York: Academic Press.

Ford, M. E. (1982). Social cognition and social competence in adolescence. *Developmental Psychology, 18,* 323–340.

French, D. C., & Waas, G. A. (1985). Behavior problems of peer-neglected and peer-rejected elementary-age children: Parent and teacher perspectives. *Child Development, 56,* 246–252.

Fromm-Reichmann, F. (1959). Loneliness. *Psychiatry, 22,* 1–15.

Furman, W., & Bierman, K. L. (1983). Developmental changes in young children's concepts of friendship. *Child Development, 54,* 549–556.

Furman, W., & Buhrmester, D. (1985). Children's perceptions of the personal relationships in their social networks. *Developmental Psychology, 21,* 1016–1024.

Goodyer, I. M., Wright, C., & Altham, P. M. E. (1989). Recent freindships in anxious and depressed school age children. *Psychological Medicine, 19,* 165–174.

Hammen, C., Ellicott, A., Gitlin, M., & Jamison, K. (1989). Sociotropy/autonomy and vulnerability to specific life events in patients with unipolar depression and bipolar disorders. *Journal of Abnormal Psychology, 98,* 154–160.

Hansell, S. (1981). Ego development and peer friendship networks. *Sociology of Education, 54,* 51–63.

Hartup, W. W. (1989). Social relationships and their developmental significance. *American Psychologist, 44,* 120–126.

Higgins, E. T. (1990). Personality, social psychology, and person-situation relations: Standards and knowledge activation as a common language. In L. A. Pervin (Ed.), *Handbook of personality: Theory and research* (pp. 301–338). New York, NY: Guilford Press.

Higgins, E. T. (1991). Development of self-regulatory and self-evaluative processes: Costs, benefits, and tradeoffs. In M. R. Gunnar & L. A. Sroufe (Eds.), *Self processes and development: The Minnesota symposia on child psychiatry,* (vol. 23), Hillsdale, NJ: Erlbaum.

Higgins, E. T., Bond, R. N., Klein, R., & Strauman, T. (1986). Self-discrepancies and emotional vulnerability: How magnitude, accessibility, and type of discrepancy influence affect. *Journal of Personality and Social Psychology, 51,* 5–15.

Higgins, E. T., Klein, R., & Strauman, T. (1985). Self-concept discrepancy theory: A psychological model for distinguishing among different aspects of depression and anxiety. *Social cognition, 3,* 51–76.

Johnson, J. H. (1988). *Life events as stressors in childhood and adolescence.* Newbury Park: Sage Publications.

Jones, R. T., & Fiore, M. (1991, Nov). *Conceptualization of self-generated stressors: Alternatives, responses, and mediators.* Paper presented at the 25th annual meeting of the Association for the Advancement of Behavior Therapy, New York, New York.

Jones, W. H. (1982). Loneliness and social behavior. In L. A. Peplau & D. Perlman (Eds.), *Loneliness: A sourcebook of current theory, research, and therapy.* New York: Wiley.

Kandel, D. B. (1978a). Homophily, selection, and socialization in adolescent friendships. *American Journal of Sociology, 84,* 427–436.

Kandel, D. B. (1978b). Similarity in real-life adolescent friendship pairs. *Journal of Personality and social Psychology, 36,* 306–312.

Kearney, C. A. (1993). Depression and school refusal behavior: A review with comments on classification and treatment. *Journal of School Psychology, 31,* 267–279.

Kindermann, T. A. (1993). Natural peer groups as contexts for individual development: The case of children's motivation in school. *Developmental Psychology, 29,* 970–977.

Kohlberg, L., LaCrosse, J., & Ricks, D. (1972). The predictability of adult mental health from childhood behavior. In B. Wolman (Ed.), *Manual of child psychopathology* (pp. 1217–1284). New York: McGraw-Hill.

Kupersmidt, J. B., Burchinal, M., & Patterson, C. J. (1995). *Developmental patterns of childhood peer relations as predictors of externalizing behavior problems. Development and Psychopathology, 7,* 825–843.

Kupersimdt, J. B., & Coie, J. D. (1990). Preadolescent peer status, aggression, and school adjustment as predictors of externalizing problems in adolescence. *Child Development, 61,* 1350–1362.

Kupersmidt, J. B., Coie, J. D., & Dodge, K. A. (1990). the role of poor peer relationships in the development of disorder. In S. R. Asher & J. D. Coie (Eds.), *Peer rejection in childhood. Cambridge studies in social and emotional development* (pp. 274–305). New York: Cambridge University Press.

Kupersmidt, J. B., DeRosier, M. E., & Patterson, C. P. (1995). Similarity as the basis for children's friendships: The roles of sociometric status, aggressive and withdrawn behavior, academic achievement, and demographic characteristics. *Journal of Social and Personal relationships, 12,* 439–452.

Kupersmidt, J. B., Griesler, P., & Patterson, C. P. (1994). *Sociometric status, aggression, and affiliation patterns of peers.* Unpublished manuscript. University of North Carolina at Chapel Hill.

Kupersmidt, J. B., & Patterson, C. P. (1991). Childhood peer rejection, aggression, withdrawal, and perceived competence as predictors of self-reported behavior problems in preadolescence. *Journal of Abnormal Child Psychology, 19,* 427–449.

La Greca, A. M., Dandes, S. K., Wick, P., Shaw, K., & Stone, W. L. (1988). Development of the Social Anxiety Scale for Children: Reliability and concurrent validity. *Journal of Clinical Child Psychology, 17,* 84–91.

Lochman, J. E., Wayland, K. K., & White, K. J. (1993). Social goals: Relationship to adolescent adjustment and to social problem solving. *Journal of Abnormal Child Psychology, 21,* 135–151.

Maccoby, E., & Jacklin, C. (1974). *The psychology of sex differences.* Stanford, CA: Stanford University Press.

O'Brien, S. F., & Bierman, K. L. (1988). Conceptions and perceived influence of peer groups: Interviews with preadolescents and adolescents. *Child Development, 59,* 1360–1365.

Oetting, E. R., & Beauvais, F. (1987). Peer cluster theory, socialization characteristics, and adolescent drug use: A path analysis. *Journal of Counseling Psychology, 34,* 205–213.

Ogilvie, D. M. (1987). The undesired self: A neglected variable in personality research. *Journal of Personality and Social Psychology, 52,* 379–385.

Ollendick, T. H., Weist, M. D., Borden, M. C., & Green, R. W. (1992). Sociometric status and academic, behavioral, and psychological asjustment: A five-year longitudinal study. *Journal of Consulting and Clinical Psychology, 60,* 80–87.

Parker, J. G., & Asher, S. R. (1987). Peer relations and later personal adjustment: Are low-accepted children at risk? *Psychological Bulletin, 102,* 357–389.

Parker, J. G., & Asher, S. R. (1993). Friendship and friendship quality in middle childhood: Links with peer group acceptance and feelings of loneliness and social dissatisfaction. *Developmental Psychology, 29,* 611–621.

Parkhurst, J. T., & Asher, S. R. (1992). Peer rejection in middle school: Subgroup differences in behavior, loneliness, and interpersonal concerns. *Developmental Psychology, 28,* 231–241.

Patterson, G. R., & Dishion, T. J. (1985). Contributions of families and peers to delinquency. *Criminology, 23,* 63–77.

Patterson, G. R., Littman, R. A., & Bricker, W. (1967). Assertive behavior in children: A step toward a theory of aggression. *Monographs of the society for research in child development.* (vol. 32, No. 5, Serial No. 113). Chicago, IL: University of Chicago Press.

Peplau, L. A., & Perlman, D. (1982). *Loneliness: A sourcebook of current theory, research, and therapy.* New York: Wiley.

Renshaw, P. D. & Asher, S. R. (1983). Children's goals and strategies for social interaction. *Merrill-Palmer Quarterly, 29,* 353–374.

Robins, C. J. (1990). Congruence of personality and life events in depression. *Journal of Abnormal Psychology, 99,* 393–397.

Robins, C. J., & Block, P. (1988). Personal vulnerability, life events, and depressive symptoms: A test of a specific interactional model. *Journal of Personality and Social Psychology, 54,* 847–852.

Rook, K. S. (1984). The negative side of social interaction: Impact on psychological well-being. *Journal of Personality and Social Psychology, 46,* 1097–1108.

Rook, K. S. (1987). Social support versus companionship: Effects on life stress, loneliness, and evaluations by others. *Journal of Personality and Social Psychology, 52,* 1132–1147.

Rook, K. S. (1988). Towards a more differentiated view of loneliness. In S. W. Duck (Ed.), *Handbook of personal relationship: Theory, research and interventions.* Chichester: Wiley.

Rubin, K. H., Fein, G. G., & Vandenberg, B. (1983). Play. In E. M. Hetherington

(Ed.), *Handbook of child psychology. Vol 4: Socialization, personality, and social development* (pp. 693–774). New York: Wiley.

Rubin, K. H., & Mills, R. S. L. (1988). The many faces of social isolation in childhood. *Journal of Consulting and Clinical Psychology, 6,* 916–924.

Russell, D., Peplau, L. A., & Cutrona, C. E. (1980). The revised UCLA Loneliness Scale: Concurrent and discriminant validity evidence. *Journal of Personality and Social Psychology, 39,* 472–480.

Schmidt, C. R., Ollendick, T. H., & Stanowicz, L. B. (1988). Developmental changes in the influence of assigned goals on cooperation and competition. *Developmental Psychology, 24,* 574–579.

Sedikides, C., & Skowronski, J. J. (1990). Toward reconciling personality and social psychology: A construct accessibility approach. *Journal of Social Behavior and Personality, 5,* 531–546.

Sedikides, C., & Skowronski, J. J. (1991). The law of cognitive structure activation. *Psychological Inquiry, 2,* 169–184.

Sewell, T. E., Farley, F. H., Manni, J. L., & Hunt, P. (1982). Motivation, social reinforcement, and intelligence as predictors of academic achievement in Black adolescents. *Adolescence, 17,* 647–656.

Sharabany, R., Gershoni, R., & Hoffman, J. E. (1981). Girlfriend, boyfriend: Age and sex differences in intimate friendship. *Developmental Psychology, 17,* 800–808.

Shaver, P., & Buhrmester, D. (1983). Loneliness, sex-role orientation, and group life: A social needs perspective. In P. B. Paulus (Ed.), *Basic group processes.* New York: Springer-Verlag.

Sherman, L. W. (1984). Social distance perceptions of elementary school children in age-heterogeneous and homogeneous classroom settings. *Perceptual and Motor Skills, 58,* 395–409.

Slaby, R. G., & Guerra, N. G. (1988). Cognitive mediators of aggression in adolescent offenders: 1, Assessment. *Developmental Psychology, 23,* 580–588.

Steinberg, L., & Silverberg, S. B. (1986). The vicissitudes of autonomy in early adolescence. *Child Development, 57,* 841–851.

Stokes, J. P. (1985). The relation of social network and individual difference variables to loneliness. *Journal of Personality and Social Psychology, 48,* 981–990.

Strauman, T. J., & Higgins, E. T. (1987). Automatic activation of self-discrepancies and emotional syndromes: When cognitive structures influence affect. *Journal of Personality and Social Psychology, 53,* 1004–1014.

Sullivan, H. S. (1953). *The interpersonal theory of psychiatry.* New York: Norton.

Tesser, A., Campbell, J., & Smith, M. (1984). Friendship choice and performance: Self-esteem maintenance in children. *Journal of Personality and Social Psychology, 46,* 561–574.

Tuma, N. B., & Hallinan, M. T. (1979). The effects of sex, race, and achievement in school children's friendships. *Social Forces, 57,* 1265–1285.

Vandell, D. L., & Mueller, E. C. (1980). Peer play and friendships during the first two years. In H. C. Foot, A. J. Chapman, & J. R. Smith (Eds.), *Friendship and social relations in children* (pp. 181–208). New York: Wiley.

Waas, G. A. (1987). Aggressive rejected children: Implications for school psychologists. *Journal of School Psychology, 25,* 383–388.

Weiss, R. S. (1973). *Loneliness: The experience of emotional and social isolation.* Cambridge, MA: MIT Press.

Weiss, R. S. (1974). The provisions of social relationships. In A. Rubin (Ed.), *Doing unto others* (pp. 17–26). Englewood Cliffs, NJ: Prentice-Hall.

Wentzel, K. R. (1991). Relations between social competence and academic achievement in early adolescence. *Child Development, 62,* 1066–1078.

Wentzel, K. R. (1993). Motivation and achievement in early adolescence: The role of multiple classroom goals. *Journal of Early Adolescence, 13,* 4–20.

Wigfield, A., & Eccles, J. S. (1992). The development of achievement task values: A theoretical analysis. *Developmental Review, 12,* 265–310.

Williams, J. G., & Solano, C. H. (1983). The social reality of feeling lonely: Friendship and reciprocation. *Personality and Social Psychology Bulletin, 9,* 237–242.

Young, J. G., Brasic, J. R., & Kisnadwala, H. (1990). Strategies for research on school refusal and related nonattendance at school. In C. Chiland & J. G. Young (Eds.), *Why children reject school: Views from seven countries. The child and his family, vol. 10 & Yearbook of the International Association for Child and Adolescent Psychiatry for Allied Professions.* (vol. 10, 199–223). New Haven: Yale University Press.

5 Motivational approaches to aggression within the context of peer relationships

Cynthia A. Erdley

For children in school, aggressive behavior often has adverse social and academic consequences. Aggressive behavior negatively impacts upon classroom functioning, as such behavior can be quite disruptive to the learning environment, both for the individual and for the class as a whole. Children who are aggressive are significantly more likely than their peers to engage in off-task, disruptive classroom behavior, and this behavior has been linked to these children experiencing academic difficulties (Coie & Krehbiel, 1984). In addition, aggressive behavior is highly visible and contributes greatly to these children earning an unfavorable image with their teachers and peers (Coie & Koeppl, 1990). Indeed, children who are excessively aggressive, hostile, and disruptive tend to be actively disliked, or rejected, by their peers (Coie, Dodge, & Kupersmidt, 1990).

It is important to note that peer rejection is associated with a variety of negative consequences for school children, including higher levels of loneliness and social dissatisfaction (Asher, Parkhurst, Hymel, & Williams, 1990) and problems with school transitions both into kindergarten (Ladd & Price, 1987) and junior high (Berndt, 1987). Furthermore, children who are rejected by their peers are more likely to drop out of school, to engage in criminal activity, and to suffer from mental health problems (Kupersmidt, Coie, & Dodge, 1990; Parker & Asher, 1987). Interestingly, however, peer acceptance and aggression show somewhat different relations to school drop-out and criminality. Specifically, whereas low peer acceptance is more predictive of dropping out of school than of criminality, aggressiveness is more predictive of later criminality than of dropping out of school (Parker & Asher, 1987). It is clear that aggressive children have a negative impact on others, and that they themselves are at risk for a variety of negative consequences, both in the short-term and the long-term. An important question, then, is what motivates children to act aggressively? An improved understanding of why children choose to behave aggressively seems to be crucial for the development of interventions that would effectively decrease aggressive behavior.

Much of the research on children's peer relationships has examined the link between children's behavior and their acceptance by peers (see Coie et al., 1990, for a review). Increasingly, however, researchers in the area of children's social behavior have been investigating how children who differ in their level peer acceptance might vary in the kinds of cognitive processes they use when responding to social situations (see Dodge & Feldman, 1990, for a review). Although links between thoughts and acceptance have been found, these links are typically not very strong. A potential explanation for these relatively weak, though significant, relations is that social-cognitive processing motivates certain behavior, and then children's behavior contributes to their acceptance level (Wentzel & Erdley, 1993). Thus, it could be hypothesized that children's thoughts about the social world would be more strongly related to children's behavior than to peer acceptance, given the more proximal links between social-cognitive processing and social behavior. Research has found that children who act aggressively among peers approach social situations with certain thought patterns that appear to motivate their aggressive behavior. This aggressive behavior, as previously noted, then seems to lead to a variety of negative consequences, such as low acceptance by peers.

In the following section, discussion focuses on how children's processing of social information relates to aspects of their social adjustment, including aggressive behavior and peer acceptance. A recent theoretical model of social-information processing is presented, followed by a review of empirical literature that provides support for this model.

Social information processing: Motivational links to children's aggressive behavior

To enhance understanding of the kinds of thought processes that underlie children's behavioral choices and the ways in which these social-cognitive constructs might operate, several models of social information-processing have been suggested (e.g., Dodge, 1986; Rubin & Krasnor, 1986). Crick and Dodge (1994) have recently proposed a model of social information-processing that is a reformulation of the model initially constructed by Dodge (1986). According to this revised model, children approach a certain social situation with a database of memories of their past social experiences, social schemas, and social knowledge. They then receive as input a set of social cues, and their behavioral response is a function of how they process those cues. These steps of processing include (1) encoding of external and internal cues, (2) interpretation of those cues, (3) selection of goals, (4) response access, and (5) response decision.

Crick and Dodge's (1994) model of social information-processing suggests several specific social-cognitive variables that may play a significant role in motivating children's selection of aggressive behavioral responses. One such variable is children's attributions of intent. As children encode and interpret social cues during the first two steps of processing, they are guided by relevant social knowledge that has been acquired through previous experiences. For example, children who have been frequently victimized by peers are apt to attribute an act, such as being tripped by a peer, to the peer's hostile intentions rather than to accidental circumstances. It seems likely that children who believe that the other has harmed them on purpose would be more motivated to respond to the provocateur in an aggressive, retaliatory manner. Another important social-cognitive variable is children's social goals, since it is hypothesized that during the third step of social information-processing, children formulate a goal for the particular situation. Presumably, children who give priority to self-defense and retaliation goals are likely to be motivated to engage in aggressive behavior in their social interactions. The fourth step of processing involves the variable of strategy knowledge, as children access possible behavioral responses to the situation from long-term memory. Children may be especially primed to implement aggressive responses if their social strategy repertoire is mostly comprised of such responses.

Several social-cognitive constructs are likely to come into play in the fifth step of social information-processing, when children must decide upon a particular behavioral response. To select a certain response for enactment, children must feel confident that they can successfully produce that behavior (i.e., feelings of self-efficacy). Furthermore, they must expect that positive outcomes will result from the behavior (e.g., If I push that child off the swing, then I will get to use the swing myself). In addition, they must make a positive evaluation of the response based on their moral rules or values (e.g., It's o.k. for me to push someone so that I can get what I want). Therefore, children are likely to be especially motivated to select an aggressive behavioral response if they think they are good at enacting aggression, if they expect that positive outcomes will result if they act aggressively, and if they believe that aggressive behavior is justified.

Using the Crick and Dodge (1994) model as a framework, I will focus on four social-cognitive variables, attributions of intent, social goals, self-efficacy perceptions, and beliefs about the legitimacy of aggression that play significant roles in the sequence of social information-processing. I will discuss how, together, these variables are likely to help in explaining children's motivation to behave aggressively. It is important to note that although Crick and Dodge propose that the path from a particular stimulus (e.g., a single provocation by a peer) to a behavioral response (e.g., retaliation) logically follows a sequence of steps, they view social information-processing as cyclical in nature, with each step of processing influencing the others through a series of feedback loops. For example, whereas children who interpret a peer's harmful behavior as intentionally committed may be motivated to pursue a goal that focuses on retaliation, it may also be that, through a feedback process, children who are primarily concerned with self-defense goals may be more likely to interpret peers' actions as hostilely motivated. Consequently, children's attributions, goals, self-efficacy perceptions, and legitimacy of aggression beliefs are not assumed to be independent of each other, and these four variables, when added together, are believed to be predictive of aggressive behavior. Although additional constructs (e.g., strategy knowledge, outcome expectations) are also likely to have an impact on children's behavioral choices, I will limit the discussion to these four social-cognitive variables.

It should be noted that this chapter is primarily concerned with *intrapersonal* processes that relate to social functioning. That is, these social-cognitive variables are viewed as key motivational constructs that influence children's decisions regarding the enactment of aggressive behavior. Nevertheless, it is important to recognize that the kinds of thought processes in which children engage are likely to be impacted by various social influences, including peers and the family. The ways in which peers interact with children are apt to affect how children process information in future social situations. For example, children who are repeatedly victimized by peers are likely to develop a propensity to attribute behaviors that harm them to their peers' hostile intentions. In addition, based on their previous negative experiences with peers, these children may feel that it is important to pursue social interaction goals that focus on retaliation. Parents and/or siblings may also influence children's social information-processing by encouraging children to take a certain kind of approach to their social interactions. For example, children may be taught to suspect that others usually have bad intentions and to believe that their own aggressive behavior is justified. Thus, although the social-cognitive constructs represent intrapersonal processes, these processes are very likely to be subject to interpersonal influences.

In the remainder of this chapter, I will review past research that has studied how children who vary in their behavioral style and/or their level of peer acceptance differ in their attributions about the intentions of others, their social goals, their self-efficacy perceptions, and their beliefs about the legitimacy of using aggression. Then, I will present some of my recent work that examines the relative contributions of these four processes in explaining the aggressive behavior of boys and girls. Also investigated in this study is the question of how these social-cognitive processes, along with children's aggressive behavior, relate to children's level of acceptance by peers. Finally, I will discuss implications for interventions that try to decrease aggressive behavior in children. Specifically, I will describe the importance of targeting social-cognitive processes that might reduce children's motivation to behave aggressively, as well as the potential difficulties in using such an approach.

Attributions of intent

Social situations are often unstructured, making it necessary for children to interpret events and decide on their behavioral responses as they are interacting with their peers (Renshaw & Asher, 1983). Different children may respond in various ways to a certain social situation because of individual differences in the attributions they make about that situation. Much of the research on children's attributions of intent has been conducted by Dodge and colleagues (e.g., Dodge, 1980; Dodge & Frame, 1982; Dodge & Newman, 1981). In this work, children are presented with various social situations, including ambiguous provocation vignettes in which the protagonist performs with ambiguous intentions some potentially provoking act that has negative consequences for them. For example, children are told to imagine that they are sitting in the lunchroom at school, and when they are not looking, a peer spills milk on them. Results of these studies, which involved boys only, have consistently shown that in response to ambiguous provocation, when compared to nonaggressive, better-accepted boys, aggressive, low-accepted boys are more likely to attribute hostile intentions to the protagonist. This same tendency to interpret a protagonist's actions as hostile has also been observed among aggressive, emotionally disturbed boys (Nasby, Hayden, & DePaulo, 1980) and highly aggressive adolescents (Graham, Hudley, & Williams, 1992; Slaby & Guerra, 1988).

In addition to attributing hostile intentions to the protagonist, aggressive, low-accepted boys are more likely to report that they would respond to the protagonist in an aggressive manner. Moreover, these boys expect to be the recipients of more aggression in the future and mistrust the protagonist more (Dodge, 1980). Based on these findings, Dodge (1980) proposed a cyclical relationship between attributions and aggressive behavior. The cycle begins with an ambiguously-motivated action that aggressive, low-accepted children attribute to the peer's hostile intentions. This attribution "confirms" the children's general image of peers as being hostile toward them and may increase their likelihood of interpreting future harmful behaviors as negatively intended. After making a hostile attribution, children will aggress against the peer, who may then aggress back, further confirming for the aggressive children that others are purposely harming them. This formulation meshes well with Berkowitz's (1977) notion that aggressive behavior is governed by the interaction of external conditions, such as behaviors observed being performed by others, and internal qualities, including the perceiver's long-lasting habits and personality traits or short-lived emotional states. Berkowitz argued that environmental cues alone usually are not enough to cause aggressive behavior. Rather, the individual must make a cognitive appraisal of the event, and the meaning given to the event will determine its cue properties and thereby control its ability to elicit particular reactions from the perceiver. Berkowitz claimed that some people are much more likely to define events as "aggression," so these events are more apt to precipitate retaliatory reactions in these individuals. The aggressive, low-accepted boys studied in Dodge's research are a good example of such a group of people.

Interestingly, when investigating factors that might influence aggressive, low-accepted boys' tendency to attribute hostile intent, Dodge and Frame (1982) found that whereas these children tended to believe that the protagonist had purposely caused harm when the negative actions or outcomes were directed at them, they did not attribute hostility when another peer was the victim of provocation. This suggests that these children have a paranoid view of others rather than a cynical view, since they seem to think that peers act with hostile intent specifically toward them, but not generally toward other people.

Although aggressive, low-accepted children exhibit systematic differences in attributing hostile intent depending on the victim (self versus peer), they continue to attribute hostility more than their nonaggressive, better-accepted peers regardless of their feelings about the protagonist. Fitzgerald and Asher (1987) presented children with a set of hypothetical ambiguous provocation situations. In some situations the protagonist was a peer highly liked by the subject, and in other situations the protagonist was a peer highly disliked by the subject. Despite the fact that children

the self, and they are less concerned with trying to preserve a positive relationship with the protagonist or deal with the problem in a constructive manner. Together, the studies that have examined the relation of children's social goals to their behavioral style suggest that children who give priority to hostile social goals, especially at the expense of prosocial goals, are more likely to be motivated to engage in aggressive interactions with peers.

Self-efficacy perceptions

In addition to the social goals children pursue, children's confidence regarding their effectiveness in being able to carry out certain actions is apt to influence their chosen behavioral responses to various social situations. Bandura (1981) defined self-efficacy as individuals' beliefs about their abilities to execute and regulate the important actions in their lives, and such self-perceived competencies affect the person's choice of what activities to undertake versus avoid. It seems quite reasonable to predict that children's goals and self-efficacy perceptions would be closely related, as individuals are likely to pursue those goals they feel most confident in attaining (see Schunk & Zimmerman, this volume).

Crick and Ladd (1990) proposed that children who are rejected by their peers focus more on instrumental goals because, based on previous social experiences, these children may feel helpless about their ability to fulfill relationship-oriented goals successfully. Such children primarily pursue instrumental goals because they are more confident about achieving successful outcomes. In contrast, children who are better-accepted by their peers predominantly pursue relationship-oriented goals. This is the case because, as a result of their generally positive interactions with peers, better-accepted children are likely to feel fairly confident about their ability to fulfill prosocial goals.

To examine how children's self-efficacy perceptions are related specifically to their behavior, as opposed to their level of peer acceptance, several studies have been conducted investigating the perceptions of children who differ in their behavioral styles. Perry, Perry, and Rasmussen (1986) compared children who were described by peers as either aggressive or nonaggressive on their ratings of how easy or difficult it would be for them to accomplish various prosocial and antisocial actions. Perry et al. found that aggressive children reported that it was easier to perform aggression and more difficult to inhibit aggressive reactions. Aggressive children were also more confident that they could achieve tangible rewards and reduce aversive treatment by others via aggression. There was no evidence that aggressive children experienced more difficulty in performing prosocial behaviors than did nonaggressive children. Nevertheless, these results suggest that aggressive children may be quite motivated to enact aggressive responses because they are fairly confident about using such behavior and expect their aggression to lead to positive outcomes for themselves.

In a recent study, Erdley and Asher (in press) investigated the self-efficacy perceptions of fourth- and fifth-grade children who varied in their predominant behavioral response (aggressive, withdrawn, or prosocial) to ten ambiguous provocation situations. In reaction to a subset of three of the situations (to which they had given their primary behavioral response), children rated the extent that they agreed or disagreed that they would be good at accomplishing various goals if they tried. Compared to the prosocial and withdrawn responders, the aggressive responders were more confident that they would be good at getting back at the other child, making the other child feel bad, and looking strong. Interestingly, the aggressive responders rated their effectiveness in staying away from the protagonist lower than did the other behavioral response groups. Finally, compared to the prosocial and withdrawn responders, the aggressive responders were less confident that they would be good at working things out peacefully with the protagonist, getting along with the other child, and taking care of the problem created by the protagonist.

Like the Perry et al. (1986) study, the Erdley and Asher (in press) study found that aggressive children were relatively more confident in their antisocial abilities. However, unlike Perry et al.'s results, in which aggressive and nonaggressive children did not differ in their confidence regarding their prosocial abilities, the Erdley and Asher study found that aggressive children felt less efficacious about their prosocial skills than did their nonaggressive counterparts. These discrepant findings may be explained by considering the situations used when assessing children's self-efficacy perceptions. In the Perry et al. study, children were asked to evaluate their prosocial abilities in situations that did not involve direct threat to the self (e.g., children rated how easy or difficult it would be for them to help a child who has a broken arm). The ambiguous provocation situations employed by Erdley and Asher may have aroused defensive reactions in the aggressive responders and consequently may have decreased aggressive responders' confidence in being able to use prosocial skills under these more emotionally-charged circumstances. The results from the Erdley and Asher study suggest that certain children are motivated to respond aggressively to provocation, not only because they think they could successfully enact aggressive behaviors, but also because they believe they are less skilled at performing prosocial actions. Interestingly, aggressive children reported that it would be relatively difficult for them to stay away from the protagonist (Erdley & Asher, in press) and that they would have problems inhibiting aggression (Perry et al., 1986). Consequently, it seems that especially when provoked, aggressive children have difficulty avoiding a confrontation, and as they approach the protagonist, it is more likely to be with hostile rather than prosocial motivations. Thus, it appears that children's aggressive behavior is influenced by their perceptions that they can use aggression successfully and that they are less skilled at enacting nonaggressive responses.

Legitimacy of aggression beliefs

An additional factor that is likely to impact upon children's decision about whether to act aggressively is their beliefs about the acceptability and legitimacy of aggression as a response to social situations. It seems quite plausible that people who vary in their beliefs about the appropriateness or moral correctness of aggression would differ in their levels of aggressive behavior. Indirect evidence for this point comes from several studies. Bandura (1979, 1986) reported that individuals who aggress typically justify their negative actions in various ways, such as blaming the victim. In other work investigating reactions to aggressive behavior, Boldizar et al. (1989) asked children to respond to hypothetical situations in which they directed aggressive acts toward peers. Children identified by peers as aggressive were less apt than nonaggressive children to make negative self-evaluations following aggressive behavior. In another study, Perry and Bussey (1977) gave children the opportunity to reward themselves after being led to believe that they had hurt another child. It was found that aggressive children rewarded themselves more than did nonaggressive children. Thus, for aggressive children, the injury of another child elicited positive self-evaluations. These studies point to the strong possibility that aggressive children believe that their aggressive behavior is justified.

Even more direct evidence concerning children's beliefs about the appropriateness of aggression comes from a study of 15-to 18-year-old adolescents by Slaby and Guerra (1988). Slaby and Guerra administered a true/false measure that assessed individuals' beliefs about whether aggression is acceptable (e.g., "It's o.k. to hit someone if he or she hits you first"). Adolescents identified by teachers as highly aggressive were more likely than their nonaggressive counterparts to believe that aggression is legitimate. In a more recent study, Erdley and Asher (1993) measured the legitimacy of aggression beliefs of fourth- and fifth-grade students. The questionnaire was a modification of the Slaby and Guerra (1988) measure (e.g., simplified wording of items, use of a rating scale rather than true/false responding). Children's behavior was assessed using both self-reports of behavior, specifically children's responses to hypothetical situations involving ambiguous provocation, and peer evaluations of children's aggressive, withdrawn, and prosocial behavior. Results from both measures of behavioral style showed that children who strongly believe in the legitimacy of aggression are more likely to engage in aggression and less apt to be prosocial or withdrawn with peers. Thus, it is clear that children's beliefs about aggression are related to their behavior. Those children who view aggressive behavior as justified seem to be particularly motivated to act aggressively and are less likely to engage in alternative, nonaggressive reponses.

A study of social-cognitive processes, aggressive behavior, and peer acceptance

From the above review, it appears that several social-cognitive variables are associated with aggressive behavior. Aggressive responses are at least partially motivated by children's attributions that others have intentionally harmed them, by their endorsement of hostile goals, by their perceptions that they can effectively enact aggressive responses, and by their beliefs that aggression is legitimate. The model proposed earlier in this chapter is that children's thoughts about the social world motivate their behavior, and their behavior then contributes to their level of acceptance by peers. The research that has been done to date has mostly focused either on how children's behavior relates to their acceptance level, how their social-cognitive processes relate to their acceptance level, or how their social-cognitive processes relate to their behavior. Rarely have all three factors been investigated in one study (see Wentzel & Erdley, 1993, for an exception). In addition, many of the studies (e.g., Dodge, 1980; Dodge & Frame, 1982; Dodge & Newman, 1981; Lochman, Wayland, & White, 1993) have included boys only.

To address some of the limitations of previous research, I conducted a study in which measures of boys' and girls' social-cognitive processes, self- and peer-assessed aggressive behavior, and level of peer acceptance were obtained. In response to six ambiguous provocation situations, 506

aggressive goals are associated with their behavior. Interestingly, for girls, none of the social-cognitive processes are associated with their general aggressive behavior.

To examine the relative contributions of these processes in explaining boys' and girls' aggressive behavior, aggressive behavior was regressed on the four social-cognitive variables. Separate analyses were conducted for self-reported and peer-assessed aggression. As can be seen in Table 5.2, for both boys and girls, attributions of intent, aggressive goals, and legitimacy of aggression beliefs were independent, significant predictors of self-reported aggressive behavior. Notably, aggressive goals were the strongest predictor of self-reported aggressive behavior for both boys and girls. When predicting peer-assessed aggressive behavior, for boys, aggressive goals were the only independent predictor, and for girls, none of the social-cognitive processes made an independent, significant contribution.

Together, these findings suggest that for both boys and girls, social-cognitive processes are strongly associated with their likelihood of reporting aggressive behavior in response to a specific kind of situation, especially a situation (ambiguous provocation) that is likely to elicit aggression in some individuals. That is, children's aggressive responses to these provocations appear to be closely related to how they view these particular situations, what they want to accomplish in these social interactions, and whether they think aggressive behavior is justified. However, children's social-cognitive processes regarding aggression show weak relations to their overall aggressive behavior, as evaluated by peers. One explanation for this finding is that peers assessed children's general level of aggressive behavior, presumably making judgments across a wide variety

Table 5.2. Results of simultaneous regressions of social-cognitive processes on the aggressive behavior of boys and girls

	Attributions of Intent	Aggressive Goals	Efficacy for Aggression	Legitimacy of Aggression	R^2
Boys' aggression					
Self-reported	.15**	.66**	−.08	.17**	.74**
Peer-assessed	.08	.20**	−.08	−.06	.05*
Girls' aggression					
Self-reported	.20**	.58**	−.01	.23**	.73**
Peer-assessed	.09	−.08	.03	.05	.01

Standardized beta weights are shown. Sample sizes for boys and girls are 247 and 259, respectively. **$p < .01$, *$p < .05$.

of situations. And, it would be expected that children's self-reported thoughts in response to a specific kind of event that is directly related to aggression would be more strongly associated with their behavior in that particular situation than with more global aspects of their behavior.

A second explanation for the weaker findings regarding the association between social-cognitive processes and peer-assessed aggressive behavior is that peers' evaluations are based on their observations and interpretations of children's actual behaviors, whereas children are focused on their planned course of action. Consequently, children may report that they would respond aggressively, but they may not really do so in actual social situations, or they may do so, but in a way that is not recognized by peers as aggressive. Interestingly, the correlation between girls' self-reported and peer-assessed aggressive behavior was not significant ($r = .11$, n.s.), but the correlation for boys was ($r = .21$, $p < .01$). This suggests that for girls, there is not a relation between what their behavioral objectives are in response to ambiguous provocation and what their peers observe regarding their actual aggressive behavior. This may help to explain why girls' thoughts regarding aggression were not found to be related to their overall aggressive behavior, although these social-cognitive processes significantly predicted to their self-reported aggressive behavior. Girls' thoughts about aggression do seem to motivate their aggressive behavior, but not necessarily in a way that is recognized as aggressive by peers. In contrast, for boys, there appears to be more consistency in their aggressive behavior across contexts and in how their social-cognitive processes relate to their aggressive behavior. Specifically, boys' self-reported aggressive behavior in response to ambiguous provocations is significantly related to their general aggressive behavior patterns, as evaluated by peers. Furthermore, boys' thought processes regarding aggression seem to motivate their aggressive behavior, both in terms of what the boys themselves report they would do and in terms of the behavioral characteristics that peers observe.

Gender differences in motivational systems regarding aggressive behavior

It is also possible that boys' and girls' social-cognitive processes regarding aggression may motivate them to engage in different forms of aggressive behavior, based on their higher-order social goals. In fact, the physical and verbal forms of aggression that were assessed in the present study appear to be more relevant to the social lives of boys than of girls. Whereas aggressive behavior has been defined as behavior that is intended to hurt or harm others (Berkowitz, 1993), Crick and Grotpeter (1995) have proposed that when attempting to inflict harm on peers, children do so in ways that best thwart or damage the goals that are valued by their respective gender groups. The goals of instrumentality and dominance have been shown to be important to boys, whereas relationship-oriented goals are more valued by girls (see Block, 1983, for a review). Crick and Grotpeter (1995) found that boys are more likely to harm others through physical and verbal aggression, whereas girls are more apt to engage in relational aggression, i.e., behaviors that are intended to damage another child's friendships, or feelings of inclusion by the peer group. Although research has consistently shown that boys are more aggressive than girls (see Parke & Slaby, 1983, for a review), Crick and Grotpeter (1995) have found that this gender gap in aggression narrows when relational as well as overt forms of aggression are assessed.

It appears that gender differences in the enactment of aggressive behavior exist because different motivational systems may be operating for boys and girls. Perhaps when boys endorse aggressive goals, they are also influenced by their higher-order goals of dominance and instrumentality as they decide how to fulfill their aggressive goals. If it is particularly important for boys to assert themselves and control peers across a variety of social situations, then they are likely to try to accomplish these goals through physical and verbal aggression. Therefore, it is likely that significant relations were found between boys' social-cognitive processes and their general aggressive behavior in the present study because the forms of aggression that were evaluated by peers are in fact more characteristic of boys' aggressive behavioral styles.

It is possible that when girls endorse aggressive thought patterns, they are also influenced by their higher-order goals of affiliation with peers. Consequently, in actual social interactions, girls may be more likely to act on their aggressive motivations by using relational aggression. For example, girls may choose to accomplish their aggressive goals by excluding a peer from participating in a group rather than by hitting the peer. Thus, perhaps part of the reason that girls' peer-evaluated aggressive behavior was not significantly predicted by their social-cognitive processes is that forms of aggression that are more relevant to girls' peer groups were not assessed in the present study. It may be that girls' social-cognitive processes are more closely tied to their enactment of relational aggression, since this form of aggression is more characteristic of them.

Relations of peer acceptance to social-cognitive processes and
aggressive behavior for boys and girls

As can be seen in Table 5.1, neither boys' nor girls' social-cognitive processes were significantly correlated with their peer acceptance level. However, for both boys and girls, aggressive behavior was significantly and negatively correlated with acceptance. Furthermore, when acceptance was regressed on attributions of intent, aggressive goals, efficacy for aggression, legitimacy of aggression beliefs, and aggressive behavior, aggressive behavior was the only significant, independent predictor of acceptance for both boys ($B = -.46$, $p < .01$) and girls ($B = -.32$, $p < .01$). Thus, it appears that there are not direct associations between thought processes and acceptance for either boys or girls. These results suggest a pathway in which social-cognitive processes motivate aggressive behavior, and then aggressive behavior contributes to reduced acceptance by peers. It may be that even stronger relations between aggression and acceptance could be found, particularly for girls, if both overt and relational forms of aggression are taken into account. It seems important that future work on motivational patterns that contribute to aggression examine the association of social-cognitive processes with relational aggression, especially to better understand girls' aggression. Furthermore, it would be interesting to investigate the relative contributions of overt and relational aggression in predicting boys' and girls' peer acceptance.

Implications for intervention

Both past research and the present study indicate that children's social-cognitive processes regarding aggression are related to their aggressive behavior. Furthermore, aggressive behavior is associated with negative consequences for children in school, including academic difficulties and social rejection by peers. Thus, it appears that to try to improve aspects of children's school adjustment, efforts must be made to decrease their aggressive behavior. One model that has been proposed by peer relationships researchers is that children who exhibit antisocial behavior and who are rejected by peers suffer from social skills deficits (Asher & Renshaw, 1981). Consequently, in many intervention studies (e.g., Ladd, 1981; Oden & Asher, 1977), children have been taught various prosocial skills (e.g., cooperation, communication, participation) thought to promote positive social interactions and peer acceptance. The social skills deficits model seems to suggest that by teaching children prosocial skills, their antisocial behavior will be replaced by more adaptive social strategies.

However, it appears important not only that prosocial skills be encouraged but also that antisocial behavior be actively discouraged (Coie & Koeppl, 1990). Indeed, in intervention work by Bierman, Miller, and Stabb (1987), children who received instruction in prosocial behavior as well as prohibitions against negative behavior displayed greater increases in prosocial behavior and decreases in antisocial behavior than children who received only one aspect of the training.

Although past intervention efforts have been fairly successful, not all children have shown improvements in behavior or gains in acceptance. One possible explanation for why these programs have not been more effective is that these interventions have focused primarily on changing children's behavior, and they have not addressed the social-cognitive variables that seem to play a significant role in motivating maladaptive social behaviors. It seems reasonable to expect that after being repeatedly reinforced for not being aggressive and being taught to use prosocial skills, children may begin to act less aggressively and more prosocially among peers. However, if these children retain the same social-cognitive patterns that initially motivated their aggression (e.g., a hostile attributional style), they are likely to return soon to a pattern of aggressive interaction with their peers.

To date, very few studies have attempted to decrease children's aggression by intervening at the social-cognitive level. However, the existing work provides evidence that such interventions can be effective in changing children's thought processes regarding aggression and in reducing their aggressive behavior. In a recent study, Hudley and Graham (1993) conducted an intervention program that was designed to reduce aggressive males' tendency to attribute hostile intentions to peers following ambiguous provocation situations. Specifically, through discussions and role play across twelve sessions, these boys were taught to identify ambiguous peer intent, to make attributions to nonhostile intent when negative social encounters were portrayed as ambiguous, and to generate nonaggressive responses given attributional uncertainty. It was found that following the attributional intervention, in response to both hypothetical situations and laboratory simulations of ambiguous provocation, aggressive boys were less likely to presume hostile intent by peers and less likely to react with aggression. In addition, intervention subjects were rated as less aggressive by their teachers following the treatment. Thus, it appears that boys' attributional styles can be modified, and such alterations in thoughts do effectively decrease their aggressive behavior, even in more generalized social contexts.

An intervention study by Guerra and Slaby (1990) likewise supports the proposition that modifying individuals' beliefs about aggression can change their behavior. In this study, adolescents incarcerated for offenses involving aggression participated in a twelve-session intervention that focused on several cognitive factors identified as correlates of aggression, including beliefs about the legitimacy of aggression. The results of the intervention were encouraging, as those adolescents who participated showed decreased endorsement of beliefs supporting aggression, decreased aggressive behavior, and increased social problem solving skills. However, following their release from the institution, the treatment groups did not have a significantly lower recidivism rate than did the nontreatment control groups. Therefore, although the intervention was effective in the short-term, it appears that its influence may have diminished in the long-term, perhaps because the adolescents returned to an environment where their aggression was once again encouraged.

Whereas past intervention efforts have focused on children's attributions of intent and beliefs about the legitimacy of aggression, results of the present study suggest that children's aggressive goals are likely to be an important target for intervention when attempting to reduce children's aggression. It appears that children who are especially focused on trying to retaliate against peers or dominate the social situation are particularly likely to engage in aggressive behavior. This suggests that attempts need to be made to restructure the social goal hierarchy of aggressive children. Such an intervention might take the form of addressing children's perceptions of the relative value of aggressive and prosocial goals and emphasizing the greater positive consequences of pursuing prosocial as opposed to aggressive goals. Moreover, it is very important that such lessons be accompanied by practice in pursuing these prosocial goals so that children can personally experience the benefits of giving priority to prosocial over aggressive goals. In an intervention study with unpopular children that may have indirectly influenced children's social goal priorities, Oden and Asher (1977) coached children on several prosocial skills (e.g., cooperation) before these children played games with peers. These skills were discussed during the coaching sessions and were also described as ways to make the games more fun to play. Thus, it seems that the coaching not only provided children with lessons about important prosocial skills, but also encouraged children to pursue a prosocial goal (having fun) in the game-playing situation rather than an aggressive goal, such as dominance.

It is possible that by focusing children on prosocial goals, and giving them the opportunity to have positive social experiences when pursuing these goals, children may eventually assign higher priority to prosocial goals in their social interactions.

Furthermore, it appears that part of the reason that children pursue aggressive goals is that they think they are good at achieving these goals, and they believe that they are not as effective in fulfilling prosocial goals, especially when they are provoked (Erdley & Asher, in press). It may be that if children have the opportunity to engage in prosocial interactions in a controlled social environment (e.g., a laboratory situation), their confidence in their prosocial skills may increase, and they may then be more likely to adopt prosocial goals in other contexts. It seems particularly important that children be given the opportunity to practice their prosocial behaviors in response to situations that are potentially emotionally arousing, such as ambiguous provocation or social failure, since these kinds of situations seem to be quite problematic for aggressive children (Dodge, McClaskey, & Feldman, 1985). Perhaps children's motivational patterns for aggression are especially primed because they perceive these situations as very threatening. Hence, if children's aggressive motivations can be successfully reduced under these types of circumstances, it is likely that their overall level of aggressive behavior would decrease as well.

Clearly, it must be recognized that modifying social-cognitive processes regarding aggression is likely to be quite challenging. This is particularly so because across development, children's experiences with various socialization influences, including the family and peers, are likely to contribute to the development and maintenance of certain social information-processing patterns. For example, children who are in a family environment that endorses antisocial behavior and promotes thoughts that support aggression are likely to receive repeated reinforcement for their more hostile approach to social interactions (Pettit, Dodge, & Brown, 1988). Moreover, in the peer context, it has been found that aggressive children not only are more likely to make hostile attributions and to react aggressively to peers but also are more likely to be victims of aggression. Thus, their perceptions of peers as hostile do have a basis in reality and are often confirmed through their experiences (Dodge & Frame, 1982). As a result of their frequent and regular use of hostile attributions, it appears that aggressive children's perception that others intend to harm them is a causal construct that remains quite active in their memories. This construct is then readily accessible in subsequent situations of attributional ambiguity, and consequently aggressive children are primed to attribute hostile intent

(Graham & Hudley, 1994). In addition to their hostile perceptions of the social world, aggressive children are likely to maintain positive beliefs regarding their own use of aggression because for many of these children, such behavior results in a variety of instrumental rewards (Perry et al., 1986), Therefore, it may be somewhat difficult to convince aggressive children that prosocial behavior is more beneficial overall than is aggressive behavior.

Together, these findings suggest that as children become older, the ways in which they process social information are likely to become solidified through years of social experiences and may become increasingly resistant to change. Perhaps future intervention efforts would be potentially more successful, particularly in the long term, if they were attempted with children at earlier ages (i.e., preschool) before thought patterns become relatively stable (see Zahavi & Asher, 1978, for a relevant intervention effort). Family-based interventions during the preschool years may be especially effective in preventing children from developing social-cognitive patterns that contribute to aggressive behavior. Moreover, peer-based interventions should take into account the possibility that, regardless of their age, aggressive children mostly associate with certain peers who encourage their aggression. Therefore, it may be important to conduct interventions with groups of children who might then reinforce one another's prosocial behavior and discourage aggressive behavior and the related aggressive thought patterns.

Children's aggressive behavior appears to be motivated by several social-cognitive processes that are related to one another. Thus, it may be that by modifying one aspect of children's motivation to act aggressively (e.g., their aggressive goals), other aspects of their thoughts that might encourage aggressive behavior (e.g., their propensity to attribute hostile intentions) may also change. However, it seems that the most effective social-cognitive interventions should try to target the variety of thought processes that are associated with aggressive behavior. That is, by simultaneously trying to alter children's attributions of intent, their endorsement of aggressive goals, their perceptions of efficacy for acting aggressively, and their beliefs that aggression is legitimate, children's motivation to engage in aggressive behavior may be decreased. Reducing the incidence of aggressive behavior of children in school is especially important because such behavior clearly has a negative impact on a variety of indices of school adjustment. The research discussed in this chapter suggests that a focus on the motivational processes that underlie children's aggression is likely to be an effective intervention strategy for decreasing children's aggressive behavior. Such decreases in aggression will then hopefully contribute to more positive outcomes for children in school, including improved academic performance and increased acceptance by classmates.

References

Asher, S. R., Parkhurst, J. T., Hymel, S., & Williams, G. A. (1990). Peer rejection and loneliness in childhood. In S. R. Asher & J. D. Coie (Eds.), *Peer rejection in childhood* (pp. 253–273). New York: Cambridge University Press.

Asher, S. R., & Renshaw, P. D. (1981). Children without friends: Social knowledge and social-skill training. In S. R. Asher & J. M. Gottman (Eds.), *The development of children's friendships* (pp. 273–296). New York: Cambridge University Press.

Bandura, A. (1979). Psychological mechanisms of aggression. In M. von Cranach, K. Foppa, W. Lepenies, & D. Ploog (Eds.), *Human ethology: Claims and limits of a new discipline* (pp. 316–379). Cambridge: Cambridge University Press.

Bandura, A. (1981). Self-referent thought: A developmental analysis of self-efficacy. In J. H. Flavell & L. Ross (Eds.), *Social cognitive development: Frontiers and possible futures* (pp. 200–239). Cambridge: Cambridge University Press.

Bandura, A. (1986). *Social foundations of thought and action: A social cognitive theory.* Englewood Cliffs, NJ: Prentice-Hall.

Berkowitz, L. (1977). Situational and personal conditions governing reactions to aggressive cues. In D. Magnusson & N. S. Endler (Eds.), *Personality at the crossroads: Current issues in interactional psychology* (pp. 165–171) New York: Wiley.

Berkowitz, L. (1993). *Aggression: Its causes, consequences, and control.* New York: Academic Press.

Berndt, T. J. (1987, April). *Changes in friendship and school adjustment after the transition to junior high school.* Paper presented at the biennial meeting of the Society for Research in Child Development, Baltimore.

Bierman, K. L., Miller, C. L., & Stabb, S. D. (1987). Improving the social behavior and peer acceptance of rejected boys: Effects of social skill training with instructions and prohibitions. *Journal of Consulting and Clinical Psychology, 55,* 194–200.

Block, J. H. (1983). Differential premises arising from differential socialization of the sexes: Some conjectures. *Child Development, 54,* 1335–1354.

Boldizar, J. P., Perry, D. G., & Perry, L. C. (1989). Outcome values and aggression. *Child Development, 60,* 17–579.

Coie, J. D., & Dodge, K. A., & Kupersmidt, J. B. (1990). Peer group behavior and social status. In S. R. Asher & J. D. Coie (Eds.), *Peer rejection in childhood* (pp. 17–59). New York: Cambridge University Press.

Coie, J. D., & Koeppl, G. K. (1990). Adapting intervention to the problems of aggressive and disruptive rejected children. In S. R. Asher & J. D. Coie (Eds.), *Peer rejection in childhood* (pp. 309–337). New York: Cambridge University Press.

Coie, J. D., & Krehbiel, G. (1984). Effects of academic tutoring on the social status of low-achieving, socially rejected children. *Child Development, 55,* 1465–1478.

Crick, N. R., & Dodge, K. A. (1994). A review and reformulation of social information-processing mechanisms in children's social adjustment. *Psychological Bulletin, 115,* 74–101.

Crick, N. R., & Grotpeter, J. K. (1995). Relational aggression, gender, and social-psychological adjustment. *Child Development, 66,* 710–722.

Crick, N. R., & Ladd, G. W. (1990). Children's perceptions of the outcomes of social strategies: Do the ends justify being mean? *Developmental Psychology, 26,* 612–620.

Dodge, K. A. (1980). Social cognition and children's aggressive behavior. *Child Development, 51,* 162–170.

Dodge, K. A. (1986). A social information processing model of social competence in children. In M. Perlmutter (Ed.), *The Minnesota Symposium on Child Psychology* (vol. 18, pp. 77–125). Hillsdale, NJ: Erlbaum.

Dodge, K. A., & Feldman, E. (1990). Issues in social cognition and sociometric status. In S. R. Asher & J. D. Coie (Eds.), *Peer rejection in childhood* (pp. 119–155). New York: Cambridge University Press.

Dodge, K. A., & Frame, C. L. (1982). Social cognitive biases and deficits in aggressive boys. *Child Development, 53,* 620–635.

Dodge, K. A., McClaskey, C. L., & Feldman, E. (1985). A situational approach to the assessment of social competence in children. *Journal of Consulting and Clinical Psychology, 53,* 344–353.

Dodge, K. A., & Newman, J. P. (1981). Biased decision-making processing in aggressive boys. *Journal of Abnormal Psychology, 90,* 375–379.

Erdley, C. A., & Asher, S. R. (in press). Children's social goals and self-efficacy perceptions as influences on their responses to ambiguous provocation. *Child Development.*

Erdley, C. A., & Asher, S. R. (1993, August). Linkages between aggression and children's legitimacy of aggression beliefs. In S. R. Asher (Chair), *Social relationships, social beliefs, and aggression.* Symposium conducted at the annual meeting of the American Psychological Association, Toronto.

Fitzgerald, P. D., & Asher, S. R. (1987, August). *Aggressive-rejected children's attributional biases about liked and disliked peers.* Paper presented at the annual meeting of the American Psychological Association, New York.

Graham, S., Hudley, C., & Williams, E. (1992). Attributional and emotional determinants of aggression among African-American and Latino young adolescents. *Developmental Psychology, 28,* 731–740.

Graham, S., & Hudley, C. (1994). Attributions of aggressive and nonaggressive African-American male early adolescents: A study of construct accessibility. *Developmental Psychology, 30,* 365–373.

Guerra, N. G., & Slaby R. G. (1990). Cognitive mediators of aggression in adolescent offenders: 2. Intervention. *Developmental Psychology, 26,* 269–277.

Hudley, C., & Graham, S. (1993). An attributional intervention to reduce peer-directed aggression among African-American boys. *Child Development, 64,* 124–138.

Kupersmidt, J. B., Coie, J. D., & Dodge, K. A. (1990). The role of poor peer relationships in the development of disorder. In S. R. Asher & J. D. Coie (Eds.), *Peer rejection in childhood* (pp. 274–305). New York: Cambridge University Press.

Ladd, G. W. (1981). Effectiveness of a social learning method for enhancing children's social interaction and peer acceptance. *Child Development, 52,* 171–178.

Ladd, G. W., & Price, J. M. (1987). Predicting children's social and school adjustment following the transition from preschool to kindergarten. *Child Development, 58,* 1168–1189.

Lochman, J. E., Wayland, K. K., & White, K. J. (1993). Social goals: Relationship to adolescent adjustment and to social problem solving. *Journal of Abnormal Child Psychology, 21,* 135–151.

Nasby, W., Hayden, B., & DePaulo, B. M. (1980). Attributional bias among aggressive boys to interpret unambiguous social stimuli as displays of hostility. *Journal of Abnormal Psychology, 89,* 459–468.

Oden, S., & Asher, S. R. (1977). Coaching children in social skills for friendship making. *Child Development, 48,* 495–506.

Parke, R. D., & Slaby R. G. (1983). The development of aggression. In E. M. Hetherington (Ed.), P. H. Mussen (Series Ed.), *Handbook of child psychology. Vol. 4: Socialization, personality, and social development* (pp.547–641). New York: Wiley.

Parker, J. G., & Asher, S. R. (1987). Peer relations and later personal adjustment: Are low-accepted children at risk? *Psychological Bulletin, 102,* 357–389.

Perry, D. G., & Bussey, K. (1977). Self-reinforcement in high- and low-aggressive boys following acts of aggression. *Child Development, 48,* 653–657.

Perry, D. G., Perry, L. C., & Rasmussen, P. (1986). Cognitive social learning mediators of aggression. *Child Development, 57,* 700–711.

Pervin, L. A. (1989). Goal concepts in personality and social psychology: A historical perspective. In L. A. Pervin (Ed.), *Goal concepts in personality and social psychology* (pp. 1–17). Hillsdale, NJ: Erlbaum.

Pettit, G. S., Dodge, K. A., & Brown, M. M. (1988). Early family experience, social problem solving patterns, and children's social competence. *Child Development, 59,* 107–120.

Rabiner, D. L., & Gordon, L. V. (1992). The coordination of conflicting social goals: Differences between rejected and nonrejected boys. *Child Development, 63,* 1344–1350.

Renshaw, P. D., & Asher, S. R. (1982). Social competence and peer status: The distinction between goals and strategies. In K. H. Rubin & H. S. Ross (Eds.), *Peer relationships and social skills in childhood* (pp. 375–395). New York: Springer-Verlag.

Renshaw, P. D., & Asher, S. R. (1983). Children's goals and strategies for social interaction. *Merrill-Palmer Quarterly, 29,* 553–574.

Rockhill, C. M., & Asher, S. R. (1992, April). *Peer assessment of the behavioral characteristics of poorly accepted boys and girls.* Paper presented at the annual meeting of the American Educational Research Association, San Francisco.

Rubin, K. H., & Krasnor, L. R. (1986). Social-cognitive and social behavioral perspectives on problem solving. In M. Perlmutter (Ed.), *The Minnesota Symposium on Child Psychology* (vol. 18, pp. 1–68). Hillsdale, NJ: Erlbaum.

Slaby, R. G., & Guerra, N. G. (1988). Cognitive mediators of aggression in adolescent offenders: 1. Assessment. *Developmental Psychology, 24,* 580–588.

Taylor, A. R., & Asher, S. R. (1984). Children's goals and social competence: Individual differences in a game-playing context. In T. Field, J. L. Roopnarine, & M. Segal (Eds.), *Friendships in normal and handicapped children* (pp.53–77). Norwood, NJ: Ablex.

Wentzel, K. R. (1991). Social and academic goals at school: Motivation and achievement in context. In M. Maehr & P. Pintrich (Eds.), *Advances in motivation and achievement* (vol. 7, pp. 185–212). Greenwich, CT: JAI Press.

Wentzel, K. R., & Erdley, C. A. (1993). Strategies for making friends: Relations to social behavior and peer acceptance in early adolescence. *Developmental Psychology, 29,* 819–826.

Zahavi, S., & Asher, S. R. (1978). The effect of verbal instructions on preschool children's aggressive behavior. *Journal of School Psychology, 16,* 146–153.

With respect to intervention, the role of the schools in promoting the development of social responsibility and caring behavior in youth can arouse controversy when educators focus on lifestyle issues and personal values (e.g., sexuality; moral and religious values). Nevertheless, there is strong support for the involvement of schools in social problems that have a clear behavioral focus and that produce significant public consequences – for example, problems relating to citizenship, public health issues, and respect for other's rights and property (Krumboltz et al., 1987). Thus, as long as educators respect these boundaries, the question is not *whether* schools should play a significant role in helping young people develop into concerned, responsible adults; rather, the question is *how* schools can best facilitate such development. This brings us back once again to the critical need for more – and more sophisticated – research on the development of social responsibility and caring behavior in youth. Such research depends in turn on the availability of a theoretically sound and pragmatically useful conceptual framework for understanding motivation and its influence on competence development. One such conceptual framework, Motivational Systems Theory, is outlined next.

Motivational systems theory

Motivational Systems Theory (MST; M. Ford, 1992) is a relatively new, integrative theory of motivation derived from Donald Ford's Living Systems Framework (LSF; D. Ford, 1987; M. Ford & D. Ford, 1987). The LSF is a comprehensive theory of human functioning and development that is designed to represent all of the biological, psychological, and behavioral processes of the person and how they are organized in complex patterns of unitary functioning in variable environments. MST elaborates on a subset of these processes, namely, those representing the three sets of phenomena that have traditionally been of concern in the field of human motivation: the selective *direction* of behavior patterns (i.e., what people want and what they are trying to accomplish), the selective *energization* of behavior patterns (i.e., how people get "turned on" or "turned off"), and the selective *regulation* of behavior patterns (i.e., how people decide to try something, stick with it, or give up.)

MST begins with the general idea that, in any given domain, effective functioning or competence can best be defined in terms of the attainment of personally and/or socially valued goals (M. Ford, 1985, 1992). MST further proposes, using a heuristic (i.e., nonmathematical) equation, that there are four basic prerequisites for goal attainment:

$$\text{Competence} = \frac{\text{Motivation} \times \text{Skill}}{\text{Biology}} \times \text{Responsive Environment}$$

In other words, valued outcomes will not occur unless (1) the person has the *motivation* needed to initiate and maintain activity directed toward those outcomes; (2) the person has the *skill* needed to construct and execute a pattern of activity that is appropriate and effective with respect to those outcomes; (3) the person's *biological structure and functioning* is able to support both the motivational and skill components; and (4) there is a *responsive environment* facilitating, or at least not excessively constraining, progress toward the desired outcomes (M. Ford, 1992). If any of these components is missing or inadequate, ineffective functioning will occur.

Because the biological and skill prerequisites for behaving in a responsible or caring manner are well within the repertoires of most older children and adolescents, the psychological literature on prosocial development has focused largely on motivational and contextual influences on social responsibility and caring behavior (e.g., Batson, 1990; Batson, Dyck, Batson, Powell, McMaster, & Griffitt, 1988; Bergin, 1987; Chapman, Zahn-Waxler, Cooperman, & Iannotti, 1987; Eisenberg & Miller, 1987; Ford, Wentzel, Siesfeld, Wood, & Feldman, 1986; Ford, Wentzel, Wood, Stevens, & Siesfeld, 1989; Hoffman, 1982; Krebs, 1975; Wentzel, 1994, this volume). This is not a well organized literature, however. Motivational processes are usually studied in isolation rather than as components of larger motivational patterns, and key concepts are often defined differently by different researchers. For example, empathy has been a dominant topic in this literature despite the fact that it is only one of many relevant motivational processes, and theorists are still struggling with some basic definitional issues. The social support literature also illustrates how conceptual narrowness and uncertainty can constrain a productive and exciting line or research. It thus seems likely that further progress will depend on the development of conceptual approaches that are both more precise and more comprehensive than existing frameworks.

In MST, motivation is understood to be a *psychological, anticipatory,* and *evaluative* phenomenon (M. Ford, 1992). In other works, motivation exists within (not outside) the person, where its job is to imagine possible future states and outcomes, and to evaluate the extent to which those future circumstances are desirable, emotionally compelling, and attainable. Based on these defining criteria, motivation is defined in MST as the organized patterning of an individual's personal goals, emotional arousal processes, and personal agency beliefs (M. Ford, 1992). This definition of motivation can be represented symbolically by the following heuristic formula:

$$\text{Motivation} = \text{Goals} \times \text{Emotions} \times \text{Personal Agency Beliefs}$$

Thus, for example, MST would predict that social responsibility and caring behavior would be largely a function of (1) the degree to which personal goals are directed toward, or at least well aligned with, prosocial actions, and achievements; (2) the degree to which compelling emotions inhibiting selfish or hurtful behavior, and facilitation caring and responsible behavior, are aroused in the pursuit of these goals; and (3) the degree to which a person believes that their skills and surrounding context will enable them to behave in a helpful or responsible manner.

Goals, emotions, and personal agency beliefs work together to guide decision making – all are necessary, and none are sufficient for goal-directed activity. Some compensation for weak elements in the equation is possible, but each motivational component has "veto power" over the rest. Strong, effective motivational messages to the "instrumental troops" (attention, perception, memory, information processing, planning, problem-solving, and action components of the person) will only result when there is reasonable agreement in "motivational headquarters" that a goal is indeed desirable, compelling, and attainable (M. Ford, 1992). Conflicts between multiple, competing goals can also produce mixed motivational messages and thereby reduce the effectiveness of ongoing behavior patterns.

With this conceptual overview, it is now possible to explicate the functional and substantive nature of each of these three sets of motivational processes.

Personal goals

In MST, goals are defined simply as thoughts about desired (and undesired) future states and outcomes (M. Ford, 1992). Such thoughts represent what the person is trying to accomplish (or avoid) in ongoing interactions with the environment. The primary function of these thoughts is to direct the other psychological and behavioral components of the person to try to produce the desired consequences. Goals thus play a leadership role in motivational patterns by defining their content and direction. They also serve as the central organizing force in social and personality development (Cantor & Harlow, 1994; Emmons, 1989; Markus & Ruvolo, 1989).

Goals that are clearly conceived and highly prioritized with respect to potentially competing goals will organize and direct people's attention and activity toward pursuit of those goals. For example, a student who values teacher acceptance and conformity to classroom rules and expectations is a good bet to behave in a socially responsible manner in school settings, even when such behavior negatively impacts evaluations from peers (Wentzel, 1994). Similarly, teenagers with a clear sense of what they are trying to accomplish at school – whether those goals are academic, social, or extracurricular – are much more likely to attend school and display patterns of meaningful engagement than are those with little personal investment in the variety of goals afforded by the school context.

In MST, the Ford and Nichols Taxonomy of Human Goals (Ford, & Nichols, 1987; 1991) is used to represent the diversity of goals that may direct people's behavior in different situations (see Table 6.1) Although people's thoughts about desired and undesired consequences are usually rather personalized and context-specific, the taxonomy serves as a useful heuristic device for researchers and practitioners who need a systematic, standardized way of representing the basic "themes" in people's concerns and priorities.

Theoretically, the goals most relevant to social responsibility and caring behavior are the four integrative social relationship goals (see Table 6.1). In the case of *belongingness*, such behavior is an expected byproduct of the individual's desire to enhance the functioning or integrity of a valued social group (e.g., family, school, or peer group) or interpersonal relationship (e.g., friend, parent, teacher). In other words, acting in a responsible, caring way toward others helps create and cement social bonds. Similarly, to the extent that participation and engagement in classroom life is seen as a means to maintaining or enhancing these bonds (e.g., with teachers or successful peers), belongingness can facilitate school achievement as well (Connell & Wellborn, 1991).

Social responsibility goals provide an alternative, more direct pathway to responsible behavior by focusing attention on personal and/or cultural standards of conduct, often independent of close relationships. Such goals are reflected in efforts to keep interpersonal commitments, fulfill social role obligations, and avoid social and ethical transgressions. These goals appear to be an important part of the motivational foundation needed to facilitate school adjustment and academic achievement (Ford, 1992; Wentzel, 1991a, 1991b, 1993a, 1993b).

Table 6.1 The Ford and Nichols taxonomy of human goals

Desired Within-Person Consequences	
Affective Goals – feelings or emotions one wishes to experience or avoid	
Arousal	Experiencing excitement or heightened arousal; Avoiding boredom or stressful inactivity
Tranquility	Feeling relaxed and at ease; Avoiding stressful overarousal
Happiness	Experiencing feelings of joy, satisfaction, or well being; Avoiding feelings of emotional distress or dissatisfaction
Bodily Sensations	Experiencing pleasure associated with physical sensations, physical movement, or bodily contact; Avoiding unpleasant or uncomfortable bodily sensations
Physical Well Being	Feeling healthy, energetic, or physically robust; Avoiding feelings of lethargy, weakness, or ill health
Cognitive Goals – mental representations one wants to construct or maintain	
Exploration	Satisfying one's curiosity about personally meaningful events; Avoiding a sense of being uninformed or not knowing what's going on
Understanding	Gaining knowledge or making sense out of something; Avoiding misconceptions, erroneous beliefs, or feeling of confusion
Intellectual Creativity	Engaging in activities involving original thinking or novel or interesting ideas; Avoiding mindless or familiar ways of thinking
Positive Self-Evaluations	Maintaining a sense of self-confidence, pride, or self-worth; Avoiding feelings of failure, guilt, or incompetence
Subjective Organization Goals – special states that one seeks to experience or avoid	
Unity	Experiencing a profound or spiritual sense of connectedness, harmony, or oneness with people, nature, or a greater power; Avoiding feelings of psychological disunity or disorganization
Transcendence	Experiencing optimal or extraordinary states of functioning; Avoiding feeling trapped within the boundaries ordinary experience

Desired Person- Environment Consequences	
Self-Assertive Social Relationship Goals – maintaining or promoting the self	
Individuality	Feeling unique, special, or different; Avoiding similarity or conformity with others
Self-Determination	Experiencing a sense of freedom to act or make choices; Avoiding the feeling of being pressured, constrained, or coerced
Superiority	Comparing favorably to others in terms of winning, status, or success; Avoiding unfavorable comparisons with others
Resource Acquisition	Obtaining approval, support, assistance, advice, or validation from others; Avoiding social disapproval or rejection

Table 6.1 Continued

Desired Person- Environment Consequences	
Integrative Social Relationship Goals – maintaining or promoting the well being of others	
Belongingness	Building or maintaining attachments, friendships, intimacy, or a sense of community; Avoiding feelings of social isolation or separateness
Social Responsibility	Keeping interpersonal commitments, meeting social role obligations, and conforming to social and moral rules; Avoiding social transgressions and unethical or illegal conduct
Equity	Promoting fairness, justice, reciprocity, or equality; Avoiding unfair or unjust actions
Resource Provision	Giving approval, support, assistance, advice, or validation to others; Avoiding selfish or uncaring behavior
Task Goals – producing desired effects or avoiding undesired effects in the relationship between the person and environment	
Mastery	Meeting a challenging standard of achievement or improvement; Avoiding incompetence, mediocrity, or decrements in performance
Task Creativity	Engaging in activities involving artistic expression or creativity; Avoiding tasks that do not provide opportunities for creative action
Management	Maintaining order, organization, or productivity in daily life tasks; Avoiding sloppiness, inefficiency, or disorganization
Material Gain	Increasing the amount of money or tangible goods one has; Avoiding the loss of money or material possessions
Safety	Being unharmed, physically secure, and free from risk; Avoiding threatening, depriving or harmful circumstances

Equity goals also promote social responsibility and caring behavior by motivating people to try to change circumstances characterized by social injustice, unequal resource distribution, and the victimization of helpless or disadvantaged individuals. Like social responsibility goals, such concerns may be manifested even in the absence of close relationships. Equity goals have not been directly linked to academic outcomes; however, it may be a question worthy of some exploration, given the demonstrated importance of other kinds of integrative social relationship goals to school achievement.

Finally, *resource provision*, with its focus on the needs and welfare of others, is the most directly implicated category of goals with respect to caring behavior. Although such goals sometimes emerge in interactions with strangers and acquaintances, they are usually embedded in social relationships involving reciprocal exchange processes (e.g., friendship or dating relationships) or in asymmetrical social roles in which one person is responsible for providing resources to another (e.g., parent-child or teacher-student relationships). Resource provision goals may also be an important feature of effective cooperative learning arrangements, perhaps in conjunction with social responsibility and resource acquisition concerns (Slavin, 1981, 1987).

Personal agency beliefs

This motivational component refers to whether a person believes that the other fundamental components of effective person-in-context functioning (i.e., the skill and "responsive environment" components) can be counted on to facilitate progress toward a goal. Thus, there are two different types of personal agency beliefs; *capability beliefs* (i.e., expectancies about whether one has the personal skill needed to attain a goal), and *context beliefs* (i.e., expectancies about whether the environment will be supportive of efforts to attain a goal) (M. Ford, 1992). Presumably, the personal agency beliefs of greatest significance for social responsibility and caring behavior are those pertaining to integrative social relationship goals. For example, one would expect students who believe they are capable of adjusting to the interpersonal expectations of the classroom, and who are confident they will be supported in their efforts to do so to be more socially and academically successful in that context than those with significant doubts about either of these prerequisites for effective functioning.

The function of personal agency beliefs is to help people decide which goals to pursue and how much time and effort they should invest in pursuit of a particular goal. This implies that, if a person is disinterested in a particular goal, his or her capability and context beliefs with respect to that goal will be of no significance. For example, if one cares little about mathematics, beliefs about the possible consequences of trying to achieve in mathematics will be moot (Meece, Wigfield, & Eccles, 1990). Conversely, personal agency beliefs can be expected to play a very influential role in the activation and inhibition of behavior when there is a strong goal in place. For example, people often do not act on deeply felt concerns about another person's welfare because they doubt their ability to act effectively or are concerned about how their actions will be interpreted.

Along these lines, it is important to keep in mind that motivation itself is only one of four major elements contributing to effective functioning. One should not assume, therefore, that strong goals and positive capability and context beliefs are sufficient for goal attainment. Ultimately, people must also have real skills and a truly responsive environment. Nevertheless, personal agency beliefs are often more fundamental than the actual skills and circumstances they represent in the sense that they can motivate people to create opportunities and acquire capabilities they do not yet possess. Thus, like personal goals, personal agency beliefs serve a crucial developmental function through their role in creating and maintaining patterns of social and academic engagement and achievement.

Emotional arousal processes

Emotions are organized functional patterns consisting of three components: an *affective* (neural-psychological) component (i.e., the general subjective feeling part of the emotion), a *physiological* component (i.e., a supporting pattern of biological processing), and a *transactional* component (i.e., expressive gestures that influence relevant aspects of the context) (D. Ford, 1987). Thus, emotions help people deal with varying circumstances by providing evaluative information about the person's interactions with the environment (affective regulatory information) and by supporting and facilitating action designed to produce desired consequences (energizing function).

Emotions provide a very potent mechanism for regulating behavior because affective experience has an immediacy to it that is hard to ignore (Frijda, 1988). For example, when people experience intense feelings of guilt or compassion, it is difficult to attend to anything else except the concern associated with those feelings (e.g., "I must make amends" or "Something needs to be done to help this person"). Emotions also gain potency by virtue of their flexibility – by interpreting situations in different ways, people can learn to associate particular emotions with almost any conceivable context (D. Ford, 1987). For example, students can learn to feel anxious in evaluative classroom situations, even when the objective consequences of a negative evaluation are imagined or trivial. Moreover, once learned, emotional associations may be generalized to other related contexts, including those that the individual has not yet encountered (e.g., other performance-related social settings).

Emotions and personal goals are highly interdependent processes. Indeed, Frijda (1988) has postulated what he calls the "Law of Concern" to characterize this interdependency: "Emotions arise in response to events that are important to the individual's goals, motives, or concerns" (p. 351). Emotions are also closely linked to personal agency beliefs, with both serving to regulate (activate or inhibit) behavior in specialized ways. Personal agency beliefs, because they are more likely to incorporate considerations about long-term consequences and the potential availability of alternative courses of action, are particularly useful for decisions about "big picture" matters, such as whether one should initiate or continue a complex, difficult, or time-consuming course of action. Emotions, on the other hand, are particularly useful when effective functioning requires immediate or vigorous action in the context of a concrete problem or opportunity, such as escape from imminent harm, removal of an obstacle to goal attainment, or inhibition of a personally or socially damaging action (M. Ford, 1992).

Because emotions are so flexible, social responsibility and caring behavior may be facilitated by a diversity of emotion patterns, both positive and negative. However, the research literature on the emotional regulation of prosocial behavior suggests that there are three emotion patterns of particular significance: empathic concern, guilt, and pride, in helping others (e.g., Batson et al., 1988; Eisenberg & Miller, 1987; Ford et al., 1989; Hoffman, 1982).

An empirical study of caring competence

In this section, the results of a recent investigation of the motivational processes associated with caring behavior in youth (Ford, Love, Chase, Pollina, & Ito, 1991) are summarized in an effort to illustrate the developmental significance of social motivation in this domain of development. Where appropriate, connections are drawn between this research and related work on adolescent social responsibility.

Participants in this study were 174 students (99 girls and 75 boys) enrolled in an ethnically diverse California (Bay Area) public high school located in an upper-middle class community. The study was designed to test the hypothesis that the three most fundamental qualities of caring behavior patterns are: (1) strong integrative goals (especially resource provision); (2) powerful emotions facilitating prosocial behavior and inhibiting selfish behavior (especially empathetic concern); and (3) positive personal agency beliefs for behaving in a caring manner. Caring competence was defined in this study as one aspect of *intergrative competence,* a broad concept representing effective efforts to promote, protect, maintain, or restore the rights, interest, or well being of another person or group of people. Within this domain, caring competence refers specifically to situations in which prosocial action is more a matter of personal choice than it is a function of social obligation. In other words, caring competence is most clearly manifested in situations for which there are no specific laws, social rules, or interpersonal commitments requiring one to behave in a prosocial manner. The concept of social responsibility represents these more obligatory aspects of integrative competence.

Caring competence

The concept of caring competence was measured in this study by seeking information from a diversity of sources. Specifically, self-ratings, teacher ratings, and peer nominations of caring competence were obtained with respect to a variety of concrete, hypothetical situations emphasizing the possibility of behaving in a helpful, supportive, or civic-minded manner. Situations were designed so that external pressures and obligations to behave in a caring manner were minimized. In each case, the caring response option required the student to behave in a socially exceptional way, either in terms of "going beyond the call of duty," resisting pressure to conform to peer norms, or overcoming the temptation to behave in a personally expedient manner.

The primary tool used to assess caring competence was the Caring Competence Nomination Form (CCNF), a six-item measure adapted from a similar instrument developed by M. Ford (1982) to assess self-assertive and integrative social competence (broadly defined). In the first part of the CCNF, students were asked to nominate up to three boys and three girls in their class (other than themselves) who would be particularly competent in a diversity of situations requiring some form of caring behavior (e.g., being a tutor or peer counselor; doing community volunteer work; supporting a teacher or student in distress). Students were then asked to respond to two questions regarding their own level of caring competence in each situation. Teachers were also asked to rate how competent each of the students in their class(es) would be in each of the six situations in the CCNF.

In addition to the CCNF, students completed a revised version of the Youth Decision-Making Questionnaire (YDMQ), an eight-item measure based on a similar questionnaire used by Ford et al. (1989) in their study of adolescent social responsibility. The revision involved the insertion of new situations into the same format used in the original questionnaire. Specifically, students were asked to indicate on a four-point scale whether they would "Definitely" or "Probably" choose to behave in a caring or noncaring response option.

As expected, correlations among the various measures of caring competence were all positive and significant, ranging from .24 to .61. This made it possible to represent this concept using a single composite variable that would presumably yield a more valid representation of students' level of caring competence than could be provided by any of the assessments taken separately.

Personal goals

Two measures were used in this study to assess the general importance of integrative goals in students' lives. The first was the Assessment of Personal Goals (APG), a self-administered paper-and-pencil measure designed to assess the strength of each of the 24 categories represented in the Ford and Nichols Taxonomy of Human Goals (see Table 6.1). Although only four of these scales (i.e., the Resource Provision, Equity, Social Responsibility, and Belongingness scales) were directly relevant to the hypotheses guiding the study, the entire measure was used to explore the possibility that caring competence might be associated with other goal categories. For example, the use of the full APG made it possible to explore the possibility that caring competence might be negatively associated with various kinds of self-enhancing goals.

The APG is composed of 24 five-item scales, with each item presented in situation-specific form. For each item, respondents are asked to indicate on a 9-point scale how likely they would be to desire a particular outcome or to be bothered by a failure to attain that outcome (e.g., "A friend of yours is moving across the country to take a new job. Would it be important to you to stay in close touch with this friend by mail or phone?").

The second measure used to assess personal goals, the Assessment of Personal Agency Beliefs (APAB), is also based on the Ford and Nichols Taxonomy of Human Goals. Although its primary purpose is to assess capability and context beliefs, respondents must first indicate for each domain, "How often is this an important goal for you in your everyday life?" The inclusion of this preliminary question is based on the theoretical premise that capability and context beliefs are uninterpretable if the goal to which they refer is unimportant to the individual.

The version of the APAB used in this study asked students to respond to 21 "Life Goals" (it has since been expanded to include all of the 24 goals included in the Ford and Nichols Taxonomy), including items representing all four intergrative goals: "Caring For and About Other People" (Resource Provision), "Working For a More Just Society), and "Having Close Personal Relationships" (Belongingness). As with the APG, the entire APAB was administered (rather than just those items referring to integrative goals) to explore the possibility that caring competence might be associated with other goal categories. This also made it possible to look for converging patterns of evidence across two somewhat different goal measures.

Personal agency beliefs

After rating the importance of each goal in the APAB, students were instructed to respond to two additional questions representing their capability and context beliefs, respectively, for attaining those goals: "Considering only *YOURSELF* – your skills, interests, and personality – do you think you are capable of being successful in this area?" and "Considering only things *OUTSIDE* of yourself – your family and friends, your school or job situation, etc. – do you think they generally make it easier or harder for you to succeed in this area?" (In a subsequent revision of the APAB, this latter question was disaggregated into a set of separate questions, one for each of the respondent's major life contexts).

Because the concept of perceived social support overlaps considerably with the concept of context beliefs (i.e., social support is a major component of environmental responsiveness), students were also asked to complete the Youth Social Support Questionnaire (YSSQ), a brief assessment designed to measure both the size of the student's social support network and the degree to which the student felt satisfied with their (perceived) level of social support. Students were asked to list the first name or initials of each person that they felt close to, or to whom they could go for help, encouragement, or advice, and then indicate how helpful each person on this list would be if the student actually sought out their support (i.e., somewhat, fairly, or extremely helpful). Finally, students were asked to indicate the extent to which they were satisfied with the size and helpfulness of their social support network.

Emotional arousal processes

In addition to providing information about self-reported caring behavior, the Youth Decision-Making Questionnaire also served as an assessment of students' anticipated emotional responses to a diversity of caring-relevant situations. Specifically, after responding to the behavioral choice question in each of the eight situations in the YDMQ, students were asked to indicate the extent to which they would anticipate feeling several different emotions (i.e., very much, a little, or not at all) if they were to choose the caring response option or the noncaring alternative (students responded to both possibilities in each situation). The specific number and wording of each category of emotion items varied somewhat across situations in order to fit the particular circumstances involved; however, in each situation there was at least one question pertaining to the emotions of empathic concern, guilt, pride/pleasure in helping others, self-focused positive emotions (e.g., relief at avoiding an uncomfortable situation), and self-focused negative emotions (e.g., fear of peer disapproval).

Hypothesis 1: Integrative goals and caring competence.   Table 6.2 summarizes the results pertaining to the importance of integrative goals as qualities of caring adolescents. As expected, both the APG and APAB versions of each goal were significantly correlated with caring competence. Moreover, the two highest correlations involved resource provision goals. Inspection of the results for the component indices of caring competence indicated that integrative goals were highly predictive of students' *decision making* with respect to caring behavior, and moderately informative with regard to the quality of their *performance* in a caring role.

Hypothesis 2: Personal agency beliefs for integrative goals and caring competence.   Tests of the proposition that caring adolescents are likely to have positive capability and context beliefs for the attainment of integrative goals are also presented in Table 6.2. As predicted, personal agency beliefs for integrative goals were reliably associated with caring competence (with the exception of context beliefs in the social responsibility domain). Unexpectedly, results were generally stronger for the capability belief variables than for the context belief measures. Although this finding may be due in part to measurement problems (recall that the APAB was later revised to enable assessment of context beliefs in different contexts), it is consistent with the profile shown by a number of the most caring students in the sample in which they saw themselves as struggling to act on others' behalf in a relatively uncaring world.

Hypothesis 3: Emotional arousal processes and caring competence.   Correlations between the five emotion variables and the various indices of caring competence are summarized in the lower half of Table 6.2. Consistent with the literature's emphasis on empathy as an antecedent of caring behavior, empathic concern was a powerful predictor of behavioral decision making in caring situations, and a moderately good indicator of how effectively a person would be likely to perform in a caring role. Guilt and

Table 6.2 Correlations between motivational processes and caring competence

	Correlation of caring competence with:			
	Integrative Goals (APG/APAB)	Capability Beliefs (APAB)	Context Beliefs (APAB)	Emotions (YDMQ)
Resource provision/caring	.54**/.49**	.36**	.15*	
Equity/more just society	.40**/.42**	.35**	.18*	
Social responsibility	.42**/.32**	.14*	−.12	
Belongingness/close relationships	.35**/.17*	.28**	.14*	
Level of social support (number of people)			.27**	
Social support satisfaction			.20*	
Empathic concern				.63**
Pride				.47**
Guilt				.53**
Positive self-focused emotions				−.45**
Negative self- focused emotions				.18*

$N = 157$–174.
*$p \leq .05$.
**$p \leq .001$.
APG = Assessment of Personal Goals; APAB = Assessment of Personal Agency Beliefs;
YDMQ = Youth Decision-Making Questionnaire

pride/pleasure in helping others manifested a similar pattern of correlations, but at a slightly lower magnitude for most of the caring competence criteria. Self-focused positive emotions (i.e., good feelings associated with selfish or uncaring choices) were also reliable predictors of caring behavior, but in the opposite direction. Self-focused negative emotions (i.e., bad feelings associated with sacrificing selfish pleasures or being unable to escape others' distress) repeated this pattern but at a much lower level.

This same set of emotions appears to be involved in motivational patterns associated with adolescent social responsibility (Ford et al., 1986; Ford et al., 1989). However, in these studies guilt emerged as the most important emotion regulating this domain of social behavior, especially in the absence of external sanctions for irresponsible behavior. This was particularly true for teenage boys, who were consistently less likely than girls to report feelings of empathic concern in situations involving negative consequences to others. The Ford et al. (1989) study also demonstrates the additive effect of combining multiple emotions supportive of responsible behavior, a phenomenon that appears to hold for caring behavior as well (see Table 6.3). Evidently, it is particularly difficult to ignore emotional

Table 6.3. Comparison of students high and low in caring competence on selected demographic and motivational variables

Probability (from 0 to 1) that high caring (N=25) and low caring (N=21) students will:	High caring	Low caring
Demographic variables		
Be a female	.75	.33
Be engaged in some form of volunteer work or school or community service	.50	.19
Report having an A or A+ GPA	.33	.24
Report having a GPA of C+ or lower	.00	.24
Intergrative goals		
Say that "Caring for and about others" (APAB) is "always" or "almost always" important	1.00	.43
Resource provision	.63	.00
Equity	.50	.20
Social responsibility	.25	.05
Belongingness	.83	.25
Score low (1–5) on the APG goals of:		
Resource provision	.08	.55
Equity	.04	.30
Social responsibility	.08	.70
Personal agency beliefs		
Say that they are "always" or "almost always" capable of caring for and about others	.83	.23
Say that they are "always" or "almost always" capable of working for a more just society	.75	.14
Score low (1 or 2 on a 5-point scale) on social support satisfaction	.04	.25
Emotions		
Score high (2.5–3) on the emotions of:		
Empathic concern	.88	.00
Pride/pleasure in helping others	.58	.05
Guilt	.29	.05
Score low (0–2) on the emotions of		
Empathic concern	.00	.33
Pride/pleasuere in helping others	.00	.52
Guilt	.00	.76
Score low (0–2) on both variables representing self-focused emotions	.63	.14
Other goals associated with caring competence		
Score high (7–9) on theAPG/APAB goals of:		
Intellectual or Task creativity (APG)	.83	.15
Unity (APG) or Spiritually (APAB)	.67	.19
Positive self-evaluations or Individuality (APG)	.75	.30

messages when there are two or more messengers providing guidance and pressure to act in a particular way.

Gender differences in motivation and behavior associated with caring competence

The female participants in this study appeared to be no more capable of caring behavior than their male counterparts; however, they were significantly more likely to *choose* to behave in a caring manner in situations calling for such behavior. Consistent with this finding, significant gender differences favoring females were observed on three of the four APG integrative goals – Resource Provision, Social Responsibility, and Belongingness – as well as the "Caring" APAB goal item. Alternatively, boys and girls had similar scores on the APG and APAB equity measures, thus providing indirect support for those who distinguish between a "justice" and "caring" orientation to morality (e.g., Noddings, 1984, 1992). Along these same lines, females had significantly higher capability and context beliefs for the goals of resource provision and belongingness, slightly more positive personal agency beliefs in the domain of social responsibility, and virtually identical capability and context beliefs with regard to equity. The girls in this study also reported having a somewhat larger social support network (on average) than did males, although no reliable gender difference in social support satisfaction was observed.

An examination of gender differences on the emotion variables revealed that, compared to males, females were significantly more likely to anticipate feeling empathic concern and positive emotions (pride/pleasure in helping) in situations where they chose to try to help someone in need or in distress. Females were also more likely to anticipate feeling empathic concern and guilt when they chose not to provide assistance or support in such situations. On the other hand, males were more likely to anticipate feeling self-focused emotions focused on the positive qualities of the noncaring alternative (e.g., relief at avoiding a socially awkward situation; excitement about engaging in a fun experience that might otherwise be sacrificed). These results precisely match those obtain by Ford et al. (1989) in their study of emotional influences on adolescent social responsibility.

Comparison of high caring and low caring students

In an effort to determine whether the qualities associated with caring behavior as revealed by correlational analyses involving the whole sample were truly characteristic of highly caring *individuals*, a further set of analyses was conducted focusing on students scoring particularly high or low in caring competence. To insure that these "exemplars" of caring and noncaring behavior were unambiguously prototypical of the groups they were intended to represent, a more stringent criterion was applied than simply scoring high or low on the caring composite variable. Specifically, high and low caring students were required to have scores at least two-thirds of a standard deviation above or below the mean (respectively) on at least three of the four variables used to create the caring composite, with the remaining score also in the same direction relative to the mean for that variable. This procedure eliminated several students who might have otherwise been selected on the strength of very high or very low scores on a subset of measures (e.g., students with highly favorable self-evaluations but less than flattering reputations among their teachers or peers; students rated highly by their teachers but rarely nominated by their classmates; students with consistently high scores on the CCNF but a relatively uncaring pattern of decision making on the YDMQ). Nevertheless, because of the overall consistency among the various indices of caring competence for those scoring toward the tails of each distribution, 28% of the sample met the criteria for membership in one of the extreme groups (i.e., 24 students in the high caring group and 21 students in the low caring group).

The results presented in Table 6.3 document the fact that the qualities most closely associated with caring competence in the group-level analyses were indeed consistently manifested in highly caring individuals. They also reveal the remarkable extent to which the variables representing these qualities discriminate between high and low caring students. In fact, a discriminant function constructed from a subset of only 14 of these variables (i.e., those most relevant to the study hypotheses) was sufficient to achieve a 100% hit rate in a classification analysis designed to predict the group membership of each student.

Among the specific findings listed in Table 6.3, several are particularly noteworthy. As one might expect from the consistent gender differences that emerged for various motivational and behavioral manifestations of caring competence, girls were three times more likely to be in the high caring group, and boys were twice as likely to be in the low caring group. The strong association between caring behavior and academic achievement, which was not readily apparent from analyses testing for linear relationships (correlations between caring competence and students' self-reported GPA ranged from .08 to .18), also appears to be worthy of further research. Inspection of the data for individual students confirmed that both the high and low ends of the caring competence continuum were well represented, even among the academically superior students in the sample. High achievement is clearly no guarantee that a student will be regarded as a caring person. However, not a single student with a GPA of C+ or lower was among those identified as part of a group of 24 caring "exemplars." In other words, although some high achieving students were identified as uncaring individuals, none of the caring exemplars in the study was a low achiever. Wentzel has observed similar results with respect to the relationship between social responsibility and academic achievement (Wentzel, 1989, 1991a, 1993a, this volume). One might speculate that the primary role of integrative social motivation in academic achievement is to (a) strengthen classroom motivation through the additive impact of multiple goals (M. Ford, 1992; Wentzel, 1989), and (b) provide some "motivational insurance" (M. Ford, 1992) in cases where other goals (e.g., exploration, understanding, mastery, intellectual or task creativity) are unreliable or absent.

Examination of the psychological variables represented in Table 6.3 suggests that the "core" of the caring adolescent is an easily activated motivational pattern characterized by strong resource provision goals, compelling feelings of empathic concern and pride or pleasure in helping others, and positive capability beliefs for caring action. Circumstances that activate this motivational pattern are likely to afford the simultaneous attainment of multiple goals that are personally compelling and rich in meaning for highly caring people.

As expected, most of the students in the high caring group had elevated scores on measures of belongingness, resource provision, and empathic concern. Moreover, virtually no one in this group had low scores on any of the goals or emotions reflecting concern for others. Surprisingly, though, these students were also relatively unlikely to score high on indices of social responsibility and guilt. In contrast, a large majority of the low caring students had unusually low scores on these measures – in some cases so low as to be frightening. This suggests that a second motivational pattern – one that is related to but qualitatively distinct from the basic caring motivational pattern – must be taken into account if one is to understand the full range of individual differences in caring competence. Specifically, it appears that a "backup" motivational pattern based on *obligation* may be needed to inhibit those with little intrinsic interest in caring from behaving in uncaring ways. In other words, some degree of desire to avoid feelings of guilt and other consequences of socially irresponsible behavior (e.g., parental disapproval or peer rejection) may be necessary to produce minimally acceptable levels of caring competence. On the other hand, this obligation pattern would rarely be sufficient to produce high levels of caring behavior – it promotes "doing one's duty" rather than "going beyond the call of duty." It is nevertheless a profoundly important component of social motivation, as it provides "motivational insurance" against dangerously low levels of social responsibility and caring behavior (M. Ford, 1992).

The role of social responsibility motivation in insuring socially acceptable levels of caring competence appears to be analogous to its role in helping students maintain satisfactory levels of academic effort and achievement (Wentzel, 1989, 1991a, 1993a, this volume). This suggests that, developmentally, social responsibility motivation may be an essential prerequisite for both academic and social success. This in turn implies that the development of strong goals, emotions, and personal agency beliefs associated with social responsibility should be a major focus of parenting and education in early childhood (Maccoby, 1992).

Individual motivational profiles were also examined in an effort to discern whether different "types" of high and low caring students could be identified within each group. At least with respect to caring competence, highly caring students seemed to be a relatively homogeneous group. They uniformly displayed most of the features associated with the prototypical caring pattern at a very high level, and generally manifested the qualities associated with the obligation pattern at a somewhat lower level – that is, caring appeared to be something they wanted to do and liked to do, not just something that they felt they had to do or ought to do.

Low caring students, on the other hand, appeared to comprise a more heterogeneous group. They were generally distinguished by their very low scores on resource provision goals and empathic concern. However, some of these students did manifest a moderate or even high degree of concern for others on certain variables. In such cases there were typically a number of very prominent personal goals that seemed to overpower the integrative concerns in the student's goal hierarchy. In particular, three different self-focused personality "types" were evident at the level of the individual low-caring student, with some students showing elements of more than one type.

One subset of cases might best be described as representing a "fun" or "feel good" type characterized by strong self-focused emotions and very high scores on the goals of Entertainment, Physical Well-Being, and Bodily Sensations. In the context of relatively weak goals and emotions reflecting concern for others, this hedonistic pattern presumably takes on a rather self-centered or even self-absorbed quality. A second subset of low-caring students seemed to manifest a "hypermasculine" pattern character-ized by very high scores on goals such as Self-determination, Superiority, and Material Gain. This pattern was coupled with low scores in an unusu-ally large number of goal categories, thus implying a rather narrow focus on goals representing power, control, and personal achievement. A third type of pattern found in some low-caring students was a "pragmatic-de-fensive" pattern focused primarily on the removal or avoidance of discrep-ancies in one's immediate affective and perceptual experience. Goals re-flecting a need for safety, emotional stability, and order were prominent in the goals hierarchies of these students.

Finally, the results summarized in Table 6.3 suggest that, compared to their less caring peers, highly caring adolescents are more likely to be in-terested in and concerned about a diversity of personal goals – social and nonsocial. Indeed, one of the distinguishing features of many students scoring low in caring competence was the relatively large number of goals they rated as unimportant. Endorsement of a broad range of goals did not necessarily mean that a student would also score high in caring compe-tence; however, highly caring students virtually never manifested the nar-rowness characterizing the goal hierarchies of many of those scoring low in caring competence.

Related to this pattern is what appears to be a strong tendency for high-ly caring youth to be particularly interested in goals pertaining to intrinsi-cally meaningful aspects of human experience – for example, creative ex-periences (Intellectual and Task Creativity); experiences reflecting feelings of unity or spiritual connectedness with people, nature, or a greater power (Unity/Spirituality); and, to a lesser extent, experiences re-lated to understanding and task accomplishment (Understanding, Mas-tery/Skill Development, and Management/Personal Productivity). Consis-tent with this interpretation, caring competence was negatively related to Material Gain, a goal commonly regarded as a more extrinsic and superfi-cial source of motivation. Thus, caring for others may be, in many cases, a part of a larger pattern of seeking to engage life in ways that are particu-larly or even profoundly rich in meaning. The strong (and unexpected) positive relationship found between caring competence and the goal of In-dividuality, which reflects a desire to feel unique, special, or different from others, may also be a part of this pattern of being attracted to experi-ences that carry enduring value and meaning (in contrast to experiences that are more transient and superficial in meaning).

Caring competence was also positively and significantly related (albeit at a somewhat lower level) to a set of goals pertaining to aspects of self-acceptance and mental, emotional, and physical well being (i.e., Positive Self-Evaluations/Self-Esteem, Happiness/Feeling Happy, Resource Acquisition/Peer Acceptance, and Physical Well-Being/Physical Fitness). Thus, it does not appear to be the case that investment in self-enhancing goals is a major factor inhibiting caring behavior. Indeed, the present results support the opposite view, namely, that people who "look after themselves" (i.e., who maintain an adequate level of self-comfort and self-acceptance) are more likely to behave in a caring manner than those who fail to do so. It may also be that for many people one of the primary rewards of helping and supporting others is increased self-acceptance and a more positive self-image.

Implications for educational research and practice

The research described in this chapter, despite some methodological limitations (e.g., use of convenience samples and relatively new measures), provides initial support for the utility of Motivational Systems Theory in guiding research on adolescent social responsibility and caring behavior. Indeed, it is hard to imagine how one could represent the multitude of motivational and nonmotivational factors involved in the development of social and academic competence without some sort of a complex systems approach (D. Ford, 1987; M. Ford, 1992).

There appear to be numerous promising directions for further research on adolescent social responsibility and caring behavior. Of particular interest are the rich goal hierarchies of highly caring adolescents. The link between social motivation and caring behavior appears to involve much more than a few goals and emotions of straightforward relevance to prosocial behavior. Rather, strong patterns of caring behavior appear to be supported by a complex web of mutually reinforcing goals that make such behavior compelling and rewarding in many different ways. This is consistent with the MST premise that strong motivational patterns will typically be anchored by more than one goal (i.e., the Multiple Goals principle; M. Ford, 1992). Application of a multiple goals perspective also provides a way of thinking about how contexts might be designed to facilitate social responsibility and caring behavior despite the vast individual differences in social motivation evident in a heterogeneous sample of adolescents.

Further research on the reciprocal relationships between social compe-

and driving; unprotected sexual activity; poor citizenship) may need to concentrate first and foremost on facilitating an obligation motivational pattern. Caring goals and emotions may also be appropriate targets of intervention, but they appear to be more relevant for promoting prosocial behavior than for inhibiting antisocial behavior. On the other hand, given the motivational strength resulting from the simultaneous operation of multiple goals and emotions, perhaps the most effective strategy for promoting both caring competence and social responsibility in youth would be to try to facilitate an optimal balance of caring and obligation motives tailored both to the goals of the intervention and the personalities of the individuals participating in the intervention.

References

Bandura, A. (1991). Social cognitive theory of moral thought and action. In W. M. Kurtines & J. L. Gewitz (Eds.), *Handbook of moral behavior and development Vol.1: Theory* (pp. 45–103). Hillsdale, NJ: Erlbaum.

Batson, C. D. (1990). How social an animal? The human capacity for caring. *American Psychologist, 45,* 336–346.

Batson, C. D., Dyck, J. L., Batson, J. G. , Powell, A. L., McMaster, M. R., & Griffitt, C. (1988). Five studies testing two new egoistic alternatives to the empathy-altruism hypothesis. *Journal of Personality and Social Psychology, 55,* 52–77.

Bergin, C. A. C. (1987). Prosocial development in toddlers: The patterning of mother-infant interactions. In M. E. Ford & D. H. Ford (Eds.), *Humans as self-constructing living systems: Putting the framework to work* (pp. 121–143). Hillsdale, NJ: Erlbaum.

Cantor, N., & Harlow, R. (1994). Social intelligence and personality: Flexible life-task pursuit. In R. J. Sternberg & P. Ruzgis (Eds.), *Personality and intelligence* (pp. 137–168). New York: Cambridge University Press.

Chapman, M., Zahn-Waxler, C., Cooperman, G. Y., Iannotti, R. (1987). Empathy and responsibility in the motivation of children's helping. *Developmental Psychology, 23,* 140–145.

Connell, J. P., & Wellbourn, J. G. (1991). Competence, autonomy, and relatedness: A motivational analysis of self-system processes. In M. R. Gunnar & L. A. Sroufe (Eds.) *Self processes and development: The Minnesota symposium on child psychology.* (vol. 23, pp. 43–78). Hillsdale, NJ: Erlbaum.

Damon, W. (1995). *Greater expectations.* New York: Free Press.

Eisenberg, N., & Miller, P. (1987). Empathy and prosocial behavior. *Psychological Bulletin, 101,* 91–119.

Eisenberg, N., & Mussen, P. H. (1989). *The roots of prosocial behavior in children.* New York: Cambridge University Press.

Emmons, R. A. (1989). The personal striving approach to personality. In L. A. Pervin (Ed.), *Goal concepts in personality and social psychology* (87–126). Hillsdale, NJ: Erlbaum.

Feldman, S., & Elliott, G. (Eds.) (1990) *At the threshold: The developing adolescent.* Cambridge, MA: Harvard University Press.

Ford, D. H. (1987). *Humans as self-constructing living systems: A developmental perspective on behavior and personality.* Hillsdale, NJ: Erlbaum.

Ford, M. E. (1992). *Motivating human: Goals, emotions, and personal agency beliefs.* Newbury Park, CA: Sage.

Ford, M. E., Chase, C., Love, R., Pollina, S., & Ito, S. (1991). Qualities associated with caring behavior in adolescence: Goals, emotions, and personal agency beliefs. Program report submitted to the Lilly Endowment, Indianapolis, IN.

Ford M. E., & Ford, D. H. (Eds.) (1987). *Humans as self-constructing living systems: Putting the framework to work.* Hillsdale, NJ: Erlbaum.

Ford M. E., & Nichols, C. W. (Eds.) (1987). A taxonomy of human goals and some possible applications. In M. E. Ford & D. H. Ford (Eds.), *Humans as self-constructing living systems: Putting the framework to work* (pp. 289–311). Hillsdale, NJ: Erlbaum.

Ford, M. E., & Nichols, C. W. (1991). Using goal assessments to identify motivational patterns and facilitate behavioral regulation and achievement. In M. L. Maehr & P. Pintrich (Eds.), *Advances in motivation and achievement, Vol. 7: Goals and self-regulatory processes* (pp. 51–84). Greenwich, CT: JAI Press.

Ford, M. E., Wentzel, K. R., Siesfeld, G. A., Wood, D., & Feldman, L. (1986). Adolescent decision making in real-life situations involving socially responsible and irresponsible choices. Paper presented at the annual meeting of the American Educational Research Association, Los Angeles.

Ford, M. E., Wentzel, K. R., Wood, D., Stevens, E., & Siesfeld, G. A. (1989). Processes associated with integrative social competence: Emotional and contextual influences on adolescent social responsibility. *Journal of Adolescent Research, 4,* 405–425.

Frijda, N. H. (1988). The laws of emotion. *American Psychologist, 43,* 349–358.

Hoffman, M. L. (1982). Development of prosocial motivation: Empathy and guilt. In N. Eisenberg (Ed.), *The development of prosocial behavior* (pp. 281–313). New York: Academic Press.

Kochanska, G. (1994). Beyond cognition: Expanding the search for the early roots of internalization and conscience. *Developmental Psychology, 30,* 20–22.

Krebs, D. L. (1975). Empathy and altruism. *Journal of Personality and Social Psychology, 32,* 1134–1146.

Krumboltz, J. D., Ford, M. E., Nichols, C. W., & Wentzel, K. R. (1987). The goals of education. In R. C. Calfee (Ed.), *The study of Stanford the schools: Views from the inside, Part II.* Stanford University: Stanford, CA.

Maccoby, E. E. (1992). The role of parents in the socialization of children: An historical overview. *Developmental Psychology, 22,* 1006–1017.

Markus, H., & Ruvolo, A. (1989). Possible selves: Personalized representations of goals. In L. A. Pervin (Ed.), *Goal concepts in personality and social psychology* (pp. 211–241). Hillsdale, NJ: Erlbaum.

Meece, J. L., Wigfield, A., & Eccles, J. S. (1990). Predictors of math anxiety and its influence on young adolescents' course enrollment intentions and performance in mathematics. *Journal of Educational Psychology, 82,* 60–70.

Noddings, N. (1984). *Caring: A feminine approach to ethics and moral education.* Berkeley, CA: University of California Press.

Noddings, N. (1992). *The challenge to care in schools: An alternative approach to education.* New York: Teachers College Press.

Radke-Yarrow, M., Zahn-Waxler, C., & Chapman, M. (1983). Children's prosocial dispositions and behavior. In E. M. Hetherington (Ed.), *Handbook of child psychology Vol. 4: Socialization, personality, and social development* (pp. 469–545). New York: Wiley.

Slavin, R. E. (1981). When does cooperative learning increase student achievement? *Psychology Bulletin, 94,* 429–445.

Slavin R. E. (1987). Developmental and motivational perspectives on cooperative learning: A reconciliation. *Child Development, 58,* 1161–1167.

Wentzel, K. R. (1989). Adolescent classroom goals, standards for performance, and academic achievement: An interactional perspective. *Journal of Educational Psychology, 81,* 131–142.

Wentzel, K. R. (1991a). Social competence at school: Relation between social responsibility and academic achievement. *Review of Educational Research, 61,* 1–24.

Wentzel, K. R.. (1991b). Relations between social competence and academic achievement in early adolescence. *Child Development, 62,* 1066–1078.

Wentzel, K. R. (1993b). Does being good make the grade? Relations between academic and social competence in early adolescence. *Journal of Educational Psychology, 85,* 357–364.

Wentzel, K. R. (1993b). Social and academic goals at school: Motivation and achievement in early adolescence. *Journal of Early Adolescence,13,*4–20.

Wentzel, K. R. (1994). Relations of social goal pursuit to social acceptance, classroom behavior, and perceived social support. *Journal of Educational Psychology, 86,* 173–182.

7   Modeling and self-efficacy influences on children's development of self-regulation

Dale H. Schunk and Barry J. Zimmerman

An essential feature of children's adjustment to school is their development of academically-related self-regulation and motivation. The question of how children acquire and internalize adult levels of self-regulatory competence and motivation has fascinated scholars since the ancient Greeks. Although philosophers, sociologists, and anthropologists have long emphasized the importance of socialization influences, until recently there has been relatively little detailed information about how such influences affect children's self-regulatory development. Since the late 1950s, researchers in the social learning tradition (Bandura & Walters, 1963) have hypothesized that children's exposure to socializing agents, especially adult or peer models, influences their behavioral and cognitive development (e.g., formation of concepts, attitudes, preferences, standards for self-reward and self-punishment). They found extensive evidence that children readily induce and transfer concepts that underlie modeling sequences (Rosenthal & Zimmerman, 1978; Zimmerman & Rosenthal, 1974).

In recent years, social cognitive theorists shifted their attention to adolescents' internalization of self-regulatory competence and studied how youngsters learn to function independently from socializing agents in an adaptive, generative, and creative manner. Bandura (1986) emphasized the importance of a number of specific self-regulatory processes. *Self-regulation* refers to processes students use to activate and sustain cognitions, behaviors, and affects, which are oriented toward the attainment of goals (Zimmerman, 1989, 1990). Academic self-regulatory processes include planning and managing time; attending to and concentrating on instruction; organizing, rehearsing, and coding information strategically; establishing a productive work environment; and using social resources effectively. In addition, self-regulation incorporates such motivational processes as setting performance goals and outcomes; holding positive

154

beliefs about one's capabilities; valuing learning and its anticipated outcomes; and experiencing pride and satisfaction with one's efforts (Schunk & Zimmerman, 1994).

This chapter focuses on the social and self origins of students' development of self-regulatory skill with special emphasis on modeling and self-efficacy beliefs. *Modeling* occurs when observers pattern their behaviors, strategies, thoughts, beliefs, and affects after those of one or more models (Schunk, 1987). *Self-efficacy* refers to beliefs about one's capabilities to learn or perform behaviors at designated levels (Bandura, 1986, in press). Recent research has demonstrated the effectiveness of modeling self-regulatory skills on students' academic achievement and associated self-efficacy beliefs (Schunk & Zimmerman, 1994).

We initially present a theoretical overview of students' development of self-regulatory competence followed by a social cognitive analysis of mature self-regulation based on Bandura's (1986) account. We then summarize research on the roles of modeling and self-efficacy in the development of self-regulatory competence. We conclude with some implications of the theory and research for educational practice.

Theoretical background

Development of self-regulatory competence

According to a social cognitive perspective, students' academic competence develops initially from social sources of academic skill and subsequently shifts to self sources in a series of levels of skill as depicted in Table 7.1 (Zimmerman & Bonner, in press). At the outset, novice learners acquire learning strategies most rapidly from social modeling, tuition, task structuring, and encouragement (Zimmerman & Rosenthal, 1974).

Table 7.1 A social cognitive analysis of primary influences on students' self-regulatory development

Levels of development	Social influences	Self influences
Observational	Modeling, verbal description	
Imitative	Social guidance and feedback	
Self-controlled		Internal standards, self-reinforcement
Self-regulated		Self-regulatory processes, self-efficacy beliefs

Although many learners can induce the major features of learning strategies from watching a model (*observational level* of academic skill), most of them will require motoric performance experiences in order for them to fully incorporate the skill into their behavioral repertoire. If the model adopts a teaching role and provides guidance, feedback, and social reinforcement during imitative practice, the observer's motoric accuracy can be improved further. During participant or mastery modeling (Bandura, 1986), the model repeats selected aspects of the strategy and guides enactment based on the learners' imitative accuracy. An *imitative level* of academic skill is attained when the learner's performance approximates the general form of the model. This does not mean that the observer is exactly copying the model (an effect termed "response mimicry"). More often, the learner emulates only the general pattern or style of the model, such as the type of question a model asks, instead of duplicating the model's words (Zimmerman & Rosenthal, 1974).

Although the source of learning of a skill is primarily social for the first two levels of academic competence, it shifts to self-influences at more advanced levels. The most apparent manifestation of a third or *self-controlled level* of academic skill is a learner's ability to use the strategy independently when performing transfer tasks. Students' use of a learning strategy becomes internalized during this phase, but it remains dependent on representational standards of a model's performance (i.e., covert images and verbal meanings) and the self-reinforcement that stems from matching them (Bandura & Jeffery, 1973).

Socialization agents expect an even higher level of self-functioning when students reach adolescence. A fourth of *self-regulated* level of academic skill is needed so learners can systematically adapt their learning strategies to changing personal and contextual conditions (Bandura, 1986). At this level of academic competence, the learner can initiate use of strategies, can incorporate adjustments based on contextual features of the applied situation, and is motivated primarily by self-efficacy perceptions of enactive success. The learner chooses when to use a strategy and varies its features self-regulatively, with little or no residual dependence on the model.

In summary, a four level analysis of self-regulatory development extends from acquiring knowledge of learning skills (observation), to using them (imitation), to their internalization (self-control), and finally to their adaptive use (self-regulation). Although this social cognitive model was initially derived from research on children's socialization processes, it has proven useful in guiding instructional efforts to teach students how to acquire and eventually self-regulate their academic learning.

Social cognitive theory of self-regulation

Triadic reciprocality. Bandura's (1986) social cognitive theory views human functioning in terms of interactions between behaviors, environmental variables, and cognitions and other personal factors. Each of these three classes of variables can influence the other and is in turn influenced by it. For example, with respect to the link between cognitions and behaviors, much research shows that students' self-efficacy beliefs influence achievement behaviors (choice of tasks, effort, persistence, achievement) (Schunk, 1989). Conversely, students' behaviors also can alter efficacy beliefs. As students work on tasks they note their progress toward their learning goals. Goal progress and accomplishment convey to students that they are capable of performing well, which enhances self-efficacy for continued learning.

Students' behaviors and classroom environments are similarly reciprocally dependent. In a typical instructional sequence, a teacher may present information and direct students' attention to material on the board. Environmental influence on behavior occurs when students respond to the board without much conscious deliberation. Conversely, students' behaviors alter their environment. When students answer incorrectly, their teacher may reteach the lesson in a different fashion rather than continue with the original material.

Finally, cognitions and environments exert reciprocal effects. When presented with the same difficult task, students with high self-efficacy may view the task as a challenge and work diligently to master it, whereas those with low efficacy may attempt to avoid it (cognition affects environment). The influence of environment on cognition is seen when teachers provide feedback to students (e.g., "That's correct. You're getting good at this.") that raises their self-efficacy and sustains their motivation to continue to improve their skills.

Self-regulatory processes. Social cognitive research has identified three major classes of self-regulation: self-observation, self-judgment, and self-reaction (Bandura, 1986; Kanfer & Gaelick, 1986). *Self-observation* involves deliberate attention to specific aspects of one's behavior (Bandura, 1986). Behaviors can be assessed on such dimensions as quantity, quality, rate, and originality. When self-observation reveals goal progress, it can motivate one to improve (Schunk, 1994). Often students with academic problems are surprised to learn that they waste much valuable study time on nonacademic distractions. Such knowledge can motivate students to reform their ways.

Self-observation is assisted with self-recording, where instances of behavior are recorded along with their time, place, and frequency of occurrence (Mace, Belfiore, & Shea, 1989). In the absence of recording, observations may be forgotten or misinterpreted. The validity of self-observation is improved if behavior is observed at regular intervals and close in time to its occurrence rather than sporadically and long after it occurs.

Self-observation is closely linked to a second self-regulatory process, *self-judgment*, which refers to comparing present performance with a standard. Self-judgments are affected by type and importance of standards employed.

Standards may be stated in absolute or normative terms. The standard for an absolute goal is fixed (e.g., write five pages in one hour). Normative standards are based on performances of others and often are acquired by observing models (Bandura, 1986). Social comparison of one's performances with those of others helps one evaluate the appropriateness of behavior. Social comparison becomes more likely when absolute standards are not in effect or are unclear (Schunk, 1994).

Self-judgments are also affected by the importance of standards. People make progress judgments for behaviors they value. They may not assess their performance or expend effort to improve their skills in areas where they care little how they perform.

Standards are informative and motivational. Comparing one's performance against standards informs one of progress. Writers who must complete a 30 page chapter in a week know they are ahead of schedule if they complete three pages during the first hour. The awareness that one is making extraordinary progress enhances self-efficacy and sustains motivation (Schunk, 1994).

Self-reaction refers to evaluations made of one's performance: good/bad, acceptable/not acceptable, beyond/below expectation. Evaluative reactions involve students' beliefs about their progress. The belief that one is making acceptable goal progress, along with the anticipated satisfaction of goal attainment, enhances self-efficacy, and sustains motivation. Negative evaluations will not decrease motivation if students believe they are capable of improving (i.e., by working harder or using more effective strategies) (Schunk, 1994). Motivation is not enhanced if students think they lack the ability to succeed and that more effort or better strategy use will not help.

Self-reactions can be augmented by tangible rewards. Students who believe they are making good progress in studying for an exam may reward themselves with two hours off from studying to watch a TV program. Tangible rewards validate the perception of progress and raise self-efficacy when they are linked to actual accomplishments.

These self-regulatory processes interact with one another. As students observe aspects of their behavior, they judge them against goal standards and react to those judgments. Their evaluations and reactions set the stage for additional observations of the same behaviors or of others. These processes also interact with environmental factors (Zimmerman, 1989). Students who judge their task progress as inadequate may react by requesting teacher assistance. Teachers may teach students a better strategy, which students then use to promote learning. This dynamic interaction of self-regulation processes is one of its central features (Schunk & Zimmerman, 1994).

Modeling processes. Modeling processes are important socialization components of self-regulation. Modeling can serve different functions: inhibition/disinhibition, response facilitation, observational learning. *Inhibition/disinhibition* means that observing a model can strengthen or weaken behavioral inhibitions. Models who perform threatening or prohibited activities without experiencing negative consequences may influence observers to perform the behaviors themselves; models who are punished may inhibit observers' responding. Inhibitory and disinhibitory effects stem from the information conveyed to observers that similar consequences are likely should they act accordingly.

Response facilitation denotes modeled actions serving as social prompts for observer behavior. Response facilitation occurs when we follow the actions of the crowd. A student who walks into a room where other students are studying quietly is apt to respond to this prompt and behave the same way.

Both inhibitory/disinhibitory and response facilitation effects are important for self-regulation because students may regulate their activities based on the social cues they observe and the consequences of modeled actions. More important for education, however, are observational learning effects. *Observational learning* through modeling occurs when observers display new behaviors that, before modeling, had no probability of occurrence, even when motivational inducements are offered (Bandura,

1986; Schunk, 1987). To learn observationally, students must attend to a model, code the information for retention, be capable of producing the demonstrated response pattern, and be motivated to perform imitatively (Bandura, 1986). An important form of observational learning occurs through *cognitive modeling*, which incorporates modeled explanations and demonstrations with verbalizations of the model's thoughts and reasons for performing the actions (Meichenbaum, 1977).

The functional value of behavior – whether modeled behaviors result in success or failure, reward or punishment – exerts strong effects on observer modeling. Modeled behaviors are likely to be performed if they previously led to rewarding outcomes, but are unlikely if they resulted in punishment.

Modeling experiences fulfill informational and motivational functions. Vicarious consequences indicate the motivational value of behavior to observers (Bandura, 1986); antecedent actions inform observers about what should be done to attain them. Most social situations are structured so that the appropriateness of behaviors depends on such factors as age, gender, or status. By observing modeled behaviors and their consequences, people formulate expectations about the likely outcomes of actions. Vicarious consequences create outcome expectations about which behaviors will be rewarded and which punished.

Perceived similarity between model and observer is hypothesized to be an important source of information to determine behavioral appropriateness and formulate outcome expectations (Schunk, 1987). The more alike observers are to models, the greater is the probability that similar actions by observers are socially appropriate and will produce comparable results. Model attributes often are predictive of the functional value of behavior. Similarity should be especially influential in situations where observers have little information about functional value. Modeled behaviors on tasks that observers are unfamiliar with or those that are not immediately followed by consequences may be highly susceptible to influence by attribute similarity.

Vicarious consequences also motivate observers. These effects depend in part on self-efficacy. Similarity to models constitutes an important source of vicarious information for gauging one's efficacy. Observing similar others succeed can raise observers' efficacy and motivate them to try the task based on the assumption that if others can succeed, they can as well. Observing similar others experiencing difficulty may lead observers to doubt their own capabilities and undermine their motivation to try the task. Model attributes provide information about what one can do. Similarity is highly influential in situations where individuals have experienced difficulties and hold doubts about performing well.

Self-Efficacy

Sources, effects, and consequences. Self-efficacy is hypothesized to influence choice of tasks, effort expenditure, persistence, and achievement (Bandura, 1986, in press; Schunk, 1989; Zimmerman, 1995) (See also Erdley, this volume, for ways in which self-efficacy is related to peer-directed aggression). Compared with students who doubt their learning capabilities, those holding a sense of efficacy for acquiring a skill or performing a task participate more readily, work harder, persist longer when they encounter difficulties, and achieve at a higher level.

Learners obtain information to appraise their self-efficacy from their performance accomplishments, vicarious (observational) experiences, forms of persuasion, and physiological reactions. Students' own performances offer reliable guides for assessing self-efficacy. Successes raise efficacy and failures lower it, although once a strong sense of efficacy develops, an occasional difficulty typically has little impact (Schunk, 1989).

Students socially acquire efficacy information by comparing their performances with those of others. Similar others offer the best basis for comparison (Schunk, 1987). Students who observe similar peers perform a task are apt to believe that they, too, are capable of accomplishing it. Information acquired vicariously typically has a weaker effect on self-efficacy than performance-based information because the former can be outweighed by subsequent failures.

Learners often receive from teachers, parents, coaches, and peers, persuasive information that they are capable of performing a task ("You can do this"). Positive persuasive feedback enhances self-efficacy, but this increase will be temporary if subsequent efforts turn out poorly. Students also acquire efficacy information from physiological reactions (e.g., sweating, heart rate). Symptoms signaling anxiety may convey that one lacks skills; conversely, students who experience less agitation feel more efficacious about performing well.

Information derived from these sources does not influence self-efficacy automatically but rather is cognitively appraised (Bandura, 1986, in press). Learners weigh and combine the contributions of many factors including perceptions of ability, task difficulty, amount of effort expended, amount and type of assistance from others, perceived similarity to models, and persuader credibility (Schunk, 1989).

Self-efficacy is important, but not the only influence on achievement behavior. High self-efficacy will not produce competent performances when requisite knowledge and skills are lacking. Outcome expectations are influential because students engage in activities they believe will lead to positive outcomes. Similarly, perceived value (importance attached to learning or what use will be made of what one learns) affects behavior because learners show little interest in activities they do not value. When students possess adequate skills, expect positive outcomes, and value what they are learning, self-efficacy is hypothesized to influence the choice and direction of much achievement behavior.

Self-efficacy and self-regulation. Effective self-regulation depends on a sense of self-efficacy for using skills to achieve mastery (Bandura, 1986, in press; Bouffard-Bouchard, Parent, & Larivee, 1991; Schunk, 1994; Zimmerman, 1989). As students work on a task, they compare their performances to their goals. Self-evaluations of progress enhance self-efficacy and keep students motivated to improve. Students who feel efficacious about learning or performing well are apt to implement various effective self-regulatory strategies, such as concentrating on the task, using proper procedures, managing time effectively, seeking assistance as necessary, and monitoring performance and adjusting strategies as needed (Schunk, 1994; Zimmerman, 1994).

Although low self-efficacy is detrimental, effective self-regulation does not require that self-efficacy be extremely high. Salomon (1984) found that lower self-efficacy led to greater mental effort and better learning than when efficacy was higher. Assuming that learners feel efficacious about surmounting problems (a very low sense of efficacy is not motivating), holding some doubt about whether one will succeed may mobilize effort and effective use of strategies more than will feeling overly confident.

Research Evidence

In this section we present a limited review of research on the social and self origins of self-regulatory competence. These categories are distinguished according to the extent they require influences in the social environment for development. Social origins include observational learning and imitative learning; self origins comprise self-instruction in achieving self control and self-regulated learning through goal setting, self-monitoring, self-evaluation, help seeking, and time management. This review is selective; readers who want a more comprehensive treatment should consult other sources (Bandura, 1986, in press; Schunk & Zimmerman, 1994; Zimmerman & Schunk, 1989).

Social origins of self-regulatory competence

Much of what we know about social origins of self-regulatory competence derives from theory and research on modeling. The research in this section on observational and imitative learning through modeling focuses on how students develop skills and access information about their competencies from exposure to adult and peer models. There is a vast literature discussed in other sources on how models affect personal relationships between students and significant adults and peers and the implications of these relationships for school adjustment (Bandura, 1986; Rosenthal & Bandura, 1978). The role of modeling also figures prominently in the current educational emphasis on mentoring and apprenticeships (e.g., Bailey, 1993).

Observational learning. Models are important sources for the initial development of self-regulation: an observational level of skill. By observing models, students acquire knowledge and strategies that they subsequently apply as they work on tasks. Modeled displays also convey to observers that they can succeed if they follow the same sequence of actions. The belief that one knows what to do to perform a task raises self-efficacy, which is increased further as observers work on the task and experience success (Schunk, 1989).

An important means of developing an observational level of competence is through cognitive modeling. Schunk (1981) gave children who had encountered difficulty in mathematics either cognitive modeling or didactic instruction. In the modeling treatment, children observed an adult model verbalize division operations while applying them to problems. The didactic treatment consisted of children reviewing instructional pages that portrayed the solution of division problems step-by-step. Both cognitive modeling and didactic instruction led to significant increases in self-efficacy, skill, and persistence, but modeling resulted in significantly higher division skill performance. Results of a path analysis showed that self-efficacy had an direct effect on both persistence and skill.

Perceived similarity to models in important attributes can raise observers' self-efficacy and motivate them to try the task because they are likely to believe that if others can succeed, they can as well (Schunk, 1987). One way to vary similarity is through the use of coping and mastery models. *Coping models* initially demonstrate the typical behavioral deficiencies and possibly fears of observers, but gradually improve their performance and gain self-confidence. These models illustrate how effort and positive thoughts can overcome difficulties. *Mastery models* demonstrate faultless performance from the outset (Schunk, 1987).

Schunk and Hanson (1985) compared peer mastery and coping models with adult teacher models and no models. Peer mastery models solved subtraction problems correctly and verbalized statements reflecting high self-efficacy and ability, low task difficulty, and positive attitudes. Peer coping models initially made errors and verbalized negative statements, but then verbalized coping statements (e.g., "I need to pay attention to what I'm doing") and eventually verbalized and performed as well as mastery models. Peer models increased self-efficacy and skill better than the teacher model or no model; teacher-model children outperformed no-model students. Although teacher models can teach students self-regulatory skills, students' self-efficacy beliefs for learning may be aided better by observation of similar peers. In turn, self-efficacy can raise motivation for skill improvement (Schunk, 1989).

Schunk, Hanson, and Cox (1987) found that observing peer coping models enhances children's self-efficacy and skillful performance more than does observing peer mastery models. Unlike the Schunk and Hanson (1985) study, these authors used a task (fractions) with which children had no prior successful performances. Coping models may be more beneficial when students have little task familiarity or have encountered previous learning difficulties. Schunk et al. (1987) also showed that multiple models (coping or mastery) promote outcomes as well as a single coping model and better than a single mastery model.

Models can convey abstract rules and concepts for self-regulation, such as self-evaluative standards. Bandura and Kupers (1964) exposed children to a model demonstrating stringent or lenient standards while playing a bowling game. Children exposed to high-standard models were more likely to reward themselves for high scores and less likely to reward themselves for lower scores compared with subjects assigned to the low-standard condition. Davidson and Smith (1982) had children observe a superior adult, equal peer, or inferior younger child set stringent or lenient standards while performing a pursuit rotor task. Children who observed a lenient model rewarded themselves for lower scores than those who observed a stringent model. Children's self-reward standards were lower than those of the adult, equal to those of the peer, and higher than those of the younger children. Age similarity may have led children to believe that peer standards were appropriate for them.

Imitative learning. Models can provide social evaluative cues, feedback, and assistance to help observers achieve an imitation level of motoric competence as well. France-Kaatrude and Smith (1985) had first and fourth graders perform a pursuit-rotor task, and children could compare their performances with a peer of higher, equal, or lower competence. Compared with children offered social comparisons with superior or inferior peers, those allowed to compare with a similarly-performing peer compared more often, demonstrated greater task persistence, and took fewer self-rewards.

Self-modeling. Self-modeling, which involves watching one's own performances, is another effective method of developing imitative competence (Dowrick, 1983). Typically, one is videotaped while performing a task and subsequently views the tape. Tapes allow for review and are especially informative for tasks one cannot watch while performing. When performances contain errors, commentary from a knowledgeable individual during tape review helps to prevent performers from becoming discouraged. The expert can explain how to execute the behavior better the next time. Tapes can convey to observers that they are becoming more skillful and can continue to make progress, which raises self-efficacy. In support of these points, Schunk and Hanson (1989) videotaped children solving problems and showed them their tapes. Subsequent self-modeling benefits were obtained as these children displayed higher self-efficacy and motivation than children who had been taped but did not observe their tapes, and those who had not been taped.

To fully achieve an imitative level of competence, adults must *fade social and instructional supports* and encourage students to work on tasks on their own. This should be done gradually, as students abstract the underlying learning strategy and receive progress feedback.

Schunk and Swartz (1993) explored the effects of learning goals and progress feedback on children's self-efficacy, self-regulatory use of writing strategies, and writing skill. Students received writing instruction and practice on different types of paragraphs over several sessions. They were taught a five-step writing strategy (e.g., choose a topic to write about, pick the main idea). Once children learned the strategy, they practiced applying it to paragraphs independently as adult support was faded out.

There were four experimental conditions: process (learning) goal, process goal plus progress feedback, product (performance) goal, general goal (instructional control). Process-goal and process-goal plus progress-feedback children received instructions emphasizing the goal of learning to use the strategy to write paragraphs. Product-goal students were told their goal was to write paragraphs; general-goal students were advised to do their best. Children assigned to the process-goal plus progress-feedback condition periodically received verbal feedback from the adult teacher that linked their use of the strategy with improved writing performance (e.g., "You're doing well because you followed the steps in order"). Feedback was given contingent on students using the strategy properly. Schunk and Swartz felt that this feedback would raise self-efficacy and motivation by informing students of their learning progress.

The results showed that the process-goal plus feedback condition was the most effective and that there also were some benefits of providing a process goal alone. Process-goal plus feedback students generally outperformed product- and general-goal students on self-efficacy and writing skill. The former subjects also reported and demonstrated the highest strategy use during the test sessions. Gains made by process-goal plus feedback students were maintained after six weeks and generalized to types of paragraphs on which students had received no instruction.

Self origins of self-regulatory competence

In this section we consider further how self-control and self-regulatory level skills develop in students. We discuss the roles of self-verbalization, goal setting, self-monitoring, self-evaluation, help seeking, and time management. It is true that each of these can be affected by social and instructional factors, and in some of the studies we discuss subtle or more direct social influences affecting students' self-regulatory activities. At the same time, there is much research showing the prominent role that students play in the development of their skills and perceptions of capabilities (Schunk, 1989), ranging from studies where students set their own goals (Schunk, 1985) to research exploring students' verbalizations as they work on achievement tasks (Schunk & Gunn, 1986). In general, then, we can say that research on self origins addresses factors that are less dependent on the social environment for development than the factors discussed in the preceding section.

Self-controlled learning. A process that can foster a self-controlled use of strategies on one's own is *verbalization* of the strategy as it is applied. Self-directed verbalization helps students attend to important task features and disregard irrelevant information. Self-verbalization also promotes encoding, such as when students must detect and integrate information needed to solve problems (Diefenderfer, Holzman, & Thompson, 1985). As a form of rehearsal, verbalization helps to instate a strategy; and the belief that one knows and can use a strategy to improve performance can raise self-efficacy and enhance motivation for strategy use (Schunk, 1989).

Schunk & Rice (1984) presented language-deficient children in grades two to four with listening-comprehension instruction. Half of the children in each grade verbalized strategic steps before applying them to questions; the other half applied but did not verbalize the steps. Strategy verbalization led to higher self-efficacy across grades, and promoted performance among all but the second graders. Perhaps the demands of verbalization interfered with the strategy encoding and retention.

In a follow-up study (Schunk & Rice, 1985), children in grades four and five with reading-comprehension difficulties received instruction and practice. Within each grade, half of the subjects verbalized a strategy before applying it. Strategy verbalization led to higher reading comprehension, self-efficacy, and ability attributions for success across grades.

Verbalization may be helpful, but to become fully self-regulating it must be internalized as private speech (Berk, 1986). In Meichenbaum's (1977) self-instructional training, for example, verbalizations made by participants while working on the task eventually are faded to whispers and covert (silent) instructions. Schunk and Cox (1986) tested the effect of faded verbalization on self-efficacy and achievement. Students with learning disabilities verbalized aloud subtraction solution steps and their application to problems. Some students verbalized continuously; others verbalized during the first half of the training program but then were advised to continue using the strategy but not verbalize aloud (discontinued verbalization); and students in a third condition did not verbalize. Continuous verbalization led to higher self-efficacy and skill than did the other two conditions. When instructed not to verbalize aloud, discontinued verbalization students might have had difficulty internalizing the strategy, and not used covert instructions to regulate their performances.

Goal setting. Goal setting is hypothesized to be an important cognitive process affecting motivation and self-regulation (Bandura, 1988; Locke & Latham, 1990; Schunk, 1989; see also Berndt & Keefe; Ford; Kupersmidt et al.; Wentzel, this volume, for other perspectives on goals). Students who set a goal on their own or have one suggested to them (e.g., by teachers) are apt to make a commitment to attempt to attain it – which is necessary for goals to affect performance – and to experience a sense of efficacy for attaining it. As they work at the task, they engage in self-regulatory activities they believe will help them attain it; for example, they use effective strategies, monitor their progress, manage their time, and seek assistance when needed. Self-efficacy is substantiated as learners observe goal progress, which conveys that they are becoming skillful (Elliott & Dweck, 1988). Providing students with feedback also raises self-efficacy (Bandura & Cervone, 1983; Schunk & Swartz, 1993). Heightened self-efficacy sustains motivation and leads to further development of self-regulatory skills.

Motivational benefits of goals depend on their properties: proximity, specificity, difficulty (Bandura, 1986, 1988; Locke & Latham, 1990). Proximal (short term) goals result in greater motivation than distant (long-term) goals because it is easier to gauge progress toward a short term goal. Specific goals improve motivation by focusing the learner's effort, and difficult but attainable goals enhance motivation more than easy goals. Self-regulatory benefits of goal setting have been obtained in several studies. Bandura and Schunk (1981) presented children with seven sets of subtraction material. Some children pursued a proximal goal of completing one set during each of seven instructional sessions; a second group was given a distant goal of completing all sets by the end of the last (seventh) session; a third group was advised to work productively (general goal). Proximal goals heightened self-efficacy, skill, motivation, and self-regulatory strategy use during instruction. The distant goal resulted in no benefits compared with the general goal. These findings support the idea that when students can gauge their goal progress, the perception of improvement enhances efficacy. Assessing progress toward a distant goal is more difficult, and uncertainty about learning will not instill a sense of efficacy for skill improvement.

Schunk (1983a) compared the effects of social comparative information with those of goal setting during mathematical instructional sessions.

Half of the children were given performance goals each session; the other half were advised to work productively. Within each goal condition, half of the subjects were told the number of problems that other similar children had completed (which matched the session goal) to convey that the goals were attainable; the other half were not given this social comparison information. Goals enhanced self-efficacy; social comparison information promoted motivation during the sessions. Students who received both goals and comparative information demonstrated the highest skill. These results suggest that providing children with a goal and social comparison information indicating that it is attainable increases self-efficacy for learning, which contributes to more productive performance during instructional sessions and greater skill acquisition.

To test the effects of goal difficulty, Schunk (1983b) provided children with either a difficult (but attainable) or easier goal of completing a given number of problems each session. To enhance motivation, half of the subjects in each goal condition were told that they could attain the goal (e.g., "You can work 25 problems"). The other half received social comparison information indicating that similar children completed that many problems. Difficult goals enhanced motivation and division skill; direct goal-attainment information promoted self-efficacy.

Allowing students to set goals may enhance goal commitment and self-efficacy. Schunk (1985) provided subtraction instruction to sixth-grade students with learning disabilities. Children who set their own performance goals and those who had goals suggested to them demonstrated greater motivation and self-regulated strategy use than students who worked without goals; self-set goals led to the highest self-efficacy and skill.

Goal setting also has proven effective over longer periods. Morgan (1985) found that proximal goals raise academic performance and intrinsic interest among college students over an academic year. Although self-efficacy was not assessed the results suggest that goal proximity may affect self-regulatory processes associated with studying over time. Further investigation is needed of students' goal setting and self-regulation of motivation over longer periods and of how self-efficacy changes as they progress toward future goals.

Earlier we discussed the benefits of providing goal progress feedback. Especially when it is difficult for students to determine whether they are making progress toward goal attainment such explicit feedback can raise self-efficacy and contribute to greater self-regulated use of learning strategies and achievement. The research by Schunk and Swartz (1993) supports the point that goal progress feedback can enhance maintenance and generalization of self-regulated strategy use and writing achievement.

Self-monitoring. Self-monitoring is an integral component of the self-regulation process (Bandura, 1986; Kanfer & Gaelick, 1986; Zimmerman & Martinez-Pons, 1990). Monitoring allows one to assess progress toward goals. The perception of progress builds self-efficacy and motivates sustained self-regulatory efforts. Monitoring often is assisted by self-recording aspects of one's behaviors.

Self-monitoring of progress can enhance self-efficacy and promote self-regulation. Sagotsky, Patterson, and Lepper (1978) had fifth- and sixth-graders periodically monitor their performances during mathematical instruction and record whether they were working on appropriate material. Other students set daily performance goals; those in a third condition received self-monitoring and goal setting. Self-monitoring increased achievement and the amount of time students spent engaged with the task; goal setting had minimal effects. For goal setting to affect performance, it may first be necessary to teach students to set challenging but attainable goals.

Schunk (1983c) provided instruction to children who had experienced difficulties acquiring subtraction skills. Self-monitoring students reviewed their work at the end of each instructional session and recorded the number of pages of problems they completed. External-monitoring subjects had their work reviewed by an adult who recorded the number of pages completed. No-monitoring subjects received the instruction and practice, but did not record pages or have them recorded.

Self- and external monitoring promoted self-efficacy, skill, and self-initiated persistence solving problems, better than did no monitoring. The two monitoring conditions did not differ on any measure. Benefits of monitoring did not depend on children's performances during the instructional sessions; the three conditions completed comparable amounts of work. The results suggest that monitoring of progress, rather than the agent, enhanced children's perceptions of their learning progress and self-efficacy for improvement.

Self-evaluation. Self-evaluation comprises self-judgments of present performance by comparing it to one's goal and self-reactions to those judgments in terms of its acceptability, noteworthiness, and so forth. Positive self-evaluations lead students to feel efficacious about learning and motivated to continue to work diligently because they believe they are capable of making further progress (Schunk, 1989). Low self-judgments of progress and negative self-reactions will not necessarily diminish self-efficacy and motivation if students believe they can succeed but that their present approach is ineffective (Bandura, 1986). They may alter their self-regulatory processes by working harder, persisting longer, adopting what they believe is a better strategy, or seeking help from teachers and peers. These and other self-regulatory activities are likely to lead to success (Zimmerman & Martinez-Pons, 1990).

An emphasis on self-evaluation during task engagement helps to develop self-regulatory skills. Research with children during learning of mathematical skills (Schunk & Hanson, 1985; Schunk et al., 1987) and writing skills (Schunk & Swartz, 1993) shows that measures of self-efficacy for learning or improving skills collected before receiving instruction predict subsequent motivation and skill acquisition. Masters and Santrock (1976) found that preschool children who verbalized self-judgmental statements during an effortful handle-turning task (e.g., "I'm really good at this") persisted longer than children who verbalized self-critical or neutral statements.

Bandura and Cervone (1983) obtained benefits of goals and self-evaluative feedback. College students pursued a goal of increasing motor-skill performance by 40% over baseline; others were given feedback indicating they increased performance by 24%; and those in a third condition received goals and feedback. Goals plus evaluative feedback had the strongest effect on performance and self-efficacy, which predicted subsequent effort. Bandura and Cervone (1986) gave subjects a goal of 50% improvement and false feedback indicating they increased by 24%, 36%, 46%, or 54%. Self-efficacy was lowest for the 24% group and highest for the 54% condition. Subjects then indicated new goals and performed the task. Effort was positively related to self-set goals and self-efficacy across conditions. A measure of self-evaluation (self-satisfaction with performance) showed that the greater the dissatisfaction and the higher the self-efficacy, the stronger was subsequent effort expenditure.

Schunk (in press) investigated how goals and self-evaluation affected motivation, self-regulated strategy use, self-efficacy, and achievement. Fourth-graders received instruction and practice on fractions and either a goal of learning how to solve problems (learning goal) or a goal of solving problems (performance goal). In the first study, half of the students in each goal condition assessed their problem-solving capabilities. The learning goal with or without self-evaluation or the performance goal with self-evaluation led to higher self-efficacy, skill, motivation for self-regulated strategy use, and learning goal orientation, than did the performance goal without self-evaluation. In the second study, all students evaluated their progress in skill acquisition. The learning goal led to higher motivation, self-regulated strategy use, self-efficacy, fractions skill, self-evaluations, self-satisfaction with progress in learning, and learning goal orientation.

Help seeking. Another important origin of self-regulatory competence comes through students' efforts to seek help when they are baffled or otherwise uncertain about the appropriateness or accuracy of their work. As Zimmerman (1989, 1990) notes, self-regulated learners are cognitively, metacognitively, and motivationally active. When confronted with a difficult task that requires assistance, self-regulated learners seek help from knowledgeable persons (Newman, 1994). Help-seeking bears a positive relation to academic achievement (Newman & Schwager, 1992).

A model of adaptive help-seeking begins with the student's awareness of a lack of understanding (Newman, 1994). The student then considers available information in deciding about the necessity for, target of, and content of the request. The help seeker expresses a need for help that is appropriate under the prevailing conditions, and finally processes the assistance in such a way as to improve subsequent performance.

Research has explored the relation of various individual characteristics to help-seeking. The most consistent findings are in the area of academic goals. Research shows that children characterized as high in intrinsic motivation for learning are more likely to seek help than are students with lower intrinsic motivation (Newman, 1994). Two dimensions of intrinsic motivation bear especially strong relations to help-seeking: striving for independent mastery and preference for challenge. Among all students, the greater the preference for challenge, the more likely students are to seek help. This relates to the importance of difficult but attainable goals for motivation. Striving for independent mastery refers to the extent of dependence on the teacher. For young children, the greater the dependence on the teacher, the greater the likelihood of seeking help; by middle school, however, this is reversed such that the stronger the striving for mastery, the greater the likelihood of seeking help.

Although help-seeking is self generated, it depends on the social environment and can be affected by social factors, especially the use of models. Teachers can model the process of seeking help by working on a task, getting stuck, deciding to ask for assistance, and posing a question. Showing children videotapes of other children engaged in a task and seeking assistance also can minimize potential inhibitions against seeking help (Newman, 1994). From a self-efficacy perspective, we might expect that knowing one can seek help if one is unsure about what to do should raise self-efficacy for performing well, but research is needed on this point.

Time management. The purposive planning, monitoring, and management of study time is another important source of students' skill in self-regulating their academic performance. To succeed in classes with implicit and explicit deadlines, students must plan their study time, feel efficacious about managing their time, and monitor their progress.

Britton and Tesser (1991) investigated the impact of college students' time management skills on cumulative grade-point-average (GPA). To evaluate the possibility that time management is merely an aspect of intelligence, they included the Scholastic Aptitude Test (SAT) as a traditional measure of intelligence. They planned to compare the separate contributions of time management skills and intelligence to the GPA. A factor analysis of the time management scale revealed three components: time attitude, short- and long-range planning. The time attitude items revealed how students felt about their efficiency of time use, their control of time use, and their skill in time self-monitoring. Britton and Tesser noted that these time attitude measures were similar to measures of self-efficacy. For example, the time attitude component includes items that directly measure the feeling of being in charge of one's time and being able to say "no" to people, in order to concentrate on homework. Britton and Tesser found that only the time attitude and short-range planning components of their scale were significant predictors of cumulative GPA. Interestingly, the effects of short-range planning and time attitude were found to be independent of and stronger predictors of GPA than the SAT. A sense of self-efficacy for managing study time is essential for effective action.

Students' perceptions of efficacy in controlling study time can have affective and somatic benefits as well as cognitive benefits. Macan, Shahani, Dipboye, and Phillips (1990) developed a questionnaire to assess time management behaviors and attitudes of college students. One of four subscales in this instrument (Perceived Control of Time) involved judgments of self-efficacy. This subscale was similar to Britton and Tesser's (1991) time attitude items, and was the most predictive of student outcomes. Students who perceived greater control of their time reported significantly higher performance evaluations, greater work and life satisfactions, less role ambiguity and overload, and fewer job-induced and somatic tensions.

Students can be taught to improve the effectiveness of their self-monitoring (Mount & Terrill, 1977). Undergraduate volunteers were assigned to various self-recording conditions in which there were two target behaviors: the amount of time that students studied for class and the amount of time they experienced "guilt" about studying when they were not engaged in it. The type of time measured did not influence the effectiveness of these self-monitoring results differentially. Students who used note cards and graph paper achieved significantly higher final examination grades than those who used either recording form alone. The authors concluded that the superiority of the combined method of self-monitoring was due to its provision of more continuous feedback than either method alone. These results show that instructions to self-monitor time use on recording forms affects college students' achievement.

Together these studies indicate that students' self-regulation of academic study time through time planning, self-efficacy beliefs, and self-monitoring significantly improves academic attainment. These findings support predictions of social cognitive theory and research results on academic self-regulation (Bandura, in press; Schunk, 1989; Zimmerman, 1989).

Implications for practice

The ideas we have presented suggest many potential implications for educational practice. Teachers should make greater use of models in the classroom by emphasizing the importance of cognitive modeling where models verbalize their thought processes, in addition to the steps they perform, as they work on a task (Zimmerman & Kleefeld, 1977). Coping models can help relieve students' fears and build their confidence by verbalizing coping statements (e.g., "I have to pay better attention") and progress statements ("I'm doing better").

Models are teachers or peers who explain and demonstrate skills and strategies in front of classes, but there are other ways to use models in the classroom. One way is in cooperative groups, in which a small number of students work jointly on a task. Responsibilities are divided so each group member is responsible for something. Groups typically are set up so that each member must master the skills and the group is not allowed to proceed until such skill mastery occurs. The characteristics of effective groups have been documented (Cohen, 1994). For our purposes it is essential that students serve as models for one another. A good way to do this is for each student to work on some aspect of the task, and then explain it to the other group members after he or she has mastered it. This type of positive peer model teaches skills and raises others' self-efficacy.

Teachers can develop student's self-regulatory skills by teaching them effective strategies, emphasizing effort and persistence, teaching students to set process goals, providing feedback on goal progress, monitoring skill acquisition, and periodically evaluating skill development. However, self-regulative mastery requires more than observational learning experience, it involves practicing those components. If teachers can incorporate many of these procedures into regular classroom instructional exercises, students will have opportunities to develop their self-regulatory skills. Teachers who have students set goals and monitor their goal progress are apt to foster these skills in students.

Students need to practice skills at home and in other contexts as well as school environments. Bruner (1985) has noted that learning to play chess, work mathematical problems, and play the flute involve such common skills as attention, memory, and maintaining frustration tolerance. Students should seek ways that self-regulatory competencies they acquire in school can be used elsewhere. Thus, goal setting learned in the context of spelling instruction may come in handy in track as students set goals for lowering their times at particular distances.

We have not discussed the role of parents in this chapter because we felt to do so would take us beyond our intended scope; however, parents are important in the development of their children's self-regulatory competencies. One way they can have a major impact is by systematically modeling skills they want their children to display. When models act one way and verbalize another type of behavior, children are more strongly influenced by the modeled behaviors than by the preaching (Bryan & Walbek, 1970). If parents want children to set goals, then parents should set goals themselves and assist children with goal setting. If parents want children to develop effort and persistence, parents must display those qualities and not give up readily on tasks.

Parents also can assist students in the selection of friends and others with whom they share academic interests and can become study partners. Friends strongly impact desirable conduct (Berndt & Keefe, 1992). Students who associate with academically-oriented peers are likely to develop more self-regulatory study skills associated with studying. By suggesting to their children friends with whom they might study and helping to arrange such opportunities, parents can help to develop children's self-regulation. To the extent that they have the resources for making such a choice, parents can aid their children's self-regulation through selection of schools or teachers.

Conclusion

In this chapter, we have discussed the roles of modeling and self-efficacy in the development of students' self-regulation to include social and self origins of self-regulatory competence. Acquisition of self-regulatory skills through modeling and social learning experiences occurs in a series of levels. We believe that educators and parents can do much to help children develop a self-regulatory level of academic skill through modeling, socially assisted motoric practice, and use of self-processes (self-verbalization, goal setting, self-monitoring, self-evaluation, help-seeking, and time management), and have suggested some ways to do this. More research is needed on how modeling and self-efficacy influence self-regulation, especially over the long term. Finally, in addition to these cognitive benefits, the attainment of self-regulatory skill is accompanied by a growing sense of self-efficacy, which is a major source of students' intrinsic interest and motivation to continue their academic learning on their own (Bandura & Schunk, 1981; Zimmerman, 1985, 1995).

References

Bailey, T. (1993). Can youth apprenticeship thrive in the United States? *Educational Researcher, 22*(3), 4–10.

Bandura, A. (1986). *Social foundations of thought and action: A social cognitive theory.* Englewood Cliffs, NJ: Prentice-Hall.

Bandura, A. (1988). Self-regulation of motivation and action through goal systems. In V. Hamilton, G. H. Bower, & N. H. Frijda (Eds.), *Cognitive perspectives on emotion and motivation* (pp. 37–61). Dordrecht, The Netherlands: Kluwer.

Bandura, A. (in press). *Self-efficacy: The exercise of control.* New York: Freeman.

Bandura, A., & Cervone, D. (1983). Self-evaluative and self-efficacy mechanisms governing the motivational effects of goal systems. *Journal of Personality and Social Psychology, 45,* 1017–1028.

Bandura, A., & Cervone, D. (1986). Differential engagement of self-reactive influences in cognitive motivation. *Organizational Behavior and Human Decision Processes, 38,* 92–113.

Bandura, A., & Jeffery, R. W. (1973). Role of symbolic coding and rehearsal processes in observational learning. *Journal of Personality and Social Psychology*, *26*, 122–130.

Bandura, A., & Kupers, C. J. (1964). Transmission of patterns of self-reinforcement through modeling. *Journal of Abnormal and Social Psychology*, *69*, 1–9.

Bandura, A., & Schunk, D. H. (1981). Cultivating competence, self-efficacy, and intrinsic interest through proximal self-motivation. *Journal of Personality and Social Psychology*, *41*, 586–598.

Bandura, A., & Walters, R. H. (1963). *Social learning and personality development*. New York: Holt, Rinehart and Winston.

Berk, L. E. (1986). Relationship of elementary school children's private speech to behavioral accompaniment to task, attention, and task performance. *Developmental Psychology*, *22*, 671–680.

Berndt, T. J., & Keefe, K. (1992). Friends' influence on adolescents' perceptions of themselves at school. In D. H. Schunk & J. L. Meece (Eds.), *Student perceptions in the classroom* (pp. 51–73). Hillsdale, NJ: Erlbaum.

Bouffard-Bouchard, T., Parent, S., & Larivee, S. (1991). Influence of self-efficacy on self-regulation and performance among junior and senior high-school age students. *International Journal of Behavioral Development*, *14*, 153–164.

Britton, B. K., & Tesser, A. (1991). Effects of time management practices on college grades. *Journal of Educational Psychology*, *83*, 405–410.

Bruner, J. S. (1985). Models of the learner. *Educational Researcher*, *14*(6), 5–8.

Bryan, J. H., & Walbek, N. H. (1970). Preaching and practicing generosity: Some determinants of sharing in children. *Child Development*, *41*, 329–354.

Cohen, E. G. (1994). Restructuring the classroom: Conditions for productive small groups. *Review of Educational Research*, *64*, 1–35.

Davidson, E. S., & Smith, W. P. (1982). Imitation, social comparison, and self-reward. *Child Development*, *53*, 928–932.

Diefenderfer, K. K., Holzman, T. G., & Thompson, D. N. (1985). Verbal self-monitoring and solution flexibility in rule induction. *Journal of Genetic Psychology*, *146*, 79–88.

Dowrick, P. W. (1983). Self-modeling. In P. W. Dowrick & S. J. Biggs (Eds.), *Using video: Psychological and social applications* (pp. 105–124). Chichester, England: Wiley.

Elliott, E. S., & Dweck, C. S. (1988). Goals: An approach to motivation and achievement. *Journal of Personality and Social Psychology*, *54*, 5–12.

France-Kaatrude, A., & Smith, W. P. (1985). Social comparison, task motivation, and the development of self-evaluative standards in children. *Developmental Psychology*, *21*, 1080–1089.

Kanfer, F. H., & Gaelick, K. (1986). Self-management methods. In F. H. Kanfer & A. P. Goldstein (Eds.), *Helping people change: A textbook of methods* (3rd ed., pp. 283–345). New York: Pergamon.

Locke, E. A., & Latham, G. P. (1990). *A theory of goal setting and task performance*. Englewood Cliffs, NJ: Prentice-Hall.

Macan, T. H., Shahani, C., Dipboye, R. L., & Phillips, A. P. (1990). College students' time management: Correlations with academic performance and stress. *Journal of Educational Psychology, 82,* 760–768.

Mace, F. C., Belfiore, P. J., & Shea, M. C. (1989). Operant theory and research on self-regulation. In B. J. Zimmerman & D. H. Schunk (Eds.), *Self-regulated learning and academic achievement: Theory, research, and practice* (pp. 27–50). New York: Springer-Verlag.

Masters, J. C., & Santrock, J. W. (1976). Studies in the self-regulation of behavior: Effects of contingent cognitive and affective events. *Developmental Psychology, 12,* 334–348.

Meichenbaum, D. (1977). *Cognitive behavior modification: A integrative approach.* New York: Plenum.

Morgan, M. (1985). Self-monitoring of attained subgoals in private study. *Journal of Educational Psychology, 77,* 623–630.

Mount, M. K., & Terrill, F. J. (1977). Improving examination scores through self-monitoring. *Journal of Educational Research, 71,* 70–73.

Newman, R. S. (1994). Academic help seeking: A strategy of self-regulated learning. In D. H. Schunk & B. J. Zimmerman (Eds.), *Self-regulation of learning and performance: Issues and educational applications* (pp. 283–301). Hillsdale, NJ: Erlbaum.

Newman, R. S., & Schwager, M. T. (1992). Student perceptions and academic help-seeking. In D. H. Schunk & J. L. Meece (Eds.), *Student perceptions in the classroom* (pp. 123–146). Hillsdale, NJ: Erlbaum.

Rosenthal, T. L., & Bandura, A. (1978). Psychological modeling: Theory and practice. In S. L. Garfield & A. E. Bergin (Eds.), *Handbook of psychotherapy and behavior change: An empirical analysis* (2nd ed., pp. 621–658). New York: Wiley.

Rosenthal, T. L., & Zimmerman, B. J. (1978). *Social learning and cognition.* New York: Academic Press.

Sagotsky, G., Patterson, C. J., & Lepper, M. R. (1978). Training children's self-control: A field experiment in self-monitoring and goal-setting in the classroom. *Journal of Experimental Child Psychology, 25,* 242–253.

Salomon, G. (1984). Television is "easy" and print is "tough": The differential investment of mental effort in learning as a function of perceptions and attributions. *Journal of Educational Psychology, 76,* 647–658.

Schunk, D. H. (1981). Modeling and attributional effects on children's achievement: A self-efficacy analysis. *Journal of Educational Psychology, 73,* 93–105.

Schunk, D. H. (1983a). Developing children's self-efficacy and skills: The roles of social comparative information and goal setting. *Contemporary Educational Psychology, 8,* 76–86.

Schunk, D. H. (1983b). Goal difficulty and attainment information: Effects on children's achievement behaviors. *Human Learning, 2,* 107–117.

Schunk, D. H. (1983c). Progress self-monitoring: Effects on children's self-efficacy and achievement. *Journal of Experimental Education, 51*, 89–93.

Schunk, D. H. (1985). Participation in goal setting: Effects on self-efficacy and skills of learning disabled children. *Journal of Special Education, 19*, 307–317.

Schunk, D. H. (1987). Peer models and children's behavioral change. *Review of Educational Research, 57*, 149–174.

Schunk, D. H. (1989). Self-efficacy and achievement behaviors. *Educational Psychology Review, 1*, 173–208.

Schunk, D. H. (in press). Goal and self-evaluative influences during children's cognitive skill learning. *American Educational Research Journal*.

Schunk, D. H., & Cox, P. D. (1986). Strategy training and attributional feedback with learning disabled students. *Journal of Educational Psychology, 78*, 201–209.

Schunk, D. H., & Gunn, T. P. (1986). Self-efficacy and skill development: Influence of task strategies and attributions. *Journal of Educational Research, 79*, 238–244.

Schunk, D. H., & Hanson, A. R. (1985). Peer models: Influence on children's self-efficacy and achievement. *Journal of Educational Psychology, 77*, 313–322.

Schunk, D. H., & Hanson, A. R. (1989). Self-modeling and children's cognitive skill learning. *Journal of Educational Psychology, 81*, 155–163.

Schunk, D. H., Hanson, A. R., & Cox, P. D. (1987). Peer model attributes and children's achievement behaviors. *Journal of Educational Psychology, 79*, 54–61.

Schunk, D. H., & Rice, J. M. (1984). Strategy self-verbalization during remedial listening comprehension instruction. *Journal of Experimental Education, 53*, 49–54.

Schunk, D. H., & Rice, J. M. (1985). Verbalization of comprehension strategies: Effects on children's achievement outcomes. *Human Learning, 4*, 1–10.

Schunk, D. H., & Swartz, C. W. (1993). Goals and progress feedback: Effects on self-efficacy and writing achievement. *Contemporary Educational Psychology, 18*, 337–354.

Schunk, D. H., & Zimmerman, B. J. (1994). *Self-regulation of learning and performance: Issues and educational applications*. Hillsdale, NJ: Erlbaum.

Zimmerman, B. J. (1985). The development of "intrinsic" motivation: A social cognitive analysis. In G. J. Whitehurst (Ed.), *Annals of child development* (pp. 117–160). Greenwich, CT: JAI.

Zimmerman, B. J. (1989). A social cognitive view of self-regulated academic learning. *Journal of Educational Psychology, 81*, 329–339.

Zimmerman, B. J. (1990). Self-regulating academic learning and achievement: The emergence of a social cognitive perspective. *Educational Psychology Review, 2*, 173–201.

Zimmerman, B. J. (1994). Dimensions of academic self-regulation: A conceptual framework for education. In D. H. Schunk & B. J. Zimmerman (Eds.), *Self-reg-*

ulation of learning and performance: Issues and educational applications (pp. 3–21). Hillsdale, NJ: Erlbaum.

Zimmerman, B. J. (1995). Self-efficacy and educational development. In A. Bandura (Ed.), *Self-efficacy in changing societies* (pp. 202–231). New York: Cambridge University Press.

Zimmerman, B. J., & Bonner, S. (in press). A social cognitive view of strategic learning. In C. E. Weinstein & B. L. McCombs (Eds.), *Skill, will, and self-regulation*. Hillsdale, NJ: Erlbaum.

Zimmerman, B. J., & Kleefeld, C. (1977). Toward a theory of teaching: A social learning view. *Contemporary Educational Psychology, 2,* 158–171.

Zimmerman, B. J., & Martinez-Pons, M. (1990). Student differences in self-regulated learning: Relating grade, sex, and giftedness to self-efficacy and strategy use. *Journal of Educational Psychology, 82,* 51–59.

Zimmerman, B. J., & Rosenthal, T. L. (1974). Observational learning of rule-governed behavior by children. *Psychological Bulletin, 81,* 29–42.

Zimmerman, B. J., & Schunk, D. H. (1989). *Self-regulated learning and academic achievement: Theory, research, and practice.* New York: Springer-Verlag.

8   Social motivation: Goals and social-cognitive processes. A comment

Carol S. Dweck

It is clear that the array of goals facing students is a daunting one. Students are typically concerned not only with academic work, but also with the liking and esteem of their teachers and peers – and with their parents' reactions to their academic and social life. Even in the best of all possible worlds, juggling this variety of concerns would be difficult. When one considers that this is often not the best of all possible worlds – for example, that what peers value is often not what parents and teachers value – then coordinating the various social and academic goals becomes even more demanding. Each of these chapters deals in an extremely thoughtful way with the psychological factors that predict how and how well students will confront these challenges.

Drawing on the wealth of research provided in the six chapters, I will use a "goal analysis" to tie together the many findings and to integrate the different perspectives represented in the chapters. I will begin by discussing the kinds of goals students may pursue in academic settings. I will then move to an examination of the factors shown by research to affect successful goal pursuit and school adjustment, and I will end by proposing a dynamic model of goals that organizes these factors into a system of coherent processes. As the work reviewed in these chapters attests, such a goal analysis can be a fruitful way to understand academic and social functioning (see Erdley; Ford; Harter; Juvonen; Kupersmidt, Buchele, Voegler, and Sedikides; and Schunk and Zimmerman chapters; see also Dodge, Asher, & Parkhurst, 1989; Pervin, 1982; 1989; Wentzel, 1991a; this volume.). Indeed, we will see how certain patterns of goal pursuit appear to foster adjustment, whereas other patterns of goal pursuit appear to undermine it.

181

What kinds of goals can students pursue in a school setting?

When we scan the array of goals available to students in a school setting, there are, first of all, skill-related goals: those related to academic-intellectual skills (and perhaps to athletic or artistic skills). In these areas, students may be primarily concerned with proving their skills and being judged favorably (performance goals), or with expanding their skills and mastering new tasks (learning goals) (Dweck & Elliott, 1983; Dweck & Leggett, 1988; Elliott & Dweck, 1988). They may also be motivated to achieve for extrinsic reasons. For example, some students may try to do well in school because parents promise good things if they do and threaten bad things if they don't. (See Harter's discussion of intrinsic vs. extrinsic motivational orientation, where the intrinsic motivational orientation involves curiosity and desire for challenge – similar to learning goals – whereas the external orientation involves a focus on such things as grades, approval, or avoiding censure – a combination of performance goals and extrinsic goals.)

Also of utmost importance are peer-oriented goals. Indeed, Wentzel (this volume) presents evidence that students value social goals in school more highly than they value learning-oriented goals. These social goals can take many forms (see Erdley; Ford; Harter; Juvonen; and Kupersmidt, et al. chapters; see also Wentzel, this volume.) One is liking and approval from others, akin to performance goals in the academic domain (see Erdley; Ford; Harter; Juvonen; Kupersmidt et al.). The negative side of this is the goal of avoiding rejection, and it is most likely to be pursued when students lose confidence in their ability to win approval (Taylor & Asher, 1984). Another social goal is to promote and develop relationships (Erdley; Wentzel, this volume). This may be seen as akin to learning goals in the academic domain in that both involve striving to develop the valued commodity rather than to win approval for it. Also in a positive vein, some students highly value the goal of helping their peers or facilitating their peers' well-being (see Ford for an extensive discussion of these goals; see also Wentzel, this volume). In contrast, some students may value the less prosocial goal of being able to control or dominate others (and they may value being known for this) (Erdley; see Ford's discussion of "hypermasculine" goals).

Some students may value personal social-moral goals, such as behaving responsibly or being a sensitive, cooperative person (Ford; Wentzel, this volume).

Others may put a high premium on instrumental goals: getting what they want when they want it or controlling valued resources. Ford also discusses a possibly related pattern: Students who pursue a hedonistic pattern of goals, striving to maximize personal pleasure above all else.

Finally, students may pursue adult-oriented goals. As noted above, they may strive to win the esteem of their teachers and parents, and they may strive to do so, for example, by excelling in skill areas, in social areas, or in their personal social-moral attributes.

This is by no means meant to be an exhaustive list of the goals students may pursue in the school setting. Yet, when one considers this diversity of goals, many of which are important to most children, it becomes clear that students cannot pursue these goals one at a time or in isolation from each other. As Dodge, Asher, and Parkhurst (1989) and Wentzel (1991a) point out (see also Ford; Harter; Juvonen; Kupersmidt et al; and Schunk and Zimmerman), most school situations present the opportunity to pursue different goals simultaneously and many situations may even *require* students to pursue several goals simultaneously.

For example, when one pursues academic-intellectual goals, these have implications for adult and peer approval – and not necessarily in the same direction. As the very interesting work by Juvonen shows, adolescents often mete out disapproval to peers who excel academically. The student who values academic achievement is thus in the position of risking peer rejection for pursuing academic goals. The student who courts peer acceptance at the expense of academic excellence risks parental sanctions, and limits future options, by doing so.

Both Ford and Wentzel (this volume) emphasize the notion that social and academic goals are not independent, but, rather, often have reciprocal effects. Both stress the degree to which having prosocial goals and successful peer relationships can foster greater engagement in school and more positive intellectual outcomes (Kupersmidt, Coie, & Dodge, 1990; Skinner & Belmont, 1993; Wentzel, 1991a,b). Thus it appears that optimal school adjustment in either the social or academic arena calls for the ability to pursue and attain goals in both arenas.

As another example of the need for goal coordination, when peer conflicts arise, a number of goals may simultaneously come to the fore. There may be the immediate instrumental goal of getting the thing one wants, there may be the goal of dominating others and showing who's boss, there may be the goal of avoiding rejection, there may be the goal of working things out fairly, and there may be the goal of fostering the relationship. All children may value these goals to some degree, but the task becomes to select among them and to coordinate effectively the ones that are selected (Dodge, Asher, & Parkhurst, 1989; Ford, Wentzel, Wood, Stevens, & Siesfeld, 1989; Rabiner & Gordon, 1992; Wentzel, 1991a). I will return to this important issue later.

What affects goal pursuit and goal persistence?

The six chapters shed considerable light on the social-cognitive factors that influence the goals students select and the vigor with which they pursue them. Below, I identify the beliefs and values that appear to be of major importance, and following this, I elaborate upon the role these factors can play in problems of goal pursuit, goal coordination, and adjustment.

Goal value

One obviously critical factor affecting whether children select and pursue a particular goal is the importance of the goal and its meaning to the self. Several of the chapters in this volume touch on this issue in various ways (Erdley; Ford; Harter; and Schunk & Zimmerman). Erdley cites a number of studies documenting the importance of control and dominance to aggressive children (see also Crick & Ladd, 1990) and the importance of avoiding rejection to withdrawn children (see Taylor & Asher, 1984). Might these be the different ways in which these children protect their self-esteem? In this vein, Harter highlights the ways in which different goals feed into self-esteem for different students. For example, for some students peer approval is paramount for maintaining self-esteem, whereas for others it appears to be of far less importance.

Kupersmidt et al. make the compelling proposal that students' psychological adjustment can be understood in terms of the value they place on various social goals or needs. Specifically, they argue that adjustment can be predicted by the discrepancy between students' valued social needs and their actual social relationships. When these social needs are not met, depression and anxiety are likely to result (see Higgins, 1987; see also Harter's chapter for a discussion of William James' contention that self-esteem is a function of the discrepancy between one's pretensions or aspirations and one's actual successes).

Ford addresses not only what students do value, but what schools ought to be teaching them to value. Here the emphasis is on making concern for others something that one prides in oneself. The implication is that some of the ills of our society may be linked to individualism run amok, to the emphasis on individuals' rights and desires over their social responsibilities.

A related factor affecting goal pursuit involves the perceived appropriateness or legitimacy of the goal. Thus some children may value a particular goal, but not pursue it because they believe it is an inappropriate one for the setting. For example, many children may value instrumental or dominance goals (gaining valued commodities, controlling other children), but they may not pursue them because they believe them to be inappropriate given their other goals, such as maintaining approval from others or being a certain kind of person. What Erdley and Asher (1993b) show (see also Slaby & Guerra, 1988) is that aggressive children not only value goals that entail aggression (e.g., dominance or retaliation), but, compared to their nonaggressive peers, they also believe that dominance or retaliation via aggression is legitimate.

Efficacy, confidence, and perceived ability

Several of the chapters emphasize the importance of students' perceived ability to attain their valued goals. Clearly, one will primarily adopt and persist at goals one believes one has the ability to pursue successfully. For example, Erdley and Asher (1993a,b) show that aggressive children have more confidence than other children that they can successfully complete goals involving aggression (see also Perry, Perry, & Rasmussen, 1986), but have less confidence than other children in their ability to succeed at prosocial goals. Personal agency beliefs play a central role in Ford's model of goal pursuit, and Schunk and Zimmerman present much compelling evidence for the role of efficacy beliefs in the goals that students adopt and in the quality of their self-regulatory processes as they work toward their achievement goals. Schunk and Zimmerman also present a fascinating analysis of how children may acquire and internalize self-efficacy beliefs and self-regulatory competencies.

Attributions

How children interpret an event can be an important determinant of whether they persist in their goal pursuit or whether they instead select other goals. The work of Weiner (e.g., Weiner, 1985, 1986; Weiner & Kukla, 1970), Dweck (e.g., Diener & Dweck, 1978; Dweck, 1975) and others has demonstrated that certain attributions can lead to the abandonment of goal striving, whereas other attributions can increase the vigor of goal pursuit. In both intellectual-academic and social situations, children who blame their abilities for failure and rejection tend to forsake active striving toward success and instead focus on minimizing the failure (Diener & Dweck, 1978; Goetz & Dweck, 1980). In contrast, those who focus on their effort or other controllable factors tend to show more effective persistence in the face of setbacks.

Attributions of intent have also been shown to play a clear role in social goal pursuit. For example, when aggressive children attribute hostile intent to their peers (which they do even for accidental or ambiguous acts), they appear to abandon prosocial goals and instead to adopt the goal of retaliation (Dodge, 1980; Dodge & Frame, 1982; Erdley & Asher, 1993a).

Thus the attributions students make play an important role in goal pursuit. I will also argue the reverse – that the goals students are pursuing affect the attributions they make. When children are overconcerned with proving themselves intellectually or socially, they may be more likely to see failure or rejection as an indictment of themselves (e.g., their intelligence or their personality) (Elliott & Dweck, 1988). In a related way, when children are overconcerned with dominance, control, or self-defense, they may be more likely to interpret others' actions as slights or provocations (see Erdley chapter).

In short, goals and attributions are likely to have important reciprocal effects, and this relation will be developed further below.

Implicit theories

Students have certain self-conceptions or implicit theories that have been shown to affect their goal choices and their goal pursuit (Dweck & Leggett, 1988). For example, some students think of their intelligence as a fixed entity (entity theory), whereas others think of it as a malleable quality that can be increased through their efforts (incremental theory). When students believe that this important trait is fixed – that they have only a certain amount of this precious commodity – they become oriented toward proving its adequacy. Thus they tend to focus on *performance goals*, in which the aim is to gain positive judgments of their intelligence.

In contrast, when students hold an incremental theory, they tend to focus more on *learning goals* – goals in which the aim is to increase their abilities. That is, believing that intelligence can be increased appears to orient students toward just that.

Moreover, Erdley, Cain, Loomis, Dumas-Hines, and Dweck (in press) have recently shown these relations to hold in the social domain as well: Those students who hold an entity theory of their personality (believe it is a fixed trait) are more concerned about judgments in social settings than those who hold an incremental theory of their personality (believe it is a malleable quality). Moreover, as in the academic domain, such a focus on performance goals leads to greater vulnerability to negative self-attributions and impaired persistence in the face of setbacks, such as rejection. Thus, the implicit theories that students favor can affect the goals they choose to pursue, as well as the persistence with which they pursue them.

As an aside, I would like to add a note on the parallels between motivational processes in the achievement and social domains. Beginning with our work on attributions (e.g., Diener & Dweck, 1978; Goetz & Dweck, 1980) and continuing through our work on implicit theories and goals (Dweck & Leggett, 1988; Elliott & Dweck, 1988), we have found that every major motivational pattern we detect in the realm of achievement has its analog in the realm of social relations. Similar self-attributions lead to a nonpersistent, helpless response in both domains, and similar implicit theories and goals appear to set up these attributions and responses in both domains. Thus the message is that researchers should look across domains (and across literatures) for clues to general patterns of motivation and adaptation (see Weiner, 1986).

Knowledge of strategies for reaching goals

It is also clear that effective goal pursuit must involve knowledge of appropriate strategies for pursuing a given goal or for coordinating goals (Erdley; Ford; Juvonen; Schunk and Zimmerman). Moreover, what the appropriate strategies are may change with age. Juvonen's research provides a beautiful example of this. Young children valuing peer approval must know that their peers approve of academic effort, but adolescents with the same goals must know that their peers disapprove of academic effort. If adolescents wish to maintain peer approval while maintaining academic excellence, they must learn to hide their effort and to project the same intellectual nonchalance as their classmates.

Juvonen provides another fine example of strategies children must learn if they wish to maintain social approval. Specifically, she shows how children learn that portraying their transgression as unintentional will mitigate the negative consequences of the transgression.

The work of Asher and his colleagues (Asher & Renshaw, 1981; Oden & Asher, 1977) provides yet another example of the importance of strategy knowledge in pursuing social goals. This work suggests that a problem for many low-accepted children is their lack of strategies for interacting with peers in ways that are rewarding to the peer. For instance, they may not know that they should show interest in what a playmate does, or they may not know how to cooperate on a task. Indeed, a major component of Oden and Asher's successful intervention with unpopular children was to coach these children to interact with peers in nonaversive ways, ways that would maximize mutual enjoyment.

Contextual variables

In addition to the personal, social-cognitive variables that affect goal pursuit and attainment, it is important to mention environmental variables that, not surprisingly, also exert major effects and can make the difference between adjustment and nonadjustment. After all, when one speaks of adjustment, one is referring to how well one adapts to particular contexts. The recent work of Eccles and her colleagues (e.g., Eccles & Midgley, 1989) points up how the environment can provide a good fit with students' own goals for themselves, for instance, giving them opportunities to achieve in ways they value or to develop the skills they value. Such a fit is found to predict favorable developmental trajectories. In contrast, students who find themselves in environments that afford them little opportunity to engage in pursuits they value are at greater risk for adjustment problems. Both Harter and Juvonen, citing this work, discuss how adolescents' educational environments, by not providing the proper fit with adolescents' emerging goals and values, can foster negative self-evaluations and negative attitudes toward learning. For example, Harter shows how the junior high school environment can account for the observed decline in students' intrinsic motivation to learn, and Juvonen shows how that environment can lead adolescents to adopt peer norms that devalue academic effort. In light of this, Juvonen makes the interesting suggestion that schools might combat the peer norms against effort by decreasing competition and fostering small group cooperation, so that effort would then be perceived as a prosocial force in the service of common achievement goals (Ames, 1992).

Schunk and Zimmerman also speak to the importance of the child's social environment as a medium for fostering self-efficacy beliefs and self-regulatory competencies. For example, they present an important series of studies demonstrating how students can develop skills and gain information about their competencies from observation of adult and peer models.

Problems of goal choice and goal persistence

Given the variables that play a clear role in the choice of appropriate goals and in the successful pursuit of those goals, we are now in a position to look in greater detail at the problems that can arise as students conduct their lives in the school setting.

One clear problem, highlighted in several of the chapters, arises when students do not have appropriate/constructive goal priorities (Erdley, Ford, Harter; see also Wentzel, this volume). For example, as noted by Oden and Asher (1977), some low-accepted children do not seem to know that having fun is one of the goals you might have when playing with other children. Or, as Erdley points out, aggressive children appear to value dominance, control, instrumental goals, and retaliation over relationship-building goals, particularly when they feel provoked (Crick & Ladd, 1990, Erdley & Asher, 1993a; Rabiner & Gordon, 1992). These goal priorities do not appear to be ones that would foster rewarding and smooth-running relationships.

Self-beliefs (e.g., efficacy beliefs, implicit theories), as noted, may play a role in the setting of goal priorities and thus may contribute to the problem of skewed goals. For example, problems of goal choice and goal coordination may be fostered by students' implicit theories, particularly by an "entity" theory, that depicts personal attributes as fixed entities (Dweck, 1991; Dweck & Leggett, 1988). As mentioned above, the belief in fixed traits (be it fixed intelligence or fixed personality) appears to promote a concern with how those traits will be judged. This preoccupation with judgments can divert students from goals involving learning and development. So, for example, those students holding an entity theory of intelligence have been shown to sacrifice meaningful learning opportunities when these opportunities pose the risk of errors or negative judgments (Dweck & Leggett, 1988). It is likely that those who hold an entity theory of their personality would avoid risky social situations, ones that hold the danger of rejection, even if those situations hold the possibility of developing desired relationships. Thus implicit theories may be seen as self-conceptions that chronically affect the value that students place on important goals. An entity theory, by making academic and social outcomes into indices of adequacy, seems to elevate the importance of performance goals to the detriment of learning/development goals, especially when the threat of failure or rejection is present.

Inappropriate goals may then set up oversensitivity to certain cues, as well as maladaptive attributions and nonconstructive responses. For example, entering a situation with dominance and control goals may make students hypersensitive to slights or threats to their dominance and may make hostile attributions, anger, and retaliation more likely (see Erdley's chapter). In a related vein, entering a situation with strong concerns about acceptance and rejection may make students hypersensitive to cues implying rejection and may foster self-blame and helpless responses in the face of rejection. In contrast, students who focus on building and maintaining relationships or on increasing their skills will be more sensitive to cues that suggest how this may best be done and will focus on varying their effort or strategies when things go amiss, rather than assigning blame and withdrawing or retaliating. In short, goals appear to be important organizers of cognitive, affective, and behavioral responses, and may help us understand why some children display strong, maladaptive reactions to seemingly mild cues.

Goals are also fluid and dynamic, so that an event like failure, conflict, or rejection can elicit new goals (or change the relative values of existing goals). Thus some students may enter a situation with a full array of goals, but may drop the appropriate ones (e.g., prosocial, relationship-maintaining goals) when they confront a difficult situation. Instead, such goals as retaliation or self-protection may come to the fore. For example, some aggressive children may value prosocial, relationship-maintaining goals, but as soon as they perceive provocation, they may relinquish these goals in favor of goals that would reestablish their control and dominance through retaliation. Or, children prone to social withdrawal may highly value the goal of developing relationships, but that goal may be easily eclipsed by the goal of avoiding rejection when social disapproval appears possible.

This problem, inappropriate abandonment of goals, may also arise when students cannot find ways to coordinate their valued goals. For example, as noted above, a real problem facing adolescents is that their peers may disapprove of academic effort or achievement. Some may learn to hide their effort or justify their achievement, but others may suppress their effort or achievement to please peers, thus limiting the schools and professions for which they will qualify in the future. Some students, in the face of conflict, may understand how to maintain their status and maintain the relationship while solving the problem at hand, but others may escape into self-protection or aggression, not because the other goals have lost their value, but because they do not understand how to pursue all of these valued goals simultaneously.

Harter brings up another interesting problem of goal coordination, and that is the necessity of coordinating goals or selves across situations.

Some students may experience little or no anxiety over the fact that they are somewhat different people who pursue somewhat different goals with, say, their parents versus their peers, or their male versus female peers. Others, however, may experience a great deal of anxiety over this, feeling perhaps that they are false or hypocritical for doing so. In this case, students must find ways either to maintain a more consistent set of roles and goals across settings or to come to terms with the different roles and goals that may be demanded in different settings.

In short, major problems can arise when students are unaware of what goals suit the situation they are in and when they are unable to maintain their pursuit of valued goals in the face of conflict or adversity.

A dynamic model of goals

Implicit in the above discussion is a model of goals, their causes, and their effects. According to this model, students enter a situation with beliefs and values that make certain goals more likely than others. Specifically, such things as their values, their implicit theories, and their efficacy beliefs will affect which goals they initially pursue. These initial goals may sensitize them to certain cues and may make certain attributions more likely. Thus as they encounter events and outcomes in the situation, the meaning of these events and outcomes is shaped by the goals students are pursuing. Then, in light of the events and outcomes and the way in which they are interpreted, students may adopt new goals for dealing with the changed situation. This model can be nicely illustrated by means of examples we have been developing throughout – the case of aggressive children and the case of withdrawn/helpless children.

In the case of aggressive children, these children may enter the situation with an array of goals, but the goals of dominance and control appear to be primary among them (Boldizar, Perry, & Perry, 1989; Crick & Ladd, 1990; Erdley & Asher, 1993a; Lochman, Wayland, & White, 1993; Rabiner & Gordon, 1992; Renshaw & Asher, 1983). As we suggested above, this focus on maintaining dominance and control may make them especially sensitive to slights and provocations and may lead them to overperceive hostile intent on the part of others. Perceiving threats to their dominance in the form of hostile provocations, in turn, may cause them to be easily angered and to adopt the goal of aggressive retaliation (Crick & Dodge, 1994).

In the case of children prone to withdrawal, these children may enter social situations with an array of goals but salient among them are the goals of gaining acceptance and avoiding rejection (social performance goals) (See Erdley). This concern with approval and disapproval of the social self may lead these children to overperceive signs of rejection and to attribute the perceived rejection to personal inadequacy (to make internal, global, stable self-attributions) (Erdley et al., in press). This, in turn, may lead them to adopt the self-protective goal of escaping from the situation in order to minimize the possibility of further rejection.

The case of children prone to helplessness in the face of academic-intellectual setbacks is a similar one. These children enter the situation with a theory of fixed intelligence and with intellectual performance goals (the goal of gaining positive judgments of their intelligence and avoiding negative ones) having a very high priority among their goals (Dweck & Leggett, 1988; Elliott & Dweck, 1988). These goals make them especially sensitive to cues signalling failure, leading them to overperceive setbacks as failures and to attribute these failures to their lack of ability. This, in turn, may set in motion not only a cycle of negative affect and performance impairment, but also the tendency to adopt defensive goals and strategies that will minimize the possibility or the meaning of further failure (such as escape from the situation or minimizing further effort) (see Juvonen's chapter; see also Covington & Omelich, 1979).

Thus, studying the dynamics of children's goals may provide insights into patterns of adaptive and maladaptive behavior. Indeed, it gives us a step-by-step way of analyzing what happens as students enter situations and experience events and outcomes in them. In such an analysis, first, we would wish to know what hierarchy of active goals students enter a situation with; how appropriate/constructive those goals are in the situation; and whether they have the strategies for attaining the more constructive goals. If the more constructive goals are low on the hierarchy, we would want to know why. Is it that children are unaware that these are the appropriate goals for the situation? Do they not have the confidence that they can pursue these goals successfully? Do they have implicit theories that foster an emphasis on particular goals at the expense of others? Have they given up on some valued goals because they perceive conflicts among goals and do not know how to coordinate them?

Next, we would want to know how that goal hierarchy changes as students experience events and outcomes, such as conflicts or setbacks. Do they maintain their full array of goals, especially the constructive ones (perhaps even adding new constructive goals and strategies to address the changed situation)? Or, alternatively, do they abandon the more constructive goals and assume a defensive posture as they focus on such goals as self-protection or retaliation? If the latter, why is this so? Is it because their attributions about the self (e.g., fixed, negative self-attributions) have caused them to lose confidence in their ability to enact the positive, constructive goals successfully? Or have their attributions about others (e.g., hostile attributions for perceived provocation) led them to feel that retaliation is the appropriate goal?

As can be seen, the goal analysis provides a way to understand the dynamics of behavior as it unfolds in a situation. It gives us a sense of the things that can go wrong and a sense of the various ways we might intervene to set them right. The goal analysis also gives us a way to organize the different social-cognitive variables psychologists study (efficacy, attributions, implicit theories, goal and strategy knowledge) into one framework and to begin to understand how they operate in concert to influence students' cognitions, behavior, and affect, and ultimately, their adjustment.

References

Ames, C. (1992). Classrooms: Goals, structures, and student motivation. *Journal of Educational Psychology, 84,* 261–271.

Asher, S. R. & Renshaw, P. (1981). Children without friends: Social knowledge and social skill training. In S. R. Asher and J. M. Gottman (Eds.) *The development of children's friendships* (pp. 273–296). New York: Cambridge University Press.

Boldizar, J. P., Perry, D. G., & Perry, L. C. (1989). Outcome values and aggression. *Child Development, 60,* 571–579.

Covington, M. V. & Omelich, C. L. (1979) Effort: The double-edged sword in school achievement. *Journal of Educational Psychology, 77,* 446–459.

Crick, N. R. & Dodge, K. A. (1994) A review and reformulation of social information-processing mechanisms in children's social adjustment. *Psychological Bulletin, 115,* 74–101.

Crick, N. R. & Ladd, G. W., (1990). Children's perceptions of the outcomes of social strategies: Do the ends justify being mean? *Developmental Psychology, 26,* 612–620.

Diener, C. & Dweck, C. S. (1978). An analysis of learned helplessness: Continuous changes in performance, strategy, and achievement cognitions following failure. *Journal of Personality and Social Psychology, 36,* 451–462.

Dodge, K. A. (1980). Social cognition and children's aggressive behavior. *Child Development, 51,* 162–170.

Dodge, K. A., Asher, S. R., & Parkhurst, J. T. (1989). Social life as a goal coordination task. In C. Ames & R. Ames (Eds.), *Research on motivation in education* (vol. 3). New York: Academic Press.

Dodge, K. A. & Frame, C. L. (1982). Social cognitive biases and deficits in aggressive boys. *Child Development, 53,* 344–353.

Dweck, C. S. (1975). The role of expectations and attributions in the alleviation of learned helplessness. *Journal of Personality and Social Psychology, 31,* 674–685.

Dweck, C. S. (1991). Self-theories and goals: Their role in motivation, personality, and development. In R. Dienstbier (Ed.), *Nebraska symposium on motivation.* (vol. 38. pp. 199–236). Lincoln NE: University of Nebraska Press.

Dweck, C. S. & Elliott, E. S. (1983). Achievement motivation. In P. Mussen & E. M. Hetherington (Eds.), *Handbook of Child Psychology.* New York: Wiley.

Dweck, C. S. & Leggett, E. L. (1988). A social-cognitive approach to motivation and personality. *Psychological Review, 95,* 256–272.

Eccles, J. & Midgley, C. (1989). Stage-environment fit: Developmentally appropriate classrooms for young adolescents. In C. Ames & R. Ames (Eds.), *Research on motivation in education* (vol. 3. pp. 139–186). New York: Academic Press.

Elliott, E. & Dweck, C. S. (1988). Goals: An approach to motivation and achievement. *Journal of Personality and Social Psychology, 25,* 109–116.

Erdley, C. A. & Asher, S. R. (1993a, April). *To aggress or not to aggress: Social-cognitive mediators of children's responses to ambiguous provocation.* Paper presented at the biennial meeting of the Society for Research in Child Development, New Orleans.

Erdley, C. A. & Asher, S. R. (1993b, August). Linkages between aggression and children's legitimacy of aggression beliefs. In S. R. Asher (Chair) *Social relationships, social beliefs and aggression.* Symposium presented at the annual meeting of the American Psychological Association, Toronto.

Erdley, C. A., Cain, K. M., Loomis, C. C., Dumas-Hines, F. & Dweck, C. S. (in press). The relations among children's social goals, implicit personality theory and response to social failure. *Developmental Psychology.*

Ford, M. E., Wentzel, K. R., Wood, D. N., Stevens, E., & Siesfeld, G. A. (1989). Processes associated with integrative social competence: Emotional and contextual influences on adolescent social responsibility. *Journal of Adolescent Research, 4,* 405–425.

Goetz, T. S. & Dweck, C. S. (1980). Learned helplessness in social situations. *Journal of Personality and Social Psychology, 39,* 246–255.

Higgins, E. T. (1987). Self-discrepancy theory: A theory relating self and affect. *Psychological Review, 94,* 319–340.

Kupersmidt, J. B., Coie, J. D., & Dodge, K. A. (1990). The role of poor peer relationships in the development of disorder. In S. R. Asher & J. D. Coie (Eds.), *Peer rejection in childhood* (pp. 274–305). New York: Cambridge University Press.

Lochman, J. E., Wayland, K. K., & White, K. J. (1993). Social goals: Relationship to adolescent adjustment and to social problem solving. *Journal of Abnormal Child Psychology, 21* 135–151.

Oden, S. & Asher, S. R. (1977). Coaching children in social skills for friendship making. *Child Development, 48,* 495–506.

Perry, D. G., Perry, L. C., & Rasmussen, P. (1986). Cognitive social learning mediators of aggression. *Child Development, 57,* 700–711.

Pervin, L. A. (1982). The stasis and flow of behavior: Toward a theory of goals. In M. M. Page (Ed.), *Nebraska symposium on motivation: Personality-current theory and research* (pp. 1–53). Lincoln NE: University of Nebraska Press.

Pervin, L. A. (1989). Goal concepts in personality and social psychology: A historical perspective. In L. A. Pervin (Ed.), *Goal concepts in personality and social psychology* (pp. 1–17). Hillsdale NJ: Lawrence Erlbaum Associates.

Rabiner, D. L. & Gordon, L. V. (1992). The coordination of conflicting social goals: Differences between rejected and nonrejected boys. *Child Development, 63,* 1344–1350.

Renshaw, P. D. & Asher, S. R. (1983). Children's goals and strategies for social interaction. *Merrill-Palmer Quarterly, 29,* 553–574.

Skinner, E. A. & Belmont, M. J. (1993). Motivation in the classroom: Reciprocal effects of teacher behavior and student engagement across the school years. *Journal of Educational Psychology, 85,* 571–581.

Slaby, R. G. & Guerra, N. G. (1988). Cognitive mediators of aggression in adolescent offenders: 1. Assessment. *Developmental Psychology, 24,* 580–588.

Taylor, A. R. & Asher, S. R. (1984). Children's goals and social competence: Individual differences in a game-playing context. In T. Field, J. L. Roopnarine, & M. Segal (Eds.), *Friendship in normal and handicapped children* (pp. 53–77) Norwood NJ: Ablex.

Weiner, B. (1985). An attribution theory of achievement motivation and emotion. *Psychological Review, 92,* 548–573.

Weiner, B. (1986). *An attributional theory of motivation,* New York: Springer-Verlag.

Weiner, B. & Kukla, A. (1970). An attributional analysis of achievement motivation. *Journal of Personality and Social Psychology, 15,* 1–20.

Wentzel, K. R. (1991a). Social and academic goals at school: Motivation and achievement in context. In M. Maehr & P. Pintrich (Eds.), *Advances in motivation and achievement* (vol. 7. pp. 185–212). Greenwich CT: JAI.

Wentzel, K. R. (1991b). Social competence at school: Relation between social responsibility and academic achievement. *Review of Educational Research, 61,* 1–24.

PART TWO

Social motivation:
Perspectives on relationships

9 Interpersonal relationships in the school environment and children's early school adjustment: The role of teachers and peers

Sondra H. Birch and Gary W. Ladd

Young children face many challenges as they attempt to adjust to new school environments, including adapting to classroom routines, performing increasingly difficult academic tasks, and negotiating the complexities of interpersonal relationships with classmates and teachers. Although children's success at negotiating these challenges may be affected by many factors, most investigators have focussed on "internal" and organismic characteristics of the child when attempting to account for early school adjustment outcomes (e.g., gender, mental age, behavioral styles; see Ladd & Kochenderfer, 1996). Further, researchers have historically defined school adjustment in terms of children's academic progress or achievement. For this reason, much of what we know about the precursors of early school adjustment has come from research on the socialization of children's cognitive skills (e.g., Lazar & Darlington, 1982).

One consequence of this research tradition is that the construct of school adjustment has been defined rather narrowly, and the search for its determinants has been restricted. To address these limitations, we have attempted to elaborate upon earlier models of school adjustment in terms of (a) the hypothesized precursors of school adjustment and (b) the conceptualization of school adjustment itself (see Ladd, 1989; 1996). As illustrated in Figure 9.1, our model is based, in part, on the assumption that successful school adjustment originates both in the child (e.g., personality and behavioral styles) as well as in the interpersonal environment (e.g., the nature of his or her relationships with parents, teachers, and peers). Certain child characteristics undoubtedly influence children's successful adjustment to school, and we propose that these characteristics may have both direct and indirect effects (e.g., the quality of children's relationships may mediate the effects of specific child characteristics on their adjustment in school contexts). More importantly, we have argued that children's interpersonal relationships may also play important roles in their

199

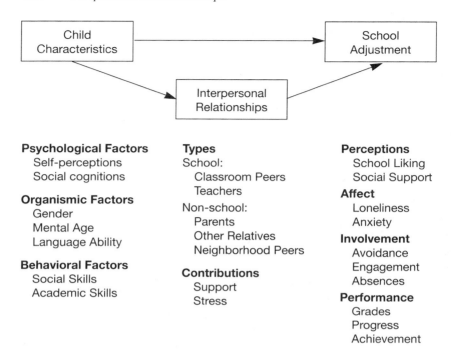

Figure 9.1. An elaborated model of early school adjustment: Hypothesized precursors and adjustment outcomes.

school adjustment and progress (see Ladd, 1996; see also Harter; Hymel et al., Juvonen, Kindermann et al., Wentzel, this volume).

Our work in this area developed from the perspective that the quality of children's classroom peer relationships may serve either as supports or stressors for young children as they attempt to adjust to the demands of new school environments (e.g., Ladd & Price, 1987). Children who are engaged in positive relationships with classmates are likely to feel more comfortable in school and may be better able to take advantage of the social and learning opportunities they encounter in this setting. On the other hand, children who experience peer rejection may develop negative attitudes toward school that may inhibit them from further exploration and development.

Conceptually, we have expanded this notion of relational supports and stressors to other individuals who are in a position to influence children's success in school (see Ladd, 1989, for further discussion of this model).

To this end, we have conducted a series of studies that examine how features of the family environment are related to children's adjustment in school contexts (e.g., Clark, 1994; Hart, Ladd, & Burleson, 1990; Ladd & Golter, 1988; Ladd & Hart, 1992; Profilet & Ladd, 1994). More recently, we have begun to investigate interpersonal features of the school environment (in addition to peers) that may facilitate or inhibit children's successful adjustment to school, namely the quality of the teacher-child relationship (Birch & Ladd, 1994, 1996b). In this line of research, we hypothesize broadly that having a supportive relationship with a significant adult figure in the school environment is likely to foster competent acclimation to school, whereas a stressful teacher-child relationship may be an obstacle to successful adjustment.

Similar developments have occurred in the field of achievement motivation research, although the focus here has tended to be on academic or educational adjustment outcomes, rather than socioemotional and other adjustment outcomes. Whereas work in this field has often concentrated on the individual's internal psychological characteristics (e.g., children's motivational orientation), recent theorists have also recognized the importance of relationships among individuals. Connell and Wellborn (1991), for example, have proposed that a sense of relatedness, or involvement (described as the quality of children's relationships with peers and teachers), may operate as a powerful motivator for children in school. Others lend support to this notion by arguing that interpersonal factors play a major role in promoting learning in school, and that learning may be optimized in interpersonal contexts characterized by support for autonomy and a sense of relatedness to others (Ryan & Powelson, 1991).

Both of these perspectives suggest that classroom relationships may motivate children to more actively explore the school environment or may inhibit children from doing so, depending on the quality of the relationships they develop in this context. Although they have developed in separate, parallel veins, both the relational approach (relationships as supports or stressors) and the motivational approach (relationships as motivational or inhibitory) have much to offer researchers investigating children's early school adjustment.

In addition to elaborating our model to include interpersonal relationships, we also propose that the concept of school adjustment be expanded to address other dimensions that may define or underlie children's educational progress, including children's perceptions of the school environment (e.g., school liking), their affective experience in school (e.g., school loneliness), their involvement or engagement in school (e.g., school avoidance), as well as other issues related to their school performance (e.g., task-related behaviors, academic readiness). Elsewhere we have argued that each of these dimensions is an important precursor of children's later educational progress (Ladd, 1989, 1996; Ladd & Price, 1987). Children with favorable school perceptions and school affect, for example, are likely to feel more comfortable in school and therefore may be better able to learn and benefit from their educational experiences. In addition, children who are positively or actively involved in the school environment, or who are not engaged in off-task behaviors, are also in a better position to optimize the learning opportunities presented to them.

Thus, the purpose of this chapter is to consider existing empirical evidence that may be consistent with the arguments above, focussing on the relationships that children form *in the school environment*. Toward this end, we will briefly discuss the types of relationships that young children form with peers and teachers, including the strategies that researchers use to define and identify them. Next, we will survey the theoretical rationales that have been advanced by researchers in these areas to explain the linkages between interpersonal relationships and school adjustment. After considering the basic premises that guide researchers' work in these domains, we will also review the results of empirical studies that might support or refute these rationales. Finally, we will discuss, on a more theoretical level, future directions for research on both teacher-child and peer relationships, their relative contributions to school adjustment, and behavioral antecedents of these two relationship systems and subsequent school adjustment.

Peer relationships and children's early school adjustment

Researchers have identified different types of peer relationships that children may form in the classroom, including friendship and peer group acceptance, and have attempted to delineate various features of these relationships. While friendship is a construct that is defined at the dyadic level, peer group acceptance uses the group as the level of analysis (see Ladd & Kochenderfer, 1996). These peer relationship constructs, and the methods used to operationalize them, are described in more detail below.

Friendship

In general, friendship refers to a voluntary, reciprocal relationship between two children. Bukowski and Hoza (1989) describe three different levels of analysis for friendships: participation (i.e., the presence or absence of friends), quantity (i.e., the breadth of the friendship network), and friendship quality (e.g., the extent to which the friendship can be characterized by certain relationship features). Much of the evidence that has been assembled on the linkages between children's friendships and their functioning in school or child-care settings comes from elementary school children (e.g., Ladd, 1990; Parker & Asher, 1993b) as well as preschool children (e.g., Howes, 1988) and infants (Vandell & Mueller, 1980).

With young children, researchers often rely on interview techniques in order to identify friendship pairs in the classroom. Children may be asked to point to pictures of, name, or write the names of their best friends in the classroom. Typically, a friendship is considered mutual when both members of a dyad have chosen each other as one of their best friends. Investigators have also relied on parents or teachers to identify children's friends or validate results obtained from other friendship assessment techniques (e.g., Ladd & Emerson, 1984). Further, with very young children, behavior observations have been used to identify children who exhibit behaviors considered characteristic of friends (e.g., spending a certain percentage of their free time together; Gershman & Hayes, 1983; Hinde, Titmus, Easton, & Tamplin, 1985; Howes, 1983).

Researchers have also attempted to study differences in the quality of children's friendships, often by measuring children's perceptions of specific relationship features (see Berndt & Perry, 1986; Furman & Buhrmester, 1985; Parker & Asher, 1993a, 1993b). Children's friendships may differ in terms of how supportive or conflictual they are, for example, and several researchers have developed interview procedures that are designed to provide information about various facets of these relationships. For example, Parker and Asher (1993a) developed a friendship quality interview for older elementary children (adapted from Bukowski, Hoza, & Newcomb, 1987) that yields reliable information about six different relationship features: validation and caring, help and guidance, companionship and recreation, intimate exchange, conflict and betrayal, and conflict resolution. Many of these same relationship features have also been reliably assessed with young children (Ladd, Kochenderfer, & Coleman, in press).

A number of propositions have been advanced about the role that friendships play in children's school adjustment. Building on research suggesting that friendships yield psychological benefits for children (e.g., Berndt, 1989; Bukowski & Hoza, 1989; Parker & Asher, 1993b), Ladd and his colleagues (e.g., Birch & Ladd, 1994; Coleman & Ladd, 1993;

Ladd, 1990; Ladd & Kochenderfer, 1996) suggest that friendship (and peer group acceptance in general) acts as a support for young children in the school environment, and may therefore help children acclimate to the school setting. Children who have a mutual friend in the classroom may be able to use that individual as a source of emotional or instrumental support or perhaps as a secure base from which they can explore the school environment (see Howes, 1988). The mere presence of or participation in a friendship with a classmate may act as a protective factor for children who might otherwise be at risk for negative school experiences (e.g., feelings of loneliness).

Findings from several recent studies can be interpreted as support for the assertion that friendships serve a supportive function for children in the school environment. Ladd (1990) found that, following the transition from preschool to grade school, kindergarten children who formed new friendships with classroom peers performed better academically than did other children, and children with friends had more positive school attitudes by the second month of school than did children without friends. Others have found that children without classroom friends were more likely to feel lonely in school than were children with friends (Parker & Asher, 1993b). Finally, Parker and Asher (1993a) report that rejected children with a friendship in the classroom felt less lonely in school than did rejected children without a classroom friendship. These findings support the view that friendship may serve a protective function for certain groups of children considered vulnerable to school adjustment difficulties.

Further, participation in friendship (i.e., the presence or absence of a friend) and friendship quality may make separate contributions to children's school adjustment. Parker and Asher (1993b) report that friendship (participation) and friendship quality made unique contributions to the prediction of loneliness in school. They found that, among children who had classroom friends, children who rated their friendships as lower on positive qualities and higher on negative qualities reported feeling more lonely in school than did children with friendships rated more positively. Related findings were obtained by Ladd, Kochenderfer, and Coleman (in press) in a study that explored the relation between the quality of kindergarten-age children's classroom friendships and their school adjustment. These investigators found that children who saw their friends as sources of validation and aid were more likely to develop positive perceptions of their classmates and favorable attitudes toward school. Further, among boys, classroom friendships that were characterized by high levels of conflict were associated with multiple forms of school maladjustment, including higher levels of school loneliness and avoidance, and lower levels of school liking and engagement. The results of these studies highlight the importance of examining the separate contributions of friendship participation and friendship quality to children's early school adjustment.

Peer group acceptance

Whereas children's friendships with classmates are dyadic, reciprocal, and voluntary, children's peer group acceptance is an index of how well children fit into the social network of the classroom. Unlike friendships, peer group acceptance is analyzed at the classroom level, and consists of unilateral nominations or ratings. Peer group acceptance is typically assessed by asking children to rate how much they like (or like to play/work with) each of their classmates (see Asher, Singleton, Tinsley, & Hymel, 1979). An average rating is computed for each child in the classroom; children who recieve higher average ratings are defined as well-accepted by their classmates. Some researchers examine children's social standing in the classroom by forming sociometric status groups (e.g., Coie, Dodge, & Coppotelli, 1982). According to this procedure, children are asked to nominate classmates that they like and don't like (or like to play/work with and don't like to play/work with). From these nominations, social preference (number of positive nominations minus number of negative nominations) and social impact (positive plus negative nominations) scores are computed. Finally, separate status groups are formed that indicate varying types of acceptance and rejection by classmates: popular, neglected, rejected, average, and controversial. Researchers establish various cut-off scores for inclusion in particular groups; however, the general nature of each sociometric status group remains the same. Specifically, popular children are children who are well-liked by many of their classmates, and disliked by few. Rejected children, on the other hand, are highly disliked and not positively regarded by many of their classmates. In contrast, neglected children are neither liked nor disliked by their classmates (i.e., their social impact is relatively low). Controversial children receive many positive and negative nominations, indicating that they are liked by some children and disliked by others.

Similar to the rationale proposed for friendships (e.g., Ladd, 1990), acceptance by the peer group may function as a support for young children. Acceptance by one's peer group may provide young children with a sense of inclusion or belongingness in the classroom, and thus facilitate exploration of and adjustment in this context (including future social relationships). On the other hand, being rejected by one's classmates may operate as a stressor, and be detrimental to children's successful adjustment to school. It is conceivable that children who are rejected by their peers develop negative "working models" of relationships that lead them to expect further rejection and discourage them from exploring potentially positive relationships with others (see Bowlby, 1982). Indeed, there is evidence that negative expectations for interpersonal relationships are associated with peer rejection (Rabiner & Coie, 1989). Peer rejection may also inhibit motivation to behave appropriately or to learn the academic and social skills necessary to successfully adapt to school. Poor peer group acceptance may foster negative feelings toward school and the schooling experience, and may result in children withdrawing from both academic and social learning situations. Additionally, children rejected by their peers may display frustration with their sociometric status by acting aggressively towards their classmates or by being disruptive during learning situations, which may perpetuate their maladjustment to school (see Coie, 1990, for further discussion of this issue).

Peer group acceptance and rejection have been linked to various aspects of young children's school adjustment, including their academic performance (e.g., Green, Forehand, Beck, & Vosk, 1980; Ladd, 1990), their school affect and attitudes (Birch & Ladd, 1994; Ladd, 1990; Parker & Asher, 1993a, 1993b), and their school avoidance (Birch & Ladd, 1994; Ladd, 1990). These studies reveal that children who are relatively well-accepted by their classmates tend to demonstrate better school adjustment than do their less well-accepted peers. Ladd (1990), for example, found that rejection by the peer group was predictive of negative perceptions of school and greater school avoidance. These findings support the assertion that poor peer relationships may act as stressors for children and restrict their ability to cope with the demands of school.

Studies in which children are classified into sociometric status groups yield similar results, indicating that children who are rejected by their classmates exhibit poorer school adjustment than do children who are not rejected (e.g., Cassidy & Asher, 1989; Coie & Dodge, 1988; Crick & Ladd, 1993; Ladd, 1990). Ladd (1990) found that rejected kindergarten children developed less positive perceptions of school, displayed higher levels of school avoidance, and exhibited lower levels of school performance than did popular, average, or neglected children. Further, Cassidy and Asher (1992) reported that first-grade children who were rejected by their peers felt more lonely in school than did children in other sociometric status groups. Crick and Ladd (1993) report similar results for third- and fifth-grade children. Rejected status has been found to be related to academic problems (Coie & Dodge, 1988) as well. Together, these studies further highlight the role of sociometrically-defined peer rejection as a potential risk factor, or precursor of young children's school adjustment difficulties.

Another form of peer rejection that may operate in the school environment and lead to poor adjustment outcomes is peer victimization. Children who are bullied by their classmates, or targeted for various forms of peer aggression, may view school as an unsafe or threatening place. They may thus develop negative feelings about this environment and seek to avoid it. Further, it is likely that these negative perceptions influence children's later adjustment; indeed, some have argued that children must perceive their environment as safe in order to successfully meet the academic demands of school (Hoover & Hazler, 1991). In addition, the victimized child may find it difficult or undesirable to become actively engaged in either academic or social classroom activities. A recent study designed to investigate links between peer victimization and children's school adjustment lends support to these assertions (Kochenderfer & Ladd, in press). In this study, peer victimization was positively associated with kindergarten children's reports of loneliness and school avoidance, and was negatively assoicated with their reports of school liking. These findings emphasize the importance of studying different forms of peer rejection in order to clarify the concomitants and precursors of children's early school adjustment difficulties.

The teacher-child relationship and children's early school adjustment

Classroom teachers are also significant figures in the school environment with whom children can form relationships, and these relationships may have important consequences for children's school adjustment (see also Harter; Wentzel, this volume). The teacher-child relationship has primarily been described from an attachment perspective (e.g., Howes & Hamiltion, 1992, 1993; Howes & Matheson, 1992), although some researchers have recently used a relationship features perspective as a framework for studying this relationship (e.g., Birch & Ladd, in 1994, 1996a, 1996b), as described below.

The teacher-child relationship as an attachment relationship

Several researchers who have studied the ties that develop between teachers and children have used the principles found in attachment theory to characterize these relationships. Howes and her colleagues (Howes & Hamilton, 1992, 1993; Howes & Matheson, 1992) rely on principal constructs from the literature on parent-child attachment relationships to describe the teacher-child relationship. In one study, for example, Howes and Hamilton (1993) identified secure, avoidant, and ambivalent children using observers' ratings of children's behaviors. These teacher-child attachment classifications were based on the parent-child attachment classifications defined by Ainsworth and her colleagues (Ainsworth, Waters, & Wall, 1978). Because of the use of the attachment perspective in this area of research, many of the examinations of the teacher-child relationship have focussed on children in preschool and kindergarten (cf. Lynch & Cicchetti, 1992).

Attachment theory has also been used by other researchers who have attempted to characterize teacher-child relationships, although the primary constructs are often not explicitly linked to the parent-child attachment literature (e.g., Lynch & Cicchetti, 1992; Pianta & Steinberg, 1992). Employing the construct of teacher-child relatedness, Lynch and Cicchetti (1992) describe five patterns of teacher-child relationships that vary in emotional quality and psychological proximity seeking: optimal, deprived, disengaged, confused, and average. These patterns were based on children's reports of their relationships with their teachers.

Alternatively, Pianta, Steinberg, and Rollins (1995) have examined features of the teacher-child relationship using teachers' perceptions of their relationships with their students. The quality of the teacher-child relationship is assessed via the Student-Teacher Relationship Scale (STRS), which is comprised of items derived from attachment theory and research on teacher-child interactions. Items were designed to tap dimensions of warmth/security, anger/dependence, and anxiety/insecurity – dimensions reminiscent of the constructs found in the parent-child attachment literature. Recent analyses of the STRS have revealed three distinct factors: closeness, dependency, and conflict.

Despite these efforts to describe the teacher-child relationship, little attention has been paid as to how this relationship might be associated with children's adjustment in school contexts. Howes and Hamilton (1992) note that one of the various roles or functions of young children's teachers is that of a caregiver who is responsible for the physical and emotional well-being of the child in the absence of the parent. By providing a secure base from which children can explore their surroundings, teachers may facilitate children's successful adaptation to the school environment. Also consistent with the attachment perspective is the notion that children may form internal working models of relationships based on the feedback that they receive during teacher-child interactions (see Bowlby, 1982; Skinner & Belmont, 1993). These models of relationships may, in turn, influence children's ability to successfully adjust to school, both socioemotionally and academically.

In one of the few studies to directly address the relation between teacher-child relationships and children's school adjustment, Pianta and Steinberg (1992) found that children who were recommended for retention in kindergarten, but who were actually not retained, had more positive relationships with their teachers than did those children who actually were retained. The use of a single index of school adjustment (e.g., retention), however, implies a relatively narrow view of school adjustment; a more comprehensive assessment of school adjustment is needed in future studies (see Birch & Ladd).

The teacher-child relationship as conceived within a relationship features perspective

Another conceptual framework that has been used to guide research on the teacher-child relationship is the relationship features perspective (see Birch & Ladd, 1994, 1996a, 1996b). This perspective has its origins in past social-psychological theory and research (see Weiss, 1974), and has recently been applied to the study of children's interpersonal relationships, especially friendships (see Berndt & Perry, 1986; Furman & Buhrmester, 1985; Parker & Asher, 1993a). Researchers who employ a relationship features perspective seek to delineate the properties of relationships (e.g., interactional processes) that create specific "provisions" for the individuals who participate in the relationship (e.g., psychological costs or benefits). Thus, relationship features can be conceptualized as dynamic processes (e.g., observable interactions) or felt properties of the relationship (e.g., perceived attributes of qualities) that may facilitate certain outcomes for the individual participants (e.g., sense of well-being, adjustment).

Although teachers and children undoubtedly form relationships that possess a myriad of features, our aim has been to identify those that make important contributions to young children's early school adjustment. As developmentalists, we recognize that the nature of children's relationships and the provisions they yield change over time. Thus, certain relationship features may emerge or become more or less important depending on the age of the child, and the types of environmental and developmental tasks the child encounters during corresponding time periods. For example, whereas certain features of the teacher-child relationship may be especially important for young children, other features may emerge over time and have greater adaptive significance as children grow older or the demands of the school environment change. Drawing upon work by Pianta, Steinberg, and Rollins (in press) and others, we have proposed three distinct features of the teacher-child relationship that are particularly important for young children, especially as they negotiate the transition to grade school: closeness, dependency, and conflict (Birch & Ladd, 1996b).

Closeness, as a feature of the teacher-child relationship, is reflected in the degree of warmth and open communication that is manifested between a teacher and a child, and it may function as a support for young children in the school environment. Indeed, our conception of closeness encompasses the extent to which children seem comfortable approaching the teacher, talking about their feelings and experiences, and using the teacher as a source of support or comfort when upset. Having warm and open communication with a significant figure in the classroom (e.g., the teacher) may facilitate positive affect and attitudes towards school. In addition, supportive teacher-child relationships may motivate children to become more involved or engaged in the school environment. In this manner, closeness may also encourage young children's learning and performance in school.

Contrasted with closeness, dependency can be construed as a relationship quality that interferes with children's successful adjustment to school. Attachment theorists have distinguished between attachment (which has positive connotations) and dependency (which has negative developmental implications; see Bowlby, 1982). Optimally, in supportive relationships, it is considered adaptive for closeness to increase over time and for dependency to decrease over time. As conceptualized in our work, dependency refers to possessive and "clingy" child behaviors that are indicative of an over-reliance on the teacher. A particular teacher-child relationship may be characterized as very close without being highly dependent as well. Likewise, some children may be quite dependent on their teachers without sharing a close relationship with them. Thus, the two constructs may make distinct contributions to children's early school adjustment.

Children who are overly dependent on the classroom teacher may be tentative in their explorations of the school environment; they may feel less motivated to explore their surroundings or other social relationships. By spending an inordinate amount of time with the teacher, children may not be engaging in learning or social tasks in the classroom. Feelings of loneliness and anxiety, as well as negative feelings about and attitudes toward school, may also be more common in children who display higher levels of dependency on the teacher.

Finally, it is likely that conflict in the teacher-child relationship functions as a stressor for children in the school environment, and may impair successful adjustment to school. Conflictual teacher-child relationships are characterized by discordant interactions and a lack of rapport between teacher and child. Children experiencing conflict in their relationships with classroom teachers may be limiting the extent to which they can rely on that relationship as a source of support. As a potential stressor in the school environment, teacher-child conflict may be emotionally upsetting to young children, yielding (or perpetuating) a variety of negative emotions (e.g., anger, anxiety) and behaviors (e.g., aggression, noncompliance). In this manner, such friction in the teacher-child relationship may be antithetical to motivating children to become positively engaged in the school environment. A conflictual teacher-child relationship may be related to children becoming disengaged or uninvolved or may foster feelings of alienation and loneliness, in addition to negative school attitudes. An aversive teacher-child relationship may be associated with academic problems as well.

In a study designed to address these issues, we found that each of these features of the teacher-child relationship was related to various aspects of kindergarten children's school adjustment (Birch & Ladd, 1996b). Teachers rated children's school perceptions (school liking), engagement in the school environment (e.g., school avoidance, self-directedness, cooperative participation), as well as the quality of their teacher-child relationships. Children's school attitudes, as reported by teachers, were correlated with all three teacher-child relationship features; specifically, children with relatively close, nondependent, and nonconflictual relationships with their teachers were seen as liking school more than were children with less positive relationships with their teachers. In addition, children's involvement in the school environment was also related to the quality of their teacher-child relationships. Higher dependency and conflict were both associated with greater school avoidance. Further, all three teacher-child relationship dimensions were linked with ratings of children's self-directedness, indicating that relatively high closeness, low dependency, and low conflict were related to more self-directed functioning in the classroom. Low conflict was also associated with higher ratings of obedience in the classroom (i.e., adapting to classroom routines). Finally, children's self-reports of school avoidance were positively related to greater dependence on the teacher.

In a related vein with older children, Wentzel (1993; this volume) found that teacher preference (i.e., teacher ratings of how much he or she would like to have the student in class again next year) was positively related to academic performance outcomes in sixth- and seventh-graders. In addition, Skinner and Belmont (1993) reported that 8-to 12-year-old children who had intimate relationships with their teachers had more positive school affect and attitudes in the classroom. These authors noted that children's working models of teacher-child relationships may be influenced by the quality of these relationships, which may influence their subsequent affective experience and engagement in the school environment.

Relationships and adjustment: Prospective theory and research

In light of the theory and research presented above, it is evident that there are a myriad of directions for future investigations of children's interpersonal relationships and their adjustment in school contexts. The discussion that follows highlights key issues that may be relevant for investigators who wish to further pursue these questions, including: (a) linkages between peer and teacher-child relationships, (b) relative contributions of peer and teacher-child relationships to children's early school adjustment, and (c) the role of children's behavior in forming relationships and adjusting to school.

Linkages between peer and teacher-child relationships

Although some researchers have alluded to the association between children's relationships with both teachers and peers, few have explicitly addressed the nature of this relation. Some research suggests that children experiencing difficulties with peers experience higher rates of interaction with their teachers (e.g., Asarnow, 1983; Dodge, Coie, & Brakke, 1982; Goldman, Corsini, & deUrioste, 1980; Howes, Phillips, & Whitebrook, 1992; Marshall & McCandless, 1957). Other investigators have found no connections between these two relational systems (e.g., Moore & Updegraff, 1964).

One of the few studies to explicitly address this issue (Howes, Matheson, & Hamilton, 1994) found that four-year-old children classified as having secure relationships with their teachers (as rated by observers) were better accepted by their peers than were children who had insecure teacher-child relationships. This relation was also explored by Birch and Ladd (1994) who found that children with relatively low conflict, low dependency, or high closeness in their teacher-child relationships were better accepted by their classroom peers than were children with high conflict, high dependency, or low closeness.

As noted above, closeness in the teacher-child relationship refers to the degree of warmth and open communication present in the relationship. Similarly, peers' sociometric ratings indicate the extent to which they want to affiliate with each of their classmates, and these ratings are also likely to be related to engaging, positive behavioral styles (characterized, for example, by warmth, open communication, friendly initiations, and so on). Thus, the two relationship systems may be positively related as a result of certain personality or behavioral characteristivs of the child (e.g., maturity, warmth, prosocial behavior) that elicit positive feelings from both teachers and peers. Alternatively, perhaps children who form close relationships with their teachers are able to use her or him as a secure base from which they can explore the classroom environment; this exploration may include the formation of social relationships with their classmates.

Dependency in the teacher-child relationship may be negatively related to competent functioning in the peer group, because children who are highly dependent on the teacher may be relatively immature or lack the social skills necessary to pursue successful relationships with their classmates. They also may be children who are relatively adult-focussed, and more interested in adult (rather than peer) attention. Because there is the expectation for children's dependency to diminish over time, children who remain highly dependent on the classroom teacher may be violating classroom norms for behavior. It is possible that children who seem highly dependent on the teacher are perceived as immature by the peer group, and thus may be less well-accepted than their more independent peers. In addition, dependency on the teacher may result in children being less available for participation in peer activities, thus producing and maintaining their social status in the classroom. It is also plausible that children who are socially withdrawn or experience impaired peer relationships might become overly dependent on the teacher as a source of validation and support.

Conflict may be present in both peer and teacher-child relationships, because some children may have an aversive style of interaction that operates across various interpersonal relationships and negatively influences the quality of relationships in both domains. Alternatively, children might construct negative working models of relationships (see Bowlby, 1982) or develop negative expectations for relationships (see Rabiner & Coie, 1989) that serve to frame all interpersonal interactions in a negative light. According to Bowlby (1982), children's working models develop from their behaviors and the feedback that they receive for these behaviors. A child exhibiting behaviors considered aversive to both teachers and peers (e.g., aggression) might experience both rejection by the peer group and a conflictual relationship with the teacher, which may serve to reinforce negative expectations for future relationships with others. This might result in a conflictual style of interaction that is counter-productive in terms of forming or maintaining positive relationships with teachers and peers.

Interpersonal features of the school environment and children's early school adjustment

Currently, there is paucity of systematic investigations into the relative contributions of these two relationship systems (peer and teacher-child) to children's early school adjustment. A preliminary study designed to address this issue yielded promising results (Birch & Ladd, 1994). In this study, the quality of children's relationships with both classroom peers and teachers emerged as important correlates of children's early adjustment to school. For example, consistent with previous research (e.g., Parker & Asher, 1993b), we found that children with higher quality peer relationships reported feeling less lonely in school. Beyond this linkage, however, our findings also revealed that conflict in the teacher-child relationship was positively correlated with children's feelings of loneliness in school. Moreover, the degree of conflict in the teacher-child relationship emerged as a significant predictor of changes in loneliness from fall to spring of the school year.

Our findings also suggest that conflict and dependency in the teacher-child relationship may be relevant to young children as they form their initial school attitudes (e.g., school liking). Children with highly dependent or conflictual teacher-child relationships reported liking school less than did their classmates with less dependent or conflictual teacher-child relationships. Peer group acceptance was not as strong a predictor of school liking as was teacher-child conflict, suggesting the need for further investigation of the relative strengths of the impact that these two relationship systems have on children's adaptation in school contexts.

Finally, children with positive relationships in both teacher-child and peer domains expressed less desire to avoid school than did children with poor relationships in both domains. The level of teacher-child conflict in the fall was further related to children's school avoidance desires in the spring semester, indicating that early discord in the teacher-child relationship continued to be associated with children's desire to avoid the school environment later in the school year. These results support the assertion that it is important to study the quality of children's relationships with both teachers and peers when considering how well they will adjust to the school environment.

These preliminary findings are consistent with the premise that both classmates and teachers have the potential to serve as emotional and instrumental supports for young children in the school environment. Positive relationships with significant figures in school are likely to promote successful adaptation to school, whereas contentious relationships with these figures may discourage effective school adjustment. Children who have positive relationships with both teachers and classmates may demonstrate better adjustment to school than those children who have poor relationships in both domains. As Connell and Wellborn (1991) have pointed out, the quality of these relationships may serve an important motivational function for children. Future studies should more explicitly examine the mechanisms by which these interpersonal features of the school environment might motivate and encourage children to successfully adapt to the school environment.

What is of greater interest, perhaps, is the type of adjustment demonstrated by children with discordance in terms of the quality of relationships in these two systems (e.g., good teacher-child and poor peer relationships or poor teacher-child and good peer relationships). It is possible that teacher-child and peer relationships may make *compensatory* contributions to various aspects of children's school adjustment. Positive peer relationships, for example, might buffer children with poor teacher-child relationships against disliking school or feeling the desire to avoid the school environment. Similarly, a close relationship with the teacher might serve as a protective factor against loneliness for children experiencing peer relationship difficulties (e.g., low acceptance, lack of a best friend). It has been shown that having even one supportive, close relationship with another person in the school environment (e.g., a best friend) can buffer children against negative school adjustment outcomes (see Parker & Asher, 1993a). Further research in this area is necessary to determine whether the benefits that accrue from being involved in positive relationships in one domain outweigh the potential for negative school adjustment outcomes that might result from having less than optimal relationships in the other domain.

Although there is some degree of overlap in terms of the functions of the relationships that young children form with peers and teachers, there are also distinctive functions that these two relationship systems serve.

According to Hartup (1989), children are involved in social relationships that can be characterized as either vertical (relationships with individuals who have greater knowledge and social power; e.g., teacher-child relationships) or horizontal (relationships with individuals who possess the same social power, characterized by reciprocity and expectations of equality; e.g., peer relationships). The functions of vertical relationships include providing protection and security (on the part of the adult), as well as modeling basic social skills. In horizontal relationships, social skills are elaborated, and themes of cooperation and competition emerge.

Thus, perhaps the quality of teacher-child relationships forecasts different adjustment outcomes than does the quality of children's peer relationships. Children may turn to significant figures in the school environment for different types of support (e.g., emotional, instrumental, academic, social) and, therefore, difficulties in one relationship domain may be reflected in some areas of school adjustment, but not others. Friction in the teacher-child relationship, for example, may be linked with poor academic performance, whereas peer rejection may be associated with feelings of loneliness in school, especially as children approach adolescence and the peer group has an increasing impact on children's development and adjustment. Other issues include consideration of whether school adjustment outcomes such as school liking, for example, are more closely tied to specific features of the teacher-child relationship (e.g., closeness) or acceptance by the peer group. In a related vein, future research should consider whether teacher-child and peer relationships make unique contributions to the same adjustment outcomes; that is, are their effects on school adjustment additive (rather than compensatory, as discussed above)? Certain aspects of children's school liking, for example, may be associated with the quality of their peer relationships (e.g., liking social activities and games), whereas other facets may be related to the quality of the teacher-child relationship (e.g., enjoying learning activities). Issues such as these have yet to be investigated; future research will help to illuminate the answers to these question.

Examining the behavioral antecedents of peer and teacher-child relationships

An extensive body of literature addresses the behavioral antecedents and correlates of children's peer relationships. Aggressive behavior (e.g., Dodge, 1983; Dodge, Coie, & Brakke, 1982) in particular has been linked to rejection by the peer group. At present, there is a substantial body of evidence indication that aggression is an important antecedent of poor peer relationships in preschool, as well as elementary school samples (see Coie, Dodge, & Kupersmidt, 1990, for a review). The link between withdrawal and peer rejection is not as clear, although some studies suggest that withdrawing from the peer group is negatively related to peer group acceptance, especially for girls (e.g., Cantrell & Prinz, 1985; La Greca, 1981). For example, Ladd (1983) found that rejected girls were three times as likely to engage in parallel play than were nonrejected girls or boys. Moreover, in preschool and kindergarten, withdrawn children exhibit less mature forms of play and are the recipients of fewer social initiations from peers than are their classmates (Rubin, 1982). As children get older, sociometric status is also associated with more subtle behaviors, including giving and receiving help, sharing, group entry skill, and honesty (Carlson, Lahey, & Neeper, 1984).

Compared to the body of evidence in the peer domain, the research identifying the behaviors associated with different types of teacher-child relationships is less clear. Wentzel (1991) notes that teachers prefer students who exhibit certain types of behaviors (e.g., cooperative, cautious, responsible) but not others (e.g., independent, assertive, disruptive; see Wentzel, 1991 for further discussion of this issue). Some researchers have used behavior observations in order to classify the types of relationships that children have with their teachers. Using the Waters and Deane Attachment Q-Sort, Howes and Hamilton (1993) identified secure, avoidant, and ambivalent/resistant children according to observers' ratings of their behaviors during teacher-child interactions. Secure children were those who scored high on many of the following behavioral indices: predominantly happy, easily comforted, comfort soliciting, and obedient. Avoidant children, in contrast, scored high on ratings of being unaware of changes in caregivers, expecting adult to be unresponsive, and demanding initiation. Finally, ambivalent children were seen as highly demanding and impatient, having distressed social interaction, and crying often, as well as being low on physical contact. It should be noted, however, that this study used behavioral observations in order to classify children into various teacher-child relationship categories (i.e., the relationship classification was determined by the children's exhibited behaviors). In this way, it differs from other studies of the behavioral correlates of teacher-child relationships, in which the quality of the teacher-child relationship is assessed using measures that are separate from the behavioral indices (e.g., Wentzel, 1993).

It is likely that some of the same behaviors associated with peer relationship difficulties are similarly associated with problematic teacher-child relationships. Aggressive and disruptive behavior, for example, may be indicative of a style of interaction that is undesirable to both teachers and peers. Indeed, Safran and Safran (1985) report that teachers find aggressive behavior to be the most disruptive to classroom order. In addition, certain types of withdrawn behavior may be characteristic of children who isolate themselves not only from the peer group, but from contact with the teacher as well (e.g., behavioral inhibition).

On the other hand, there may be some behavioral styles that are conducive to forming and maintaining positive relationships in one domain, but promote negative relationships in the other domain. Behaviors that lead children to become "teachers' pets," for example, might be inimical to peer group acceptance or lead to resentment by the peer group (e.g., compliance that may be perceived as submissive behavior by peers). Making peers laugh might be associated with peer group acceptance, but may be problematic for teachers if this behavior is disruptive and interferes with learning activities. Indeed, such behaviors seem to have inconsistent outcomes even within the peer culture; behaviors such as being funny and making peers laugh are related to controversial sociometric status (i.e., children who are liked by a number of children and also disliked by a number of children; Coie, Finn, & Krehbiel, 1984). Further, as children move toward adolescence, teachers (and other adults) and peers may have increasingly divergent behavioral expectations, and children's ability to successfully negotiate these competing demands may be challenged (see also Juvonen, this volume). Although the influence of teachers may be more significant to young children, the peer group may become increasingly influential as children grow older. Some investigators have started to examine how children coordinate multiple social and academic goals, and how this goal pursuit is related to their acceptance by teachers and peers (e.g., Wentzel, 1994); however, further discussion of the goal coordination literature is beyond the scope of the present chapter (see Ford; Wentzel, this volume).

We recently examined how children's early behavioral styles are related to the types of relationships that they form with classroom teachers and peers (Birch & Ladd, 1996a) both concurrently (i.e., fall of kindergarten) as well as at two later points in time (i.e., spring of kindergarten and spring of first grade). At all three assessment times, aggression and hyperactivity were associated with problematic relationships with teachers and peers, and prosocial behavior was linked to better relationships in both domains. Asocial behavior was negatively related to children's peer group acceptance, and was associated with poorer quality teacher-child relationships (especially for girls). Finally, anxious-fearful behavior was not related to acceptance by the peer group, but was negatively associated with harmonious teacher-child relationships (particularly for girls). These findings suggest that the behaviors that children exhibit early in kindergarten have enduring relationship outcomes, even with new teachers and peers (in first grade). Additionally, many of the same behaviors that are linked to the level of children's acceptance by the peer group were also associated with the quality of the relationships that they have with their classroom teachers. These data also suggest that there are important gender differences in the behaviors that are related to children's interpersonal relationships in the school environment, and these differences warrant further investigation.

Finally, there is also the need for a comprehensive examination of the links between classroom behavior, relationships with teachers and peers, and adjustment in school contexts. Researchers have found early aggressive and disruptive behavior in elementary school to be associated with school adjustment difficulties in high school, including poor grades (Feldhusen, Thurston, & Benning, 1970) and dropping out of school (see Parker & Asher, 1987 for a comprehensive review). Other correlational studies have found appropriate behaviors to be associated with positive academic outcomes (see Wentzel, 1991).

We propose that behavior may be associated with young children's early school adjustment in at least two ways. First, behavior may be directly linked to how well children respond to the demands of the school environment. Specifically, it is possible that certain behaviors have direct effects on children's school adjustment (e.g., aggressive behavior may lead to children being removed from learning and social situations, which may result in impaired academic performance and more negative school attitudes). Second, behavior may be indirectly associated with school adjustment outcomes, mediated by the quality of the relationships that children have with teachers and peers. Perhaps the behaviors that children exhibit in the classroom influence the quality of the relationships that children form with teachers and peers, and the quality of these relationships, in turn, is predictive of young children's adjustment in school contexts. Again, future investigations will elucidate these issues and, in fact, exploration of this question is a central objective of our research program.

Other researchers have developed similar models to examine related issues in older children. Wentzel (1993), for example, examined direct and indirect connections between two types of behavior (prosocial and antisocial), teacher preferences for students, and students' academic competence in sixth- and seventh-grades. The results indicate direct links between behavior and academic adjustment outcomes, but did not show teacher preferences for students to be mediating a relation between behavior and academic outcomes. Future studies that examine specific features of the teacher-child relationship and use a broader definition of school adjustment, however, may yield different results.

In sum, in addition to describing the current state of the literature regarding the association between interpersonal features of the school environment and children's adjustment in school contexts, we have also delineated various avenues for future investigation, which will do much to advance our understanding of the nature of these connections. The social relationships children form with significant others in the school environment (i.e., peers and teachers) may serve important motivational functions for young children as they form their initial opinions of and attitudes towards school. If these relationships are characterized by acceptance, children's motivation to be actively and appropriately engaged in the classroom may be optimized. If, on the other hand, relationships with peers and teachers are typified by conflict and rejection, children's motivation may be suppressed or extinguished. Exploration of the aforementioned issues will further illuminate these propositions.

Note

Preparation of this chapter was supported by National Institute of Mental Health Grant MH-49223 to Gary Ladd. Correspondence concerning this chapter should be addressed to Sondra Birch or Gary Ladd, 183 Children's Research Center, 51 Gerty Drive, Champaign, Illinois 61820.

References

Ainsworth, M. D. S., Waters, E., & Wall, S. (1978). *Patterns of attachment: A psychological study of the strange situation.* Hillsdale, NJ: Erlbaum.

Asarnow, J. R. (1983). Children with peer adjustment problems: Sequential and nonsequential analysis of school behaviors. *Journal of Consulting and Clinical Psychology, 51,* 709–717.

Asher, S. R., Singleton, L. C., Tinsley, B. R., & Hymel, S. (1979). A reliable sociometric measure for preschool children. *Developmental Psychology, 15,* 443–444.

Berndt, T. J. (1989). Contributions of peer relationships to children's development. In T. J. Berndt & G. W. Ladd (Eds.), *Peer relationships in child development* (pp. 407–416). New York: Wiley.

Berndt, T. J., & Perry, T. B. (1986). Children's perceptions of friendships as supportive relationships. *Developmental Psychology, 22,* 640–648.

Birch, S. H., & Ladd, G. W. (1994, April). *The relative contributions of peer and teacher-child relationships to children's early school adjustment.* Paper presented at the 13th Biennial conference on Human Development, Pittsburgh, PA.

Birch, S. H., & Ladd, G. W. (1996a). *Behavioral correlates of children's relationships with classroom peers and teachers.* Manuscript under review.

Birch, S. H., & Ladd, G. W. (1996b). The teacher-child relationship and children's early school adjustment. *Journal of School Psychology.*

Bowlby, J. (1982). *Attachment.* New York: Harper Collins.

Bukowski, W. M., & Hoza, B. (1989). Popularity and friendship: Issues in theory, measurement, and outcome. In T. J. Berndt & G. W. Ladd (Eds.), *Peer relationships in child development* (pp. 15–45). New York: Wiley.

Bukowski, W. M., Hoza, B., & Newcomb, A. F. (1987). *Friendship, popularity, and the "self" during adolescence.* Unpublished manuscript, University of Maine, Orono.

Cantrell, V. L., & Prinz, R. J. (1985). Multiple perspectives of rejected, neglected, and accepted children: Relation between sociometric status and behavioral characteristics. *Journal of Consulting and Clinical Psychology, 53,* 884–889.

Carlson, C. L., Lahey, B. B., & Neeper, R. (1984). Peer assessment of the social behavior of accepted, rejected, and neglected children. *Journal of Abnormal Child Psychology, 12,* 189–198.

Clark, K. E. (1994). *Connectedness and autonomy in parent-child relationships: Linkages to children's socioemotional orientation and peer relationships.* Unpublished doctoral dissertation, University of Illinois, Urbana-Champaign.

Cassidy, J., & Asher, S. R. (1992). Loneliness and peer relations in young children. *Child Development, 63,* 350–365.

Coie, J. D. (1990). Toward a theory of peer rejection. In S. R. Asher & J. D. Coie (Eds.), *Peer rejection in childhood* (pp. 365–401). New York: Cambridge University Press.

Coie, J. D., & Dodge, K. A. (1988). Multiple sources of data on social behavior and social status in the school: A cross-age comparison. *Child Development, 59,* 815–829.

Coie, J. D., Dodge, K. A., & Coppotelli, H. (1982). Dimensions and types of social status: A cross-age perspective. *Developmental Psychology, 18,* 557–570.

Coie, J. D., Dodge, K. A., & Kupersmidt, J. B. (1990). Peer group behavior and social status. In S. R. Asher & J. D. Coie (Eds.), *Peer rejection in childhood* (pp.17–59). New York: Cambridge University Press.

Coie, J. D., Finn, M., & Krehbiel, G. (1984, September). *Controversial children: Peer assessment evidence for status category distinctiveness.* Paper presented at annual meeting of the American Psychological Association, Toronto.

Coleman, C. C., & Ladd, G. W. (1993, April). How children who dislike school feel about their classroom peer relationships. Paper presented at the annual meetings of the American Educational Research Association, Atlanta, GA.

Connell, J. P., & Wellborn, J. G. (1991). Competence, autonomy, and relatedness: A motivational analysis of self-system processes. In M. R. Gunnar & L. A. Sroufe (Eds.), *Self processes in development: Minnesota Symposium on Child Psychology* (vol. 23, pp. 43–77). Hillsdale, NJ: Erlbaum.

Crick, N. R., & Ladd, G. W. (1993). Children's perceptions of their peer experiences: Attributions, loneliness, social anxiety, and social avoidance. *Developmental Psychology, 29,* 244–254.

Dodge, K. A. (1983). Behavioral antecedents of peer social status. *Child Development, 54,* 1386–1399.

Dodge, K. A., Coie, J. D., & Brakke, N. P. (1982). Behavior patterns of socially rejected and neglected preadolescents: The roles of social approach and aggression. *Journal of Abnormal Child Psychology, 10,* 389–410.

Feldhusen, J. F., Thurston, J. R., & Benning, J. J. (1970). Longitudinal analyses of classroom behavior and school achievement. *Journal of Experimental Education, 38,* 4–10.

Furman, W., & Buhrmester, D. (1995). Children's perceptions of the personal relationships in their social networks. *Developmental Psychology, 21,* 1016–1021.

Gershman, E. S., & Hayes, D. S. (1983). Differential stability of reciprocal friendships and unilateral relationships among preschool children. *Merrill-Palmer Quarterly, 29,* 169–177.

Goldman, J. A., Corsini, D. A., & deUrioste, R. (1980). Implications of positive and negative sociometric status for assessing the social competence of young children. *Journal of Applied Developmental Psychology, 1,* 209–220.

Green, K. D., Forehand, R., Beck, S., & Vosk, B. (1980). An assessment of the relationship among measures of children's social competence and children's academic achievement. *Child Development, 51,* 1149–1156.

Hart, C. H., Ladd, G. W., & Burleson, B. R. (1990). Children's expectations of the outcomes of social strategies: Relations with sociometric status and maternal disciplinary styles. *Child Development, 61,* 127–137.

Hartup, W. H. (1989). Social relationships and their developmental significance. *American Psychologist, 44,* 120–126.

Hinde, R. A., Titmus, G., Easton, D., & Tamplin, A. (1985). Incidence of "friendship" and behavior toward strong associates versus nonassociates in preschoolers. *Child Development, 56,* 234–245.

Hoover, J., & Hazler, R. J. (1991). Bullies and victims. *Elementary School Guidance and Counseling, 25,* 212–219.

Howes, C. (1983). Patterns of friendship. *Child Development, 54,* 1041–1053.

Howes, C. (1988). Peer interaction of young children. *Monographs of the Society for Research in Child Development, 53* (1, Serial No. 217).

Howes, C., & Hamilton, C. E. (1992). Children's relationships with child care teachers: Stability and concordance with parental attachments. *Child Development, 63,* 867–878.

Howes, C., & Hamilton, C. E. (1993). The changing experience of child care: Changes in teachers and in teacher-child relationships and children's social competence with peers. *Early Childhood Research Quarterly, 8,* 15–32.

Howes, C., & Matheson, C. C. (1992). Contextual constraints on the concordance of mother-child and teacher-child relationships. *New Directions for Child Development, 57,* 25–40.

Howes, C., Matheson, C. C., & Hamilton, C. E. (1994). Maternal, teacher, and child care history correlates of children's relationships with peers. *Child Development, 65,* 264–273.

Howes, C., Phillips, D. A., & Whitebrook, M. (1992). Thresholds of quality in child care centers and children's social and emotional development. *Child Development, 63,* 449–460.

Kochenderfer, B. J., & Ladd, G. W. (in press). Peer victimization: Manifestations and relations to school adjustment in kindergarten. *Journal of School Psychology.*

La Greca, A. M. (1981). Peer acceptance: The correspondence between children's sociometric scores and teachers' ratings of peer interactions. *Journal of Abnormal Child Psychology, 9,* 167–178.

Ladd, G. W. (1983). Social networks of popular, average, and rejected children in school settings. *Merrill-Palmer Quarterly, 29,* 283–307.

Ladd, G. W. (1989). Children's social competence and social supports: Precursors of early school adjustment? In B. H. Schneider, G. Attili, J. Nadel, & R. P. Weissberg (Eds.), *Social competence in developmental perspective* (pp. 277–291). Amsterdam: Kluwer Academic Publishers.

Ladd, G. W. (1990). Having friends, keeping friends, making friends, and being liked by peers in the classroom: Predictors of children's early school adjustment? *Child Development, 61,* 1081–1100.

Ladd, G. W. (1996). Shifting ecologies during the 5–7 year period: Predicting children's adjustment during the transition to grade school. In A. Sameroff & M. Haith (Eds.), *The Five to Seven Year Shift* (pp. 363–386). Chicago: University of Chicago Press.

Ladd, G. W., & Emerson, E. S. (1984). Shared knowledge in children's friendships. *Developmental Psychology, 20,* 932–940.

Ladd, G. W., & Golter, B. S. (1988). Parents' management of preschoolers' peer relations: Is it related to children's social competence? *Developmental Psychology, 24,* 109–117.

Ladd, G. W., & Hart, C. H. (1992). Creating informal play opportunities: Are parents' and preschoolers' initiations related to children's competence with peers? *Developmental Psychology, 28,* 1179–1187.

Ladd, G. W., & Kochenderfer, B. J. (1996). Linkages between friendship and adjustment during early school transitions. In W. M. Bukowski, A. F. Newcomb, & W. W. Hartup (Eds.), *The company they keep: Friendship in childhood and adolescence* (pp. 322–345). New York: Cambridge University Press.

Ladd, G. W., Kochenderfer, B. J., & Coleman, C. C. (in press). Friendship quality as a predictor of young children's early school adjustment. *Child Development.*

Ladd, G. W., & Price, J. M. (1987). Predicting children's social and school adjustment following the transition from preschool to kindergarten. *Child Development, 58,* 1168–1189.

Lazar, I., & Darlington, R. (1982). Lasting effects of early education: A report from the Consortium for Longitudinal Studies. *Monographs of the Society for Research in Child Development, 47,* (2–3), Serial Number 195.

Lynch, M., & Cicchetti, D. (1992). Maltreated children's reports of relatedness to their teachers. *New Directions for Child Development, 57,* 81–108.

Marshall, H. R., & McCandless, B. R. (1957). Relationships between dependence on adults and social acceptance by peers. *Child Development, 28,* 413–419.

Moore, S., & Updegraff, R. (1964). Sociometric status of preschool children related to age, sex, nurturance-giving, and dependency. *Child Development, 35,* 519–524.

Parker, J. G., & Asher, S. R. (1987). Peer relations and later personal adjustment: Are low-accepted children at risk? *Psychological Bulletin, 102,* 357–389.

Parker, J. G., & Asher, S. R. (1993a). Beyond peer group acceptance: Friendship and friendship quality as distinct dimensions of peer adjustment. In W. H. Jones & D. Perlman (Eds.), *Advances in personal relationships* (vol. 4, pp. 261–294). London: Kinglsley Press.

Parker, J. G., & Asher, S. R. (1993b). Friendship and friendship quality in middle childhood: Links with peer group acceptance and feelings of loneliness and social dissatisfaction. *Developmental Psychology, 29,* 611–621.

Pianta, R. C., & Steinberg, M. (1992). Teacher-child relationships and the process of adjusting to school. *New Directions for Child Development, 57,* 61–80.

Pianta, R. C., Steinberg, M., & Rollins, K. (1995). The first two years of school: Teacher-child relationships and deflections in children's school adjustment. *Development and Psychopathology, 7,* 295–312.

Profilet, S. M., & Ladd, G. W. (1994). Do mothers' perceptions and concerns about preschoolers' peer competence predict their peer management practices? *Social Development, 3,* 205–221.

Rabiner, D. L., & Coie, J. D. (1989). Effect of expectancy inductions on rejected children's acceptance by unfamiliar peers. *Developmental Psychology, 25,* 450–457.

Rubin, K. H. (1982). Social and social-cognitive developmental characteristics of young isolate, normal, and sociable children. In K. H. Rubin & H. S. Ross (Eds.), *Peer relationships and social skills in childhood* (pp. 353–374). New York: Springer-Verlag.

Ryan, R. M., & Powelson, C. L. (1991). Autonomy and relatedness as fundamental to motivation and education. *Journal of Experimental Education, 60,* 49–66.

Safran, S. P., & Safran, J. S. (1985). Classroom context and teachers' perceptions of problem behaviors. *Jorunal of Educational Psychology, 77,* 20–28.

Skinner, E. A., & Belmont, M. J. (1993). Motivation in the classroom: Reciprocal effects of teacher behavior and student engagement across the school year. *Journal of Educational Psychology, 85,* 571–581.

Vandell, D. L., & Mueller, E. C. (1980). Peer play and friendship during the first two years. In H. C. Foot, A. J. Chapman, & J. R. Smith (Eds.), *Friendship and social relations in children* (pp. 181–208). New York: Wiley.

Weiss, R. (1974). The provisions of social relationships. In Z. Rubin (Ed.), *Doing unto others* (pp. 17–26). Englewood Cliffs, NJ: Prentice-Hall.

Wentzel, K. R. (1991). Social competence at school: Relation between social responsibility and academic achievement. *Review of Educational Research, 61,* 1–24.

Wentzel, K. R. (1993). Does being good make the grade? Social behavior and academic competence in middle school. *Journal of Educational Psychology, 85,* 357–364.

Wentzel, K. R. (1994). Relations of social goal pursuit to social acceptance, classroom behavior, and perceived social support. *Journal of Educational Psychology, 86,* 173–182.

same general findings in that adaptive classroom behavior in elementary school predicts grades and test scores in high school, over and above early achievement or IQ (Feldhusen, Thurston, & Benning, 1970; Lambert, 1972; Safer, 1986). Findings from longitudinal studies also link social responsibility with educational attainment. Based on a comprehensive review of both follow-up and follow-back studies, Parker and Asher (1987) conclude that antisocial and aggressive (i.e., socially irresponsible) behavior in the early grades is a strong predictor of dropping out in high school. Finally, intervention studies suggest that teaching children appropriate social responses to instruction such as attending, following instructions, and volunteering answers can lead to significant and stable gains in academic achievement (Cobb & Hopps, 1973; Coie & Krehbiel, 1984; Hopps & Cobb, 1974).

Summary and implications

Displays of prosocial and socially responsible behavior (e.g., tendencies to be cooperative, helpful, compliant, and nonaggressive) have been related consistently and positively to children's academic accomplishments. Several explanations for these associations are possible. First, social competence might set the stage for academic competencies to develop. Second, academic competencies might lead to displays of socially appropriate behavior. Third, social and academic competencies might influence each other in reciprocal fashion. Finally, social and academic competence might not be causally related but rather, an additional variable or set of variables might account for the significant correlations between social and academic outcomes.

There is scant evidence to support any one of these explanations. The longitudinal studies provide initial evidence in support of the first model. In addition, intervention studies indicate that the promotion of socially responsible behavior often results in higher levels of academic performance rather than the reverse (Cobb & Hopps, 1973; Coie & Krehbiel, 1984; Hops & Cobb, 1974). Research on the underlying processes that might contribute to social as well as academic outcomes also has not been extensive. However, from a motivational perspective, those processes that appear to motivate children to behave in prosocial and responsible ways also appear to motivate academic performance. In the following section, social goal pursuit will be discussed as a potentially critical motivational process that links children's social adjustment to their academic performance at school.

Social goal pursuit and children's adjustment at school

Personal goals have been of central importance in explanations of motivational orientations and patterns of behavior (see Pervin, 1982; Ford, th⁺ᵤ volume). Goals have been described with respect to their content (Fᵤrd & Nichols, 1991; Wentzel, 1993a, 1994b), orientation (Dweck & Leggett, 1988; Nicholls, 1984), levels of challenge, proximity, and specificity (Bandura, 1986), and their relations to each other (Wentzel, 1991c). Central to all of these descriptions is the notion that people do set goals for themselves and, as cognitive representations of future events, these goals can be powerful motivators of behavior.

The notion that goals organize and regulate behavior also has been central to research linking achievement motivation to academic performance and learning-related outcomes. Students' goal orientations most often associated with academic outcomes are described as concerns with either task-intrinsic or extrinsic outcomes. Task-intrinsic outcomes such as task-involved (Nicholls, 1984) or learning (Dweck & Leggett, 1988) goals reprᵉsent outcomes reflecting the actual process of learning. Such goals can take the form of increased knowledge or task mastery. Task-extrinsic goals such as ego-involved (Nicholls, 1984) or performance (Dweck & Leggett, 1988) goals are those derived from social expectations or values associated with the consequences of task performance. In this case, desired outcomes can take the form of praise or tangible rewards.

For the most part, research on achievement goal orientations has generated discussions concerning the educational benefits of task-involved and learning goals relative to ego-involved and performance goals. Several authors, however, have focused on the broader social context of the classroom, suggesting that school adjustment requires the pursuit of multiple and often complementary goals, both social and academic. Early work in this area identified the need for approval as an important social motivatior of classroom learning (e.g., Maehr, 1983; Veroff, 1969). More recent work has recognized a broader range of social concerns as important aspects of school-related motivation. For instance, Kozeki (1985; Kozeki & Entwisle, 1984) proposes three dimensions of school motivation: an affective domain represented by motives to maintain relationships with parents, teachers, and peers; a moral domain represented by motives to establish trust, compliance, and social responsibility; and a cognitive domain represented by motives for independence, competence, and interest.

Most recently, Connell and his colleagues (Connell & Wellborn 1991; Deci & Ryan, 1991) have developed a model of student motivation based on three basic needs: competence, autonomy, and relatedness. With respect to social aspects of motivation, Connell and Wellborn (1991) suggest that a sense of social relatedness contributes to the adoption of goals promoted by social groups or institutions, whereas a lack of relatedness or disaffection can lead to a rejection of such goals. In other words, the pursuit of social goals that promote group cohesion and positive interpersonal interactions (such as to be prosocial and responsible), depends in large part on feeling like one is an integral part of the social group.

In the following sections, the literature on children's pursuit of social goals at school will be reviewed. Then, relations between social goal pursuit and academic accomplishments will be discussed.

Children's pursuit of social goals at school

In my own work, I have taken the perspective that as in other socialization contexts, children are required to pursue goals to conform to rules for social conduct and to behave in socially appropriate ways when they are at school. Moreover, I view the classroom as a social context that affords students the opportunity to pursue other social goals related to social interaction and relationship development. Empirical work on social goal pursuit as an integral part of classroom life has not been extensive. However, Ford (1982) found that the pursuit of goals to establish and maintain social relationships is an important school-related activity for adolescents. In an ethnographic study of 9th graders, Allen (1986) also found that the pursuit of socializing goals is an integral part of classroom life. Similarly, in a study of 9th through 12th graders, I found that adolescents reported trying to achieve social goals to make friends, have fun, and be dependable and responsible more often than learning-related goals (Wentzel, 1989).

In recent work on students' pursuit of prosocial and responsibility goals, I have found that middle school students also pursue prosocial and responsibility goals with greater frequency than either learning-related goals or goals to socialize with peers (Wentzel, 1991c, 1992). In this research, social goal pursuit was operationalized as students' self-reported efforts to help, share, and cooperate with teachers and peers (prosocial goals) and to follow rules and keep interpersonal promises and commitments (social responsibility goals). Pursuit of these social goals has also been related to social acceptance by classmates and teachers (Wentzel, 1991c, 1994b). Social acceptance among classmates was measured using sociometric techniques designed to identify popular, rejected, neglected, controversial, and average status children (see Wentzel, 1991a). To assess teachers' acceptance of students, teachers were asked to rate how much they would like to have each of their students in their class again next year. When compared with average status children, popular children (those with many friends and who are disliked by few of their classmates) reported trying to achieve prosocial goals significantly more often, neglected children (those who have few friends but are not disliked) reported trying to achieve both prosocial and compliance goals significantly more often, and controversial children (those with many freinds but who are also disliked by many of their peers) reported trying to achieve compliance goals significantly less often. In the case of teacher acceptance, students reporting high levels of effort to achieve social responsibility goals were preferred by teachers significantly more than other students (see Wentzel, 1991a).

Social goal pursuit and academic outcomes

Findings linking social goal pursuit to academically-relevant behavior have been inconsistent. Early work in this area suggests that the pursuit of goals to be compliant and responsible is associated with outcomes often antagonistic to learning (Kozeki & Entwistle, 1984; Kozeki, 1985). In contrast, other findings suggest positive relations between a need for approval and academic outcomes depending on the age of students (Crandall, 1966; Veroff, 1969), and whether these goals were pursued in conjunction with or in opposition to more academically-relevant goals (Nakamura & Finck, 1980).

In my own research, the pursuit of goals to behave in prosocial and socially responsible ways has been related consistently and positively to academic motivation as well as performance. In a study of adolescents from a suburban high school (Wentzel, 1989), students' self-reported efforts to achieve six classroom goals were related significantly and positively to student grades. These goals represented social as well as cognitive outcomes: to be a successful student, be dependable and responsible, learn new things, understand things, do your best, and get things done on time. Self-reported efforts to have fun were related negatively to students' grades.

In addition, relations between academic performance and student reports of effort could be explained more precisely by the *sets* of goals that students tried to achieve at school. In particular, 84% of the highest achieving students reported always trying to be a successful student, to be dependable and responsible, and to get things done on time; only 13% of the lowest achieving students reported always trying to achieve these three goals. Moreover, although the highest achieving students reported frequent pursuit of academic goals (i.e., to learn new things, to understand things), less frequent pursuit of these goals did not distinguish the lowest achieving from average achieving students. Rather, an unwillingness to try to conform to the social and normative standards of the classroom uniquely characterized the lowest achieving students.

A second study of 6th and 7th grade middle school students and their teachers was conducted in a predominantly working class, midwestern community (Wentzel, 1993a). In this research, two academic goals reflecting efforts to master new and challenging tasks and to earn positive evaluations, and two social goals reflecting efforts to be prosocial and to be socially responsible were investigated. As in the first study, I found that goal pursuit differed as a function of students' levels of academic achievement. Findings also indicated a significant relation between combinations of goal pursuit and academic achievement: 59% of the high-achieving students reported frequent efforts to achieve both social and academic goals whereas only 38% of the average achievers and 34% of the low-achieving students reported similar levels of effort to achieve these goals.

Summary and implications

There is growing evidence to suggest that students' pursuit of prosocial and social responsibility goals is related to their levels of social acceptance by peers and teachers. In addition, results linking the pursuit of prosocial and social responsibility goals to the pursuit of academic goals as well as to actual levels of academic performance suggest that social goal pursuit might be a necessary (albeit insufficient) requirement for achievement in both social and academic domains of functioning. Given the seemingly critical role of prosocial and socially responsible goal pursuit and behavior for multiple aspects of classroom adjustment, it therefore becomes important to understand the socialization processes that might contribute to the development of these motivational orientations and to their expression in classroom settings.

Research on classroom factors that directly promote the pursuit of these social goals is rare. However, the literature on family socialization suggests that behaving in prosocial and responsible ways might represent an important social competency that links the quality of family functioning and parent-child relationships to children's school adjustment. In the following section, I will review this literature, adopting a perspective that children's tendencies to behave in socially appropriate ways at school can be understood by examining socialization experiences at school that parallel those that occur within the context of family relationships.

Socialization processes contributing to social goal pursuit at school

In the developmental literature, models of self and social skills development have posited that personal goals play a key role in the organization and direction of social information processing and behavioral regulation (Dodge, 1986; Dweck & Leggett, 1988; Ford, 1992). Models of socialization stress the process of adopting and internalizing societal and parental goals as a critical part of children's socialization into adult roles (see Grusec & Goodnow, 1994; Maccoby & Martin, 1983). The ability to pursue multiple goals, especially the ability to resolve conflicts between personal goals and those of others, is considered to be an integral part of this process. In the following sections, socialization processes that might explain children's pursuit of social goals at school will be discussed.

Models of socialization within the family

Perhaps most relevant for understanding *why* children are motivated to behave in socially appropriate ways are models of socialization that focus on processes that promote children's general compliance and internalization of rules and norms for behavior. In support of a motivational interpretation, Maccoby (1992) suggests that "socialization does not merely involve the inculcation of socially acceptable habits, but also of *motives, so that* children willingly adopt and enact appropriate behavior patterns without constant surveillance . . ." (p. 172).

Research based on family socialization models typically has examined the quality of parent-child interactions and relationships, or specific parental disciplinary styles, in relation to a broad range of children's social, emotional, and cognitive outcomes (see Maccoby & Martin, 1983). Baumrind, for instance, found that four dimensions of parent-child interactions could predict reliably children's social adjustment (Baumrind, 1971; 1991). *Parental control* reflects consistent enforcement of rules, provision of structure to children's activities, and persistence in gaining child compliance; *maturity demands* reflect expectations to perform up to one's potential, and demands for self-reliance and self-control; *clarity of communication* reflects the extent to which parents solicit children's opinions and feelings, and use reasoning to obtain compliance; and *nurturance* reflects parental expressions of warmth and approval as well as conscientious protection of children's physical and emotional well-being. Other family socialization models are compatible with this approach (see Grusec & Goodnow, 1994).

Research based on these models suggests that a child is more likely to behave in prosocial and responsible ways if her parents are warm and nurturing, responsive to her wishes and point of view, and minimize external pressures to comply by using inductive reasoning rather than power assertive methods of discipline (Baumrind, 1971, 1991; Maccoby & Martin, 1983). It is beyond the scope of this chapter to discuss the precise mechanisms by which these practices lead to the internalization of social goals. In general, however, it is believed that these aspects of parent-child interactions contribute to the pursuit of socially valued goals because they (1) provide the structure necessary for learning appropriate forms of social behavior; (2) communicate expectations that a child's behavior will reflect his best intentions and abilities; (3) provide opportunities for autonomous decision making and the development of feelings of self-determination; and (4) support the development of positive feelings of self-worth (Grusec & Goodnow, 1994).

Interestingly, this work has not identified mechanisms that can explain the generalization and transfer of socially competent behavior from the family setting to that of the classroom. On the one hand, socialization models would suggest that goals internalized as a result of family socialization processes motivate children to behave in prosocial, responsible ways in nonfamilial contexts (see Wentzel, 1994a). On the other hand, children's goals and behavior are not always consistent across settings. Therefore, alternative or complementary models of classroom socialization need to be developed that can explain classroom-specific social competence.

One way to address the issue of transfer and generalization is to identify social processes in the classroom that correspond to those known to promote positive social behavior and the internalization of socially integrative goals within the family. Recent research indicates that children's relationships with peers and teachers might provide them with valuable resources similar to those provided by relationships with parents. In the following section, this literature will be reviewed and parallels between family and school socialization processes will be drawn. In particular, the degree to which teachers and peers provide stable and consistent structure and guidance, opportunities for democratic decision making, high standards for performance, and nurturance will be discussed.

Socialization processes in the classroom

Research on classroom processes that directly correspond to those known to promote prosocial and socially responsible behavior within the context of parent-child relationships has not been extensive. However, the history of American education suggests that the development of socially integrative skills has long been a primary function of the schooling process (e.g., Dreeben, 1968; Jackson, 1968; Wentzel, 1991b). At the policy level, socially responsible and prosocial behavior in the form of moral character, conformity to social rules and norms, cooperation, and positive styles of social interaction has been a stated educational objective for American schools. In fact, character development and social responsibility in general have been explicit objectives for public schools in almost every educational policy statement since 1848, being promoted with the same frequency as the developement of academic skills (see Wentzel, 1991b).

The suggestion that the development of prosocial and socially responsible behavior is an important educational goal is also supported by literature indicating that teachers as well as students provide socialization experiences that promote displays of socially competent behavior. For example, with respect to Baumrind's parenting dimensions, instances of *control, maturity demands,* and *democratic communication styles* have been observed on the part of teachers and students. Indeed, teachers appear to have common social rules and norms that they expect students to follow (e.g., Hargreaves, Hester, & Mellor, 1975). Blumenfeld and her colleagues have documented teacher communications to students concerning *why* they ought to behave in socially appropriate ways and what will happen if they do not (Blumenfeld, Hamilton, Bossert, Wessels, & Meece, 1983). Shultz and Florio (1979) describe how teachers indicate to students when they need to pay attention as a function of which contexts they are in. Although rarely linked to academic performance, teacher provision of structure and guidance has been related positively to elementary school-aged students' engagement in classroom activities (Skinner & Belmont, 1993).

For the most part, classroom rules and teacher communications are designed to establish classroom order and the hierarchical nature of teacher-student relationships. However, teachers establish norms for peer relationships that also focus on considerate, cooperative, and morally responsible forms of behavior (Hargreaves et al., 1975; Sieber, 1979). Students themselves have been observed to contribute to social order in the classroom. This occurs most often when they are held accountable for the behavior of each other or when teachers use peer group leaders to monitor the class when they must leave their classroom (Seiber, 1979). Students also have been observed to monitor each other by ignoring irrelevant or inappropriate behavior and responses during group instruction, and by private sanctioning of inappropriate conduct (Sieber, 1979).

Children also appear to provide each other with instrumental help and guidance that directly facilitates adherence to teachers' expectations for behavior and academic performance. For instance, students frequently clarify and interpret their teacher's instructions and provide mutual assistance (Sieber, 1979). Classmates also provide each other with information by modeling both academic and social competencies and establishing normative standards for performance (Schunk & Zimmerman, this volume).

Finally, teachers and peers can also be valuable sources of *nurturance*. Studies of perceived social support from peers suggest that young adolescents are primarily sources of companionship for each other (Burmester & Furman, 1987; Reid, Landesman, Treder, & Jaccard, 1989; Youniss & Smollar, 1989). Within the context of these relationships, however, peers tend to provide each other with nurturance and emotional support by serving as buffers against stress in unfamiliar surroundings and bolstering perceptions of self-worth and self-esteem. With respect to academic outcomes, evidence suggests that positive relationships with peers can provide emotional security and incentives to achieve (e.g., Ladd & Price, 1987), whereas the loss of a familiar peer group can have negative effects on self-esteem and general interest in school (Miller, 1983). Also, perceived isolation from peers as well as perceived lack of control in obtaining social support at school have been related to low levels of achievement (Epperson, 1963).

Although research on social support from teachers has been less frequent (see Birch & Ladd and Harter, this volume, for exceptions), young adolescents report that teachers can be valuable sources of help and guidance outside the home (Burmester & Furman, 1987). However, young adolescents report declines in the quality of teacher-student relationships after the transition to middle school; these declines correspond to declines in academic motivation and achievement (Feldlaufer, Midgley, & Eccles, 1988; Midgley, Feldlaufer & Eccles, 1989).

Experiences with peers and teachers as motivators of social goal pursuit

The literature reviewed in the previous section describes ways in which teachers and peers provide students with socialization experiences conducive to the development of socially competent classroom behavior. Few studies have documented relations between these socialization experiences and student motivation (see Berndt & Keefe and Birch & Ladd, this volume, for exceptions). As suggested by models of family socialization, however, one reason why social interactions with teachers and peers might be related to aspects of school adjustment is that they promote positive motivational orientations toward prosocial behavior and respect for classroom rules and norms.

My recent work has begun to explore ways in which students' pursuit of goals to be prosocial and responsible is related to interpersonal resources from teachers and peers (Wentzel, 1994b). In this research, interpersonal support is reflected in perceptions that peers and teachers care about the student as a person and as a learner. Results indicate that middle school students' pursuit of goals to help and cooperate (prosocial goals) and to follow classroom rules and norms (social responsibility goals) is related to perceived social support from teachers as well as peers. These findings were robust even when taking into account actual levels of social acceptance by teachers and peers, and students' sex, ethnicity, and family structure. In a second study of middle school students, perceived support from teachers and peers was related negatively to students' emotional distress and positively to interest in school (Wentzel, 1996).

These findings support the notion that interpersonal support from teachers and peers (i.e., perceiving that teachers and peers care about them) are related positively to social and motivational aspects of school adjustment (see also Goodenow, 1993; Midgley et al., 1989; Wentzel & Asher, 1995). In an effort to relate these results to a family socialization perspective, I conducted a third study that examined students' characterizations of "caring." I asked students to list three things that teachers do to show that they care about them and three things that teachers do to show that they don't care. Students then repeated this process for peers.

For teachers, student responses were coded along dimensions reflecting those typically studied in the parenting literature. Responses reflecting three of the four dimensions emerged from the data: democratic interaction styles as demonstrated by respect, recognition of social and academic

Table 10.1. *Students' descriptions of caring and uncaring teachers*

Characteristics of caring teachers	Percentage of total responses
Democratic interaction styles	
Communication	25
Respect	4
Recognition of individual differences	
Personal	15
Academic	13
Expectations for achievement	30
Positive encouragement and feedback	11
Other (e.g., generic helping, being nice)	6
Characteristics of uncaring teachers	
Lack of democratic interaction styles	
Lack of communication	46
Lack of respect	9
Lack of recognition of individual differences	
Personal	8
Academic	7
Low expectations for achievement	18
Criticism and negative feedback	10
Other (e.g., negative personality traits)	2

individual differences, and solicitation of student input and opinions; high expectations for achievement; and positive encouragement and feedback (see Table 10.1). These categories of responses correspond to Baumrind's dimensions of clarity of communication, maturity demands, and nurturance, respectively.

In contrast to adult-child relationships that are predominantly hierarchical, the nature of peer relationships is relatively egalitarian. Therefore, dimensions of support from peers differ somewhat from those of parents or other adults. Consequently, characterizations of "caring" and "uncaring" peers were coded along four dimensions derived from work by Burmester & Furman (1987): companionship, help, reliable alliance, and emotional support (see Table 10.2). However, provision of help and a stable and reliable source of guidance correspond roughly to parental control in that both represent a source of consistent and reliable support. Emotional support corresponds to nurturance in that it represents concern with promoting and maintaining positive levels of emotional well-being.

The findings shown in Tables 10.1 and 10.2 are relevant for understanding ways in which socialization experiences in the classroom parallel

Table 10.2. *Students' descriptions of caring and uncaring peers*

Characteristics of caring peers	Percentage of total responses
Companionship	32
Academic help	24
Reliable allies	15
Emotional support (positive regard & concern)	29
Characteristics of uncaring peers	
Lack of companionship	17
Lack of academic help	9
Unreliable allies	13
Emotionally unsupportive	
Lack of concern	8
Verbal and physical aggression	53

those of the family. Specifically, these results indicate that students characterize positive relationships with peers and teachers in ways that are similar to positive parent-child relationships. Of interest, however, is that students tend to perceive teachers and peers as sources of different types of experiences and support. Students seem to look to teachers primarily for opportunities for self-expression and autonomous decision making (democractic interaction styles), and for standards for performance. In contrast, students tend to look to peers primarily for companionship and emotional support.

Of final interest is that preliminary findings indicate that these dimensions of social support from teachers and peers are related to social and motivational outcomes. Specifically, students who define uncaring teachers as failing to provide nurturance and autonomy support are not highly motivated to behave in prosocial and socially responsible ways, whereas those who define caring peers as emotionally supportive are those who tend to be motivated to be prosocial and socially responsible.

Conclusions and future directions

The literature reviewed in this chapter suggests that social competence in the form of prosocial and socially responsible behavior is a critical aspect of school adjustment that is valued by teachers as well as students. Prosocial and responsible behavior also has been linked consistently with academic accomplishments. Second, students who pursue multiple goals re-

flecting social as well as academic objectives are those who are most successful at school. Moreover, pursuit of goals to behave in prosocial and responsible ways appear to be an underlying variable that links social adjustment with positive academic outcomes. Finally, students' pursuit of
these goals appears to be motivated, in part, by the quality of support derived from relationships with teachers and peers.

In addition, I have proposed that access to interpersonal resources and
social support promotes prosocial and socially responsible behavior in
both family and school settings. This proposition, however, reflects several important assumptions. First, it assumes that all children value prosocial and socially responsible behavior and that all that is necessary to elicit pursuit of goals to behave in this manner is the existence of certain
interpersonal resources. Related to this notion is the assumption that provisions of specific types of support by teachers and peers will provide students with continuity between home and school. Finally, it is assumed that
once a child adopts goals to be prosocial and socially responsible, she will
be able to achieve those goals. Each of these assumptions will be discussed in turn.

Where do goals come from?

A central theme of this chapter has been that children's willingness and
desire to pursue goals to be cooperative and compliant is an important aspect of social motivation that contributes to the stability and maintenance
of their respective social groups. Little is known, however, about how children come to value these particular goals in the first place. As suggested
in the socialization literature, children will adopt those goals that are valued by individuals with whom they have warm and supportive relationships. Therefore, an examination of the content of family goals and how
children come to adopt them as their own seems to be especially important for understanding children's reactions to and adoption of social rules
and norms in other social settings such as the classroom.

Research on the content of family goals might be especially relevant
for understanding the achievement of children from minority cultures who
are expected to comply with rules and norms for classroom behavior that
might be inconsistent with those espoused by their families and community (see, e.g., Ogbu, 1985). Alternatively, research on goals promoted by
supportive peer groups might also help to explain the motivational orientations of children who do not experience warm and nurturant relationships with their parents.

Developmental issues also need to be considered. For instance, the transition from elementary to middle school is often marked by heightened levels of mistrust between teachers and students, student perceptions that teachers no longer care about them, and a decrease in opportunities for students to establish meaningful relationships with teachers and peers (Eccles & Midgley, 1989). Therefore, perceived social support at school might be an especially critical factor that motivates students to pursue socially adaptive goals at this time.

In addition, we know very little about how goals develop over the course of the school years or about the relative contribution of schooling and family socialization processes to individual differences in children's adoption and pursuit of these goals. Whereas parents and teachers might influence the internalization of goals and values in the early years, peers might play an increasingly important role as children reach adolescence. This might be especially true if peers become the primary source of emotional support and nurturance as children make their way through middle school and high school.

Continuity across contexts

An assumption drawn from research on family socialization processes is that relationships characterized by authoritative parenting styles are enjoyed by most children and that this style leads to the most adaptive outcomes for all children. However, it is clear that many children do not have relationships with parents that are authoritative in nature. Moreover, authoritative parenting styles are not always related significantly to aspects of children's school adjustment. This is especially true for children from nonwhite, nonmiddle class families (Steinberg, Dornbusch, & Brown, 1992). Therefore, we must begin to explore the nature of similarities and differences between home and school settings and carefully examine what happens when children experience discontinuities between home and school in the socialization processes and types of social supports they experience.

Social skills and self-regulatory processes

The adoption of social goals is dependent on several important social cognitive factors. For instance, the pursuit of these goals reflects an ability to perceive and understand social rules and conventions and to judge when and where these rules are appropriate to follow. In addition, active pursuit of socially integrative goals often requires an ability to recognize the existence of conflicting goals (those that a child *wants* to achieve and those that a child is *supposed* to achieve) and then, to coordinate them in ways that satisfy both personal and social objectives (Ford, Wentzel, Wood, Stevens, & Seisfeld, 1989).

Reasons why conflicts between parents and children arise (Smetana, 1988), and ways in which these problems are resolved might also shed additional light on young adolescents' classroom goal pursuit. Research on how students perceive and consequently resolve conflicts between their own personal goals and those that contribute to a positive instructional classroom climate is especially needed in this regard.

Finally, although the literature reviewed in this chapter suggests that the pursuit of social goals is related significantly and positively to social as well as academic outcomes, it tells us little about the processes that link these efforts to tangible results. Clearly, having good intentions is important, but students must also be able to accomplish what they set out to achieve. The processes by which goals are linked to social acceptance and academic accomplishments are not well understood. Theoretical models have suggested various psychological processes that regulate goal pursuit and that mediate the initial adoption of goals and subsequent displays of goal-directed behavior (e.g., Dodge, 1986; Ford, 1992). The next step is to examine empirically the role of these self-regulatory and self-control processes in linking social goal-setting to socially competent behavior in the classroom.

Acknowledgment

I would like to thank Martin Ford for his constructive and insightful comments on an earlier version of this chapter.

References

Allen, J. D. (1986). Classroom management: Students' perspectives, goals, and strategies. *American Educational Research Journal, 23,* 437–459.

Bandura, A. (1986). *Social foundations of thought and action: A social cognitive theory.* Englewood Cliffs, NJ: Prentice-Hall.

Baumrind, D. (1971). Current patterns of parental authority. *Developmental Psychology Monograph, 4,* (1, Pt.2).

Baumrind, D. (1991). Effective parenting during the early adolescent transition. In P. A. Cowan & M. Hetherington (Eds.), *Family transitions* (pp. 111–164). Hillsdale, NJ: Erlbaum.

Blumenfeld, P. C., Hamilton, V. L., Bossert, S. T., Wessels, K., & Meece, J. (1983). Teacher talk and student thought: Socialization into the student role. In J. M. Levine & M. C. Wang (Eds.), *Teacher and student perceptions: Implications for learning* (pp. 143–192). Hillsdale, NJ: Erlbaum.

Burmester, D., & Furman, W. (1987). The development of companionship and intimacy. *Child Development, 58,* 1101–1113.

Cobb, J. A., & Hopps, H. (1973). Effects of academic survival skills training on low achieving first graders. *The Journal of Educational Research, 67,* 108–113.

Coie, J. D., & Krehbiel, G. (1984). Effects of academic tutoring on the social status of low-achieving, socially rejected children. *Child Development, 55,* 1465–1478.

Connell, J. P., & Wellborn, J. G. (1991). Competence, autonomy, and relatedness: A motivational analysis of self-system processes. In M. R. Gunnar & L. A. Sroufe (Eds.), *Self processes and development: The Minnesota symposia on child development* (vol. 23, pp. 43–78). Hillsdale, NJ: Erlbaum.

Crandall, V. J. (1966). Personality characteristics and social and achievement behaviors associated with children's social desirability response tendencies. *Journal of Personality and Social Psychology, 4,* 477–486.

Deci, E. L., & Ryan, R. M. (1991). A motivational approach to self: Integration in personality. *Nebraska symposium on motivation 1990* (pp. 237–288). Lincoln, NE: University of Nebraska Press.

Dodge, K. A. (1986). A social information processing model of social competence in children. In M. Perlmutter (Ed.), *Minnesota symposium on child psychology* (vol. 18, pp. 77–126). Hillsdale, NJ: Erlbaum.

Dreeben, R. (1968). *On what is learned in school.* Menlo Park, CA: Addison-Wesley.

Dweck, C. S., & Leggett, E. L. (1988). A social-cognitive approach to motivation and personality. *Psychological Review, 95,* 256–272.

Eccles (Parsons), J., Adler, T. F., Futterman, R., Goff, S. B., Kaczala, C. M., Meece, J. L., & Midgley, C. (1983). Expectancies, values, and academic behaviors. In J. T. Spence (Ed.), *Achievement and achievement motivation* (pp. 75–146). San Francisco: W. H. Freeman.

Eccles, J., & Midgley, C. (1989). Stage-environment fit: Developmentally appropriate classrooms for young adolescents. In C. Ames & R. Ames (Eds.), *Research on motivation in education,* (vol. 3, pp.139–186). New York: Academic Press.

Epperson, D. C. (1963). Some interpersonal and performance correlates of classroom alienation. *School Review, 71,* 360–376.

Feldhusen, J. F., Thurston, J. R., & Benning, J. J. (1970). Longitudinal analyses of classroom behavior and school achievement. *Journal of Experimental Education, 38,* 4–10.

Feldlaufer, H., Midgley, C., & Eccles, J. S. (1988). Student, teacher, and observer perceptions of the classroom before and after the transition to junior high school. *Journal of Early Adolescence, 8,* 133–156.

Feldman, S. S., & Wentzel, K. R. (1990). The relationship between family interaction patterns, classroom self-restraint, and academic achievement. *Journal of Educational Psychology, 82,* 813–819.

Ford, M. E. (1982). Social cognition and social competence in adolescence. *Developmental Psychology, 18,* 323–340.

Ford, M. E. (1992). *Motivating humans: Goals, emotions, and personal agency beliefs.* Newbury Park, CA: Sage.

Ford, M. E., & Nichols, C. W. (1991). Using goal assessments to identify motivational patterns and facilitate behavioral regulation and achievement. In M. L. Maehr & P. Pintrich (Eds.), *Advances in motivation and achievement* (vol. 7, pp. 51–84). Greenwich, CT: JAI.

Ford, M. E., Wentzel, K. R., Wood, D. N., Stevens, E., & Siesfeld, G. A. (1989). Processes associated with integrative social competence: Emotional and contextual influences on adolescent social responsibility. *Journal of Adolescent Research, 4,* 405–425.

Goodenow, C. (1993). Classroom belonging among early adolescent students: Relationships to motivation and achievement. *Journal of Early Adolescence, 13,* 21–43.

Grusec, J. E., & Goodnow, J. J. (1994). Impact of parental discipline methods on the child's internalization of values: A reconceptualization of current points of view. *Developmental Psychology, 30,* 4–19.

Hargreaves, D. H., Hester, S. K., & Mellor, F. J. (1975). *Deviance in classrooms.* London: Routledge & Kegan Paul.

Hartup, W. W. (1983). Peer relations. In P. H. Mussen (Ed.), *Handbook of child psychology,* (vol. 4, pp. 104–196). New York: Wiley.

Hopps, H., & Cobb, J. A. (1974). Initial investigations into academic survival-skill training, direct instruction, and first-grade achievement. *Journal of Educational Psychology, 66,* 548–553.

Horn, W. F., & Packard, T. (1985). Early identification of learning problems: A meta-analysis. *Journal of Educational Psychology, 77,* 597–607.

Jackson, P. W. (1968). *Life in classrooms.* New York: Holt, Rinehart & Winston.

Kozeki, B. (1985). Motives and motivational style in education. In N. Entwistle (Ed.), *New directions in educational psychology: 1. Learning and teaching* (pp. 189–199). Philadelphia: Falmer Press.

Kozeki, B., & Entwistle, N. J. (1984). Identifying dimensions of school motivation in Britain and Hungary. *British Journal of Educational Psychology, 54,* 306–319.

Ladd, G. W., & Price, J. M. (1987). Predicting children's social and school adjustment following the transition from preschool to kindergarten. *Child Development, 58,* 1168–1189.

Lambert, N. M. (1972). Intellectual and non-intellectual predictors of high school status. *Journal of Special Education, 6,* 247–259.

Maccoby, E. E. (1992). Trends in the study of socialization: Is there a Lewinian heritage? *Journal of Social Issues, 48,* 171–185.

Maccoby, E. E., & Martin, J. A. (1983). Socialization in the context of the family: Parent-child interaction. In P. H. Mussen (Ed.), *Handbook of child psychology,* (vol. 4, pp. 1–101). New York: Wiley.

Maehr, M. L. (1983). On doing well in science: Why Johnny no longer excels; why Sarah never did. In S. G. Paris, G. M. Olson, & H. W. Stevenson (Eds.), *Learning and motivation in the classroom* (pp. 179–210). Hillsdale, NJ: Erlbaum.

Midgley, C., Feldlaufer, H., & Eccles, J. (1989). Student/teacher relations and attitudes toward mathematics before and after the transition to junior high school. *Child Development, 60,* 981–992.

Miller, N. (1983). Peer relations in desegrated schools. In J. L. Epstein & N. Karweit (Eds.), *Friends in school* (pp. 201–217). New York: Academic Press.

Nakamura, C. Y., & Finck, D. N. (1980). Relative effectiveness of socially oriented and task-oriented children and predictability of their behaviors. *Monographs of the Society for Research in Child Development, 45,* (Nos. 3–4).

Nicholls, J. G. (1984). Achievement motivation: Conceptions of ability, subjective experience, task choice, and performance. *Psychological Review, 91,* 328–346.

Ogbu, J. U. (1985). Origins of human competence: A cultural-ecological perspective. *Child Development, 52,* 413–429.

Parker, J. G., & Asher, S. R. (1987). Peer relations and later personal adjustment: Are low-accepted children at risk? *Psychological Bulletin, 102,* 357–389.

Pervin, L. A. (1982). The stasis and flow of behavior: Toward a theory of goals. In M. M. Page (Ed.), *Personality-Current theory and research* (pp. 1–53). Lincoln, NE: University of Nebraska Press.

Reid, M., Landesman, S., Treder, R., & Jaccard, J. (1989). "My family and friends": Six- to twelve-year-old children's perceptions of social support. *Child Development, 60,* 896–910.

Safer, D. J. (1986). Nonpromotion correlates and outcomes at different grade levels. *Journal of Learning Disabilities, 19,* 500–503.

Schunk, D. H., & Zimmerman, B. J. (1996). Modeling and self-efficacy influences on children's development of self-regulation. In J. Juvonen & K. R. Wentzel (Es.), *Social motivation: Understanding children's school adjustment.* pp. 154–180. New York: Cambridge.

Shultz, J., & Florio, S. (1979). Stop and freeze: The negotiation of social and physical space in a kindergarten/first grade classroom. *Anthropology and Education Quarterly, 10,* 166–181.

Sieber, R. T. (1979). Classmates as workmates: Informal peer activity in the elementary school. *Anthropology and Education Quarterly, 10,* 207–235.

Skinner, E. A., & Belmont, M. J. (1993). Motivation in the classroom: Reciprocal effects of teacher behavior and student engagement across the school year. *Journal of Educational Psychology, 85,* 571–581.

Smetana, J. G. (1988). Concepts of self and social convention: Adolescents' and parents' reasoning about hypothetical and actual family conflicts. In M. R. Gunnar (Ed.), *Minnesota symposium on child psychology* (pp. 79–122). Hillsdale, NJ: Erlbaum.

Steinberg, L., Dornbusch, S. M., & Brown, B. B. (1992). Ethnic differences in adolescent achievement: An ecological perspective. *American Psychologist, 47,* 723–729.

Veroff, J. (1969). Social comparison and the development of achievement motivation. In C. P. Smith (Ed.), *Achievement-related motives in children* (pp. 46–101). New York: Russell Sage.

Weiner, B. (1985). An attribution theory of achievement motivation and emotion. *Psychological Review, 92,* 548–573.

Wentzel, K. R. (1989). Adolescent classroom goals, standards for performance, and academic achievement: An interactionist perspective. *Journal of Educational Psychology, 81,* 131–142.

Wentzel, K. R. (1991a). Relations between social competence and academic achievement in early adolescence. *Child Development, 62,* 1066–1078.

Wentzel, K. R. (1991b). Social competence at school: The relation between social responsibility and academic achievement. *Review of Educational Research, 61,* 1–24.

Wentzel, K. R. (1991c). Social and academic goals at school: Achievement motivation in context. In M. Maehr & P. Pintrich (Eds.), *Advances in motivation and achievement* (vol. 7, pp. 185–212). Greenwich, CT: JAI.

Wentzel, K. R. (1992). Motivation and achievement in adolescence: A multiple goals perspective. In J. Meece & D. Schunk (Eds.), *Student perceptions in the classroom: Causes and consequences* (pp. 287–306). Hillsdale, N. J.: Erlbaum.

Wentzel, K. R. (1993a). Social and academic goals at school: Motivation and achievement in early adolescence. *Journal of Early Adolescence, 13,* 4–20.

Wentzel, K. R. (1993b). Does being good make the grade? Relations between academic and social competence in early adolescence. *Journal of Educational Psychology, 85,* 357–364.

Wentzel, K. R. (1994a). Family functioning and academic achievement in middle school: A social-emotional perspective. *Journal of Early Adolescence, 14,* 268–291.

Wentzel, K. R. (1994b). Relations of social goal pursuit to social acceptance, classroom behavior, and perceived social support. *Journal of Educational Psychology, 86,* 173–182.

Wentzel, K. R. (1996). Social Support and Achievement: The Role of Parents, Teachers, and Peers. Unpublished manuscript, University of Maryland.

Wentzel, K. R., & Asher, S. R. (1995). Academic lives of neglected, rejected, popular, and controversial children. *Child Development, 66,* 754–763.

Wentzel, K. R., & Feldman, S. S. (1993). Parental predictors of boys' self-restraint and motivation to achieve at school: A longitudinal study. *Journal of Early Adolescence, 13,* 183–203.

Wentzel, K. R., Weinberger, D. A., Ford, M. E., & Feldman, S. S. (1990). Academic achievement in preadolescence: The role of motivational, affective, and self-regulatory processes. *Journal of Applied Developmental Psychology, 11,* 179–193.

Youniss, J., & Smollar, J. (1989). Adolescents' interpersonal relationships in social context. In T. Berndt & G. Ladd (Eds.), *Peer relationships in child development* (pp. 300–316). New York: Wiley.

11   Friends' influence on school adjustment: A motivational analysis

Thomas J. Berndt and Keunho Keefe

Best friends can have a powerful influence on children's attitudes toward school, behavior in class, and academic achievement. The influence of friends has long been a concern of educators and educational researchers. Several decades ago, James Coleman (1961) argued that most high-school students care more about being popular with peers than about doing well in school, in part because their peers emphasize academic success less than social success. Many recent writers have echoed this theme (e.g., Bishop, 1989).

By contrast, other writers have emphasized the positive effects of friendships on children's adjustment and development. Piaget (1932/1965) proposed that interactions with friends or other peers are crucial for the development of a mature morality. Sullivan (1953) suggested that intimate friendships among preadolescents contribute to high self-esteem and to social understanding (Buhrmester & Furman, 1986). More recently, many researchers have tested the hypothesis that support from friends enhances the social and academic adjustment of children and adolescents (e.g., Berndt & Keefe, 1995).

Both perspectives on friends' influence capture part of the truth, but both are incomplete and therefore misleading. Friends influence children and adolescents through two distinct pathways (Berndt, 1992). First, students at all grade levels are influenced by the attitudes, behavior, and other characteristics of their friends. This influence is not always negative. Students whose friends have positive characteristics, such as high grades, are likely to improve their own grades over time (Epstein, 1983). One goal of our chapter is to outline various motives that account for friends' influence by this pathway.

Second, students are influenced by the quality of their friendships. For example, friendships are higher in quality when they are more intimate (Sullivan, 1953). Friendships are lower in quality when the friends often

248

engage in conflicts or hostile rivalry with one another (Laursen, 1993). The quality of students' friendships affects their social and emotional adjustment. It can, in turn, affect their adjustment to school. The second goal of our chapter is to outline motives related to friendship quality. Identifying these motives should increase understanding of this second pathway of influence.

Before proceeding, we should say more precisely what we mean by motives and by school adjustment. Weiner (1992) proposed that the domain of motivation includes all questions about why organisms think and behave as they do. This broad definition includes motives that actors themselves report. For example, students sometimes say that their goal at school is trying to do what a teacher asks (Wentzel, 1991a). The definition also includes motives of which a person may not be aware. Unconscious motives are emphasized not only in psychoanalytic theories, but also in some learning theories and social-psychological theories (see Nisbett & Wilson, 1977; Weiner, 1992). Both types of motives are considered in the chapter.

Like motivation, school adjustment is a broad construct. Our focus is on three facets of adjustment. First, students' adjustment to school is reflected by their attitudes toward their classes, their teachers, and other experiences at school. Well-adjusted students value what they are learning and are positively involved in classroom activities (Berndt & Miller, 1990; Wentzel, 1993). Second, students' adjustment is reflected by their classroom behavior. Well-adjusted students behave appropriately and are rarely disruptive (Berndt & Keefe, in press; Dubow, Tisak, Causey, Hryshko, & Reid, 1991). Third, students' adjustment is reflected by their academic achievement. Well-adjusted students learn what is taught in school, and so receive high grades and test scores.

Friends may affect all three facets of school adjustment through both influence pathways outlined earlier. The first pathway is the focus of the next section of the chapter. We emphasize that many motives contribute to the influence of friends' characteristics. The second pathway is the focus of the following section. We emphasize that friends have goals not only for themselves as individuals, but for themselves and their friends viewed as a unit. An outline of the two pathways of influence and their associated motives is given in Table 11.1.

Also discussed in the initial sections is how friends' influence through the two pathways might change with age. Unfortunately, little evidence on such changes is available, and the evidence is not always consistent. We summarize the conclusions that can be drawn, and then use our motivational analysis to suggest new perspectives on the issue.

Table 11.1. *Motives contributing to friends' influence through two pathways*

Pathway I: Influences of friends' characteristics	Pathway II: Effects of friendship quality
1. The need for approval 2. Identification with friends 3. The self-enhancement motive 4. The need to be correct	1. Relationship ("we") motives (related to positive features) 2. Individualistic/competitive motives (related to negative features)

In a third section, we consider implications of the motivational analysis for educational practice. We focus specifically on strategies for dealing with friends who negatively influence one another. Our recommended strategies must be interpreted cautiously, because many questions about friends' influence remain open. In the final section, we suggest directions for future research on these questions.

Motives related to the influence of friends' characteristics

Both popular and scholarly writers have suggested that pressure from peers contributes to drug use, delinquent behavior, and apathy toward school (Ansley & McCleary, 1992; Bishop, 1989; Steinberg & Silverberg, 1986). These writers rarely say which peers are the presumed source of this negative pressure, but other data suggest that close friends have more influence than do other peers (Downs, 1987). Nevertheless, many kinds of evidence show that this view of friends' influence is seriously distorted.

We begin this section by examining evidence related to the notion of friends' pressure. Then we consider four motives that better explain why students' friends affect their adjustment to school. Finally, we review the few existing studies of developmental changes in this pathway of influence.

Inaccurate ideas about friends' pressure

The notion that pressure from friends has strong and negative effects on children and adolescents is inaccurate in three major ways. First, this notion exaggerates the magnitude of friends' influence. A popular magazine recently published a survey that was completed by more than 100,000 adolescents (Ansley & McCleary, 1992). One question asked, "How much peer pressure are you under to do things that probably are wrong?" Although the reporters who summarized the results concluded that "peer pressure is a big problem," the adolescents' responses suggest otherwise. Most adolescents (66%) said the amount of pressure they were under was "not much." Another 14% said they were under no pressure to do things that are wrong. Only 20% of the adolescents said they were under "a lot" of pressure.

More systematic research confirms that strong pressure from friends to engage in specific behaviors is rare. Naturalistic observations of adolescents' interactions with friends have shown that most decisions are reached by consensus rather than coercive pressure (Suttles, 1968). Usually, the friends discuss various options until they agree on what to do. Rarely is one adolescent pressured to conform to the rest of the group.

Research on friends' pressure and school adjustment is limited. Coleman's (1961) evidence for negative effects of peers on academic achievement was indirect, and writers such as Bishop (1989) mentioned no empirical data at all. We obtained relevant data with two samples of junior-high-school students (Berndt, Miller, & Park, 1989). We asked students how much influence their friends had on the three aspects of school adjustment defined earlier: attitudes, behavior in class, and academic achievement. Most students said their friends did not affect these aspects of their school adjustment. Evidence presented later implies that the students underestimated their friends' influence on them, but the students' comments suggest that any influence of friends did not result from overt pressure.

A second inaccuracy in popular ideas about friends' pressure concerns the direction of its effects. For most students, these effects are more likely to be positive than negative. High-school students in several large samples reported that their friends discouraged drug and alcohol use, delinquent activities, and other types of antisocial behavior more than they encouraged them (Brown, Clasen, & Eicher, 1986; Keefe, 1994). The students also said their friends encouraged studying for school subjects more than they discouraged studying.

The third inaccuracy in popular ideas about friends' pressure concerns the motives that account for friends' influence. These ideas imply that students conform to their friends because they fear they will be punished if they don't. However, students can escape any punishment by ending those friendships and making new friends. Furthermore, neither children nor adolescents are as lacking in independence as is often suggested. When completing surveys, many adolescents report that they make their own decisions rather than relying on the advice of parents or friends (Sebald, 1986). In experimental studies, some children and adolescents show anticonformity, rejecting their peers' judgments and making different ones (Hartup, 1983).

According to Piaget (1932/1965), friendships have features that limit both the use and the effectiveness of coercive pressure. Friends assume that their relationship is based on equality and mutual respect, so decisions must be made through negotiation rather than domination by one person. Adolescents in our previous study suggested this kind of mutual respect when explaining why their friends had no influence on their school adjustment (Berndt et al., 1989). For example, one boy said that his friend "doesn't try to change my opinions, and I don't try to change his."

This argument should not be carried too far. Although students' adjustment to school does not depend greatly on their response to friends' pressure, friends do influence attitudes, behavior, and achievement in school (Berndt & Keefe, in press; Epstein, 1983; Kandel, 1978). By drawing upon a long tradition of developmental and social-psychological research, we can identify the motivation that accounts for these effects of friends' characteristics.

Four motives that underlie friends' influence.   For decades, questions about interpersonal influence have been explored by social psychologists interested in persuasion, attitude change, decision making in groups, and other phenomena (Chaiken, Liberman, & Eagly, 1989; Zanna, Olson, & Herman, 1987; Zimbardo & Leippe, 1991). These questions have also been explored by developmental psychologists interested in social learning, conformity to peers and parents, basic socialization processes, and other topics in social development (Bandura & Walters, 1963; Hartup, 1983; Maccoby & Martin, 1983).

Not surprisingly, a strong consensus about the motives responsible for interpersonal influence does not exist. The lack of consensus is due partly to researchers' use of different terms to refer to the same or overlapping constructs. In addition, multiple motives are linked to social influence, and many researchers have focused on only one. We argue that four motives should be considered when trying to understand how students are affected by their friends' adjustment to school (see Table 1). Some writers might propose motives other than the four that we present, but we assume other motives are less important than the following four or are largely synonymous with them (see, however, Erdley; Ford; Kupersmidt et al., Wentzel, this volume, for alternative perspectives on social goals).

The first motive that underlies the influence of friends' characteristics is students' need for social approval (Hoving, Hamm, & Galvin, 1969; Juvonen & Weiner, 1993) or their impression motivation (Chaiken et al., 1989). Students want to be liked by their friends, so they try to do things that will meet the friends' expectations or make a positive impression on them. This motive is associated theoretically with the idea of social reinforcement. Praise and other kinds of positive comments from friends can function as rewards for specific behaviors by students and so increase the likelihood of those behaviors (Hartup, 1983). In the broadest sense, this motive relates to Skinner's principle of positive reinforcement, a principle common to all learning theories.

The category of positive reinforcement includes both material rewards and social reinforcers like praise. However, for understanding the influence of friends, praise and other social reinforcers are more important than are material rewards. Friends rarely give things to one another as rewards for specific behaviors. Therefore, the construct of social approval corresponds to the attributes of friends' interactions more precisely than does the broader construct of positive reinforcement.

In the domain of school adjustment, the importance of the needs for social approval was first emphasized by Crandall, Katkovsky, and Preston (1960). They argued that "the basic goal of achievement behavior is the attainment of approval and the avoidance of disapproval" (p. 791). They assumed that approval comes from both teachers and peers, but little of their research focused directly on this motive. In particular, they did not explore whether the need for approval is related to friends' influence on school adjustment.

Many studies in laboratory settings have shown the effects of peer reinforcement on children's behavior (Hartup, 1983). Therefore, it is reasonable to assume that reinforcement from friends and other classmates also affects students' attitudes, behavior, and achievement in school. Whether friends typically encourage a positive or a negative adjustment to school is a controversial question. Consistent with the positive view is the evidence mentioned earlier that students say friends encourage them to study hard at school (Brown et al., 1986). Also consistent with this view is evidence that students higher in academic achievement are usually more popular with peers (Coie, 1990).

There is conflicting evidence, however. The eighth graders in one recent study (Juvonen & Murdock, 1993; see also Juvonen, this volume) said they thought a peer who got good grades would generally be more popular than a peer who got bad grades. However, the eighth graders thought a peer who got bad grades but who was very smart and tried very hard would be more popular than a peer with the same attributes who got good grades. To explain this finding, the researchers speculated that the eighth graders might have assumed the high-achieving student would "set the curve" for the class and make them look worse. Alternatively, the eighth graders might have viewed the high achiever as accepting tradition-al expectations about the value of school achievement that they them-selves rejected. Notice that these two explanations differ in that they sug-gest that students generally value, or are disdainful of, high academic achievement.

Other findings indicate that students' level of academic achievement affects their selection of friends. Friendship selection, in turn, affects the attitudes and behavior for which students receive friends' praise (Ball, 1981; Schwartz, 1981). High-achieving students are usually friends with classmates who encourage them to get good grades and not to misbehave in class. Low-achieving students are usually friends with classmates who express no interest in getting good grades and who often misbehave in class. Moreover, students shift over time toward their friends' attitudes and behavior. The shift can be attributed partly to the students' need for their friends' approval.

A second motive that partly accounts for the influence of friends is the desire of students to think and behave like their friends. Students normally choose best friends who have characteristics or talents that the students admire (Hallinan, 1983). This admiration motivates students to act as their friends do.

Kelman (1961) described the process leading to emulation of an ad-mired individual as identification. The concept of identification originat-ed in Freudian theory, where it had multiple meanings (Mischel, 1970). Identification was used to refer to actual imitation of another's behavior, to the mechanisms leading to imitation, to a motive to be like another, and to a belief that one has the same attributes as the other. Later, social learn-ing theorists argued that the core meanings of identification were the same as their principles of observational learning and imitation (Bandura, 1969). That is, people learn how and when to perform certain behaviors by observing other people.

Observational learning is different from Kelman's (1961) concept of identification, however. Social learning theorists assume that people imi-tate others' behavior mainly because they believe they will be rewarded for doing so (Bandura, 1977). By contrast, Kelman retained Freud's as-sumption that identification depends on a specific motive to be like the other person. It depends, therefore, on having a special relationship with the other person.

Kelman also argued that identification involves a continuing relation-ship between the person being influenced and the person who is the source of influence. One byproduct of this continuing relationship is that the behavior of the person being influenced changes whenever the other person's behavior changes. For example, when students are strongly identified with particular friends, they will change their own interests and activities whenever those of their friends change. When the friends express dislike for a particular teacher, the students will also form negative attitudes toward that teacher. If the friends later begin to like that teacher for some reason, the students will also develop greater liking for the teacher. By contrast, the principle of observational learning does not imply that students will track the variations in their friends' behavior so closely, because it does not assume such enduring links between models and observers.

Several experimental studies of observational learning from peers have been done (Hartup, 1983). Few studies, however, have focused on aspects of school adjustment or examined the influence of friends in particular. The effects of peer models on students' achievement and self-efficacy have been demonstrated (e.g., Schunk, Hanson, & Cox, 1987), but these studies did not use friends as models. In addition, friends' similarity in academic achievement and educational aspirations has often been attributed to modeling (e.g., Kandel & Andrews, 1987). However, the processes leading to friends' similarity have not been assessed directly.

Despite the absence of direct evidence, few researchers or educators would deny that students' identification with friends has some effect on their school adjustment. Students' desires to behave exactly like their friends may often be exaggerated, but students certainly pay attention to how their friends talk about school, behave in school, and achieve academically.

Moreover, the motive to identify with friends is theoretically significant because it falls within the category of intrinsic motivation. Students do as their friends do, not because their friends provide rewards for imitation, but because the friends have positive characteristics that the students want to have. Thus, this motive contrasts sharply with the notion that friends have influence because they punish students who try to resist their coercive pressure.

A third motive related to friends' influence is self-enhancement. Students partly judge their own competence by comparing their performance with that of their classmates. According to Veroff (1969), social comparison increases students' motivation to achieve and contributes to aggressive competition with classmates. Veroff proposed that students who are the winners in academic competition often receive approval from peers as well. This social approval further enhances their social comparison motivation.

Veroff's ideas are intriguing because they contrast sharply with the more recent speculations of Juvonen and Murdock (1993; see also Juvonen, this volume). Recall that these researchers assumed competition in academics is resented by classmates and reduces a student's popularity. These opposing viewpoints also exist when the question is focused on friends rather than all peers. As noted earlier, friendships are based on equality, which makes friends likely targets for social comparison (Berndt, 1986). Veroff's (1969) theory implies that these comparisons enhance students' efforts to achieve academically, to prove they are as good as, or better than, their friends. Juvonen and Weiner's (1993) ideas imply that these comparisons make students less eager to achieve academically, because their success might make their friends resentful.

Tesser's (1984) self-esteem maintenance model suggests a resolution to this controversy. He argues that students try to show their superiority to friends in areas most relevant to their self-esteem, while admitting their friends' superiority to them in less relevant areas. Thus, fifth and sixth graders who consider mathematics as very important also rate their performance in math more highly than that of their friends. Fifth and sixth graders who consider mathematics as relatively unimportant rate their friends' performance in math more highly than their own (Tesser, Campbell, and Smith, 1984).

However, students are not completely free to define domains of achievements as unimportant. For example, not all parents would accept their child's assertion that getting a "C" in math is unimportant. For this reason, students cannot always avoid direct comparisons with friends. In addition, they cannot always escape the academic competition that such comparisons provoke.

Ethnographic research suggests that friends' competition takes different forms, depending on a student's level of achievement. High-achieving students often compete with friends to get the best grades on tests (Ball, 1981; Schwartz, 1981). These students express the self-enhancement motive by trying to show their academic superiority to friends. Low-achieving students often compete with friends in misbehavior, trying to enhance their self-esteem by creating the greatest disruption in class or by challenging teachers' authority most directly (Ball, 1981; Schwartz, 1981). In short, the motive to distinguish oneself – as a scholar or as a scoundrel – can partly explain both students' own behavior and a route by which friends influence them.

The fourth motive that partly accounts for friends' influence is the need to be correct (Hoving et al., 1969), or validity-seeking (Chaiken et al.,

1989). This motive refers to a person's desire to hold correct beliefs and make reasonable decisions. Deutsch and Gerard (1955) suggested the distinction between this motive and the three previous ones when they contrasted processes of normative and informational influence.

Normative influence depends on a person's desire to conform to the positive expectations of others. Viewed narrowly, it is the same as the need for social approval. This category has been expanded to include all influence processes that involve a person's reactions to other people's opinions and behavior (Isenberg, 1986). This broad definition encompasses all three motives discussed earlier.

By contrast, informational influence depends on a person's acceptance of another person's arguments as evidence about reality (Deutsch & Gerard, 1955). In other words, the person focuses on the accuracy of those arguments rather than their source. This category has been expanded in more recent research to include all influence processes that involve a person's comprehension and evaluation of relevant arguments (Isenberg, 1986).

Many types of studies show that the need to be correct provides a partial explanation of friends' influence on children and adolescents. Its importance is perhaps most obvious in research on peer collaboration during problem solving (Damon & Phelps, 1989). Students often show improved performance on cognitive problems after working on them with a peer. This improvement is not due entirely to observational learning, that is, poorer students learning from better students. Often, two students who are working together both gain a better understanding of cognitive problems after listening to one another's arguments (Tudge, 1992).

Studies of peer collaboration can partly explain the influence of friends on one another's academic achievement (Epstein, 1983). This influence must depend partly on the friends' collaboration on class work or homework assignments. But informational influence goes beyond academic work itself. A need to be correct, or to hold valid opinions, also provides a partial explanation of friends' influence on attitudes about school.

In a recent study (Berndt, Laychak, & Park, 1990), junior high school students made decisions on hypothetical dilemmas that pitted doing school work against social activities or more free time. For example, on one dilemma students had to decide whether to go to a rock concert one evening or to stay home and study for an exam. After making decisions independently, students in one condition discussed the decisions with a close friend and tried to agree on them. In another condition, students discussed topics unrelated to school, such as where to go on a summer vacation.

After the discussions, the students again made decisions on the dilemmas independently. The independent decisions of friends who had discussed the dilemmas were more similar than those of friends who had not, showing that friends influenced one another's decisions. Students also shifted after the discussions toward the decisions that were accompanied by the most reasons during the discussions. These findings imply that during adolescence, friends' influence depends on information exchange and the motive to be correct, just as is true in adulthood (Chaiken et al., 1989; Isenberg, 1986).

Age changes in the influence of friends

Does the influence of friends' characteristics change with age? To answer this question, a few researchers asked students to read about hypothetical situations in which friends supposedly encouraged them to engage in specific behaviors (Berndt, 1979; Brown et al., 1986; Steinberg & Silverberg, 1986). Then students reported whether they would conform to the friends' suggestions. Most often, apparent conformity to friends increased between middle childhood and mid-adolescence, or around ninth grade. Conformity then decreased between mid-adolescence and late adolescence, or the end of high school. However, this developmental trend was not significant in all samples (Brown et al., 1986).

Other approaches to the estimation of friends' influence have also yielded mixed results. A few researchers have tried to assess the increase in friends' similarity that results from their influence on each other. In one study (Urberg, Cheng, & Shyu, 1991), friends seemed to influence eighth-graders' cigarette smoking more than that of eleventh graders. In another study (Epstein, 1983), friends' influence on school-related attitudes and on academic achievement seems to change little between fourth and twelfth grade.

Another way to explore the question of developmental changes would be to examine the strength of the various motives that underlie friends' influence. Unfortunately, this approach has not often been adopted. Researchers once assumed that students' need for social approval could be estimated from their conformity to peers on certain types of judgments. However, the available data on peer conformity are difficult to interpret (Hartup, 1983). Our second motive, to identify with friends or want to be like them, has rarely been examined directly. Furthermore, few researchers have examined age changes in the related process of observational learning from peers. Therefore, it is impossible to say whether this motive changes in strength as children grow older.

The self-enhancement motive may become more important during middle childhood. A few studies suggest that children's self-evaluations are more strongly affected by social comparisons with peers with increasing age (e.g., Ruble, Boggiano, Feldman, & Loebl, 1980). This age trend is consistent with evidence that self-esteem decreases during middle childhood, as children better appreciate how their performance in various domains compares with that of their peers (Marsh, 1989). Veroff (1969) suggested that this trend is partly reversed in early adolescence, as social comparison is integrated with autonomous motives for achievement. Unfortunately, little research has been done on this hypothesis.

Finally, some data suggest that group discussions are more rational, or based more on informational influence, as children move into adolescence (Berndt, McCartney, Caparulo, & Moore, 1983-1984; Smith, 1973). Adolescents give more reasons for their opinions than children; they also resolve conflicts during discussions more effectively.

More research on the age changes in motives linked to friends' influence would be valuable. Nevertheless, it is important to recognize that friends can have a strong influence on certain aspects of school adjustment throughout the school years. Even in the elementary grades, students' behavior is affected by the disruptive behavior of their friends (Schwartz, 1981). Near the end of high school, students' educational aspirations are affected by their friends' aspirations (Davies & Kandel, 1981). More research is needed on how much friends affect each aspect of school adjustment during each phase of schooling.

Motives related to the effects of friendship quality

To understand the effects of friendship quality on students' adjustment, the construct of friendship quality must first be defined. In this section, we provide a definition that links features of friendship to their associated motives. Then we review research that indicates the effects of friendships on school adjustment. Next, we consider the limited research on developmental changes in the effects of friendships.

High-quality friendships: Features and motives

Piaget (1932/1965) and Sullivan (1953) assumed that friendships are high in quality when they are intimate, egalitarian, and based on mutual respect. To supplement these definitions, other writers have suggested that high-quality friendships are high in prosocial behavior (sharing and helping), trust, loyalty, affection, companionship, and caring (Berndt & Perry,

1986; Bukowski, Hoza, & Boivin, 1994; Furman & Buhrmester, 1992; Parker & Asher, 1993).

Few writers have explicitly discussed the motives associated with high-quality friendships. However, Sullivan's analysis of friendship included a few suggestions about these motives. He referred to a close friend as a *chum*, and suggested that children who have a chum say to themselves, "What should I do to contribute to the happiness or to support the prestige and feeling of worth-whileness of my chum?" (p. 245). That is, their motive is to make the friend happy and boost the friend's self-esteem.

As a complement to this apparently altruistic motive, Sullivan suggested that high-quality friendships fulfill a need for interpersonal intimacy. During intimate conversations, friends share their concerns and are assured that they are respected by peers whom they also respect. Sullivan implied, however, that high-quality friendships do not involve a combination of altruistic and self-interested motives. The goal of friends' interaction is collaboration, or "the pursuit of increasingly identical – that is, more and more nearly mutual – satisfactions" (p. 246).

When friends aim for mutually satisfying interactions, they reject the distinction between the goals of self and of friend. In this sense, the primary motive of persons involved in high-quality friendships is qualitatively different from the individualistic motives (e.g., the need for approval) considered earlier (see Table 11.1). In high-quality friendships, these individualistic motives are replaced by motives for both partners in the relationship. They focus not on what "I" want, but what "we" want (Hartup, 1992).

Of course, actual friendships fall short of the complete mutuality described by Sullivan. Aristotle (Ostwald, 1962) said that some people want friends who increase their own pleasure. Other people want friends who are useful to them, who will do favors for them and help them make valuable contacts with other people. Aristotle believed that perfect friendships, which have the kind of intimacy and mutuality described by Sullivan, are extremely rare.

Nevertheless, Aristotle assumed that most close friendships have some features of a perfect friendship. Researchers who assess the positive features of students' friendships are exploring how well these friendships match the ideal in classical and modern writings. That is, they are examining the degree to which friends adopt relationship motives, thinking not of "me" and "you" but of "us."

Friendships also have negative features. Earlier, we mentioned the forces that lead to competition between friends (Tesser, 1984). Students often compare their performance in academic and other activities to that of their friends. For example, friends often compare their grades on tests in school and take the results as an indicator of who is the smartest. Because their self-esteem is at stake, friends sometimes compete more intensely with one another in such situations than nonfriends do (Berndt, 1986; Berndt, Hawkins, & Hoyle, 1986).

Competition between friends may not only affect each friend's behavior, as discussed earlier. This competition may also affect the quality of their friendship. Recall that Piaget (1932/1965) assumed peer relationships are based on equality. Friends, especially, view themselves as equal in all important respects (Berndt, 1986; Youniss & Smollar, 1985). But when students are high in competitive motivation, they may reject this view and try to prove their superiority to friends. Then the quality of their friendships is likely to suffer.

Other types of conflicts between friends arise for various reasons (Laursen, 1993). The root of many conflicts may be students' emphasis on individualistic goals (Asher & Renshaw, 1981; Putallaz & Sheppard, 1990). Stated informally, some students would rather get what they want and lose a friend than vice versa. Measures of negative friendship features reflect the degree to which friends favor competitive and individualistic goals over the goal of mutually satisfying outcomes.

Negative interactions between friends are less common in friendships with many positive features, but the correlation is weak. Especially as children move into adolescence, their reports about the positive and negative features of their friendships become more independent (Berndt & Keefe, in press; Berndt & Perry, 1986). Therefore, the quality of a friendship should be judged from separate assessments of its positive and negative features. The effects of the two aspects of friendship quality on school adjustment should also be judged separately.

Effects of friendship quality on school adjustment

Children and adolescents whose friendships have more positive features are higher in self-esteem and prosocial behavior, are more popular with peers, and less often suffer from emotional problems (Berndt & Savin-Williams, 1993; Hartup, 1992). They also have more positive attitudes toward school, are better behaved, and are higher in academic achievement than other students (Berndt & Keefe, in press; Dubow et al., 1991; Kurdek & Sinclair, 1988). In addition, students whose friendships have more negative features report less classroom involvement and more disruptive behavior. By contrast, the number of best friends that students report usually is only weakly correlated with their social and school adjustment (Savin-Williams & Berndt, 1990). In research with adults, measures of number of friendships are usually less strongly related to indicators of psychological health than are measures of the support those relationships provide (Sarason, Sarason, & Pierce, 1990). In sum, relationship quality matters more than quantity.

Correlations between friendship features and school adjustment do not prove that friendship quality affects school adjustment. Students' adjustment to school could instead affect the quality of the friendships they can form. To distinguish between these alternatives, a few researchers have examined the relations of friendship quality to the changes over time in students' adjustment. In one recent study (DuBois, Felner, Brand, Adan, & Evans, 1992), a measure of support from friends was not related to the changes over two years in adolescents' grades. In a second study (Dubow et al., 1991), friends' support was not related to the changes over two years in younger students' behavioral and academic adjustment.

The two studies might have yielded null results because the interval between assessments was too long. Best friendships among children and adolescents usually last for several months, but not for years (Hallinan, 1978/1979). With an interval of two years, researchers may have been trying to assess effects of friendships that ended months before.

Another possible explanation for the null results is that the measures of friends' support were too general. In one study (Dubow et al., 1991), the items referred to support from classmates as well as friends. In the other study (DuBois et al., 1992), the items referred to friends but not specifically to best friends. Both measures included items about positive features but not negative ones.

Recently, we completed a longitudinal study that was less subject to these problems (Berndt & Keefe, in press). In the fall of a school year, junior-high-school students described the positive and negative features of their three best friendships. The students also reported their involvement in classroom activities and their disruptive behavior at school. Teachers rated the students on their involvement and disruptive behavior, and reported their report-card grades. These assessments were repeated in the following spring, about six months later. The data were analyzed in a hierarchical regression analysis that took into account the continuity in school adjustment. Therefore, the results can be interpreted as evidence regarding the effects of friendship quality on school adjustment.

Students' reports on the positive features of their very best (or closest) friendship were related to the changes during their year in their self-re-

Table 11.2. *Predicting students' adjustment from the features of their friendships*

	Very best friend			Multiple friends		
	R^2	R^2 change	Beta	R^2	R^2 change	Beta
Time 2 involvement (self-reported)						
Step 1: Time 1 involvement	.384	.384	.62***	.385	.385	.62***
Step 2: Time 1 Friendship Features						
Positive features	.393	.009	.09*	.390	.005	.08
Negative features	.388	.004	−.06	.389	.004	−.06
Time 2 disruption (self-reported)						
Step 1: Time 1 disruption	.389	.389	.62***	.389	.389	.62***
Step 2: Time 1 Friendship Features						
Positive features	.391	.002	−.04	.389	.000	−.01
Negative features	.407	.018	.13**	.410	.021	.15**

For each Time 2 measure of adjustment, the values listed in Step 2 are from two separate analyses, one including only the variable for positive features and the other including only the variable for negative features. For all analyses, Ns = 293 – 296.
*$p < .05$. **$p < .01$. ***$p < .001$.

ported involvement (Table 11.2). These data imply that having a very best friendship with many positive features increased students' involvement. A plausible explanation for this finding is that a close friendship high in quality strengthens motives to seek mutually satisfying interactions with the best friend and other people. Students with such friendships may be more willing to join classmates in academic activities and more eager to participate in class discussions. To test this hypothesis, researchers might assess the school-related motives of students with friendships varying in quality. The motives and goals identified by Wentzel (1989, 1991b) and other researchers (Asher & Renshaw, 1981; Nicholls, Patashnick, & Nolen, 1985) would be good candidates for this assessment.

Students' reports on the negative features of both their very best friendships and the average of their three best friendships were related to the changes during the year in their self-reported disruption. These data imply that having friendships high in conflicts and rivalry increased students' disruptive behavior. Negative interactions with friends apparently spilled over to affect students' behavior toward other classmates and teachers. Sullivan (1953) suggested that some children compete so often with peers that competitive motivation becomes a prominent part of their personality. Apparently, students in more competitive friendships acquire a habit of competing with others in many activities. These students probably look for chances to "put down" other classmates; they probably respond forcefully to actions by others that seemed aimed at putting them down. Similarly, students who have many conflicts with friends may try harder to defend their perceived rights than to adapt to others. These students may not seek mutually satisfying resolutions to conflicts because their friends had rarely done so with them.

The influence of friendship quality on school adjustment should not be exaggerated. Table 11.2 shows that the measures of friendship features accounted for only a small (but significant) amount of the variance in students' involvement and disruption. Moreover, like previous researchers, we did not find a significant effect of friendship quality on students' grades. Even so, evidence that friendship quality is a predictor of changes in some aspects of school adjustment is both theoretically and practically significant.

Age changes in the effects of friendship quality

As one aspect of positive friendship quality, intimacy first becomes an important feature of friendships in early adolescence (Berndt & Savin-Williams, 1993; Hartup, 1992). The intimacy of friendships increases further during adolescence, as time spent with friends increases (Csikszentmihalyi & Larson, 1984; Sharabany, Gershoni, & Hofman, 1981). Moreover, as adolescents approach adulthood, their friendships develop more positive features and become more like the ideal friendships of classical literature (Furman & Buhrmester, 1992).

Less information is available on the negative features of friendships. On structured tasks, adolescents sometimes compete less intensely with friends than do elementary-school children (Berndt et al., 1986). Conflicts with friends change little in frequency during the elementary and middle-school years, but they may decrease during the senior-high years (Berndt & Perry, 1986; Furman & Buhrmester, 1992; Laursen & Collins, 1994).

Changes in friendship features might be accompanied by changes in the effects of friendship. As adolescents develop friendships higher in quality, and friends start to interact more often, variations in friendship quality could have a greater influence on their behavior and development. Thus far, only one study has tested this hypothesis.

Buhrmester (1990) asked early adolescents (10- to 13-year-olds) and middle adolescents (14- to 16-year-olds) about the intimacy of one of their closest friendships. The adolescents also reported on their sociability, hostility, and other aspects of their socioemotional adjustment. The correlations of intimacy with socioemotional adjustment were stronger in middle adolescence than in early adolescence. Although other interpretations are possible, these findings are consistent with the hypothesis that friendship quality has stronger effects on students' psychological adjustment as they grow older. Furthermore, both empirical research and everyday observations show that friendships become more important *to* students as they move through adolescence. Thus it is reasonable to assume that friendship quality also becomes more important *for* students' adjustment.

Implications of friends' influence for educational practice

Many teachers face the practical issue of whether to intervene in the friendships of students who are a bad influence on each other. Should the friends be moved to different parts of the classroom? If their new locations do not end their misbehavior, should one of them be transferred to another class? For a full answer to these questions, we need again to consider both pathways of friends' influence.

Changing the influence of friends' characteristics

Friends certainly can have a negative influence on one another (Berndt & Keefe, in press; Epstein, 1983; Kandel, 1978). For example, friends can discourage students' involvement in class activities. These negative influences can be reduced by separating students from their friends. Ball (1981) observed classrooms for early adolescents before and after academic tracking was eliminated from a school. When tracking was the norm, low-achieving students typically attended classes and formed friendships with other low-achieving students. In these classes, students and their friends usually had negative attitudes toward school. The classes were so disruptive that teachers found them extremely unpleasant.

After tracking was eliminated, many disruptive and low-achieving students found themselves in classrooms with other students average or high in achievement. The other students typically had positive attitudes toward school, and they did not go along with the low achievers' disruptive behavior. Moreover, the disruptive students did not have enough friends in the new classrooms to form cohesive groups.

Ball's observations suggest that weakening friendships among disruptive students by eliminating tracking can reduce negative influences of friends on students' behavior. Because his study was not an experiment, however, other explanations for the results are possible. For example, the changes in students' behavior might be attributed to other positive effects of eliminating tracking (see Oakes, 1985), rather than a decrease in the negative effects of disruptive friends. The alternative explanations are not especially relevant to our chapter, but the general issue of teachers' interference with students' friendships is relevant.

What happens to disruptive students when teachers' intervention weakens their friendships? These students may find it hard to make new friends, because students who misbehave in class are usually unpopular with peers (Coie, 1990; Wentzel, 1991a). If the students have difficulty making new friends, they may also have difficulty satisfying their need for social approval. Without friends to give them praise and encouragement, these students are likely to drop out of school, officially or unofficially (Parker & Asher, 1987).

Instead of trying to break up friendships among students who are poorly adjusted to school, teachers might try to correct students' misperceptions about their friends' attitudes and behavior. Research on alcohol and drug abuse has shown that adolescents often assume their friends have more positive attitudes toward the use of alcohol and other drugs than they actually do (Cook, Anson, & Walchli, 1993). Substance-abuse interventions are effective partly because they reduce these misperceptions. In other words, they give adolescents accurate information about how their friends think and act. By doing so, they reduce adolescents' motivation to seek social approval or self-enhancement by using drugs themselves.

Similar misperceptions may exist in the realm of school adjustment. Students may believe that their friends like school less and approve of misbehavior more than is actually true. If teachers asked all students to report their attitudes toward school, both they and their students might discover that pro-school attitudes are widely shared. Doing such a survey and giving students the results could reduce students' misperceptions that their friends admire classmates who are poorly adjusted to school. Reducing these misperceptions could, in turn, enhance the positive effects of friends on school adjustment.

Changing friendship features

When faced with friends who are a bad influence on one another, teachers might also consider the quality of these friendships. As noted earlier, students who are poorly adjusted to school often have friendships that are low in quality (Berndt & Keefe, in press; Dubow et al., 1991). Instead of trying to end these friendships or, conversely, taking a completely hands-off attitude toward them, teachers might try to improve them and so improve students' adjustment to school.

To improve students' friendships, teachers could use cooperative-learning techniques for academic instruction (Cohen, 1994; Furman & Gavin,

1989). Placing students in small groups and asking them to work together on academic tasks has been viewed mainly as a means of raising students' achievement (Slavin, 1983). But cooperative-learning programs also enhance prosocial behavior and tolerance of other people while reducing competition between classmates (Furman & Gavin, 1989).

Cooperative-learning programs are not foolproof. Teachers need to prepare students carefully and monitor interactions among the students in a group. Otherwise, students with low status in the classroom may continue to be treated negatively in their small group (Cohen, 1994). Yet with appropriate monitoring, the use of cooperative learning may not only improve classroom climate but also contribute to the formation of high-quality friendships (Hansell & Slavin, 1981).

Programs for training social skills might also affect friendship quality (Coie & Koeppl, 1990; Mize & Ladd, 1990). Students can be trained to ask polite questions, to make suggestions, and to offer support to their classmates. In addition, students can be trained to avoid unnecessary conflicts with peers and to resolve conflicts effectively when they arise. One strategy for training emphasizes anger control, or avoiding impulsive action when upset by a classmate's behavior. Another strategy emphasizes social problem solving, or thinking about ways to resolve conflicts without using aggression (Lochman, 1985). Because conflicts with friends spill over to affect students' behavior toward other people (Berndt & Keefe, in press), training in conflict resolution could reduce behavior problems in the classroom.

One limitation in most social-skills training programs is a lack of emphasis on students' motivation. The programs teach students how to behave in social situations, but not why they should behave that way. Some students, however, may enjoy competing more than compromising, or be more motivated to get things they want than to develop positive relationships with peers (Putallaz & Sheppard, 1990). These students need to be persuaded that improving their friendships is worth the effort.

Trying to increase students' motivation to develop high-quality friendships could be seen as risky. As students' interest in having good friendships increases, their interest in strictly academic aspects of school might be expected to decrease. Low-achieving students typically endorse the goals of making friends and having fun at school more than do students with high grades (Wentzel, 1989). At first glance, intervening to improve students' friendships might be thought to enhance this contrast. The intervention might encourage poorly adjusted students to work even less on their school work than on their social life.

This concern reflects a misunderstanding of the proposed intervention.

It is designed not to increase the time students spend with friends but to improve the quality of their friendships. Low-achieving students already interact frequently with friends (Csikszentmihalyi & Larson, 1984). The problem is that their friendships are often low in positive features and high in negative features. Giving these students the motivation to be more supportive to friends and to have more harmonious interactions with friends is not likely to reduce their school adjustment. On the contrary, the change in motivation should enhance students' social and academic competence.

Unanswered questions and future directions

Currently, evidence on the motives underlying friends' influence is largely indirect. Few researchers have tried to assess the motives that account for the influence of friends' characteristics. Even fewer have tried to examine the motives that explain how and why friendship quality affects school adjustment.

This state of affairs is problematic. Without direct assessments of motives, it is difficult to propose convincing alternatives to the idea that students usually conform to friends' pressure because of fear of punishment. Without direct assessments of motives, it is difficult to explain why friendship quality affects some aspects of school adjustment more than others.

Two methods of assessing motives might be used in future research. The first is an experimental approach. For many years, social psychologists have used experimental manipulations to probe the motives underlying people's behavior. For example, many experiments have been done to see whether group discussions affect people's decisions because people are motivated to seek social approval or because they want to make correct decisions (Isenberg, 1986). Interest in these two types of motives remains strong within social psychology (e.g., Wood, Lundgren, Ouellette, Busceme, & Blackstone, 1994). Adapting the experimental manipulations used in this research to study friends' influence on students' adjustment to school could be very productive.

The second method of assessing students' motives is to ask them directly. As mentioned earlier, this method has been used to examine motives or goals associated with classroom behavior and academic achievement (Nicholls et al., 1985; Wentzel, 1989, 1991a, b). One limitation of the method is that students may not be aware of the motives that govern their behavior. Some students may also be unwilling to report their motives to a researcher. Nevertheless, these limitations should not be overestimated. Previous studies have shown that valuable information can be obtained with direct questions about motivation. Extensions of the research to explore the motives underlying friends' influence should also be rewarding.

Another direction for future research would be a thorough analysis and investigation of relationship motives. Sullivan's (1953) proposals about friends' collaboration in pursuit of mutually satisfying outcomes were novel in 1953, and they are still unusual. Few theories of motivation take account of people's social relationships; even fewer include motives that apply to partners in a relationship as a unit (see Weiner, 1992). Theories of motivation generally deal with only two classes of motives, individualistic (or self-centered) and altruistic (or other-centered).

The individualistic motives that affect friendship quality have sometimes been examined systematically. Students have been asked to do tasks with a partner and then to say whether they tried to compete with the partner, to get many rewards for themselves, or to pursue other goals (see Berndt et al., 1986). Other researchers have constructed tasks that allow the assessment of students' motives from their actual behavior rather than from their self-reports (e.g., Knight, Dubro, & Chao, 1985). Extensions of this work to probe the motives of students with friendships high in negative features would be worthwhile.

Motives associated with positive features of friendship, with a concern for what "we" need instead of what "I" need, have so far not been examined directly. We have argued that these relationship motives are stronger when friendships are more intimate, egalitarian, and have other positive features. This argument should be evaluated more carefully.

One direction for research would be to explore the parallel between relationship motives and collectivist values. Many researchers have assumed that Western cultures emphasize individualistic values like personal freedom, whereas collectivist cultures emphasize responsibility to the other members of an ingroup such as the family (Triandis, 1989; 1990). People in collectivist cultures are assumed not to distinguish between their personal goals and the goals of their small group. They are assumed to view the success of everyone in their ingroup as their greatest goal. In this sense, they are like close friends who seek not their own satisfaction but mutually satisfying outcomes.

To document the contrast between individualistic and collectivist cultures, researchers have often used or adapted Rokeach's (1973) survey of values. Researchers have also devised items for assessing attitudes consistent with these two orientations (see Triandis, 1990). This research could provide not only some specific ideas but also a general approach to the study of relationship motives. This approach could be doubly rewarding because variations in friendships and cultural variations could be explored simultaneously (cf. Miller, Bersoff, & Harwood, 1990).

Finally, throughout this chapter we have emphasized the distinction between the two pathways of friends' influence. This distinction may be absolute. That is, the influence of friends' characteristics may be entirely independent of the effects of friendship features. Consider, for example, students who have high-quality friendships with peers who have negative attitudes toward school. Our argument to this point is that these students will be positively affected by the quality of their friendships and negatively affected by their friends' attitudes toward school. The net effect will depend on the strength of the two separate effects.

An alternative hypothesis is that the quality of students' friendships modifies the influence of friends' characteristics. When students trust and admire their friends, the friends' characteristics should have an especially powerful influence on the students' adjustment (Hallinan, 1983). Cauce and Srebnik (1989) applied this general hypothesis to the case of school adjustment. They argued that students' adjustment to school may worsen greatly if they have highly supportive friendships with peers who are poorly adjusted to school.

Cauce and Srebnik (1989) cited only correlational data in support of their hypothesis. Findings consistent with the hypothesis were also obtained in one experimental study (Berndt et al., 1990). As mentioned earlier, this study included pairs of friends who discussed dilemmas concerning school work. The similarity of friends' decisions increased after the discussions, showing that they influenced one another's decisions. Friends' similarity increased most when their interactions were judged by observers as most cooperative and least aggressive. Friends' similarity increased least when they reported that their friendships were high in conflicts and rivalry. These results imply that friends were more influenced by their discussions when their friendships were high in positive features and low in negative features.

This experiment cannot be taken as conclusive because the findings are inconsistent with those from other studies. Hundreds of studies have suggested that supportive social relationships almost invariably have positive effects on psychological adjustment and even on physical health (Sarason et al. 1990). Moreover, data from our longitudinal study (Berndt & Keefe, in press) did not support the hypothesis that high friendship quality can magnify the negative influence of poorly adjusted friends. We looked for interactions between the effects of friends' characteristics and of friendship features. That is, we checked to see whether the effects of friends' characteristics varied with the quality of students' friendships, but we found no interactions of this type.

The available data are too limited to answer questions about the relations between the two influence pathways. More attention to the contrasting hypotheses is needed, because they are linked to critical assumptions in important theories of social influence. The contrasting hypotheses also have important practical implications. Their systematic comparison should be a central focus of future research.

Conclusions

One message of the chapter is that friends' influence on students' adjustment to school is a more complex phenomenon than most popular and scholarly writers have implied. Interactions with friends affect students' attitudes toward school, behavior in class, and academic achievement through two distinct pathways. The effects of influence via each pathway may be either to increase or to decrease students' adjustment to school. Most importantly, influence via each pathway depends on multiple motives.

The influence of friends' characteristics has been emphasized by popular writers who express concern about the negative effects of friends' pressure on students' behavior. Our review of empirical research has shown that coercive pressure is rarely applied in friendship groups. Students are affected by their friends' characteristics, but fear of punishment for nonconformity to friends' pressure is not the primary motive underlying this influence. More important are students' need for social approval, their identification with friends, a motive for self-enhancement, and the need to be correct or make reasonable decisions. Evidence for these four motives is indirect, but their importance cannot be questioned.

The second pathway of influence, through the quality of students' friendships, is linked to theories of social and personality development. The quality of a friendship is indicated by its intimacy, by the friends' prosocial behavior toward each other, and by the frequency of other types of positive interactions. Negative interactions also occur between friends, and friendship quality is lower when conflicts and rivalry are frequent and intense. Ideally, interactions between friends are governed by a motive to seek mutually satisfying outcomes. That is, friends think about what "we" want, not what "I" want. In real life, friends often have motives to get their own way or to compete with each other. Students develop more positive attitudes toward school when their friendships are higher in quality. Students become more disruptive at school when their friendships are lower in quality. The connections of these effects to differences in motives have not been documented precisely, and more research on these connections is needed.

Information about the two influence pathways and their associated motives has clear implications for educational practice. One set of issues concerns friends who negatively influence one another's adjustment to school. Breaking up these friendships, for example, by transferring the students to different classes, can reduce this problem, but this solution is not ideal. A better alternative is making all students more aware of their classmates' attitudes toward school and beliefs about acceptable behavior. In addition, teachers can try to improve the quality of students' friendships by using cooperative learning or social skills training.

Our recommendations for teachers are offered tentatively, because their basis in research is limited. Our motivational analysis derives more from theories of social influence than from specific studies. Systematic exploration of the motives underlying friends' influence is needed. Research on possible links between the two influence pathways is also needed. Future research should not only answer basic questions about how friends influence one another during childhood and adolescence. This research should also clarify how this influence can be channeled to enhance students' adjustment to school.

References

Ansley, L., & McCleary, K. (1992, August 21–23). Do the right thing. *USA Weekend*, 4–7.

Aristotle (1962). *Nicomachean ethics* (M. Ostwald, trans.). New York: Bobbs-Merrill, 1962.

Asher, S. R., & Renshaw, P. D. (1981). Children without friends: Social knowledge and social skill training. In S. R. Asher & J. M. Gottman (Eds.), *The development of children's friendships* (pp. 273–296). Cambridge, England: Cambridge University Press.

Ball, S. J. (1981). *Beachside comprehensive*. Cambridge, England: Cambridge Press.

Bandura, A. (1969). Social learning theory of identificatory processes. In D. A. Goslin (Ed.), *Handbook of socialization theory and research* (pp. 213–262). Chicago: Rand-McNally.

Bandura, A. (1977). *Social learning theory*. Englewood Cliffs, NJ: Prentice Hall.

Bandura, A., & Walters, R. (1963). *Social learning and personality development.* New York: Holt, Rinehart and Winston.

Berndt, T. J. (1979). Developmental changes in conformity to peers and parents. *Developmental Psychology, 15,* 608–616.

Berndt, T. J. (1986). Sharing between friends: Contexts and consequences. In E. C. Mueller and C. Cooper (Eds.), *Process and outcome in peer relationships* (pp. 129–160). New York: Academic.

Berndt, T. J. (1992). Friendship and friends' influence in adolescence. *Current Directions in Psychological Science, 1,* 156–159.

Berndt. T. J., Hawkins, J. A., & Hoyle, S. G. (1986). Changes in friendship during a school year: Effects on children's and adolescents' impressions of friendship and sharing with friends. *Child Development, 57,* 1284–1297.

Berndt, T. J. & Keefe, K. (1995). Friends' influence on adolescents' adjustment to school. *Child Development, 66,* 1312–1329.

Berndt, T. J., & Laychak, A. E., & Park, K. (1990). Friends' influence on adolescents' academic achievement motivation: An experimental study. *Journal of Educational Psychology, 82,* 664–670.

Berndt, T. J., McCartney, K. A., Caparulo, B. K., & Moore, A. M. (1983-1984). The effects of group discussions on children's moral decisions. *Social Cognition, 2,* 343–360.

Berndt, T. J., & Miller, K. A. (1990). Expectancies, values, and achievement in junior high school. *Journal of Educational Psychology, 82,* 319–326.

Berndt, T. J., Miller, K. A., & Park, K. (1989). Adolescents' perceptions of friends' and parents' influence on aspects of school adjustment. *Journal of Early Adolescence, 9,* 419–435.

Berndt, T. J. & Perry, T. B. (1986). Children's perceptions of friendships as supportive relationships. *Developmental Psychology, 22,* 640–648.

Berndt, T. J., & Savin-Williams, R. C. (1993). Variations in friendships and peer-group relationships in adolescence. In P. Tolan & B. Cohler (Eds.), *Handbook of clinical research and practice with adolescents* (pp. 203–219). New York: Wiley.

Bishop, J. H. (1989). Why the apathy in American high schools? *Educational researcher, 18*(1), 6–10.

Brown, B. B., Clasen, D. R., & Eicher, S. A. (1986). Perceptions of peer pressure, peer conformity dispositions, and self-reported behavior among adolescents. *Developmental Psychology, 22,* 521–530.

Buhrmester, D. (1990). Intimacy of friendship, interpersonal competence, and adjustment during preadolescence and adolescence. *Child Development, 61,* 1101–1111.

Buhrmester, D., & Furman, W. (1986). The changing functions of friends in childhood: A neo-Sullivanian perspective. In V. J. Derlega & B. A. Winstead (Eds.), *Friendship and social interaction* (pp. 41–62). New York: Springer-Verlag.

Bukowski, W. M., Hoza, B., & Boivin, M. (1994). Measuring friendship quality during pre- and early adolescence: The development and psychometric properties of the Friendship Qualities Scale. *Journal of Social and Personal Relationships, 11*, 471–484.

Cauce, A. M., Srebnik, D. S. (1989). Peer networks and social support: A focus for preventive effects with youth. In L. A. Bond & B. E. Compas (Eds.), *Primary prevention and promotion in the schools* (pp. 235–254). Newbury Park, CA: Sage.

Chaiken, S., Liberman, A., & Eagly, A. H. (1989). Heuristic and systematic processing within and beyond the persuasion context. In J. S. Uleman & J. A. Bargh (Eds.), *Unintended thought* (pp. 212–252). New York: Guilford.

Cohen, E. G. (1994). Restructuring the classroom: Conditions for productive small groups. *Review of Educational Research, 64*, 1–35.

Coie, J. (1990). Toward a theory of peer rejection. In S. R. Asher and J. D. Coie (Eds.), *Peer rejection in childhood* (pp. 365–402). Cambridge, England: Cambridge University Press.

Coie, J. D., & Koeppl, G. K. (1990). Adapting intervention to the problems of aggressive and disruptive rejected children. In S. R. Asher and J. D. Coie (Eds.), *Peer rejection in childhood* (pp. 309–337). Cambridge, England: Cambridge University Press.

Coleman, J. S. (1961). *The adolescent society*. New York: Free Press.

Cook, T. D., Anson, A. R., & Walchli, S. B. (1993). From causal description to causal explanation: Improving three already good evaluations of adolescent health program. In S. G. Millstein, A. C. Petersen, & E. O. Nightingale (Eds.), *Promoting the health of adolescents* (pp. 339–374). New York: Oxford University Press.

Crandall, V. J., Katkovsky, W., & Preston, A. (1960). A conceptual formulation for some research on children's achievement development. *Child Development, 31*, 787–797.

Csikszentmihalyi, M., & Larson, R. (1984). *Being adolescent*. New York: Basic Books.

Damon, W., & Phelps, E. (1989). Strategic uses of peer learning in children's education. In T. J. Berndt & G. W. Ladd (Eds.), *Peer relationships in child development* (pp. 135–157). New York: Wiley.

Davies, M., & Kandel, D. B. (1981). Parental and peer influences on adolescents' educational plans: Some further evidence. *American Journal of Sociology, 87*, 363–387.

Deutsch, M., & Gerard, H. B. (1955). A study of normative and informational social influences upon individual judgment. *Journal of Abnormal and Social Psychology, 51*, 629–636.

Downs, W. R. (1987). A panel study of normative structure, adolescent alcohol use, and peer alcohol use. *Journal of Studies on Alcohol, 48*, 167–175.

DuBois, D. L., Felner, R. D., Brand, S., Adan, A. M., & Evans, E. G. (1992). A prospective study of life stress, social support, and adaptation in early adolescence. *Child Development, 63*, 542–557.

Dubow, E. G., Tisak, J., Causey, D., Hryshko, A., & Reid, G. (1991). A two-year longitudinal study of stressful life events, social support, and social problem-solving skills: Contributions to children's behavioral and academic adjustment. *Child Development, 62,* 583–599.

Epstein, J. L. (1983). The influence of friends on achievement and affective outcomes. In J. L. Epstein & N. Karweit (Eds.), *Friends in school: Patterns of selection and influence in secondary schools* (pp. 177–200). New York: Academic Press.

Furman, W., & Buhrmester, D. (1992). Age and sex differences in perceptions of networks of personal relationships. *Child Development, 63,* 103–115.

Furman, W., & Gavin, L. A. (1989). Peers' influence and adjustment and development: A view from the intervention literature. In T. J. Berndt & G. W. Ladd (Eds.), *Peer relationships in child development* (pp. 319–340). New York: Wiley.

Hallinan, M. T. (1978/1979). The process of friendship formation. *Social Networks, 1,* 193–210.

Hallinan, M. T. (1983). Commentary: New directions for research on peer influence. In J. L. Epstein & N. Karweit (Eds.), *Friends in school: Patterns of selection and influence in secondary schools* (pp. 219–231). New York: Academic Press.

Hansell, S., & Slavin, R. E. (1981). Cooperative learning and the structure of interracial friendships. *Sociology of Education, 54,* 98–106.

Hartup, W. W. (1983). Peer relations. In P. H. Mussen (Series Ed.), E. M. Hetherington (Vol. Ed.), *Handbook of child psychology. Vol. 4. Socialization, personality, and social development* (pp. 103–196). New York: Wiley.

Hartup, W. W. (1992). Friendships and their developmental significance. In H. McGurk (Ed.), *Contemporary issues in childhood social development.* Hove, England: Erlbaum.

Hoving, K. L., Hamm, N., & Galvin, P. (1969). Social influence as a function of stimulus ambiguity at three age levels. *Developmental Psychology, 1,* 631–636.

Isenberg, D. J. (1986). Group polarization: A critical review and meta-analysis. *Journal of Personality and Social Psychology, 50,* 1141–1151.

Juvonen, J., & Murdock, T. B. (1993). How to promote social approval: Effects of audience and achievement outcome on publicly communicated attributions. *Journal of Educational Psychology, 85,* 365–376.

Juvonen, J., & Weiner, B. (1993). An attributional analysis of students' interactions: The social consequences of perceived responsibility. *Educational Psychology Review, 5,* 325–345.

Kandel, D. B. (1978). Homophily, selection, and socialization in adolescent friendships. *American Journal of Sociology, 84,* 427–436.

Kandel, D. B., & Andrews, K. (1987). Processes of adolescent socialization by parents and peers. *International Journal of the Addictions, 22,* 319–342.

Keefe, K. (1994). Perceptions of normative social pressure and attitudes toward alcohol use: Changes during adolescence. *Journal of Studies on Alcohol*, *55*, 46–54.

Kelman, H. C. (1961). Processes of opinion change. *Public Opinion Quarterly*, *25*, 57–78.

Knight, G. P., Dubro, A. F., & Chao, C.-C. (1985). Information processing and the development of cooperative, competitive, and individualistic social values. *Developmental Psychology*, *21*, 37–45.

Kurdek, L. A., & Sinclair, R. J. (1988). Adjustment of young adolescents in two-parent nuclear, stepfather, and mother-custody families. *Journal of Consulting and Clinical Psychology*, *56*, 91–96.

Laursen, B. (1993). Conflict management among close peers. In B. Laursen (Ed.), *Close friendships in adolescence* (pp. 39–54). San Francisco, CA: Jossey-Bass.

Laursen, B., & Collins, W. A. (1994). Interpersonal conflict during adolescence. *Psychological Bulletin*, *115*, 197–209.

Lochman, J. E. (1985). Effects of different treatment lengths in cognitive behavioral interventions with aggressive boys. *Child Psychiatry and Human Development*, *16*, 45–56.

Maccoby, E. E., & Martin, J. A. (1983). Socialization in the context of the family: Parent-child interaction. In E. M. Hetherington (Ed.), *Socialization, personality, and social development. Vol. 4. Handbook of child psychology* (pp. 1–101). New York: Wiley.

Marsh, H. W. (1989). Age and sex effects in multiple dimensions of self-concept: Preadolescence to early adulthood. *Journal of Educational Psychology*, *81*, 417–430.

Miller, J. G., Bersoff, D. M., & Harwood, R. L. (1990). Perceptions of social responsibilities in India and in the United States: Moral imperatives or personal decisions? *Journal of Personality and Social Psychology*, *58*, 33–47.

Mischel, W. (1970). Sex typing and socialization. In P. H. Mussen (Ed.), *Carmichael's Manual of Child Psychology. Vol. II* (pp. 3–72). New York: Wiley.

Mize, J., & Ladd, G. W. (1990). Toward the development of successful social skills training for preschool children. In S. R. Asher and J. D. Coie (Eds.), *Peer rejection in childhood* (pp. 338–361). Cambridge, England: Cambridge University Press.

Nicholls, J. G., Patashnick, M., & Nolen, S. B. (1985). Adolescents' theories of education. *Journal of Educational Psychology*, *77*, 683–692.

Nisbett, R. E., & Wilson, T. D. (1977). Telling more than we can know: Verbal reports on mental processes. *Psychological Review*, *84*, 231–259.

Oakes, J. (1985). *Keeping track*. New Haven: Yale University Press.

Parker, J. G., & Asher, S. R. (1987). Peer relations and later personal adjustment: Are low-accepted children "at risk"? *Psychological Bulletin*, *102*, 357–389.

Parker, J. G., & Asher, S. R. (1993). Friendship and friendship quality in middle childhood: Links with peer group acceptance and loneliness. *Developmental Psychology*, *29*, 611–621.

Piaget, J. (1965). *The moral judgment of the child.* New York: The Free Press. (Originally published, 1932.)

Putallaz, M., & Sheppard, B. H. (1990). Social status and children's orientations to limited resources. *Child Development, 61,* 2022–2027.

Rokeach, M. (1973). *The nature of human values.* New York: Free Press.

Ruble, D. N., Boggiano, A. K., Feldman, N. S., & Loebl, J. H. (1980). Developmental analysis of the role of social comparison in self-evaluation. *Developmental Psychology, 16,* 105–115.

Sarason, B. R., Sarason, I. G., & Pierce, G. R. (Eds.) (1990). *Social support: An interactional view.* New York: Wiley.

Savin-Williams, R. C., & Berndt, T. J. (1990). Friendships and peer relations during adolescence. In S. S. Feldman & G. Elliott (Eds.), *At the threshold: The developing adolescent* (pp. 277–307). Cambridge, MA: Harvard University Press.

Schunk, D. H., Hanson, A. R., & Cox, P. D. (1987). Peer-model attributes and children's achievement behaviors. *Journal of Educational Psychology, 79,* 54–61.

Schwartz, F. (1981). Supporting or subverting learning: Peer group patterns in four tracked schools. *Anthropology and Education Quarterly, 13,* 99–121.

Sebald, H. (1986). Adolescents' shifting orientations toward parents and peers: A curvilinear trend over recent decades. *Journal of Marriage and the Family, 48,* 5–13.

Sharabany, R., Gershoni, R., & Hofman, J. E. (1981). Girlfriend, boyfriend: Age and sex differences in intimate friendship. *Developmental Psychology, 17,* 800–808.

Slavin, R. E. (1983). When does cooperative learning increase student achievement. *Psychological Bulletin, 94,* 429–445.

Smith, H. W. (1973). Some developmental interpersonal dynamics through childhood. *American Sociological Review, 38,* 543–552.

Steinberg, L., & Silverberg, S. R. (1986). The vicissitudes of autonomy in early adolescence. *Child Development, 57,* 841–851.

Sullivan, H. S. (1953). *The interpersonal theory of psychiatry.* New York: Norton.

Suttles, G. D. (1968). *The social order of the slum.* Chicago: University of Chicago Press.

Tesser, A. (1984). Self-evaluation maintenance processes: Implications for relationships and for development. In J. C. Masters & K. Yarkin-Levin (Eds.), *Boundary areas in social and developmental psychology* (pp. 271–299). New York: Academic Press.

Tesser, A., Campbell, J., & Smith, M. (1984). Friendship choice and performance: Self-esteem maintenance in children. *Journal of Personality and Social Psychology, 46,* 561–574.

Triandis, H. C. (1989). The self and social behavior in differing cultural contexts. *Psychological Review, 96,* 506–520.

Triandis, H. C. (1990). Cross-cultural studies of individualism and collectivism. *Nebraska Symposium on Motivation, 37,* 41–133.

Tudge, J. R. H. (1992). Processes and consequences of peer collaboration: A Vygotskian analysis. *Child Development, 63,* 1364–1379.

Urberg, K. A., Cheng, C.-H., & Shyu, S.-J. (1991). Grade changes in peer influence on adolescent cigarette smoking: A comparison of two measures. *Addictive Behavior, 16,* 21–28.

Veroff, J. (1969). Social comparison and the development of achievement motivation. In C. P. Smith (Ed.), *Achievement-related motives in children* (pp. 46–101). New York: Russell Sage Foundation.

Weiner, B. (1992). *Human motivation: Metaphors, theories, and research.* Newbury Park, CA: Sage.

Wentzel, K. R. (1989). Adolescent classroom goals, standards for performance, and academic achievement: An interactionist perspective. *Journal of Educational Psychology, 81,* 131–142.

Wentzel, K. R. (1991a). Relations between social competence and academic achievement in early adolescence. *Child Development, 62,* 1066–1078.

Wentzel, K. R. (1991b). Social competence at school: Relation between social responsibility and academic achievement. *Review of Educational Research, 61,* 1–24.

Wentzel, K. R. (1993). Does being good make the grade? Social behavior and academic competence in middle school. *Journal of Educational Psychology, 85,* 357–364.

Wood, W., Lundgren, S., Ouellette, J. A., Busceme, S., & Blackstone, T. (1994). Minority influence: A meta-analytic review of social influence processes. *Psychological Bulletin, 115,* 323–345.

Youniss, J., & Smollar, J. (1985). *Adolescent relations with mothers, fathers, and friends.* Chicago: University of Chicago Press.

Zanna, M. P., Olson, J. M., & Herman, C. P. (Eds.). (1987). *Social influence.* Hillsdale, NJ: Erlbaum.

Zimbardo, P. G., & Leippe, M. R. (1991). *The psychology of attitude change and social influence.* Philadelphia: Temple University Press.

12   Peer networks and students' classroom engagement during childhood and adolescence

Thomas A. Kindermann, Tanya L. McCollam,
and Ellsworth Gibson, Jr.

If one asks parents and teachers about important influences on children's motivation and adjustment to school, answers will likely suggest four sets of factors: the teacher and the general school environment, the psychological make-up of the individual child himself or herself, the family environment, and the child's relationships with his or her peers in school. In fact, research on school motivation and adjustment has examined all four influences. However, if one looks at current discussions of motivation and school adjustment (e.g., Ames & Ames, 1984, 1985), most research seems to concentrate on the first two factors, namely, the school and the child; some efforts target the family, and only comparatively few include children's peers.

Characteristics of schools, classrooms, teachers, and students have been prime targets of motivational studies (Skinner & Belmont, 1993). In general, it is educational researchers who have focused on school and classroom contexts (for reviews, see Ames & Ames, 1985; Brophy, 1983; 1986), such as the role of teacher behaviors, teaching styles, or evaluation strategies (Boggiano & Katz, 1991; Brophy, 1985, 1986; Graham & Barker, 1990; Grolnick & Ryan, 1987; Keller, 1983; Midgley, Feldlaufer, & Eccles, 1989; 1990; Moely et al., 1992), and the overall classroom environment and organization (Ames, 1984; Eccles, Midgley, & Adler, 1984; Johnson & Johnson, 1985).

Psychological research has focused more on children themselves (for reviews see Ames & Ames, 1984; Dweck & Elliott, 1983; Stipek, 1993), specifically on their understanding and explanations of their own role in the school environment. Key constructs are children's attributions (Weiner, 1979, 1985, 1986), their beliefs about themselves and the extent to which they feel in control (Chapman, Skinner, & Baltes, 1990; Patrick, Skinner, & Connell, 1993; Skinner, Wellborn & Connell, 1990; Weisz & Cameron, 1985), and their self-efficacy in the school environment

(Schunk, 1991). Often, this is combined with examinations of children's perceived abilities or competencies (McIver, Stipek, & Daniels, 1991), goal orientations (Elliott & Dweck, 1988; Meece & Holt, 1993; Nicholls, 1984; Wentzel, 1989), learning strategies (Ainley, 1993; Pintrich & De Groot, 1990), and interests (Schiefele, 1991), or of children's self-concept or self-worth (Covington, 1984; Wigfield & Karpathian, 1991). Last but not least, there is increasing interest in children's intrinsic motivation for academic activities and their sense of autonomy within the school environment (Connell & Wellborn, 1991; Corno & Rohrkemper, 1985; Deci & Ryan, 1985).

Compared to both of these areas, research on other context influences on student motivation and adjustment is relatively sparse. Family oriented researchers have examined childrearing practices (e.g., DeBaryshe, Patterson, & Capaldi, 1993; Dishion, 1990), parents' provision of autonomy support and involvement (Connell, Spencer, & Aber, 1994; Gottfried, Fleming, & Gottfried, 1994; Grolnick, Ryan, & Deci, 1991), parental values, expectations, and standards (Stevenson et al., 1990), as well as parents' explanations for children's success and failure (Holloway & Hess, 1982).

However, even this relatively small body of empirical work is large compared to the amount of research dedicated to the study of peer influences on school motivation and adjustment. Although the study of peer relationships has a long-standing theoretical and empirical tradition among developmentalists who are interested in social development (for reviews see Asher & Coie, 1990; Hartup, 1978; 1983), most attention has been directed toward variables like social adjustment, social behavior, and, if related to the academic domain, to achievement outcomes.

The fact that the current volume exists can be taken as evidence that this is changing, and that social relationships are accorded a more important role by many as a factor relevant for motivational development and adjustment to school. In this chapter, we hope to contribute a specific perspective. Our chapter aims to examine the role of children's and adolescents' affiliations with *peer groups* in their developing school motivation during elementary and high school. After outlining our general framework, which is based on a contextual understanding of development and oriented toward a self-system view of motivation, we will describe methods that aim to identify students' peer contexts and show promise for examining their influences for students' motivation in school. To illustrate this perspective and these methods, we will use data from two studies, one focusing on 4th and 5th grade children (Kindermann, 1993), and a new study on adolescents. Specific attention will be paid to two motivationally relevant processes, namely processes of how children and adolescents *select* other students as peer contexts for themselves, and processes of how these peer contexts, in turn, can *influence* the students' own subsequent motivational development.

Peer influences on motivation and achievement

There are many indications suggesting that children's peer relationships can have an important role in their school adjustment and motivation, in addition to students' own psychological profiles and their interactions with teachers. From a motivational standpoint, theoretical expectations exist that children's need for belongingness (Weiner, 1990), their connectedness to a "community of learners" (Skinner & Belmont, 1993), and feelings of relatedness to others in the classroom (Connell & Wellborn, 1991) do extend to peers as well as adults.

Thus, many of the characteristics of students' peer relations that are assumed to be influential for their social development can also be regarded as influential for their motivational development. Particularly prominent is the *sociometric tradition*, which focuses on student's overall standing and popularity in the classroom (e.g., Coie, Dodge, & Copotelli, 1982). Research has shown that a child's sociometric standing among his or her classmates is a strong predictor of his or her further development (for reviews, see Newcomb, Bukowski, & Pattee, 1993; Parker & Asher, 1987; Price & Dodge, 1989). Of specific interest for this chapter are findings that point to a relation between low social status and variables like risks for school dropout (cf. Parker & Asher, 1987) and academic failure (Green, Forehand, Beck, & Vosk, 1980).

A second tradition is the study of children's and adolescents' *friendships* (e.g., Berndt, 1989; Berndt, Laychak, & Park, 1990; Cohen, 1977; Hallinan & Williams, 1990; Ladd 1990; Kandel, 1978a; b; Tesser, Campbell, & Smith, 1984). Friendship researchers emphasize that adjustment does not depend only on how well one is liked or accepted overall, but also on more reciprocal aspects of peer relationships. Hence, adjustment depends on the individual as much as on the specific others with whom the individual becomes affiliated. Friendship researchers argue that different kinds of children have different kinds of friends and that friends have important functions for children's adjustment to school. For example, at early ages, the quantity and quality of children's friendships was found to be a predictor of their adjustment to school (Ladd, 1990). At older ages, friends seem to become even more important. From childhood to adolescence, there is some increase in the amount of time that individuals spend with their friends (Larson & Richards, 1991), an increase in the emotional quality during interactions with one's friends (Csikszentmihalyi & Larson, 1984), and an increase in the extent to which the quality of one's close friendships is related to social adjustment (Buhrmester, 1990).

One line of friendship research that is of special interest for the present discussion is represented by studies that examine which kinds of children or adolescents become friends with one another, and the specific processes of influence that occur between them. For example, Hallinan and Williams (1990) examined (about 1400) reciprocal friendships of adolescents for their effects on college aspirations and actual college attendance. As was found in many other studies, reciprocal friends were highly similar to one another, and the extent of similarity that existed among friends was related to their academic behavior. Friends who were most similar with regard to gender, racial characteristics, and academic tracks also had very similar college aspirations. Interestingly, adolescents who had friends across gender, race, or tracking barriers tended to have higher college aspirations than others.

Our perspective is most closely related to a third tradition, namely, the study of children's *peer group networks*. Students' close friends may be only part of the picture. Teachers and parents often believe that it is not just children's best friends who exert a powerful influence on their adjustment in school, but the larger group of peers with whom they affiliate. Of interest are processes of influence that may exist within networks of peers (e.g., Cairns, Cairns, & Neckerman, 1989; Feiring & Lewis, 1989; Furman, 1989), and specifically, processes of peer selection (Who becomes a member of a peer group?) and socialization (Do a child's peer group members have an influence on that child?). Like friendship researchers, proponents of a network approach have also investigated school-related behavior in their studies. For example, Cairns and colleagues (1989) found that 7th grade students who later dropped out of school were likely to be members of peer networks that consisted of students who were also at risk for drop out.

Defining school motivation: The concept of engagement

Our studies were guided by a conceptualization of school motivation in terms of self-system processes (e.g., Connell, 1990; Connell & Wellborn, 1991; Skinner et al., 1990). According to this model, motivational processes within the child are neither solely products of the child's own characteristics, nor of his or her context, but outcomes of dialectical relations between children's psychological needs and their experiences in interactions with their environment.

Engagement in the classroom is seen as the prime indicator of school motivation, and as the outcome of the extent to which children's needs are met by environmental characteristics at school (Connell & Wellborn, 1991). Typically, engaged children are described as selecting tasks at the border of their competencies, taking initiative when there is an opportunity, exerting effort and concentration when working on tasks, and persisting when tasks demand more than routine effort. On the opposite pole, children whose needs are not met by their school environment are likely to become *disaffected*. These children are passive, do not try hard, and give up easily when faced with tasks that demand more than routine exertion (Wellborn, 1991).

Students' engagement in classroom activities has considerable long-term consequences. On the one hand, the extent to which students are engaged in ongoing learning activities sets the stage for their academic achievement and adjustment; for example, engagement was shown to be related to perceptions of control in the school environment as well as to children's sense of autonomy in the classroom (Patrick et al., 1993; Skinner et al., 1990). On the other hand, students' behavior is also likely to influence their social interactions with teachers as well as with other students in the classroom. For example, students' classroom behavior can influence teachers' opinions about their competencies (Bennett, Gottesman, Rock, & Cerullo, 1993), as well as teachers' expectations of their further success (e.g., Brophy, 1983; Jussim, 1989). Across time, engaged students are more likely to experience support from their teachers, and tend to become even more engaged, while disaffected students are likely to experience interactions with teachers negatively and to further decrease in motivation (Skinner & Belmont, 1993).

Challenges of studying peer network contexts and motivation

If there is reason to believe that peer contexts are important influences for students' motivation in school, why have these contexts not been studied more? Peer contexts have three properties that make them quite distinct from any other context studied traditionally.

First, they are *self-selected* to a large extent. Teachers and parents are contexts that are assigned to an individual child, whereas peer contexts usually are not. Within the constraints of a given setting, children are relatively free to affiliate with others according to their own needs and desires. However, these constraints may change from childhood to adolescence. In adolescence, for example, the age composition in mixed-grade classrooms may present constraints on peer selection processes within these classrooms, while at the same time a larger range of choices may exist, because students move across different classrooms during the school day.

Second, peer contexts consist of *multiple* and *overlapping groups* of individuals. Students need to be regarded both as individuals and as contexts for the other individuals with whom they share networks. In comparison to the contexts traditionally studied as influential for student motivation, these characteristics make peer context hard to identify.

Third, although teachers typically remain stable contexts for a school year, and one's parents for a lifetime, children's peer affiliations may *change* quite *rapidly* and unexpectedly. This change may occur in (at least) two ways. Peer affiliations may change in terms of who does or does not belong to a group. In addition, the members of a child's or adolescent's peer groups are other children or adolescents, and we need to assume that they themselves change and develop at the same rate as our target individuals under study.

Identifying peer group networks

Researchers in the area of peer relationships are generally well aware of these problems. The methods for identifying categories of rejected, popular, or neglected children within a classroom have been the topic of considerable discussion (cf. Asher & Hymel, 1981; Hymel & Rubin, 1985; Newcomb et al., 1993). So have the criteria for identification of social networks (e.g., Cairns, Gariépy, & Kindermann, 1990; Wellman & Berkowitz, 1988; Wasserman & Galaskiewicz, 1994). Perhaps the only area within this literature that can be relatively certain about definitional criteria is the research on children's friendships (e.g., Ladd, 1990). In friendship research, the phenomenon is usually restricted to friendships on which two children agree reciprocally. However, as soon as we leave the age of childhood, the definition of a friendship usually can not be left any more to the subjects themselves, and definitional problems are recognized (cf. Adams, 1989).

With regard to peer groups, it is an even more critical issue to identify who, among a group of candidates, can be assumed to be important for a given individual. While social network researchers usually also rely on the traditional strategy of obtaining children's reports of their own affiliations with others, we made use of a new assessment strategy. Cairns, Perrin, and Cairns (1985; see also Cairns, Cairns, Neckerman, Gest, & Gariépy, 1988; Cairns et al., 1989) have developed a method for assessing children's peer networks among each other that employs children as *expert observers* of their whole classroom. Children are probably better informed about what peers are doing than most adults (or researchers), and the goal of this method is to assess what is publicly known about existing peer associations. Students are asked to report about "who hangs around with whom?" in a classroom. These reports are usually based on free recall; groups of any size can be reported, and students can be nominated as belonging to any number of groups at the same time. In response to the probe, students typically generate lists of names of students who belong to groups. For example one informant may recall students ALI, BEV, and CAR to be in one group, whereas another adds a second group consisting of GIL, HAL, and FIN. With children, we used the original interview procedure; with adolescents, we used a paper-and-pencil adaptation that was administered in a group format.

Two specific advantages of the method should be noted before we go into the details of its use. One advantage is that informants do not just report about themselves, but about all the social configurations that are known in the classroom. This allows us to examine peer groups in classrooms in which not all students participate as informants themselves; usually, participation rates of at least 50% are recommended (Cairns et al., 1985). A second advantage is that it becomes possible to assess the consistency of the individual reports with the extracted map of publicly known group affiliations in the setting.

Analyzing group nominations

In most cases, the reports will be too complex for just a qualitative analysis, and researchers may want to use reliability criteria for decisions about students' network memberships. Identification procedures usually proceed in two steps. First, a matrix is formed of co-nominations among students. This is a matrix of conditional nomination frequencies, given that a specific student is nominated to have a group himself or herself (see also Breiger's, 1988, *P*-matrix of "person-to-person relations"). Table 12.1 gives an example of conominations in a classroom that consisted of adolescents from 9th through 11th grade.

The second step is to identify students' actual affiliates. Many statistical tools can be used to identify patterns in conomination matrices. Usually, these have the goal to identify overall network structures and to obtain

Table 12.1 Matrix of conominations for groups in a classroom attended by 9th through 11th graders.

	ALI	BEV	CAR	DAR	EVE	FIN	GIL	HAL	INA	JIL	KEN	LES	MIK	NIC	OLA	PAT	QIA	RIA	SAL	TIA	ULA	Total Nominations
ALI	—	18	19	19	18	0	0	0	0	0	0	0	0	0	0	0	0	0	0	0	0	20
BEV	18	—	17	17	16	0	0	0	0	0	0	0	0	0	0	0	0	0	0	0	0	18
CAR	19	17	—	20	17	0	0	0	0	0	0	0	0	0	0	0	0	0	0	0	0	20
DAR	19	17	20	—	17	0	0	0	0	0	0	0	0	0	0	0	0	0	0	0	0	20
EVE	18	16	17	17	—	0	0	0	0	0	0	0	0	0	0	0	0	0	0	0	0	18
FIN	0	0	0	0	0	—	20	20	5	3	3	3	2	0	0	0	0	0	0	0	0	29
GIL	0	0	0	0	0	20	—	20	5	4	4	4	3	0	0	0	0	0	0	0	0	21
HAL	0	0	0	0	0	20	20	—	5	3	3	3	2	0	0	0	0	0	0	0	0	20
INA	0	0	0	0	0	5	5	5	—	7	14	5	7	0	0	0	0	0	0	0	0	17
JIL	0	0	0	0	0	3	4	3	7	—	11	14	15	0	0	0	0	0	0	0	0	16
KEN	0	0	0	0	0	3	4	3	14	11	—	9	11	0	0	0	0	0	0	0	0	33
LES	0	0	0	0	0	3	4	3	5	14	9	—	13	0	0	0	0	0	0	0	0	14
MIK	0	0	0	0	0	2	3	2	7	15	11	13	—	0	0	0	0	0	0	0	0	16
NIC	0	0	0	0	0	0	0	0	0	0	0	0	0	—	8	8	8	2	2	2	1	11
OLA	0	0	0	0	0	0	0	0	0	0	0	0	0	8	—	9	16	5	4	2	2	18
PAT	0	0	0	0	0	0	0	0	0	0	0	0	0	8	9	—	9	2	2	1	1	12
QIA	0	0	0	0	0	0	0	0	0	0	0	0	0	8	16	9	—	5	2	0	0	16
RIA	0	0	0	0	0	0	0	0	0	0	0	0	0	2	5	2	5	—	9	3	2	12
SAL	0	0	0	0	0	0	0	0	0	0	0	0	0	2	4	2	2	9	—	5	4	11
TIA	0	0	0	0	0	0	0	0	0	0	0	0	0	2	2	1	0	3	5	—	11	13
ULA	0	0	0	0	0	0	0	0	0	0	0	0	0	1	2	1	0	2	4	11	—	11

Matrix shows the number of times each student in the classroom was reported to be in a group together with any other student. A considerable number of conominations with students from other classrooms is omitted. Across all classrooms, 323 groups were generated by 73 informants; the total of group nominations was 1082. Six students were not nominated to be in any group in this classroom.

a structural description of an entire setting (see, for example, Cairns et al., 1990; Wellman & Berkowitz, 1988). However, we approached the question from a different angle, namely, from the perspective of individuals. Our question was not about network structures in general, but about who, among many candidates, can be considered to be a relevant context for a target child, and who cannot. Thus, there was little need to describe the *overall* environment, as is usually attempted by sociologists and social network researchers. Instead, the goal is to identify the exact peers with whom a student is affiliated.

Borrowing from strategies for analyzing social interactions (e.g., Bakeman & Gottmann, 1986; Sackett, Holm, Crowley, & Henkins, 1979), we focused on conditional probabilities in patterns of conominations: Given that a specific individual has been nominated to be in a group with other students, how likely is it that any other individual is nominated to belong to the same group? And, are the conditional probabilities for these other individuals higher than could be expected by chance? Chance expectations are based on the nominations that the candidates had received among *all* group nominations. Discrepancies between observed (conditional) probabilities and their (expected) base rates can be tested via binomial z-tests (or using Fisher's exact test in cases of low expected frequencies; for ease of computation we use Stirling's approximation formula; see von Eye, 1990).

To give an example (see also Table 12.1) in a classroom of 9th through 11th grade adolescents, student ALI was nominated 20 times, and student BEV was nominated 18 times to be a member of a group, out of a total of 323 groups that were generated by the respondents. Thus, the expected rate for BEV to be nominated in any group of students was .06 (18/323). However, given that ALI was nominated to belong to a group, BEV was nominated to be a member of the same group in 18 of the 20 cases, yielding a conditional probability of .90; the z-score of 16.99 is highly significant, denoting that ALI and BEV are members of the same group. These tests were conducted for all combinations of students in the classrooms under study. Connections that were found to be significant at the 5% level are depicted in Figure 12.1.

It should be noted that in this figure, no distinction is made with regard to individuals' centrality in the whole setting or within their networks; individuals' positions are arbitrary and based on drawing convenience only. The method should mainly be considered as a tool to partition social ecologies into different kinds of contexts, namely, a context that can be considered to be central for a specific individual (one's own network of

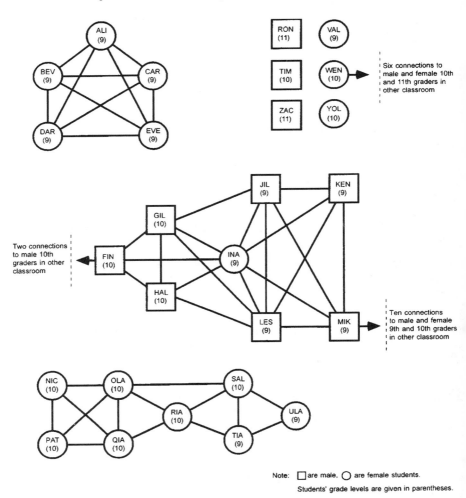

Figure 12.1. Map of social networks in a science classroom attended by 9th through 11th graders ($p < .05$)

"buddies") and another context that is assumed to be of minor relevance (one's other classmates, or "bystanders").

Peer group profiles as descriptors of groups' motivational characteristics

Classical accounts (e.g., Moreno, 1934) as well as current sociological strategies of network analysis (see Wasserman & Galaskiewicz, 1994; Wellman & Berkowitz, 1988) usually focus on structural characteristics to describe peer networks, as, for example, group size, cohesiveness, individuals' centrality within groups, or groups' centrality within the larger setting. However, we were more interested in the *psychological characteristics* of peer groups than in their structural parameters.

An assumption that became central for our efforts to describe peer affiliations was that groups can be described as a joint function of the characteristics of their members. This may be debatable, because it leads to aggregation of scores across all of the individual members of a given student's peer group. However, aggregation has several advantages. One advantage is the possibility of forming a group score or *profile* in order to express group characteristics in one variable. A second advantage is that this group score then allows us to compare networks that differ in terms of structural characteristics (size, overlapping memberships, etc.). Third, across time, group change is likely to involve turnover in group memberships, and we may not want to limit ourselves to examining influences only within stable networks.

A simple strategy for capturing the composite profile of a child's peer group(s) is to average the scores of the members of his or her network. In the example in Figure 12.1, this means that ALI's peer group score is the average of the scores of BEV, CAR, DAR, and EVE. All members of her peer group are considered to be of equal importance. However, alternative strategies are also possible; individual weights can be used in the averaging procedure if there is reason to assume that some individuals carry more weight than others, or standard deviations can be used if target questions are directed at examining group diversity.

Examining peer group processes

What we have discussed so far is a way to identify a student's networks of peers at some level of reliability, and a way to form a representation for the characteristics of this entire peer group. Taken together, these methods offer strategies to examine two basic processes of peer group dynamics: peer selection and socialization.

Peer selection processes

Theorizing about the nature of selection processes can be characterized by one statement: homophily rules. In childhood, as well as in adolescence or adulthood, friends and self-selected members of peer groups are usually more similar to one another than they are to people who are not friends or not members of the group (cf. Cairns et al., 1989; Cohen, 1977; East et al.,

1992; Hallinan & Williams, 1990; Jackson et al., 1991; Kandel, 1978a; Wright, Giammarino, & Parad, 1986).

Most findings about peer selection processes, when considering both the friendship and the social network research literatures, suggest that homophily may go in positive as well as negative directions. Traditionally, much attention has been paid to how deviant adolescents affiliate with deviant others (e.g., Cairns et al., 1988; 1989; Cohen, 1977; Dishion, Patterson, Stoolmiller, & Skinner, 1991; Kandel, 1978a). However, there is also research that focuses on the positive side of peer affiliations, and among these are studies that include attention to academic characteristics (e.g., Cohen, 1977; Hallinan & Williams, 1990; Kandel, 1978a).

How can selection processes be examined? A simple way is to inspect correlations between scores of individuals and of the members of their peer group(s). This can be done by using peer profile scores, or by using intra-class correlations between individuals and the members of their peer group(s). If group profiles are used, the correlation of individuals' own scores with the profile of their peer group can be interpreted in analogy to item-total correlations, in which an individual would be an item, and the group the total. Thus, these correlations give information about the extent to which individuals are similar to their peer group members.

Alternative strategies are also possible. In cases in which there is not much overlap across groups and not many individuals who hold memberships in many groups at the same time, analyses of variance can be used in order to test whether variances within groups are smaller than those across groups (see Kindermann, 1993). Alternatively, peer group profiles can be based directly on the variance of the scores of a student's network members (instead of their average), and this variance can be compared with the variance across the other students who were not in this student's peer group (i.e., forming a nonpeer group profile). Group homogeneity would again be denoted by differences between the group profiles and the nongroup variances.

Peer socialization processes

Many motivational researchers assume that peers exert socialization influences on students' motivational development in school (e.g., Dweck & Goetz, 1978). Peer networks have been labeled "socialization templates" that define students' opportunities for interactions, opportunities for observing others in interactions, and their access to situations and activities (Feiring & Lewis, 1989, p. 125).

Strong socialization effects have been found in studies in which selection effects were experimentally controlled, as, for example, in the classic study by Sherif, Harvey, White, Hood, and Sherif (1961), in which children were assigned to different groups in a summer camp. However, when groups of peers were self-selected, rather than experimentally assigned, indications for socialization effects were found in some studies (e.g., Kandel, 1978b), whereas other studies caution us that these effects may be small (e.g., Berndt et al., 1990), or even negligible compared to selection processes (e.g., Cohen, 1977).

In the peer relationships literature, notions of socialization processes usually imply expectations that members of a group become more similar to one another across time. For example, Hall and Cairns (1984) found effects of social modeling by peers in an analogy to Bandura's classic bobo-doll study on aggression. Modeling of a peer was found to have stronger effects than the experimental manipulations themselves; it was the behavior of the peer that predicted most strongly whether aggression occurred. With regard to motivation, Berndt and colleagues (1990) found that discussions among pairs of friends influenced their decisions in motivation-related dilemmas (e.g., whether to go to a rock concert or to complete a homework assignment) and made friends more similar in their decisions.

Often, however, socialization researchers are more interested in a further hypothesis, namely, that individuals in different groups do not just change toward the mean of their own group, but change in a way that magnifies the existing differences between groups. Thus, in a specific variable under study, the initially "rich" should become "richer" across time, and the "poor" should become "poorer." Accordingly, in the study by Berndt and colleagues, initially highly motivated students were expected to become more motivated, whereas low motivated students were expected to decrease in motivation. While this hypothesis was not supported in this specific study, it is nevertheless central to many investigations, especially to studies focusing on the negative role of peer group affiliations.

How can these socialization expectations be examined? If a students' peers influence his or her motivational development such that affiliations with highly motivated peers have a positive effect, while being with disaffected peers has a negative effect, change in this student's motivation across time should be related to the motivational profile of his or her peer group at an earlier point in time. Regression analyses can be used to examine whether students' peer group scores can predict their own engagement at a later point in time, over and above their own earlier engagement. Significant correlations would indicate that the motivational composition of a student's peer group is related to change in his or her motivation across time.

Availability of same-aged peers and selection and socialization processes in adolescence

Peer selection processes are known to be based primarily on similarity among candidates. The extent to which candidates are available in a classroom who are highly similar to target students is an important factor in these processes. In fact, Kandel (1978a) found that among adolescents, similarity in grade levels was the one criterion in which friendship dyads showed most similarity. Although this is not a critical issue in traditional elementary classrooms, in which children are usually of the same grade or age and peer group members can be selected from equals, this can be of major importance in classrooms that include students of different grades or ages, as is often the case for adolescents.

Thus, if a classroom of adolescents is mainly attended by students from a lower grade, but only by some students from higher grades, this can limit the latter students' access to peers who are most similar to them. Even if many classmates were of the same developmental level as a target student, or similar to him or her in terms of academic interests, differences in grade levels or age may nevertheless make these peers quite inaccessible (or unacceptable) as potential members of that student's peer group.

Not much is known about the influences of classroom's age composition on student development in general, and even less about influences on academic variables. Most of the available information pertains to childhood. While reviews suggest that mixed-age playgroups and classrooms can have positive effects for young children (Bailey, Burchinal, & McWilliam, 1993; Howes & Farver, 1987; Urberg & Kaplan, 1986) and in later childhood (Miller, 1990; Pratt, 1986), this is much less clear with regard to adolescence. Often, negative expectations prevail with regard to adolescents who affiliate with older peers (cf. Magnusson, 1988).

Because mixed-age classrooms can impose constraints on peer group formation processes in terms of availability of most similar others (i.e., of classmates of the same age), analyses of selection and socialization processes should be able to incorporate differential expectations in adolescents' classrooms. For example, subgroups of students with different amounts of mixed-age peer group networks can be compared if sample sizes are large enough. Alternatively, proportions can be used of students' peer group members who are of the same age (versus different ages). These proportions can be used as controls in regression analyses, if it is of interest whether peer homogeneity exists over and above an average level of mixed-age affiliations overall. Alternatively, they can be used as weights if it is of interest whether the amount of same-age (or cross-age) affiliations contributes to overall peer group homogeneity.

Similarly, the peer groups' age composition can be also taken into consideration for socialization analyses. Usually, controlling for same-age or cross-age affiliations will be helpful if differential effects are not of interest; weighting procedures will be helpful if expectations exist that cross-age (or same-age) affiliations exert especially powerful socialization influences.

Illustration: Peer groups and engagement across the school year in children and adolescents

The second part of this chapter will illustrate the use of the peer network identification method and the procedures we use to examine motivationally relevant peer selection and socialization processes. Data from two studies will be used: a study on 4th and 5th grade children (Kindermann, 1993), and an unpublished study of 9th through 12th grade adolescents.

In terms of its participants, the adolescents' study is quite different from the children's study. We had two goals with this study: One goal was to examine the use of the network identification and description methods in this age range, and to find evidence for similar processes of motivationally based peer selection and socialization processes. The second goal was to do this in a less homogeneous setting, in which students were from a more diverse sociodemographic and ethnic background.

In the children study, two 4th and two 5th grade classrooms ($n = 115$) were targeted in a rural suburban school district in upstate New York. Students were lower-middle to middle class and almost equally divided by grade, classroom, and gender. The adolescents' study took place in an urban school district in Oregon, targeting five mixed-grade science classes ($n = 102$) that were attended by students from 9th through 12th grade. Slightly more than half of the students were male, and about half of the students were 9th graders. The classrooms exhibited a wide range of ethnic diversity; about 30% of the students were African American and about 30% of Hispanic or Asian origin.

All adolescents' classes were taught by the same teacher, who had the explicit goal of encouraging group work and cooperative learning. Many students in these classes had previously experienced problems with science classes; in fact, these classes were part of an effort to restructure the school's science curriculum. We hoped that in such a setting peer group structures would be more pronounced, that their relations to classroom engagement would become more clear, and that, by working with one single teacher, interindividual differences in teachers' standards would be held constant.

Peer groups at the beginning of the school year

In the 4th and 5th grade classrooms, 57 children were individually interviewed about peer networks at the beginning of the year. In the adolescents' study, 68 students from the five classrooms filled out network assessments in a paper-and-pencil format. In these classrooms, candidates could also be freely chosen, but in contrast to the children's study, adolescents were encouraged to think about science work-groups in their reports. (Work groups were usually self-selected, with little guidance from the teacher.) Accordingly, there was some overlap in nominations across classrooms; however, adolescents did not include peers who did not attend any of the five science classes. (Figure 12.1 depicts one of the adolescents' classrooms.)

In general, networks of adolescents were more complex than those of children. For children, although their networks were quite complex in some classrooms, there were mostly dyads, and larger networks were rare (nevertheless, there was one with 7 members). For adolescents, although peer group structures were often larger, they were also more distinct and less overlapping; there were many dyads and triads, and there was one cluster that consisted of 14 students. Among both children and adolescents, there were students who were not connected to a peer group (13 children, 11 adolescents).

On average, a child had about 2.2 other students included in his or her group; group sizes did not differ across grades. In comparison, an adolescent had 3.2 students in his or her group, and group size decreased with increasing grade levels (from 4.3 for 9th graders, to 1.7 for the 11th and 12th graders combined). Nevertheless, there were no indications of grade differences in the number of students who were not found with a peer group.

We had also expected to see the "gender gap" in students' peer groups decrease with age. For children, groups were exclusively comprised of peers of the same sex; among adolescents, there were cases in which groups bridged across genders. Often, just one student of a different sex was included in an otherwise same-sex group. On average, 80% of an adolescent's peer group members were of the same gender.

Reliability of peer group assessments

Examinations of the extent to which maps of identified groups were consistent with individual students' nominations focused on errors of commission only. Thus, students who knew just about some groups but not about others were still considered accurate if they agreed with their classmates on those accounts that they did report. The overall kappa indices were .70 for children and .84 for adolescents.

Engagement at the beginning of the school year

Students' school motivation was measured using self-reports as well as reports by their teachers. Connell and Wellborn (1991) have developed a ten-item scale that assesses students' perceptions of their own behavior in the classroom (e.g., "I try as hard as I can in school," or "When I'm in class, I just act like I'm working"). A parallel scale exists for measuring teacher-perceptions of students' engagement (Skinner et al., 1990; Wellborn, 1991; e.g., "In my class, this student just tries to look busy," or " . . . works as hard as he/she can"). In previous studies, the scales were shown to have high internal consistency and stability across a school year (Skinner & Belmont, 1993), to be moderately intercorrelated, and correlated with grades and achievement scores in mathematics, language, and science (Skinner et al., 1990; Wellborn, 1991).

In both studies, students' self-reported engagement was initially measured about one month after the beginning of the school year; 109 children and 90 adolescents participated. With regard to teacher reports of motivation, the four teachers of the children's classrooms provided reports for all participating students; in the adolescents' study, the science teacher reported on 47 students from three of the five classrooms.

We had only partial success in securing a wider range of motivational scores in the adolescents' data than were obtained with children. On average, children had a self-reported motivation score of 3.2 (the scale ranges from 1 to 4), and adolescent's average motivation score was 2.9. Also, the ranges of individuals' scores were more comparable than we had expected (for children, they ranged from 1.33 to 4.0; for adolescents from 1.46 to 4.0; SD's = .49 and .44).

As was the case in the children's data, the adolescents' teacher also tended to regard her students' motivation to be significantly lower than they did themselves. However, adolescents' classrooms showed a *smaller* range of engagement scores (SD = .44; average 2.62) than did the children's classrooms (*SD* = .59; average 3.00). This may have been due to the decision to work with one teacher only. It should be noted that the teacher had not paid selective attention to specifically high or low motivated adolescents; the 47 students with teacher-reports did not differ in their self-reports from the other students on whom no reports were available.

Grade differences

In the literature, there is ample evidence for a decline in children's motivation for school with increasing grade level (e.g., Skinner & Belmont, 1993). In the children's study, there had also been differences favoring younger children (self-report averages: 3.24 for 4th, and 3.07 for 5th graders). We found further decreases for adolescents (from 3.0 in 9th grade down to 2.7 for the 11th and 12th graders combined). However, as was true for the children's study, there were no grade differences in adolescents' teacher-reported engagement. Thus, adolescents in higher grades felt *less* motivated, but did not appear so to the teacher.

Peer groups and motivation at the beginning of the school year

Our main questions were about the *motivational composition* of children's peer groups in elementary school and of adolescents' peer groups in mixed-age classrooms. We were first interested in the extent to which students were affiliated with others who shared a similar motivational orientation to school. Group similarity is an important indicator that peer selection processes proceed according to motivational criteria.

Peer group selection

As descriptors for the motivational profiles of students' peer groups, we used the average of their members. Analyses of variance showed that, for either children or adolescents, there were no significant differences between individual students' scores and their peer group scores. As indicators of the extent to which selection processes had led students to select members for their peer groups who were similar to themselves, we used correlations between individuals' scores and the scores of their peer network profiles. For both children and adolescents, individuals' own scores corresponded significantly to the profile scores of their networks with regard to self-reported motivation (with .28 and .27). With regard to teacher perceptions, group homogeneity was present for children ($r = .55$), but not adolescents ($r = .23$).

Grade differences

There were little grade differences in children's or adolescents' peer groups. The only exception was found with regard to teacher reports of adolescents' motivation; 11th and 12th graders' peer groups were perceived as significantly *more* motivated than groups of students in grades 9 and 10 combined (profile averages 3.25 versus 2.52). This was contrary to our expectations, because there had been declines with grade in adolescents own self-reported engagement. We concluded that students in higher grades, although they were less motivated themselves, were nevertheless affiliated with peers who were not less motivated than the peer group members of students from lower grades.

With regard to peer group homogeneity, there were no grade differences for children. Across adolescents' grades however, peer group homogeneity was pronounced for the 9th graders (self-report: $r = .50$, $n = 36$, $p < .01$; teacher-report: $r = .78$, $n = 17$, $p < .001$.), but did not exist in higher grades. Group similarity seemed to decrease with increasing grade level in the mixed-grade classrooms. Although students in lower grades had succeeded in seeking out others who were motivationally similar to themselves, adolescents in higher grades may not have had the same opportunity to do so. This was also evident in the proportions of mixed-grade versus grade-homogenous peer affiliations. On average, 9th graders had 90% of their affiliations with other 9th graders, 10th graders had 60% from the same grade, but 11th and 12th graders had 60% of their peer group members from grades *outside* their own.

In sum, there was evidence that children were affiliated with peer groups that were similar to themselves at the beginning of the school year. However, for adolescents in the mixed-grade classrooms there were differences with regard to grade levels. Students in 9th grade were more highly motivated themselves, usually had larger networks that more often included other 9th graders, and there was considerable homogeneity within these groups. Adolescents in higher grades, who were less motivated themselves, had fewer classmates with whom they were affiliated, a higher percentage from lower grades, and their groups were less homogeneous with regard to their motivational composition. Nevertheless, it appears that some of these students were able to compensate for their own low motivation by affiliating with others who were at least as motivated as the group members of students from lower grades.

Peer groups across the school year

At the end of the school year, 27 of the children from one 4th grade class-room were individually reinterviewed about peer networks in the class-room. In the adolescents' study, 28 students participated again from three of the five classrooms that were studied initially ($n = 61$). Although the number of reports in the adolescent study appears to be low, the reliability index of the composite map across the individual reports at the end of the year ($\kappa = .88$) indicates that the composite map is nevertheless reliable.

All of the children who had been without a group at the beginning of the year in the one longitudinal 4th grade classroom had acquired mem-bership in a group by the end of the school year. For adolescents in the longitudinal classrooms, 6 of the 8 students who had been without a group at the beginning of the year were still without a group at the end; only two students had gained membership in a group across the year. However, there were 19 additional adolescents who had lost all of their initial affili-ations. (All of these were not present at the second measurement point of the study.)

Group stability

Across time, stability of children's peer group membership was low; about 50% of a child's peer group members were exchanged. Adolescents' groups showed even larger instability and a 75% rate of member turnover. Whereas children's membership changes were mostly due to additions of new members (on average, group size increased from 2.2 to 2.64 mem-bers), adolescents' peer group changes were characterized by loss of members (on average, group size decreased from 3.16 to 1.85 members). However, this does not imply that change was random; there were some groups that stayed entirely stable across the year (e.g., the cluster of stu-dents ALI to EVE in Figure 12.1). Also, stability of adolescents' peer group memberships decreased significantly with increasing grade level; for students who were above grade 9, more than 80% of their peer group members were exchanged or lost across time.

Engagement across the school year

Within a month of the end of the school year, all of the children of the lon-gitudinal 4th grade classroom participated again in a second questionnaire assessment. In the adolescent study, 28 students from the three longitudi-nal classrooms participated again; 23 students were not present during any of the three days when the survey took place. According to their records, these students had not dropped out of school but were just absent. Seven other students were excluded who had left the school or had shifted to different classrooms that were not part of the study; the status of three missing students could not be determined.

Across the school year, there were no significant changes in children's or adolescents' motivation. There were also no grade differences in engagement scores at the end of the school year for either children or adolescents. Analyses of variance showed that this was an outcome of differential attrition in the sample. The students from the longitudinal classrooms who were present at the second measurement point had already been more engaged at the beginning of the study in terms of self-reports as well as teacher-reports.

Peer group selection and socialization processes across the year

For purposes of examining peer selection processes across the year, we treated individual students' motivation as if it had remained constant across the school year. In order to construct peer group profiles for the end of the school year, we used students' own engagement scores from the beginning of the school year in combination with the information on their group affiliations at the end of the year. Thus, correlations between students' peer group profiles at the beginning and end of the year give information about the extent to which group member turnover had an influence on the groups' motivational composition across time, when students' intraindividual motivational change across time was controlled.

Children's as well as adolescents' peer groups had remained quite stable across the year in terms of their motivational composition, despite the fact that at least half of the members had been exchanged. Correlations between group scores across time were significant for self-reported engagement in children ($r = .47$; $p < .05$, $n = 25$) and adolescents ($r = .45$, $p < .01$, $n = 37$), as well as for teacher-reports (children: $r = .80$, $p < .001$, $n = 25$; adolescents: $r = .69$, $p < .001$, $n = 31$). Thus, although many of the members of a student's peer network were exchanged, there was nevertheless considerable continuity in the motivational make-up of students' groups.

With regard to adolescents, an additional indication for peer group continuity across time can be seen in the fact that stable peer groups also led to a higher probability that students participated in the second measurement point of the study. On average, nearly 40% of the stable members of a student's group were present in the classroom again at the end of the year. However, among students' ties that were not maintained across the year, 95% of these were associations with peers who were not present at the end of the year.

Finally, we examined potential *socialization influences* of students' peer groups on their own motivational development. For these analyses, we used students' group profiles from the beginning of the year in combination with their individual self-reports of engagement from both the beginning and the end of the school year.

For children, there were clear indications of motivational socialization through peer groups. Regression analyses examined the extent to which individuals' engagement at the end of the year could be predicted from their peer group scores at the beginning of the year, when their own engagement at this earlier time was controlled. The results showed that changes in children's own engagement could be predicted by the initial composition of their peer networks ($\beta = .15$, $t = 2.06$, $p < .05$, $n = 96$). For the adolescent study, we had originally hoped for stronger effects, because we expected a broader range of self-reported engagement scores. We did not find such a broad range in our sample. In addition, we needed to revise our expectations, because of the very high rate of membership turnover that existed overall. Probably, little can be expected in terms of peer group socialization if the overwhelming majority of one's group members do not remain stable socialization agents across time.

Hence, we included two further refinements in the analyses. First, socialization effects were expected to be stronger in adolescent peer groups that stayed together for a longer time, and we included an index of *network stability* across time for our analyses. This index was the percentage of individuals who remained stable members of a student's group across time, and was used as a control. Thus, socialization effects were examined under the assumption that all students had the same number of stable peer group members. By the same token, adolescents who did not have at least one stable member were excluded from the analysis.

Secondly, we took the *mixed-grade* design of the adolescent classrooms into consideration. Students' grade differences were of less interest to us than the question of whether the mixed-grade design of the classrooms offered opportunities for some students in terms of their motivational development. Since some (but not all) of the peer groups in our adolescent classrooms consisted of students from different grades, we wanted to examine whether the grade-composition of students' peer networks contributed to changes in students' engagement in combination with the motivational characteristics of these groups. In order to do so, we included the proportion of an individuals' peer group members that were in different grades as a weighting factor in the analysis.

Thus, we examined whether an individual student's peer group profile at the beginning of the year, when weighted with the proportion of his or her peer group members who were in a different grade, and controlling for the level of stability within his or her group, allowed us to predict how that student's own motivation would change across time. The results were consistent with our expectations: Students who were with highly motivated peer groups and who had many of their members from grades that were different from their own were likely to increase in motivation across time (on average by about .20 points on the 4-point scale). Students who were affiliated with groups that were low on motivation and showed little grade diversity decreased slightly across time ($\beta = .48$; $t = 2.51$, $n = 18$, $p < .05$). We regard this as an indication that the mixed-grade design of the classrooms (as well as the teacher's encouragement to form groups that work together) had indeed offered some advantages for those students who managed to bridge across grade barriers in their peer networks.

Discussion: Peer group selection and socialization processes in elementary school and high school classrooms

The goal of this chapter was to describe a method for identifying students' peer groups in school as well as its applications for studying peer selection and socialization processes in childhood and adolescence. Specifically, we wanted to examine the use of this method in a setting of adolescents that was characterized by a large amount of ethnical diversity. In adolescence, classrooms are quite common in which students differ with regard to age and grade level, although these classrooms may be more homogeneous with regard to students' performance or academic achievement. As was the case in the current study, these classroom environments are often formed with the specific goal of encouraging students' to learn from one another, both in terms of social and academic development.

The results of both studies indicated that at the beginning of the school year, *self-selection* processes among the students led to peer groups that were quite homogeneous in terms of their motivational composition. The major difference between children and adolescents was that there were grade differentiations in adolescents' (mixed-grade) classrooms. Peer group homogeneity was stronger for 9th graders and for students who had more peer group members from their own grade.

Across the school year, children's peer groups remained moderately stable in terms of peer group memberships, whereas adolescents' groups were characterized by an enormous turnover rate. This rate of change matched perceptions of the teacher, who also reported that adolescents' groups changed greatly in terms of work group membership. Nevertheless, the *motivational make-up* of students' peer groups remained quite stable across time. Peer group members seem to have been replaced, dropped, or newly integrated into networks in a way that left the motivational composition of these groups intact.

Peer socialization processes were examined as the extent to which the motivational profile of a student's peer group members at the beginning of the school year allowed for the prediction of that child's own motivational change across time. For children, we found clear evidence that self-selected peer group contexts can have socializing effects on individuals across time: Children who were affiliated with highly motivated groups changed positively across the school year, while children who were with less motivated groups changed negatively. For adolescents, the evidence for socialization effects was clearer for those students who had peer networks that included many peers from different grades. Although this needs to be taken with caution, because our survivor sample of students who participated at both measurement times had been relatively highly motivated right from the start, the results are nevertheless encouraging. Despite the differences, there are clear similarities with regard to the general finding that the motivational composition of students' peer groups at the beginning of the school year was indicative of these student's own motivational development across the year.

School motivational and peer selection and socialization processes. Because these findings are correlational, there can be doubts whether students' motivational characteristics can really be regarded to be direct targets of selection and socialization processes. What appear to be indications of selection and socialization processes according to motivational criteria may be by-products of processes that do not directly target school motivation, but are directed toward other criteria that are more salient in interactions among students.

Indeed, studies by Cohen (1977) and Kandel (1978a) caution us that academic variables may not be the characteristics on which peer group members may be most similar to one another. For example, selection processes may be more based on sociodemographic variables, achievement, intelligence, or on classroom behavior that is openly observable by others, at least at the beginning of a school year. Similarly, socialization processes may also not target motivation directly, but rather academic or social behaviors. Some of these behaviors may be facilitative of (or compatible with) classroom engagement and others may be incompatible with classroom engagement. Considering that there are relations between students' social behavior in the classroom and their academic achievement (cf. DeBaryshe et al., 1993; Wentzel, 1991; Wentzel, 1993), it may well be that peer selection and socialization processes are more directed towards social behaviors, rather than academic motivation.

The extent to which this is the case may be a matter of the specific classroom settings in which peer processes are studied, of the classrooms' agenda, and of the specific goals of the teacher, but also of the kinds of students who attend the classrooms. For example, it seems likely that students' age can play a role in the extent to which peer groups are influential for their own motivational development. However, in our understanding, all of these variables will mostly affect the *strength* with which peer selection or socialization processes pertain to school motivation. In other words, if motivational change is a by-product of peer group processes, links to peer selection and socialization processes can be expected to be weaker than if motivation was a direct target of these processes.

Integrating the strands of peer relationships research

Our studies point to peer group selection processes as key processes by which children and adolescents seem to select contexts for themselves in the classroom, which then, via socialization processes, have implications for their own further motivational development. On this general level, our results seem to be entirely compatible with results of other researchers, such as, for example, studies of children's or adolescents' friendship patterns. Nevertheless, we think that the current framework can provide some additional information.

The methods presented for peer group identification seem to be especially promising if they are combined with existing frameworks from the friendship and sociometrics literatures. By combining network methods with sociometric classification systems (e.g., Coie et al., 1982; Newcomb & Bukowski, 1983), we could find out about the role of sociometric popularity within and across peer groups. Do individuals who belong to popular, neglected, or rejected categories of children share associations with each other, or do they also belong to different parts of the social world in the classroom? Are popular children "stars" who have connections to all kinds of different other children, whereas rejected children are more isolated? Are neglected children "satellites," and unlikely candidates for group inclusion who have outlier positions in otherwise more coherent networks? Are the children within one's network perceived to be more likeable than children on the outside?

Further questions could also be addressed by combining network methods with methods used in the friendship literature (e.g., Ladd, 1990). Are one's friends usually members of one's network, or is friendship something special, and one's close friends are as likely to be members of one's peer network as they are to be outsiders? Are friends more influential in terms of socializing influences than the larger group of one's peer network members?

Combining these methods could also help in addressing more specific questions about the motivational relevance of the processes under study. Processes of how students select members for work groups in school may be affected by the peers' overall popularity, and so may the peers' socializing influences on individuals. Work groups that include one's friends may have stronger socializing influences than work groups that do not. In particular, a student's peers may have influences on the formation or maintenance friendships, and it is entirely possible that resulting friendships have socializing influences that are stronger and more specific than those that emanate from network members who do not become this student's close friends.

Peer group networks as socialization contexts for motivational development

We have started our chapter by pointing out that contemporary research on school motivation is mainly oriented toward intraindividual explanations, or toward explanations that focus on the teacher as the central motivating force. In contrast, our framework focuses on students' social relationships with peers, and on processes of peer selection and socialization. Because peers are students themselves who are developing at the same rate as target students under study, it is essential that a framework for studying their influences pays attention to the notion that individuals' development proceeds within contexts that change themselves, and that individuals can have an active role in determining who or what will be a socialization context for their development (Kindermann & Skinner, 1992; Kindermann & Valsiner, 1995).

On a large scale, the methods presented in this chapter have two general objectives. The first goal was to show that it is possible to partition the social ecology of a student in the classroom into sub-units that can be expected to be particularly influential contexts for this student's further development. The second goal was to demonstrate how specific pathways of reciprocal person-context influences can be examined across time.

Findings that children's and adolescents' peer groups change rapidly across the time span of a school year can make it difficult to study their influences. A large amount of member turnover in students' peer groups across time can be regarded as a sign that nothing stays stable in these contexts, and that changes are rather unpredictable. We regard our findings as indicating that this depends on how we conceive students' peer contexts in school. While the individual "faces" of students' peer networks may change rapidly, there can nevertheless be considerable continuity in the psychological characteristics of these groups. In our findings, not only did the motivational profiles of children's and adolescents' peer networks remain quite unaffected by vast changes in who was a member of these groups at different points in time; in addition, there also were indications that the motivational characteristics of students' were indicative of students' own motivational change across time.

The methods presented in this chapter seem to offer ways to identify contextual agents as well as to examine their developmentally influential characteristics at different points in time. These methods also seem to allow us to examine how changes within individuals are related to changes within their contexts. The specifics of these methods may be in need of further refinement and elaboration. However, for studies of the role of self-selected peer networks on student's development, we think that it is this *perspective* on developing person-context relationships, over and above the specifics of the methods used, that may be most useful for future research on the social determinants of students' school adjustment and motivation.

Acknowledgment

We want to thank Robert B. Cairns from the University of North Carolina at Chapel Hill, who developed the network assessment method on which this chapter is based, and Ellen A. Skinner from Portland State University and James P. Connell from the Institute for Research and Reform in Education, Philadelphia, PA, for methodological advice. We also want to thank the students who participated in the studies. Special thanks go to Dawn Oostman, the teacher of the adolescents' classrooms, Christine Borgford from Portland State University, Joan E. Crosby, Vice-Principal, and Fred Rectanus, Coordinator of the Institute for Science and Mathematics at Grant High School for their support for the study. Matthew B. Hall from Portland State University and Meredith Boatsman from Lewis & Clark College deserve our thanks for their help with the data collection.

Note

This research was supported by a Faculty Development Grant from Portland State University, and a grant from the National Institutes of Health (NICHD, 1R15HD31687-01).

References

Adams, R. G. (1989). Conceptual and methodological issues in studying friendships of older adults. In R. G. Adams and R. Blieszner (Eds.), *Older adult friendship: Structure and process* (pp. 17–41). Newbury Park, CA: Sage.

Ainley, M. D. (1993). Styles of engagement with learning: Multidimensional assessment of their relationship with strategy use and school achievement. *Journal of Educational Psychology, 85,* 395–405.

Ames, C. (1984). Competitive, cooperative, and individualistic goal structures: A cognitive-motivational analysis. In R. E. Ames & C. Ames (Eds.), *Research on motivation in education* (vol. 1. pp. 177–207). *Student motivation.* Orlando, FL: Academic Press.

Ames, C., & Ames, R. E. (Eds.), (1985). *Research on motivation in education.* (vol. 2). *The classroom milieu.* Orlando, FL: Academic Press.

Ames, R. E., & Ames, C. (Eds.), (1984). *Research on motivation in education. Student motivation* (vol. 1). Orlando, FL: Academic Press.

Asher, S. R., & Coie, J. D. (Eds.) (1990). *Peer rejection in childhood.* New York: Cambridge University Press.

Asher, S. R., & Hymel, S. (1981). Children's social competence in peer relations: Sociometric and behavioral assessment. In J. D. Wine & M. D. Smye (Eds.), *Social competence* (pp. 125–157). New York: Guilford.

Bailey, D. B., Burchinal, M. R., & McWilliam, R. A. (1993). Age of peers and early childhood development. *Child Development, 64,* 848–862.

Bakeman, R., & Gottman, J. M. (1986). *Observing interaction: An introduction to sequential analysis.* Cambridge, England: Cambridge University Press.

Bennett, R. E., Gottesman, R. L., Rock, D. A., & Cerullo, F. (1993). Influence of behavior perceptions and gender on teacher's judgments of students' academic skill. *Journal of Educational Psychology, 85,* 347–356.

Berndt, T. J. (1989). Friendships in childhood and adolescence. In W. Damon (Ed.), *Child development today and tomorrow* (pp. 332–348). San Francisco, CA: Jossey-Bass.

Berndt, T. J., Laychak, A. E., & Park, K. (1990). Friends' influence on adolescents' academic achievement motivation: An experimental study. *Journal of Educational Psychology, 82,* 664–670.

Boggiano, A. K., & Katz, P. (1991). Maladaptive achievement patterns in students: The role of teachers' controlling strategies. *Journal of Social Issues, 47,* 35–51.

Breiger, R. L. (1988). The duality of persons in groups. In B. Wellman & S. D. Berkowitz (Eds.), *Social structures: A network approach* (pp. 83–98). New York: Cambridge University Press.

Brophy, J. (1983). Research on the self-fulfilling prophecy and teacher expectations. *Journal of Educational Psychology, 70,* 154–166.

Brophy, J. (1985). Teacher's expectations, motives, and goals for working with problem students. In C. Ames & R. E. Ames (Eds.), *Research on motivation in education The classroom milieu.* (vol. 2, pp. 175–214). Orlando, FL: Academic Press.

Brophy, J. (1986). Teacher influences on student achievement. *American Psychologists, 41,* 1069–1077.

Buhrmester, D. (1990). Intimacy of friendship, interpersonal competence, and adjustment during preadolescence and adolescence. *Child Development, 61,* 1101–1111.

Cairns, R. B., Cairns, B. D., & Neckerman, J. (1989). Early school dropout: Configurations and determinants. *Child Development, 60,* 1437–1452.

Cairns, R. B., Cairns, B. D., Neckerman, H. J., Gest, S. D., & Gariépy, J.-L. (1988). Social networks and aggressive behavior: Peer support or peer rejection? *Developmental Psychology, 24,* 815–823.

Cairns, R. B., Gariépy, J. L., & Kindermann, T. A. (1990). *Identifying social clusters in natural settings.* Unpublished manuscript: University of North Carolina at Chapel Hill.

Cairns, R. B., Perrin, J. E., & Cairns, B. D. (1985). Social structure and social cognition in early adolescence: Affiliative patterns. *Journal of Early Adolescence, 5,* 339–355.

Chapman, M., Skinner, E. A., & Baltes, P. B. (1990). Interpreting correlations between children's perceived control and cognitive performance: Control, agency, or means-ends beliefs? *Developmental Psychology, 23,* 246–253.

Cohen, A. K. (1977). Sources of peer group homogeneity. *Sociology of Education, 50,* 227–241.

Coie, J. D., Dodge, K. A., & Coppetelli, H. (1982). Dimensions and types of social status. *Child Development, 59,* 815–829.

Connell, J. P. (1990). Context, self, and action: A motivational analysis of self-system processes across the life-span. In D. Cicchetti & M. Beeghly (Eds.), *The self in transaction: Infancy to childhood* (pp. 61–97). Chicago, IL: University of Chicago Press.

Connell, J. P., Spencer, M. B., & Aber, J. L. (1994). Educational risk and resilience in African-American youth: Context, self, action, and outcomes in school. *Child Development, 65*, 493–506.

Connell, J. P., & Wellborn, J. G. (1991). Competence, autonomy, and relatedness: A motivational analysis of self-system processes. In M. R. Gunnar & L. A. Sroufe (Eds.), *Minnesota symposium on child psychology*, (vol. XXIII, pp. 43–77). Hillsdale, NJ: Erlbaum.

Corno, L., & Rohrkemper, M. M. (1985). The intrinsic motivation to learn in classrooms. In C. Ames, & R. E. Ames (Eds.), *Research on motivation in education* (vol. 2, pp. 53–90). *The classroom milieu*. Orlando, FL: Academic Press.

Covington, M. V. (1984). The motive for self-worth. In R. E. Ames & C. Ames (Eds.), *Research on motivation in education* (vol. 1, pp. 77–113). *Student motivation*. Orlando, FL: Academic Press.

Czikszentmihalyi, M., & Larson, R. (1984). *Being adolescent*. New York: Basic Books.

DeBaryshe, B. D., Patterson G. R., & Capaldi, D. M. (1993). A performance model for academic achievement in early adolescent boys. *Developmental Psychology, 29*, 794–804.

Deci, E. L., & Ryan, R. M. (1985). *Intrinsic motivation and self-determination in human behavior*. New York: Plenum.

Dishion, T. J. (1990). The family ecology of boys' peer relations in middle childhood. *Child Development, 61*, 874–892).

Dishion, T. J., Patterson, G. R., Stoolmiller, M., & Skinner, M. L. (1991). Family, school, and behavioral antecedents to early adolescent involvement with antisocial peers. *Developmental Psychology, 27*, 172–180.

Dweck, C. S., & Elliott, E. S. (1983). Achievement motivation. In P. Mussen (Series. Ed.) & E. M. Hetherington (Volume Ed.), *Handbook of child psychology* (vol. 4, pp. 103–196). *Socialization, personality, and social development*. New York: Wiley.

Dweck, C. S., & Goetz, T. (1978). Attributions and learned helplessness. In J. Harvey, W. Ivkes, & R. Kidd (Eds.), *New directions in attribution research* (pp. 157–179). Hillsdale, NJ: Erlbaum.

East, P. L., Lerner, R. M., Lerner, J. V., Soni, R. T., Ohannessian, C. M., & Jacobson, L. P. (1992). Early adolescent-peer group fit, peer relations, and psychosocial competence: A short-term longitudinal study. *Journal of Early Adolescence, 12*, 132–152.

Eccles, J., Midgley, C., & Adler, T. F. (1984). Grade-related changes in the school environment: Effects on motivation. In J. G. Nicholls (Ed.), *The development of achievement motivation* (pp. 283–331). Greenwich, CT: JAI.

Elliott, E. S., & Dweck, C. S. (1988). Goals: An approach to motivation and achievement. *Journal of Personality and Social Psychology, 54*, 5–12.

Feiring, C., & Lewis, M. (1989). The social networks of girls and boys from early through middle childhood. In D. Belle (Ed.), *Children's social networks and social support* (pp. 119–150). New York: Wiley.

Furman, W. (1989). The development of children's social networks. In D. Belle (Ed.), *Children's social networks and social support* (pp. 151–172). New York: Wiley.

Gottfried, A. E., Fleming, J. S., & Gottfried, A. W. (1994). Role of parental motivational practices in children's academic intrinsic motivation and achievement. *Journal of Educational Psychology*, *86*, 104–113.

Graham, S., & Barker, G. P. (1990). The downside of help: An attributional-developmental analysis of helping behavior as a low-ability cue. *Journal of Educational Psychology*, *82*, 7–14.

Green, K. D., Forehand, R., Beck, S. J., & Vosk, B. (1980). An assessment of the relationship among measures of children's social competence and children's academic achievement. *Child Development*, *51*, 1149–1156.

Grolnick, W. S., & Ryan, R. M. (1987). Autonomy in children's learning: An experimental and individual difference investigation. *Journal of Personality and Social Psychology*, *52*, 1–9.

Grolnick, W. S., Ryan, R.M., & Deci, E. L. (1991). Inner resources for school achievement: Motivational mediators of children's perceptions of their parents. *Journal of Educational Psychology*, *83*, 508–517.

Hall, W. M., & Cairns, R. B. (1984). Aggressive behavior in children: An outcome of modeling or social reciprocity? *Developmental Psychology*, *20*, 739–745.

Hallinan, M. T., & Williams, R. A. (1990). Students' characteristics and the peer-influence process. *Sociology of Education*, *63*, 122–132.

Hartup, W. W. (1978). Children and their friends. In H. McGurk (Ed.), *Childhood social development* (pp. 181–271). London: Methuen.

Hartup, W. W. (1983). Peer relations. In P. Mussen (Series. Ed.) & E. M. Hetherington (Volume Ed.), *Handbook of child psychology* (vol. 4, pp. 103–196). *Socialization, personality, and development.* New York: Wiley.

Holloway, S. D., & Hess, R. D. (1982). Causal explanations for school performance: Contrasts between mothers and children. *Journal of Applied Developmental Psychology*, *3*, 319–327.

Howes, C., & Farver, J. (1987). Social pretend play in a 2-year old: Effects of age of partners. *Early Childhood Research Quarterly*, *2*, 305–314.

Hymel, S., & Rubin, K. H. (1985). Children with peer relationships and social skills problems: Conceptual, methodological, and developmental issues. In G. Whitehurst (Ed.), *Annals of child development* (vol. 2, pp. 251–297). Greenwich, CT: JAI.

Jackson, S., Brett, J. F., Sessa, V. I., Cooper, D. M., Julin, J. A., & Peyronnin, K. (1991). Some differences make a difference: Individual dissimilarity and group heterogeneity as correlates of recruitment, promotions, and turnover. *Journal of Applied Psychology*, *76*, 675–689.

Johnson, D. W., & Johnson, R. (1985). Motivation processes in cooperative, competitive, and individualistic learning situations. In C. Ames & R. E. Ames

(Eds.), *Research on motivation in education. The classroom milieu.* (vol. 2, pp. 249–288). Orlando, FL: Academic Press.

Jussim, L. (1989). Teacher expectations, self-fulfilling prophecies, perceptual biases, and accuracy. *Journal of Personality and Social Psychology, 57,* 469–480.

Kandel, D. B. (1978a). Similarity in real-life adolescent friendship pairs. *Journal of Personality and Social Psychology, 36,* 306–312.

Kandel, D. B. (1978b). Homophily, selection, and socialization in adolescent friendships. *American Journal of Sociology, 84,* 427–436.

Keller, J. (1983). Motivational design of instruction. In C. M. Reigeluth (Ed.), *Instructional design theories and models: An overview of their current status.* (pp. 383–434). Hillsdale, NJ: Erlbaum.

Kindermann, T. A. (1993). Natural peer groups as contexts for individual development: The case of children's motivation in school. *Developmental Psychology, 29,* 970–977.

Kindermann, T. A., & Skinner, E. A. (1992). Modeling environmental development: Individual and contextual trajectories. In J. B. Asendorpf & J. Valsiner (Eds.), *Stability and change in development: A study of methodological reasoning* (pp. 155–190). Newbury Park, CA: Sage.

Kindermann, T. A., & Valsiner, J. (1995). (Eds.) *Development of person-context relations.* Hillsdale, NJ: Erlbaum.

Ladd, G. W. (1990). Having friends, keeping friends making friends, and being liked by peers in the classroom: Predictors of children's early school adjustment. *Child Development, 61,* 108–1100.

Larson, R., Richards, M. H. (1991). Daily companionship in late childhood and early adolescence: Changing developmental contexts. *Child Development, 62,* 284–300.

Magnusson, D. (1988). *Individual development from an interactional perspective.* Hillsdale, NJ: Erlbaum.

McIver, D. J., Stipek, D. J., & Daniels, D. H. (1991). Explaining within-semester changes in student effort in junior high school and senior high school courses. *Journal of Educational Psychology, 83,* 201–211.

Meece, J. L., & Holt, K. (1993). A pattern analysis of students' achievement goals. *Journal of Educational Psychology, 85,* 582–590.

Midgley, C., Feldlaufer, H., & Eccles, J. (1989). Change in teacher efficacy and student self-and task related beliefs in mathematics during the transition to junior high school. *Journal of Educational Psychology, 81,* 247–258.

Miller, B. A. (1990). A review of the quantitative research on multigrade instruction. *Research in Rural Education, 7,* 1–8.

Moely, B. E., Hart, S. S., Leal, L., Santulli, K. A., Rao, N., Johnson, T., & Hamilton, L. B. (1992). The teacher's role in facilitating memory and study strategy development in the elementary school classroom. *Child Development, 63,* 653–672.

Moreno, J. L. (1934). *Who shall survive? A new approach to the problem of human interrelations.* Washington, DC: Nervous and Mental Disease Publishing.

Newcomb, A. F., & Bukowski, W. M. (1983). Social impact and social preference as determinants of peer group status. *Developmental Psychology, 19,* 856–867.

Newcomb, A. F., Bukowski, W. M., & Pattee, L. (1993). Children's peer relations: A meta-analytic review of popular, rejected, neglected, controversial, and average sociometric status. *Psychological Bulletin, 113,* 99–128.

Nicholls, J. G. (1984). Concepts of ability and achievement motivation. In R. E. Ames & C. Ames (Eds.), *Research on motivation in education. Student motivation* (vol. 1, pp. 39–73). Orlando, FL: Academic Press.

Parker, J. G., & Asher, S. R. (1987). Peer relations and later personal adjustment: Are low-accepted children at risk? *Psychological Bulletin, 86,* 357–389.

Patrick, B. C., Skinner, E., A., & Connell, J. P. (1993). What motivates children's behavior and emotion? Joint effects of perceived control and autonomy in the academic domain. *Journal of Personality and Social Psychology, 65,* 781–791.

Pintrich, P. R., & De Groot, E. V. (1990). Motivational and self-regulated learning components of classroom performance. *Journal of Educational Psychology, 82,* 33–50.

Pratt, D. (1986). On the merits of multiage classrooms. *Research in rural education, 3,* 111–115.

Price, J. M., & Dodge, K. A. (1989). Peers' contributions to children's social maladjustment: description and intervention. In T. J. Berndt & G. W. Ladd (Eds.), *Peer relationships in child development* (pp. 341–370). New York: Wiley.

Sackett, G. P., Holm, R., Crowley, C., & Henkins, A. (1979). A FORTRAN program for lag sequential analysis of contingency and cyclicity in behavioral interaction data. *Behavior Research Methods & Instrumentation, 11,* 366–378.

Schiefele, U. (1991). Interest learning and motivation. *Educational Psychologist, 26,* 299–324.

Schunk, D. H. (1991). Self-efficacy and academic motivation. *Educational Psychologist, 26,* 207–232.

Sherif, M., Harvey, O. J., White, B. J., Hood, W. R., & Sherif, C. W. (1961). *Intergroup conflict and cooperation: The robbers cave experiment.* Norman, OK: Institute of Group Relations.

Skinner, E. A., & Belmont, M. J. (1993). Motivation in the classroom: Reciprocal effects of teacher behavior and student engagement across the school year. *Journal of Educational Psychology, 85,* 571–581.

Skinner, E. A., Wellborn, J. G., & Connell, J. P. (1990). What it takes to do well in school and whether I've got it: The role of perceived control in children's engagement and social achievement. *Journal of Educational Psychology, 82,* 22–32.

Stevenson, H. W., Lee, S. Chen, C., Lummis, M., Stigler, J., Fan, L., & Ge, F. (1990). *Mathematics achievement of children in China and the United States.* Child Development, 61, 1053–1066.

Stipek, D. J. (1993). *Motivation to learn.* Boston, MA: Allyn and Bacon.

Tesser, A., Campbell, J., & Smith, M. (1984). Friendship choice and performance: Self-esteem maintenance in children. *Journal of Personality and Social Psychology, 46,* 561–574.

Urberg, K. A., & Kaplan, M. G. (1986). Effects of classroom age composition on the play and social behaviors of preschool children. *Journal of Applied Developmental Psychology, 7,* 403–415.

von Eye, A. (1990). *Introduction to configural frequency analysis: The search for types and antitypes in cross-classifications.* New York: Cambridge University Press.

Wasserman, S., Galaskiewicz, J. (Eds.), (1994). *Advances in social network analysis.* Thousand Oaks, CA: Sage.

Weiner, B. (1979). A theory of motivation for some classroom experiences. *Journal of Educational Psychology, 71,* 3–25.

Weiner, B. (1985). An attribution theory of achievement and emotion. *Psychological Bulletin, 92,* 548–573.

Weiner, B. (1986). *An attributional theory of motivation and emotion.* New York: Springer.

Weiner, B. (1990). History of motivational research in education. *Journal of Educational Psychology, 82,* 616–622.

Weisz, J. R., & Cameron, A. M. (1985). Individual differences in the student's sense of control. In C. Ames & R. E. Ames (Eds.), *Research on motivation in education. The classroom milieu.* (vol. 2, pp. 93–140). Orlando, FL: Academic Press.

Wellborn, J. G. (1991). *Engaged vs. disaffected action: Conceptualization and measurement of motivation in the academic domain.* Unpublished Doctoral Dissertation, Graduate School of Human Development and Education. Rochester, NY: University of Rochester.

Wellman, B., & Berkowitz, S. D. (Eds.), (1988). *Social structures: A network approach.* Cambridge, England: Cambridge University Press.

Wentzel, K. R. (1989). Adolescent classroom goals, standards for performance, and academic achievement: An interactionist perspective. *Journal of Educational Psychology, 81,* 131–142.

Wentzel, K. R. (1991). Relations between social competence and academic achievement in early adolescence. *Child Development, 62,* 1066–1078.

Wentzel, K. R. (1993). Does being good make the grade? Social behavior and academic competence in middle school. *Journal of Educational Psychology, 85,* (2), 357–364.

Wigfield, A., & Karpathian, M. (1991). Who am I and what can I do? Children's self-concepts and motivation in academic situations. *Educational Psychologist, 26,* 233–262.

Wright, J. C., Giammarino, M., & Parad, H. W. (1986). Social status in small groups: Individual-group similarity and the social "misfit". *Journal of Personality and Social Psychology, 50,* 523–536.

13   Academic failure and school dropout: The influence of peers

Shelley Hymel, Colin Comfort, Kimberly Schonert-Reichl, and Patricia McDougall

Academic failure and school dropout pose serious obstacles to the pursuit of educational success and represent a loss for both the individual and society. Recent data indicate that in the United States in 1992, about 11% of individuals age 16–24 had not completed high school, representing approximately 3.4 million individuals (Center for Education Statistics, 1993). In urban areas such as Chicago, the dropout rate can reach as high as 50% for ethnic minority students (Hahn, 1987). In Canada, an estimated 30% of 15- to 20-year-olds do not complete high school, as compared with an estimated dropout rate of less than 10% in Germany, and less than 2% in Japan (Employment and Immigration, 1990; Statistics Canada, 1993). The consequences of early school leaving are quite negative, as dropouts are more likely to experience unemployment and acquire less secure and satisfying work than graduates (McCaul, Donaldson, Coadarci, & Davis, 1992; Rumberger, 1987). Biemiller and Meichenbaum (1993) and Catterall (1985) remind us that the existing dropout rate also has direct implications for society in general, not only in terms of loss of potential of these individuals as contributors to our society, but also in terms of the cost incurred from unemployment, welfare and assistance programs, housing, health care, and so on.

   Although studies of the causes of school dropout have identified a wide range of contributing factors, institutional as well as individual, the primary emphasis in this literature has been on academic and familial factors. Far less attention has been given to the role of social factors in contributing to and/or protecting against school failure and dropout. Accordingly, in this chapter, we consider the impact of social factors on the likelihood of academic failure and school dropout, with particular interest in the role of peers. Our focus on the peer group is based on an extension of a recent model of school motivation proposed by Ryan and Powelson (1991), who emphasize that feelings of relatedness (among other things)

313

are critical to education and learning. Although relatedness between students and their parents and teachers has been emphasized in research to date, we suggest that students' relations with peers provide another critical, but often overlooked, sphere of influence. We begin with a brief overview of the extant literature on school dropout. Against this backdrop, we then review research on the role of peers in early school withdrawal, considering four distinct aspects of peer influence: (1) prior social acceptance and rejection, (2) social isolation versus involvement, (3) the negative influence of peers, and (4) aggression and antisocial behavior. Viewing dropout as a final act in a gradual process of school disengagement, we end with a discussion of how peer influences may interact with other variables to contribute ultimately to the likelihood of school withdrawal versus completion.

Correlates and predictors of school dropout

To date, research on the correlates of school dropout has focused on characteristics of the student, particularly academic and familial factors, with the implication that the causes of dropout must lie primarily in the scholastic failure of the individual or difficulties within the family. For instance, students who drop out are more likely to exhibit lower levels of intellectual ability (Combs & Cooley, 1968; Howell & Frese, 1982; Lloyd, 1978), poorer achievement and grades (Barrington & Hendricks, 1989; Dryfoos, 1990; Ekstrom, Goertz, Pollack, & Rock, 1986; Ensminger & Slusarcick, 1992; Statistics Canada, 1993), higher rates of truancy (Wehlage & Rutter, 1986), grade retention (Cairns, Cairns, & Neckerman, 1989; Center for Education Statistics, 1993; Ekstrom et al., 1986; Howell & Frese, 1982; Statistics Canada, 1993) and school transfers (Stroup & Robins, 1972). With regard to familial variables, dropout rates are found to be disproportionately higher among lower income families and some racial minorities (Hahn, 1987), although research by Rumberger (1983) indicates that the effect of race/ethnicity decreases when socioeconomic level is held constant, and recent U.S. data indicate that dropout rates do not differ significantly across ethnic groups (Center for Education Statistics, 1993). Dropouts are also more likely to come from single-parent and no-parent homes (Rumberger, 1983; Statistics Canada, 1993), from homes that provide less support for educational success (Ekstrom et al., 1986; Howell & Frese, 1982), less involvement in parent-school organizations, and less strict rules regarding school (Ensminger & Slusarcick, 1992). As well, parents of dropouts tend to exhibit lower levels of educational attainment (Lloyd, 1978; Statistics Canada, 1993).

Academic and familial factors certainly play a significant role in school dropout. However, we are concerned that this primary focus within the literature reflects (perhaps implicitly) an individual deficit model of school failure that emphasizes characteristics of the student (e.g., socioeconomic status, family characteristics, learning problems, absenteeism) as the major "cause" of academic failure and early school leaving. Moreover, these factors do not represent a complete picture of the problem, and alone cannot account for the current rate of school dropout. Even data used to support the influence of familial and academic factors suggests that these variables only account for a portion of the dropouts surveyed. For example, although school leavers are found to perform more poorly in school than graduates (as reflected in reported grades), most dropouts performed satisfactorily in school and only some reported problems with school work as a primary reason for leaving school (Center for Education Statistics, 1993; Statistics Canada, 1993). With regard to familial variables, a recent study comparing school leavers and graduates indicated that most dropouts (61%) as well as graduates (83%) came from two-parent homes (Statistics Canada, 1993). Moreover, although dropout rates are higher among low income families, the majority of dropouts come from middle income families (Center for Education Statistics, 1993). Thus, the individual factors which have been highlighted in previous research do not appear to characterize the majority of dropouts surveyed. As well, many of the individual variables identified as predictors of school leaving are nonmanipulable (e.g., SES) and thus do not easily lend themselves to intervention efforts. It therefore becomes imperative to consider a broader range of factors that also play a role in the decision to drop out of school early.

What reasons do *students* give for dropping out? This question becomes crucial in light of concerns expressed by Zaslow and Takanishi (1993) that much of the extant research on adolescence has bypassed the step of giving students a "voice" and has failed to consider students' own perceptions of their school experiences. Recent studies in both the U.S. (Center for Education Statistics, 1993) and Canada (Statistics Canada, 1993) indicate that students' reasons for dropping out of school are quite varied. In addition to academic and familial concerns, dropouts also highlight job- or work-related concerns, the desire to travel, and drug/alcohol problems as reasons for dropout. It is important to note, however, that dissatisfaction with the school milieu and other school-related problems top the list of reasons for leaving school early (Goertz, Ekstrom, & Rock, 1991; O'Sullivan, 1990). Indeed, about 40% of dropouts cite school-related concerns and not liking school as a major factor in dropping out (Center for Education Statistics, 1993; Statistics Canada, 1993).

Because such a large proportion of dropouts attribute leaving school early to school concerns, the critical question becomes "what about school was disliked?" To date, the most obvious answer has been that students dislike the work they are required to do in school. Still, fewer than one-third of recent U.S. dropouts indicated not being able to keep up with schoolwork as a reason for dropping out (Center for Education Statistics, 1993). Dislike of school and school work can also manifest itself in generalized reports of boredom (Farrell, 1990), as students question the personal relevance of school for their daily lives. A second, but often overlooked, reason for disliking school involves the social climate of the school. A substantial proportion of recent dropouts suggested that they could not get along with teachers (22.8%) or other students (14.5%), that they did not feel that they belonged (24.2%), or that they did not feel safe at school (6.0%) (Center for Education Statistics, 1993). Another 8% indicated that their friends had dropped out. These data suggest that a substantial number of dropouts do not feel a sense of connectedness or belonging within the school context. Thus, it is important to consider how aspects of the educational system, in addition to academic and familial difficulties, contribute to the likelihood of school dropout.

In an effort to broaden our understanding of the factors that underlie school dropout, some researchers have examined aspects of the school system which may, in part, contribute to early withdrawal. For example, Fine (1991) suggests that many so-called "dropouts" are better labeled "pushouts," since they have been "encouraged" to leave school early. As well, Crespo and Michelena (1981) suggest that the school practice of streaming students into varying tracks or levels is significantly predictive of dropout, even after controlling for intellectual ability, academic performance, and age. There is also evidence to suggest that dropout rates are lower in smaller as opposed to larger schools (Pittman & Haughwout, 1987), and in schools with neighborhood rather than system-wide attendance boundaries (Toles, Schulz, & Rice, 1986). Although these studies reflect a greater appreciation of the range of factors that contribute to school dropout, the role of peers in school dropout has not been adequately considered to date.

A theoretical model of school motivation

In a recent model of school motivation, Ryan and Powelson (1991) argue that three basic needs are fundamental to learning: feelings of *competence, autonomy,* and *relatedness.* These researchers begin with the assumption that students come to school with a natural and innate curiosity and interest in learning, which manifests itself as a basic need for feelings of competence and autonomy as a primary basis for motivation (Ryan, 1991; White, 1963). In their model, *competence* refers to one's sense of mastery and accomplishment when challenged optimally (see Harter, 1983; White, 1960). *Autonomy* refers to the idea of self-regulation or self-determination (see deCharms, 1968; Deci & Ryan, 1985, 1987). However, there is another, equally important and natural tendency that is critical to education – the need to develop connections and associations within a social matrix, which Ryan and Powelson refer to as a psychological need for *relatedness. Relatedness* refers to the interpersonal attachments and bonds developed between individuals, and is based on a fundamental striving for contact and alliance with others, enhancing the well-being of all involved. Ryan (1991) further suggests that the need for relatedness is a social motive that is evident in one's concern for "what others look for in and from us" (Ryan, Connell, & Grolnick, 1992, p. 172).

In an historical analysis of the changing context of education, moving from learning through apprenticeship and participation in adult work, to the modern day institutions of education (schools), Ryan and Powelson (1991) suggest that "the institutionalization of education in the modern era removed the processes of learning and cultural transmission from contexts in which children were often guided by adults to whom they were closely attached and from activities of significance in everyday life" (p. 49). Despite the obvious benefits of modern education, this transition created a school context in which children are more isolated from the adult world, and learn skills that often have no clear or immediate purpose in their daily lives. Ryan and Powelson also suggest that learning has evolved into an individualized and/or competitive experience, despite arguments for the efficacy of more cooperative and interpersonal learning approaches (see Hymel, Zinck, & Ditner, 1993). Such changes have effectively reduced the likelihood that the educational system can maintain students' feelings of autonomy and relatedness and, in failing to do so, may contribute to the academic failure of at least some students.

Thus, Ryan and Powelson (1991) direct our attention to two fundamental aspects of education beyond the basic goal of fostering learning or academic competence. The need for *autonomy* has implications for how classroom environments are structured (see Eccles et al., 1993). The need for *relatedness* has implications for students' interpersonal relationships with both adults and peers. There is ample evidence to support the notion that teaching practices that foster student autonomy versus control (the classroom "climate") are related to greater academic motivation, achievement, and feelings of competence (e.g., Boggiano & Katz, 1991; Boggiano, Main, Flink, Barrett, Silvern, & Katz, 1989; Deci, Schwartz, Scheinman, & Ryan, 1981; Eccles et al., 1990, 1993; Grolnick & Ryan, 1987; Ryan & Connell, 1989; Ryan & Grolnick, 1986).

Far less empirical support is available for the notion that feelings of *relatedness* are important in maximizing student learning, although a few recent studies suggest that relatedness to parents as well as teachers is important for school success. Ryan, Stiller, and Lynch (1994) examined how students' feelings of relatedness to parents, teachers, and peers were related to school functioning (positive coping, autonomy, perceived control, and general self-esteem). Results indicated that the quality of reported relatedness to both teachers and parents independently predicted various aspects of school functioning. No predictive relations were obtained for feelings of relatedness to peers, although Ryan et al. suggest that this may be due to the fact that peers can exert either a positive or negative influence on school success. Thus, when the influence of all peers is considered, an overall positive or negative influence is not clearly evident. Goodenow (1993), however, has demonstrated that feelings of classroom belonging and peer/teacher support in middle school are significant predictors of school motivation and expectations for academic success.

There has been growing recognition of the importance of peer relations for school engagement. In discussing early school adjustment, Ladd (personal communication, 24 Sept., 1994) suggests that peers are the "glue" that solidifies students' initial involvement in the educational enterprise (see also Ladd, 1990). The importance of peers does not diminish and may even increase with age. For example, in our own research we have found that the transition from elementary to middle school is easier for those students who report positive peer support, and more difficult for students who are lonely and dissatisfied with their current peer relations (McDougall & Hymel, 1995). From interviews with urban high school students, Firestone and Rosenblum (1988) suggest that school "is where students can come to be with their friends or where they find activities other than educational ones to keep them occupied" (p. 10). Andersson (1994) reports that 70% of Swedish adolescents surveyed indicated that the "best thing" about school is peers, and more than 40% indicated that if it were not for their peers, they would not be able to "stand school." Thus, Andersson suggests that peers may be more important than teachers in fostering school engagement.

Consistent with the model proposed by Ryan and Powelson (1991), our view is that student participation and involvement in school (factors that may protect the student against school dropout) are to a large degree dependent on how much the school environment contributes to students' feelings of both autonomy and relatedness which, in turn, contribute to positive academic performance and feelings of competence. Like Ryan and Powelson, we feel that both parents and teachers play a critical role in maximizing student feelings of both autonomy and relatedness. However, although parents and teachers have traditionally been viewed as the primary agents of children's scholastic motivation (e.g., Blumenfeld, 1992), developmental and educational psychologists have increasingly recognized the role of peers in the socialization process (e.g., Asher, 1983; Berndt & Ladd, 1989; Hartup, 1983; Hartup & Sancilio, 1986; Ladd, 1988; Parker & Asher, 1987). The influence of peers may be particularly critical during adolescence, when peers take on added significance in one's life (e.g., Berndt & Ladd, 1989; Brown, 1990; Buhrmester, 1990; Claes, 1992; Csikzentmihalyi & Larson, 1994; Hartup, 1993; Larson & Richards, 1991). Adolescents reportedly spend twice as much time with peers than with their family (Csikzentmihalyi & Larson, 1984; Larson & Richards, 1991), and peers fulfill a developmental need that cannot be met by parents or other adults (Berndt, 1982; Hartup, 1993; Seltzer, 1982). Moreover, Steinberg, Dornbusch, and Brown (1992) suggest that although parents play a critical role in students' long-term educational plans and goals, "peers are the most potent influence on their day-to-day behaviors in school (e.g., how much time they spend on homework, if they enjoy coming to school each day, and how they behave in the classroom)" (p. 727). Thus, especially during adolescence, peers may be particularly important in providing an educational context in which the student can feel a sense of belonging and affiliation (relatedness). Although few studies have directly examined the impact of feelings of peer relatedness on school functioning, there is a growing body of evidence to suggest that various aspects of peer relationships are important in determining the likelihood of school dropout.

The influence of peers on school dropout

Studies have demonstrated consistent links between social competence and various academic outcomes, suggesting that children who are poorly accepted and/or aggressive are at greater risk for academic failure than their more popular or prosocial peers (e.g., Dishion, 1990; Green, Forehand, Beck, & Vosk, 1980; Lambert, 1972; Vosk, Forehand, Parker, & Rickard, 1982). Given evidence (reviewed above) that academic difficulties are a significant predictor of later school dropout, these findings lead to the question of whether social factors are themselves directly related to the likelihood of school dropout. Although limited, there is a growing body of evidence to suggest that peer relationships do indeed play a critical role. In our review, we distinguish four aspects of peer influence: prior social acceptance within the peer group, social isolation versus involvement, the negative influence of peers, and aggressive and antisocial behavior.

Prior social acceptance within the peer group

The importance of good peer relations has been most convincingly demonstrated in studies showing that children who are rejected by peers are at greater risk for a variety adjustment difficulties in adolescent and adult life (see Parker & Asher, 1987, for a review). Of interest here is whether early peer difficulties, as assessed by indices of peer acceptance/rejection during the elementary years, place the student at greater risk for later school dropout. Several older studies have demonstrated direct associations between early social status and later dropout (Barclay, 1966; Gronlund & Holmlund, 1958; Kuhlen & Collister, 1952; Lambert, 1972; Ullmann, 1957). For example, Gronlund and Holmlund (1958) found that 54% of low accepted boys and 35% of low accepted girls subsequently dropped out of school, as compared with 19% and 4% of more accepted boys and girls, respectively. Similarly, Barclay (1966) reported that students who were not well accepted by peers were two to three times more likely later to drop out of school than their more accepted classmates. In more recent studies, using sociometric measures that allow for the distinction of various social status subgroups (e.g., rejected, neglected, controversial, popular, average), there is also evidence to suggest that children who are rejected during the elementary years are at greater risk for later school dropout. Specifically, Ollendick et al. (1992) found that 18% of the children classified as sociometrically rejected (generally disliked) in grade four had dropped out of school by grade nine, as compared with 5% of popular students, 6% of average status students, 3% of neglected students, and 9% of controversial status students. Given evidence that students are more likely to drop out in the later grades of high school (Center for Education Statistics, 1993; Statistics Canada, 1993), rejected children may be even more likely to drop out of school than suggested by the Ollendick et al. results. Further, Ollendick et al. found that, relative to popular peers, rejected students were also more likely to later exhibit problems of adolescent delinquency, conduct disturbance and substance abuse, to obtain lower achievement test scores in grade eight, and more grade retentions by grade nine, all factors which have been shown to predict school dropout (e.g., Barrington & Hendricks, 1989).

Not all studies, however, have demonstrated significant links between early social status and later dropout. Following 112 fifth grade students through high school, Kupersmidt and Coie (1990) reported no significant differences in later dropout rates as a function of sociometric status (using a categorical modeling analysis). However, consistent with earlier studies, they reported that about 30% of rejected fifth graders later dropped out, compared to 20% of average status students, 7% of popular students, and 0% of students who were neglected in grade five. Moreover, Kupersmidt and Coie provide a footnote indicating that results of a logistic regression analysis, conducted with only a White subsample, revealed that social preference among grade five peers (the degree to which they are liked rather than disliked) did emerge as a significant predictor of later dropout. Using a different assessment procedure, Cairns et al. (1989) also evaluated whether early social difficulties predicted later dropout. Although social status has typically been evaluated using peer assessments, Cairns et al. used teacher reports to assess popularity in 475 seventh grade students and followed them through grade eleven. Peer assessments were used to assess social isolation. In this study, neither popularity nor social isolation was found to predict subsequent dropout. The failure to demonstrate a relation between social status and later dropout may be attributable to the use of teacher rather than peer assessments of popularity, or to the examination of social status during middle, rather than elementary school.

Although findings are somewhat mixed, the majority of these studies do suggest a link between early problems in peer relations and later school withdrawal. As well, in a small-scale meta-analysis of the seven available studies examining peer status (popularity, acceptance, rejection) and later school dropout, Comfort and Kishor (1994) reported a significant mean effect size of $r = .19$. Although the overall effect size is not large, it does suggest that status among peers plays a role in subsequent school dropout. Several questions remain, however, regarding the mechanisms underlying the relations between early rejection and later dropout. Peer rejection has generally been shown to be a rather stable phenomenon from one year to the next (Coie & Dodge, 1983), but such data do not suggest that children who are rejected within the elementary school classroom are destined to be rejected throughout their academic years. Thus, it is not appropriate to assume that early rejection leads to continued rejection, which is itself predictive of school dropout. Clearly, more extensive longitudinal research on the stability of peer rejection across the elementary to high school years is needed, as is research on whether *concurrent* peer rejection is related to school dropout. To our knowledge, such data do not presently exist.

Recent research on the functions of peer group formation and peer cultures during adolescence may offer, in part, an hypothesis regarding the social trajectories of rejected children. As Erikson (1959) and others (e.g., Marcia, 1980) have noted, one of the major developmental tasks of adolescence is to develop a sense of identity – adolescents must determine who they are, what they are all about, and what they are going to do in the future. As students move from the smaller, homogeneous classrooms of the elementary school to the larger social world of the secondary school, the number and variety of peers and cliques available to them increases substantially. In their search for identity, then, adolescents are able to choose from a wider array of possibilities than was afforded within the elementary context. These diverse opportunities for affiliation may provide a chance to overcome the early rejection experienced by some students during the elementary years. Support for this contention comes from a qualitative study by Kinney (1993) who examined the everyday experiences of adolescents whose high school peers had labeled them as unpopular during their earlier school years. Through extensive interviews, Kinney identified a pattern whereby students who were previously labeled as unpopular "nerds" in middle school were able to obtain a more positive perception of themselves as "normal" and accepted by at least some peers within the more differentiated social context of the high school. Kinney suggested that one of the mechanisms responsible for this transformation from "nerd" to "normal" was the quest for identity formation – a need to find a peer group niche with whom one can identify. Adolescents seemed to experience the transition from middle to high school as a time of increased opportunities to find a peer group niche, recalling that such opportunities "provided alternative domains to achieving school-wide popularity in which students could feel adequate and successful" (p. 30). Thus, the transition to high school may provide some students with an opportunity to rid themselves of the stigma of peer rejection and find a peer group which offers support for school-related goals.

Other research on peer cultures and adolescent subgroups, however, suggests that the opposite effect can take place as well – that the peer group with whom one comes to identify can advocate a value system that does *not* support school involvement and participation. For example, Eckert (1989), in her work on social categories in high schools, has identified a subgroup of "burnouts" – students who were alienated from the social and academic functioning of school. Such subgroups often fostered the development of "anti-school" feelings and a dislike for all aspects of school, such as rules, teachers, and school activities. Thus, the shift to the larger social world of secondary school may afford students an opportunity to change their social status, but the effects of such a shift may vary depending on the value system supported by the newly-found social niche, a point to which we will return shortly. Future research may benefit from consideration of whether dropout rates vary across peer subgroups within the high school community.

In summary, it is not clear whether peer rejection constitutes a highly stable phenomenon that persists through the elementary years and into adolescence, directly contributing to the likelihood of school dropout, or whether early peer rejection is merely a precursor to other forms of disengagement from school, serving as one of many factors that together make school an undesirable context for some students. Consistent with the latter hypothesis, Kupersmidt, Coie, and Dodge (1990), in reviewing research on the prediction of school dropout from indices of earlier social status, conclude that "social rejection might play a unique, incremental role in this prediction. One reason for this may be that being rejected by the peer group may make coming to school an aversive experience for adolescents and thus motivate them to think of leaving school" (p. 290). Still, several authors suggest that perceived social isolation or peer rejection per se leads to school dropout (e.g., Pittman, 1986; Valverde, 1987). In the next section, we review evidence concerning the relation between *perceived* social isolation (as opposed to actual peer rejection) and the likelihood of school dropout.

Social isolation versus involvement

Although the preceding review suggests that early peer rejection is predictive of later school dropout, not all rejected children drop out of school, and some well-accepted students also drop out. One possibility is that only those students who *perceive themselves* to be rejected or isolated within the peer group are at risk for dropout. Research on children's social self-perceptions suggests that actual and perceived peer rejection may not be synonymous. For example, studies have shown that rejected children are significantly more likely to report feelings of loneliness and social dis- satisfaction than their more accepted peers, but there is also considerable variability in children's social self-perceptions, especially among rejected children (Asher, Parkhurst, Hymel, & Williams, 1990). Perhaps only those students who acknowledge their social difficulties and who feel isolated are more likely to dropout, regardless of actual levels of peer rejection. Many have suggested that students at risk for dropout experience feelings of alienation, disenfranchisement, or isolation (see Finn, 1989), yet sur- prisingly few empirical studies have directly examined perceptions of so- cial isolation among dropouts.

As an initial means of evaluating the degree to which feelings of social isolation play a role in the decision to drop out of school, we can examine the reasons students offer for their decision to leave school early. When asked about their reasons for leaving, a substantial number of dropouts emphasize peer-related factors, although generalizations are difficult, giv- en the variable ways in which reasons for dropping out have been catego- rized across studies. For example, results of some studies (Pittman, 1986; Rumberger, 1983) suggest that perceived rejection by peers is not neces- sarily a major reason for school dropout, as far as reports by dropouts themselves are concerned, although problems with peers may well have been subsumed within other categories such as "disliked school" (Rum- berger, 1983) or "unhappy school experience" (Pittman, 1986). Gastright (1987) reported that only 3% of dropouts indicated that "other students" were a reason for dropping out. In contrast, in a recent U.S. sample (Cen- ter for Education Statistics, 1993), 14.5% of dropouts indicated that not getting along with other students was a reason for dropping out, and 24.2% of dropouts reported that feeling like they did not belong was a contributing factor in their decision to drop out. Thus, when open-ended questions are used to assess reasons for school dropout, with researchers free to categorize responses in their own way, the degree to which students cite interpersonal difficulties as a major factor in their dropout decision is difficult to ascertain, although some reports suggest that peer difficulties may be a factor for a number of dropouts.

Discrepant findings are also evident when more direct evaluation methods are used. When dropouts were asked to indicate the degree to which they agreed with various reasons for dropping out, Tidwell (1988) found that 20.5% agreed that "students at the school" were a reason for leaving school. In contrast, McCaul (1989), using a similar methodology, reported that only 6.3% of dropouts agreed that not getting along with students was a reason for their dropping out.

Results of several retrospective studies also provide some support for the notion that school dropouts are more likely to feel socially isolated or alienated within the high school. Seidel and Vaughn (1991) found that Learning Disabled (LD) dropouts reported greater social alienation from peers than did LD nondropouts, although the generalizability of these findings to non-LD students is questionable. Dohn (1991) found that Danish dropouts reported feeling more excluded by their classmates than did nondropouts. In an inner-city sample, Fagan and Pabon (1990) observed that dropouts were more socially isolated than graduates, as indicated by self-reported immersion in friendship networks combined with reported participation in social activities. In a qualitative study comparing Hispanic dropouts versus graduates, Valverde (1987) found that dropouts reported more feelings of alienation/rejection and fewer friendships than did graduates (see also Williams, 1987). Although results of these studies suggest a relation between feelings of social isolation and school dropout, the retrospective nature of these studies makes it difficult to determine whether these self-perceptions existed before the decision to leave school, or whether they emerged in a post hoc fashion as a rationalization for the decision to leave school early.

Other studies have examined whether students' feelings of isolation, alienation, or lack of belonging predict school dropout using experimenter-developed, self-report instruments (e.g., Pittman, 1991). Information on the psychometric properties of these measures is not always reported, and the conceptual underpinnings of these scales are not always clear. For example, Wehlage and Rutter (1986) reported that dropouts feel alienated and rejected in school, but their measure of alienation was embedded within a larger set of items, including perceived teacher interest and discipline practices. Elliott and Voss (1974) reported that students who would later drop out reported greater feelings of social isolation, but the majority of items in their assessment reflected school participation and extracurricular involvement rather than feelings of isolation per se. Although a lack of school participation may stem from feelings of isolation (or vice versa), it may also be the result of other factors, such as job- or family-related demands.

Several authors have argued that involvement in school and extracurricular activities constitutes an index of social integration within the school context (e.g., Kelly & Pink, 1972; Tinto, 1975). Although somewhat distinct from feelings of social isolation as discussed here, there is ample evidence to suggest that dropouts are significantly less likely to participate in school-based extra-curricular activities and/or sports than are students who do not drop out (Ekstrom et al., 1986; Elliott & Voss, 1974; Hinojosa & Miller, 1984; Kelly & Pink, 1972; Pittman, 1991; Smith, Tseng, & Mink, 1971; Statistics Canada, 1993; Thomas, 1954; Walters & Kranzler, 1970). Whether this lack of participation in school activities is a cause, a consequence, or even a correlate of social isolation is unclear, but these findings do suggest that the dropout is less involved in the social aspects of the high school.

In summary, despite suggestions that dropouts may feel socially isolated, there is little *unequivocal* empirical support for this notion within the current dropout literature. For example, when we examine the spontaneous reasons students give for leaving school early, some studies indicate no clear relations between early school leaving and reported peer difficulties (e.g., Pittman, 1986; Rumberger, 1983), whereas other studies show that a substantial number of dropouts (24.2%) report feeling that they did not belong as a factor contributing to their decision to leave school early (Center for Education Statistics, 1993). Results of several retrospective studies consistently demonstrate that feelings of social isolation are more likely among dropouts than among graduates, but the retrospective nature of these findings makes it difficult to determine whether perceived social isolation is an antecedent of school dropout or a rationalization which emerges after the fact, owing perhaps to a need to cut ties with one's school friends *after* leaving school. There is considerable evidence indicating that dropouts are less likely to participate in extracurricular activities and/or sports within the school context, suggesting that, at least to some extent, dropouts are not well-integrated or involved in the social activities afforded by schools. However, it is not clear whether a lack of social involvement stems from feelings of social isolation or from other demands such as work or family. More extensive research is needed, particularly prospective, longitudinal studies, before definitive conclusions can be reached.

In the absence of clear evidence that perceived social isolation contributes to the likelihood of school dropout, we consider a somewhat different hypothesis regarding the social relations that characterize the early school leaver. That is, the high school dropout may in fact experience a reasonable degree of social integration and may enjoy a number of established peer relationships, but with peers who do not identify with or participate in the school context and who do not encourage school completion. These arguments are consistent with Finn's (1989) "participation-identification model" of school dropout, which suggests that students who drop out are less likely to be active participants in school and classroom activities, and thus fail to develop a feeling of identification with or "bonding" to school. Consistent with Ryan and Powelson's (1991) notion of relatedness, Finn reviews evidence to suggest that students typically develop an internalized feeling of belonging within the school. Two distinct components are critical here: belonging and valuing. Students must feel a part of the social world of the school and must value educational success. As indicated above, research has demonstrated a rather consistent relation between lack of participation in school and subsequent school dropout. Thus, dropouts do not appear to be engaged in or committed to the social activities that typify most educational institutions. At the same time, many dropouts evidently do not necessarily feel socially isolated, suggesting that they *are* involved in some form of satisfying social networks. As Finn suggests, the social affiliations that characterize early school leavers may not be ones that enhance feelings of belonging or identification with school and may not foster the maintenance of positive school values. Research relevant to these hypotheses is reviewed in the next section.

The negative influence of peers

If most school dropouts are not the socially isolated individuals that some suggest them to be, what is the nature of their social affiliations during the high school years? Some have suggested that potential dropouts tend to affiliate with others who are also at risk for early school leaving, and together disengage from school (e.g., Mensch & Kandel, 1988; Pittman, 1991). Consistent with this hypothesis, Cairns et al. (1989) found that students who would eventually drop out tended to affiliate with other students who were also at risk for school dropout. Thus, although school dropouts may not be socially isolated, they may be victims of negative peer influence. There is some evidence to support these speculations.

First, results of a recent national survey of school dropouts (Statistics Canada, 1993) indicated that students who leave school early are more likely to have friends outside of school than are students who graduate. In addition, most graduates (80%) reported having friends who believed that high school completion was very important, and only a few graduates (2%) reported having friends who felt that completing high school was

unimportant. In contrast, fewer than half of the dropouts surveyed reported having friends who believed completing high school was important,
and 12% of dropouts reported that their friends felt high school completion was not very important. Similar findings have emerged from qualitative studies of school dropout (Delgado-Gaitan, 1986; Farrell, Peguero,
Lindsey, & White, 1988), suggesting that involvement in peer groups that
embrace a noneducational orientation can contribute to the decision to
drop out of school early. Research has also shown that students who have
friends who like school (Hinojosa & Miller, 1984), who get good grades
and are interested in school or attend classes regularly (Ekstrom et al.,
1986) are more likely to graduate from high school. Using a path analysis,
Pittman (1991) provides evidence to suggest that of all the variables he examined in the High School and Beyond data set, peers' interest in school
had the largest impact on students' own interest in school which, in turn,
had the largest direct influence on later school dropout. Other research indicates that dropouts tend to have lower educational and occupational expectations than do graduates (Wehlage & Rutter, 1986), and that they perceive their friends to have lower educational aspirations as well (Ekstrom
et al., 1986; Rumberger, 1983). Results of retrospective studies have also
shown that dropouts were significantly more likely to have friends who
had dropped out of high school than were graduates (Alpert & Dunham,
1986; Dunham & Alpert, 1987), although only a small proportion of
dropouts (2.5%, McCaul, 1989; 8%, U.S. Center for Education Statistics,
1993) acknowledge that one of the reasons that they dropped out was that
their friends were dropping out. It may be that students who are at high
risk for dropping out of school simply share a number of negative school
values with like-minded friends who are also at risk for school dropout or
who have already left school. These findings underscore the importance
of determining the role that peers play in the socialization of educational
values.

To understand the roles that peers might play, we must first understand
the general developmental trajectory of academic motivation across the
adolescent years. Results of several studies suggest a general increase in
negative attitudes toward learning and achievement (Eccles, Midgley, &
Adler, 1984) and a gradual decline in academic motivation over the early
adolescent years (see Eccles & Midgley, 1989, 1990, for reviews). In particular, Harter (1981) has shown that, as students move through our educational system, there is a gradual shift from an intrinsic interest in learning
during the elementary years to a more extrinsic motivational orientation
by adolescence. These general declines do not characterize all adoles-

cents, however, with a large proportion of students exhibiting no major change in motivation and some showing increases in intrinsic motivation (Harter, Whitesell, & Kowalski, 1986, as cited in Harter, 1992).

There is some evidence to suggest that academic motivation may be socialized within students' self-selected peer networks. For example, studies have shown that students tend to associate with classmates who exhibit a similar level of school performance (Tesser, Campbell, & Smith, 1984) and/or a similar motivational orientation toward school (Kindermann, 1993). Such self-selected peer affiliations may set the stage for enhancing or decreasing students' value for school. At least two studies have examined whether students' motivational orientation can be modified by peer group experiences. In a small N study, Kindermann (1993) demonstrated that the motivational orientation of children's peer groups was preserved over a school year (despite considerable changes in group membership), and that the motivational orientation of the group influenced individual changes in motivation across the year. Berndt, Laychak, and Park (1990) demonstrated that discussions with friends about achievement-related dilemmas can increase similarity in achievement-related decisions, especially if the friendship is characterized by greater cooperation and acceptance, and less aggression and conflict.

More recent models of academic motivation have moved from consideration of two contrasting motivational orientations (intrinsic versus extrinsic) to a third orientation: internalized motivation (Harter, 1992, this volume; Ryan et al., 1992). According to Harter (1992), internalized motivation represents the effects of socialization within the culture, such that academic behaviors that are initially controlled by extrinsic rewards gradually become internalized, as the student comes to view these behaviors and attitudes, valued by significant others, as important for the self. Although internalized motivation is not the idealized intrinsic motivation that characterizes the very young student's natural curiosity and interest in learning, it does represent a self-directed or self-regulated motivational orientation, one that operates in absence of extrinsic rewards. Our view is that internalized motivation is particularly likely to be influenced by significant others in one's life, most notably, parents, teachers, and peers. As noted earlier, research has shown that students who drop out of school are more likely to associate with peers who do not value educational excellence or do not view high school graduation as important (e.g., Cairns et al., 1989; Delgado-Gaitan, 1986; Farrell et al., 1988; Statistics Canada, 1993), and who are perceived to have lower educational aspirations (Ekstrom et al., 1986; Rumberger, 1983). Thus, students at risk for dropout may be more likely to affiliate with peers who do not positively influence the internalization of culturally prescribed values, or who fail to contribute positively to the socialization of internalized motivation.

Given arguments that an internalized motivational orientation is socialized by significant others in one's life, it is also important to remember that students who drop out tend to come from families that provide less encouragement for educational success (Ekstrom et al., 1986; Howell & Frese, 1982) and have parents who themselves exhibit lower levels of educational attainment (Lloyd, 1978; Statistics Canada, 1993). Thus, the influence of both parents and peers on the development of an internalized motivational orientation may be less likely for the dropout. Steinberg et al. (1992) specifically suggest that both parenting practices and peer support for academic attainment play critical roles in determining school outcomes. Although Steinberg et al. did not address the issue of school dropout per se, they concluded that "youngsters whose friends and parents both support achievement perform better than those who receive support only from one source but not the other, who in turn perform better than those who receive no support from either" (p. 727). They further suggest that the relative availability of parental and peer support for academic attainment varies across ethnic groups, with the "congruence of parent and peer support [being] greater for White and Asian-American youngsters than for African-American and Hispanic adolescents" (p. 727). Thus, Steinberg et al. conclude that parents and peers can offset or compensate for the influence of each other on school values.

In summary, results of several studies indicate that dropouts are more likely to affiliate with peers outside of school, with peers who have themselves dropped out, and/or with peers who are also at risk for dropout. Further, dropouts tend to associate more with peers who evidence less positive educational values, interest, or motivation, and who have lower educational aspirations. It may be that early peer rejection (during the elementary years) constitutes the beginning of a cycle in which rejected students who are not well integrated within the mainstream classroom begin to associate with similar others – those who do not support the "school game" – and together these students gradually disengage from school. On the basis of these findings, we suggest that the peer group plays a critical role in the socialization of educational values and academic motivation, a relationship that to date has been relatively unrecognized within the literature. Although parents and teachers have traditionally been seen as the primary agents of socialization with regard to school motivation, our review suggests that students' academic motivation and perceived school value are also influenced by those peers with whom they are closely associated, and this influence can be either positive or negative. The peer group may also play an important role in the socialization of aggressive and antisocial behavior, a characteristic that has also been linked to the likelihood of school dropout, as discussed in the next section.

Aggression and antisocial behavior

Considerable evidence exists regarding the relationship between aggressive behavior and school dropout. Although aggressive behavior cannot be considered an aspect of peer influence per se, it does reflect students' difficulty in getting along with peers and therefore is considered relevant to the present review. Studies comparing dropouts with graduates consistently demonstrate that dropouts are rated by both teachers and peers as exhibiting more aggressive behavior than graduates (Kuhlen & Collister, 1952; Lambert, 1972; see Parker & Asher, 1987, for a review). Moreover, ratings of aggressive behavior during elementary school (Ensminger & Slusarcick, 1992; Kupersmidt & Coie, 1990) as well as early adolescence (Cairns et al., 1989) have been shown to be a strong predictor of subsequent school dropout, even after the influence of other variables such as gender, race, peer rejection, excessive absences, and low grades (Kupersmidt & Coie, 1990), or race, SES, grade retention, maturation, and popularity (Cairns et al., 1989) are taken into account. As is the case for indices of early peer rejection, however, the studies reviewed herein have been concerned with *early* aggressive behavior as a predictor of subsequent dropout, and have not addressed the *concurrent* relations between aggressive or antisocial behavior and school dropout. In addition to aggressive behavior, school dropouts report more regular alcohol and drug use than do graduates, and also are more likely to have criminal records than are graduates (Ekstrom et al., 1986; Elliott & Voss, 1974; Mensch & Kandel, 1988; Steinberg, Blinde, & Chan, 1984; Statistics Canada, 1993).

Finn (1989) suggests that these negative social behaviors may be a reaction to the frustration some students feel within the school context. Specifically, in his "frustration-self-esteem model" of school dropout, Finn suggests a cycle that begins with poor school performance (attributable to student academic deficits and/or poor instruction), which leads to low self-esteem on the part of the student in response to the frustration and embarrassment caused by school failure. These feelings of personal failure fuel reactive opposition to the school context, which is held responsible, observed in the form of various kinds of disruptive or oppositional behavior (aggression, delinquency, classroom disruption, skipping class). According to Finn, some versions of this model suggest that, as the resulting oppositional behavior becomes more disruptive with age, school personnel direct greater attention toward the behavior problems themselves, with less and less attention directed toward the learning difficulties that underlie them. As a result, the student falls further behind academically, and behavior problems escalate, becoming increasingly entrenched. Other versions of this model suggest that low self-esteem leads to a search for alternate activities (such as oppositional behavior) in which the student might feel some form of success. Even though such activities and behaviors are less socially sanctioned by the schools, they may garner the approval of similar nonparticipant or antisocial peers (see Elliott & Voss, 1974; Finn, 1989 for relevant supportive literature). In the end, the frustrated student is at increased risk for school dropout. According to this model, then the negative and antisocial behavior that characterizes some dropouts emerges as a response to academic frustration, but may be maintained and supported through associations with like-minded peers. Thus, selective peer affiliations may contribute to the socialization of antisocial, aggressive behavior in the same way as they contribute to the socialization of negative school values.

Relative and cumulative effects

In light of evidence reviewed thus far, it seems clear that academic, familial, school, and social variables may all play a role in the decision to leave school early. Although the relative contribution of these factors has not been determined in research to date, we may be better able to understand the underpinnings of school dropout if we consider the process to be a gradual, sequential, or cumulative one, resulting from multiple contributing factors (e.g., Farrell, 1990; Finn, 1989). Yet few studies examining the relative contribution of various factors in predicting school dropout have included consideration of social factors, as reviewed below.

The relative impact of social and academic factors has been considered in a model of dropout from higher education proposed by Tinto (1975) and recently applied to the phenomenon of high school dropout (e.g., Pittman, 1991). According to Tinto, the decision to drop out is largely influenced by two constructs: academic integration and social integration. Academic integration refers to the degree to which a student identifies with "those environmental features that are part of the school's academic mission" (Pittman, 1991, p. 209), as reflected in such things as grades, teacher evaluations, etc.; whereas social integration refers to the "student's identity within the school's social structure" (Pittman, 1991, p. 209), as reflected by social involvement, participation, integration, etc. Applying Tinto's framework to higher education in a college setting, Pascarella and colleagues (e.g., Pascarella & Chapman, 1983) have demonstrated that these two factors exhibit what they term "compensatory relationships" in predicting subsequent dropout. Thus, academic difficulties may be more critical to the decision to drop out for students who are not well integrated socially, whereas social difficulties may be more critical for students who are not doing well academically.

Despite the appeal of Tinto's model, few researchers have attempted to explore the relative or interactive influence of both social and academic variables on school dropout within the high school setting. However, results of these studies do support the idea that social and academic factors may interact in important ways in predicting the likelihood of school dropout. Kelly and Pink (1972) considered the combined effect of grade point average and participation in extracurricular activities on early school withdrawal. Although no statistical analyses were presented, results did suggest a combined effect, with reported dropout rates of 2% for students with both high grades and high social participation, 5% for students with high grades and low social participation, 22% for students with high social participation and low grades, and 38% for students with both low grades and low social participation. More recent studies by Cairns et al. (1989) and Kupersmidt and Coie (1990) have used logistic regression analyses to examine the relative contribution of academic and social variables to later dropout, and both found aggressive behavior, in combination with academic indicators, to be a significant predictor of dropout. Specifically, Kupersmidt and Coie found that the probability of dropout was lowest (9.8%) for students who were neither excessively absent from school nor aggressive, and higher for students who were either only excessively absent from school (27%) or only aggressive (45%), but highest (73.7%) for students who were *both* excessively absent *and* highly aggressive. Similarly, Cairns et al. found that students who were viewed by teachers as exhibiting low aggressiveness and average to high academic competence were least likely to drop out of school (7.5%), whereas students who were viewed by teachers as exhibiting both high aggressiveness and low academic competence were the most likely to dropout (64%). In between these extremes were students who were viewed by teachers as low in academic competence but not aggressive (22% dropped out), and students who were viewed as average to high in academic competence but highly aggressive (31.3% dropped out). Taken together, results of these studies underscore the value of exploring the relative and combined influence of social and academic variables on the decision to drop out of school. Future research would benefit from consideration of the independent and overlapping contributions of a wider variety of social as well as academic variables, as well as the relative influence of familial and other variables in this regard.

It may also be important to consider the relative contribution of social factors and characteristics of the school environment to early school withdrawal. As noted, academic motivation tends to decline over the early adolescent years (Eccles & Midgley, 1989, 1990), with a gradual shift from an intrinsic to a more extrinsic motivational orientation by adolescence (Harter, 1981), although not all students show such a decline (Harter, Whitesell, & Kowalski, 1986, as cited in Harter, 1992). Harter (1992) reviews evidence to suggest that these changes in motivational orientation are related to changes in students' self-perceptions of their ability (with students who viewed themselves as increasing in academic competence showing corresponding increases in academic motivation), as well as to perceived changes in the educational environment. In particular, the shift toward a more extrinsic and less intrinsic motivational orientation was associated with perceived changes in educational practices from the elementary to the high school setting, including greater emphasis on academic performance, competence evaluation, and social comparison, all of which served to highlight variations in ability. With regard to the present emphasis on peer influence, we suggest that the perceived increase in the salience of social comparison among students, coupled with the generally competitive nature of the educational enterprise, creates a situation in which classmates are increasingly viewed as adversaries rather than partners in learning. Thus, characteristics of the school environment that foster competition rather than cooperation among students may serve to disenfranchise some students from the larger social milieu of the school and may inadvertently reduce the positive influences of peer support for academic success.

Conclusions

The decision to drop out of school appears to involve an interplay of academic, familial, school, and social factors. The influence of these factors may be additive, with each contributing to the likelihood of dropout, or may vary across individuals, with particular factors being more critical for some students than others. Moreover, the decision to drop out of school does not occur overnight, but likely reflects the cumulative impact of a variety of experiences over an extended period of time. In the present chapter, we have attempted to highlight the role of peers in this process, arguing that peer influences have been relatively neglected within the dropout literature to date. Based on arguments put forward by Ryan and Powelson (1991) that feelings of relatedness are critical to academic functioning and school success, we propose that feelings of relatedness with *peers* may be particularly important during adolescence, and that peers may play a critical role in encouraging students to stay in school or drop out. We do not wish to dismiss the importance of academic, familial, and school factors, which has been clearly documented in the literature extant. Notwithstanding, the purpose of the present review was to highlight yet another factor in the decision to drop out or stay in school – the role of peers.

In support of our arguments, we reviewed research demonstrating that various aspects of students' peer relationships are related to school dropout. First, it seems that early peer rejection during the elementary school years places students at greater risk for later dropout, although the mechanisms underlying this association are unclear. It may be simply that students who are rejected do not feel a sense of relatedness with their peers and, as a result, disengage from school and drop out. However, there are no data at present to suggest that dropouts are rejected at the time that they decide to leave school, although future research should examine this possibility. Nor are there clear data to suggest that dropouts feel socially isolated (although there is suggestion that some of them do). Thus, the hypothesis that continued peer rejection (or perceived isolation) itself constitutes a major factor in the decision to drop out remains a question for future research.

Given evidence that early social difficulties are to some extent related to academic problems, it may be that only socially rejected students who experience academic failure are at increased risk for dropout. We suggest that both academic and social integration are critical for school success. Although few studies have directly examined the "compensatory relationships" that may exist between social and academic integration, results of these studies show that students who experience *both* social and academic failure are at considerably higher risk for later dropout. Thus, future research should attempt a more in-depth examination of the combined effects of academic and social problems on the likelihood of school dropout, as well as the additional influence of familial and school variables.

Other research reviewed in this chapter, however, suggests that the in-

fluence of early peer rejection on subsequent dropout may be more complex. Based on the preceding review, it appears that a more plausible suggestion is that the student who experiences rejection during the early school
years may be at greater risk for developing associations during adolescence
with like-minded classmates who fail to socialize positive academic values,
who discourage active school participation, and who may actively support
or encourage deviant behavior, all of which are factors known to be associated with school dropout. Although this proposed developmental trajectory
must be considered speculative at present, the available supportive evidence suggests that further research on this possibility is warranted.

In considering the influence of peers on the decision to leave school
early, it is important to recognize that there may be multiple pathways that
students can traverse as they negotiate their way to the completion of high
school. Although a high school education seems necessary for survival in
today's society, for some students the decision to leave school early may
be entirely appropriate for their circumstances and may ultimately represent a positive life choice. For most students, however, the decision to
drop out of school may be the lamentable result of a number of factors,
one of which concerns involvement with peers. Given the research reviewed herein, several different pathways can be suggested. For some students, early peer rejection may be one of a number of factors that together
contribute to students' feelings of alienation and isolation within the
school context, and eventually lead them to view school as an undesirable
place to stay. As Finn (1989) suggests in his "participation-identification"
model of school dropout, such students fail to participate actively in
school and classroom activities and fail to "bond" to the school enterprise,
increasing the likelihood of dropping out. For other students, early peer
rejection, coupled with academic difficulties, may lead to a reduced sense
of self-esteem, which in turn leads to increased oppositional behavior, as
suggested in Finn's "frustration-self-esteem" model of school dropout. Together, these factors may enhance the likelihood of identification and affiliation with other aggressive and antisocial students who devalue the importance of school generally and the completion of a high school
education in particular. Similarly, early peer rejection and aggression may
also mark the beginning of a cycle in which students begin to affiliate
with other at-risk students who together disengage from school. These examples represent only three of a potentially larger number of pathways
that may lead a student to drop out of school. If the additional influences
of familial and school variables are also considered, the possible trajectories become even more numerous.

The present review suggests that the likelihood of school dropout depends on a number of factors, some of which reflect characteristics of the student (e.g., academic and familial factors, as implied in an individual deficit model of dropout) and others that reflect characteristics of the social context of the school. We live in a social world, and adolescence marks a period during which the triadic interplay of the individual, the family and the peer group becomes particularly salient. Accordingly, the decision to leave school is perhaps most appropriately viewed, not as the result of deficits in the individual, but as an interaction of student characteristics (academic competence, motivation), familial background and support, and the influence of the peer group with whom one interacts on a daily basis. It becomes imperative, then, that future research consider the relative and compensatory contributions of each of these, in terms of both identifying the causes of school dropout and developing preventive efforts to keep students in school. As one example, we are currently involved in an ongoing partnership with an inner-city high school to explore the multiple factors associated with school dropout. In this prospective, longitudinal study, we began by identifying students who are perceived to be at high risk for school dropout according to teacher-, peer-, and self-reports, and are examining whether these students differ on a variety of factors including academic performance, motivation, familial characteristics, as well as current peer rejection, social isolation, school involvement, and aggressive behavior. As the entire sample is followed over time, we hope to examine the complex interplay of individual and social variables as they predict actual dropout.

Our hope is that by highlighting the influence of peers in determining student motivation to stay in school, we will stimulate further research on the relative impact of multiple factors, including peers, on school dropout. Although our review of this literature has focused primarily on the potentially negative influence of peers, there is another perspective that also must be recognized. Just as peers can encourage early school leaving, or fail to foster positive school values and motivation, it is equally possible for peers to positively influence students to value school and to complete their education. For example, Rebane and Schonert-Reichl (1994) have developed a unique classroom for grade nine students identified by the school staff as being at high risk for subsequent dropout. In this "Bridge" class-room, the teacher has used the principles of a "just community" (e.g., Kohlberg & Higgins, 1987) to develop a democratic classroom aimed at developing a sense of community and collective solidarity among students and between the students and the teacher. Interviews with the students at the end of the first year suggest that this experimental classroom was effective in developing more positive attitudes toward school among these students. The students attributed such changes to several differences they perceived between the "Bridge" classroom and the regular school program, including positive peer and teacher-student relationships, opportunities for democratic decision-making, and opportunities to negotiate their own academic curriculum. This experimental "democratic" classroom had a marked influence on improving school attendance, especially in the "Bridge" classes, which may be a first step toward reducing dropout risk. In the words of one student, "I just hope that I'll still be in this class next year. If it wasn't for Bridge class, I wouldn't be in school." (Rebane & Schonert-Reichl, 1994, p. 3). Consistent with Ryan and Powelson (1991), our hope is that by fostering the development of both autonomy and relatedness, we can improve students' sense of school belonging. And this sense of community and belonging may, for some students, be a key factor in the decision to stay in school. As we begin to appreciate the impact of peers on school dropout, we may be better able to maximize the positive rather than negative influence of peers, especially with regard to school engagement.

Acknowledgment

Preparation of this chapter was supported in part by a Faculty of Education Partnership Research Grant from the University of British Columbia, in conjunction with the British Columbia Ministry of Education to authors Schonert-Reichl and Hymel.

References

Alpert, G., & Dunham, R. (1986). "Keeping academically marginal youths in school" A prediction model. *Youth and Society, 17,* 346–361.

Andersson, B. (1994, February). *School as a setting for development – a Swedish example.* Paper presented at the biennial meeting of the Society for Research on Adolescence, San Diego, CA.

Asher, S. R. (1983). Social competence and peer status: Recent advances and future directions. *Child Development, 54,* 1427–1434.

Asher, S. R., Parkhurst, J. T., Hymel, S., & Williams, G. A. (1990). Peer rejection and loneliness in childhood. In S. R. Asher and J. D. Coie (Eds.), *Peer rejection in childhood* (pp. 253–273). NY: Cambridge University Press.

Barclay, J. R. (1966). Sociometric choices and teacher ratings of school dropout. *Journal of Social Psychology, 4,* 40–45.

Barrington, B. L., & Hendricks, B. (1989). Differentiating characteristics of high school graduates, dropouts, and nongraduates. *Journal of Educational Research, 82,* 309 – 319.

Berndt, T. J. (1982). The features and effects of friendship in early adolescence. *Child Development, 53,* 1447–1460.

Berndt, T. J., & Ladd, G. W. (1989). *Peer relationships in child development.* NY: Wiley.

Berndt, T. J., Laychak, A. E., & Park, K. (1990). Friend's influence on adolescents' academic achievement motivation: An experimental study. *Journal of Educational Psychology, 82,* 664–670.

Biemiller, A., & Meichenbaum, D. (1993). *How to make destreaming work: Towards successful integration.* Unpublished manuscript, University of Toronto.

Blumenfeld, P. C. (1992). Classroom learning and motivation: Clarifying and expanding goal theory. *Journal of Educational Psychology, 84,* 272–281.

Boggiano, A. K., & Katz, P. (1991). Maladaptive achievement patterns in students: The role of teachers' controlling strategies. *Journal of Social Issues, 47,* 35–51.

Boggiano, A. K., Main, D. S., Flink, C., Barrett, M., Silvern, L., & Katz, P. A. (1989). A model of achievement in children: The role of controlling strategies in helplessness and affect. In R. Schwarzer, H. V. van der Ploeg, & C. D. Spielberger (Eds.), *Advances in test anxiety research* (pp. 13–26). Lisse, Netherlands: Swets & Zeitlinger.

Brown, B. B. (1990). Peer groups and peer cultures. In S. S. Feldman & G. R. Elliott (Eds.), *At the threshold: The developing adolescent* (pp. 171–196). Cambridge, MA: Harvard University Press.

Buhrmester, D. (1990). Friendship, interpersonal competence, and adjustment in preadolescence and adolescence. *Child Development, 61,* 1101–1111.

Cairns, R. B., Cairns, B. D., & Neckerman, J. J. (1989). Early school dropout: Configurations and determinants. *Child Development, 60,* 1437–1452.

Catterall, J. S. (1985). *On the social costs of dropping out of school* (CERAS Report No. 86–SEP–3). Stanford, CA: Stanford University, School of Education.

Catterall, J. S. (1987). An intensive group counseling dropout prevention intervention: Some cautions on isolating at-risk adolescents within high schools.*American Educational Research Journal, 24,* 521–540.

Center for Education Statistics (September, 1993). *Dropout Rates in the United States: 1992,* U.S. Department of Education, Office of Educational Research and Improvement.

Claes, M. E. (1992). Friendship and personal adjustment during adolescence. *Journal of Adolescence, 15,* 39–55.

Coie, J. D., & Dodge, K. A. (1983). Continuities and changes in children's social status: A five-year longitudinal study. *Merrill-Palmer Quarterly, 29,* 261–282.

Combs, J., & Cooley, W. W. (1968). Dropouts: In high school and after school. *American Educational Research Journal, 5,* 343–363.

Comfort, C., & Kishor, N. (1994, June). *Relations of self-esteem, alienation and popularity to school dropout: A meta-analysis.* Paper presented at the annual meeting of the Canadian Society for the Study of Education. Calgary, Alberta.

Csikzentmihalyi, M., & Larson, R. (1984). *Being adolescent.* NY: Basic Books.

Crespo, M., & Michelena, J. (1981). Streaming, absenteeism and dropping-out. *Canadian Journal of Education, 6,* 40–55.

deCharms, R. (1968). *Personal causation: The internal affective determinants of behavior.* NY: Academic.

Deci, E. L., & Ryan, R. M. (1985). *Intrinsic motivation and self-determination in human behavior.* NY: Plenum.

Deci, E. L., & Ryan, R. M. (1987). The support of autonomy and the control of behavior. *Journal of Personality and Social Psychology, 53,* 1024–1037.

Deci, E. L., Schwartz, A. J., Sheinman, L., & Ryan, R. M. (1981). An instrument to assess adults' orientations toward control versus autonomy with children: Reflections on intrinsic motivation and perceived competence. *Journal of Educational Psychology, 74,* 642–650.

Delgado-Gaitan, C. (1986). Adolescent peer influence and differential school performance. *Journal of Adolescent Research, 1,* 449–462.

Dishion, T. J. (1990). The family ecology of boys' peer relations in middle childhood. *Child Development, 61,* 874–892.

Dohn, H. (1991). "Drop-out" in the Danish high school (gymnasium): An investigation of psychological, sociological and pedagogical factors. *International Review of Education, 37,* 415–428.

Dryfoos, J. G. (1990). *Adolescents at risk.* NY: Oxford University Press.

Dunham R. G., & Alpert, G. P. (1987). Keeping juvenile delinquents in school: A prediction model. *Adolescence, 22,* 45–57.

Eccles, J. S., McCarthy, K. A., Lord, S. E., Harold, R., Wigfield, A., & Aberbach, A. (1990, April). *The relationship of family factors to self-esteem and teacher-rated adjustment following the transition to junior high school environment.* Paper presented at the annual meeting of the Society for Research on Adolescence, Atlanta, GA.

Eccles, J. S., & Midgley, C. (1989). Stage/environment fit: Developmentally appropriate classrooms for early adolescents. In R. Ames & C. Ames (Eds.) *Research on Motivation in Education* (vol. 3). San Diego, CA: Academic.

Eccles, J. S., & Midgley, C. (1990). Changes in academic motivation and self-perception during early adolescence. In R. Montemayor, G. Adams, & T. P. Gullotta (Eds.), *From Childhood to Adolescence: A transitional period?* (pp. 134–155). Newbury Park: Sage.

Eccles, J. S., Midgley, C., & Adler, T. F. (1984). Grade-related changes in the school environment: Effects on achievement motivation. In J. G. Nicholls (Ed.), *The development of achievement motivation* (pp. 283–331). Greenwich, CT: JAI.

Eccles, J. S., Midgley, C., Wigfield, A., Buchanan, C. M., Reuman, D., Flanagan,

C., & MacIver, D. (1993). Development during adolescence: The impact of stage-environment fit on young adolescents' experiences in schools and in families. *American Psychologist, 48,* 90–101.

Eckert, P. (1989). *Jocks and burnouts: Social categories and identity in the high school.* NY: Teachers College Press, Columbia University.

Ekstrom, R. B., Goertz, M. E., Pollack, J. M., & Rock, D. A. (1986). Who drops out of high school and why? Findings from a national study. *Teachers College Record, 87,* 356–373.

Elliott, D. S., & Voss, H. L. (1974). *Delinquency and dropout.* Lexington, MA: D. C. Heath.

Employment and Immigration Canada (1990). *A National Stay-In-School Initiative.* Ottawa, ONT.: Minister of Supply and Services.

Ensminger, M. E., & Slusarcick, A. L. (1992). Paths to high school graduation or dropout: A longitudinal study of a first-grade cohort. *Sociology of Education, 65,* 95–113.

Erikson, E. H. (1959). *Identity and the life cycle* (revised edition). NY: W. W. Norton.

Fagan, J., & Pabon, E. (1990). Contributions of delinquency and substance use to school dropout among inner-city youth. *Youth and Society, 21,* 306–354.

Farrell, E. (1990). *Hanging in and dropping out: Voices of at-risk high school students.* NY: Teachers College Press.

Farrell, E., Peguero, G., Lindsey, R., & White, R. (1988). "Giving voice to high school students" Pressure and boredom, Ya no what I'm saying'? *American Educational Research Journal, 25,* 489–502.

Fine, M. (1991). *Framing dropouts: Notes on the politics of an urban public high school.* Albany, NY: State University of New York Press.

Finn, J. D. (1989). Withdrawing from school. *Review of Educational Research, 59,* 117–142.

Firestone, W. A., & Rosenblum, S. (1987, April). *First year project: A study of alienation and commitment in five urban districts.* Paper presented at the annual meeting of the American Educational Research Association, Washington, D. C.

Gastright, J. F. (1987). *Profile of students at-risk.* (ERIC Document Reproduction Service, No. 313 465).

Goertz, M. E., Ekstrom, R. B., & Rock, D. (1991). Dropouts, high school: Issues of race and sex. In R. M. Lerner, & J. Brooks-Gunn (Eds.), *Encyclopedia of adolescence,* (vol. 1). NY: Garland.

Goodenow, C. (1993). Classroom belonging among early adolescent students: Relationships to motivation and achievement. *Journal of Early Adolescence, 13,* 21–43.

Green, K. D., Forehand, R., Beck, S. J., & Vosk, B. (1980). An assessment of the relationships among measures of children's social competence and children's academic achievement. *Child Development, 51,* 1149–1156.

Grolnick, W. S., & Ryan, R. M. (1987). Autonomy in children's learning: An experimental and individual difference investigation. *Journal of Personality and Social Psychology, 52,* 890–898.

Gronlund, N., & Holmlund, W. (1958). The value of elementary school sociometric status scores for predicting pupils' adjustment in high school. *Education Administration Supervision, 44,* 225–260.

Hahn, A. (1987). Reaching out to America's dropouts: What to do? *Phi Delta Kappan,* Dec., 256–263.

Harter, S. (1981). A new self-report scale on intrinsic versus extrinsic orientation in the classroom: Motivational and informational components. *Developmental Psychology, 17,* 300–312.

Harter, S. (1983). Developmental perspectives on the self-system. In E. M. Hetherington (Ed.), *Handbook of child psychology. vol. 4, Socialization, personality and social development,* (4th edition, pp. 275–386). NY: Wiley.

Harter, S. (1992). The relationship between perceived competence, affect, and motivational orientation within the classroom: Processes and patterns of change. In A. K. Boggiano & T. W. Pitman (Eds.), *Achievement and motivation: A social-developmental perspective* (pp. 77–114). NY: Cambridge.

Hartup, W. W. (1983). Peer relations. In E. M. Hetherington (Ed.), P. H. Mussen (Series Ed.), *Handbook of child psychology. vol. 4: Socialization, personality, and social development* (pp. 103–196). NY: Wiley.

Hartup, W. W. (1993). Adolescents and their friends. In B. Laursen (Ed.), *Close friendships in adolescence* (pp. 3–22). San Francisco, CA: Jossey-Bass.

Hartup, W. W., & Sancilio, M. F. (1986). Children's friendships. In E. Schopler & G. B. Mesibov (Eds.), *Social behavior in autism* (pp. 61–79). NY: Plenum.

Hinojosa, D., & Miller, L. (1984). Grade level attainment among migrant farm workers in south Texas. *Journal of Education Research, 77,* 346–350.

Howell, F. M., & Frese, W. (1982). Early transition into adult roles: Some antecedents and outcomes. *American Educational Research Journal, 19,* 51–73.

Hymel, S., Zinck, B., & Ditner, E. (1993). Cooperation versus competition in the classroom. *Exceptionality Education Canada, 3,* 103–128.

Kelly, D. H., & Pink, W. T. (1972). Academic failure, social involvement, and high school dropout. *Youth and Society, 4,* 47–59.

Kinderman, T. A. (1993). Natural peer groups as contexts for individual development: The case of children's motivation in school, *Developmental Psychology, 29,* 970–977.

Kinney, D. A. (1993). From nerds to normals: The recovery of identity among adolescents from middle school to high school. *Sociology of Education, 66,* 21–40.

Kohlberg, L., & Higgins, A. (1987). School democracy and social interaction. In W. M. Kurtines & J. L. Gewirtz (Eds.), *Moral development through social interaction* (pp. 102–128). NY: Wiley.

Kuhlen, R., & Collister, E. G. (1952). Sociometric status of sixth and ninth-graders who fail to finish high school. *Educational and Psychological Measurement, 12,* 632–637.

Kupersmidt, J. B., & Coie, J. D. (1990). Preadolescent per status, aggression, and school adjustment as predictors of externalizing problems in adolescence. *Child Development, 61,* 1350–1362.

Kupersmidt, J. B., Coie, J. D., & Dodge, K. A. (1990). The role of poor peer relationships in the development of disorder. In S. R. Asher & J. D. Coie (Eds.), *Peer rejection in childhood* (pp. 274–308). NY: Cambridge.

Ladd, G. W. (1988). Friendship patterns and peer status during early and middle childhood. *Journal of Developmental and Behavioral Pediatrics, 9,* 229–238.

Ladd, G. W. (1990). Having friends, keeping friends, making friends, and being liked by peers in the classroom: Predictors of children's early school adjustment? *Child Development, 61,* 1081–1100.

Larson, R., & Richards, M. (1991). Daily companionship in late childhood and early adolescence: Changing developmental contexts. *Child Development, 62,* 284–300.

Lambert, N. A. (1972). Intellectual and nonintellectual predictors of high school status. *Journal of Scholastic Psychology, 6,* 247–259.

Lloyd, D. N. (1978). Prediction of school failure from third-grade data. *Educational and Psychological Measurement, 38,* 1193–1200.

Marcia, J. E. (1980). Identity and adolescence. In J. Adelson (Ed.), *Handbook of Adolescent Psychology* (pp.145–160). NY: Wiley.

McCaul, E. (1989). Rural public school dropouts: Findings from High School and Beyond. *Research in Rural Education, 6,* 19–24.

McCaul, E. J., Donaldson, G. A., Coadarci, T., & Davis, W. E. (1992). Consequences of dropping out of school: Findings from High School and Beyond. *Journal of Educational Research, 85,* 198–207.

McDougall, P., & Hymel, S. (1995, April). *The transition to middle school: The voice of the consumer.* Paper presented at the annual meeting of the American Educational Research Association, San Francisco, CA.

Mensch. B. S., & Kandel, D. B. (1988). Dropping out of high school and drug involvement. *Sociology of Education, 61,* 95–113.

Ollendick, T. H., Weist, M. D., Borden, M. C., & Greene, R. W. (1992). Sociometric status and academic, behavioral, and psychological adjustment: A five-year longitudinal study. *Journal of Consulting and Clinical Psychology, 60,* 80–87.

O'Sullivan, R. G. (1990). Validating a method to identify at-risk middle school students for participation in a dropout prevention program. *Journal of Early Adolescence, 10,* 209–220.

Parker, J. G., & Asher, S. R. (1987). Peer relations and later personal adjustment: Are low-accepted children at risk? *Psychological Bulletin, 102,* 357–389.

Pascarella, E. T., & Chapman, D. W. (1983). A multi-institutional, path analytic validation of Tinto's model of college withdrawal. *American Educational Research Journal, 20,* 87–102.

Pittman, R. B. (1986). Importance of personal, social factors as potential means for reducing high school dropout rate. *The High School Journal,* 7–13.

Pittman, R. B. (1991). Social factors, enrollment in vocational/technical courses, and high school dropout rates. *Journal of Educational Research, 84,* 288–295.

Pittman, R. B., & Haughwout, P. (1987). Influence of high school size on dropout rate. *Educational Evaluation and Policy Analysis, 9,* 337–343.

Rebane, K., & Schonert-Reichl, K. A. (1994, November). *Fostering a moral community among "at-risk" secondary students: Implication for promoting school success.* Paper presented at the annual meeting of the Association for Moral Education, Banff, Alberta.

Rumberger, R. W. (1983). Dropping out of high school: The influence of race, sex and family background. *American Educational Research Journal, 20,* 199–220.

Rumberger, R. W. (1987). High school dropouts: A review of issues and evidence. *Review of Educational Research, 57,* 101–121.

Ryan, R. M. (1991). The nature of the self in autonomy and relatedness. In G. R. Goethals & J. Strauss (Eds.), *Multidisciplinary perspectives on the self* (pp. 208–238). NY: Springer-Verlag.

Ryan, R. M., Connell, J. P., & Grolnick, W. S. (1992). When achievement is *not* intrinsically motivated: A theory of internalization and self-regulation in school. In A. K. Boggiano & T. S. Pittman (Eds.), *Achievement and motivation: A social-developmental perspective* (pp. 167–188). NY: Cambridge.

Ryan, R. M., & Grolnick, W. S. (1986). Origins and pawns in the classroom: Self-report and projective assessments of individual differences in children's perceptions. *Journal of Personality and Social Psychology, 50,* 550–558.

Ryan, R. M., & Powelson, C. L. (1991). Autonomy and relatedness as fundamental to motivation and education, *Journal of Experimental Education, 60,* 49–66.

Ryan, R. M., Stiller, J. D., & Lynch, J. H. (1994). Representations of relationships to teachers, parents and friends as predictors of academic motivation and self-esteem. *Journal of Early Adolescence, 14,* 226–249.

Seidel, J. F., & Vaughn, S. (1991). Social alienation and the learning disabled school dropout. *Learning Disabilities Research and Practice, 6,* 152–157.

Seltzer, V. C. (1982). *Adolescent social development: Dynamic functional interaction.* Lexington, MA: Lexington Books.

Smith, J. E., Tseng, M. S., & Mink, O. G. (1971). Prediction of school dropouts in Appalachia: Validation of a dropout scale. *Measurement and Evaluation in Guidance, 5,* 31–37.

Statistics Canada (September, 1993), *Leaving School,* Report for Human Resources and Labour Canada.

Steinberg, L., Blinde, P. L., & Chan, K. S. (1984). Dropping out among language minority youth. *Review of Educational Research, 54,* 113–132.

Steinberg, L., Dornbusch, S. M., & Brown, B. B. (1992). Ethnic differences in adolescent achievement: An ecological perspective. *American Psychologist, 47,* 723–729.

Stoup, A. L., & Robins, L. N. (1972). Elementary school predictors of high school dropout among black males. *Sociology of Education, 45,* 212–222.

Tesser, A., Campbell, J., & Smith, M. (1984). Friendship choice and performance: Self-esteem maintenance in children. *Journal of Personality and Social Psychology, 46,* 561–574.

Thomas, R. J. (1954). An empirical study of high school drop-outs in regard to ten possibly related factors. *Journal of Educational Sociology, 28,* 11–18.

Tidwell, R. (1988). Dropouts speak out: Qualitative data on early school departures. *Adolescence, 23,* 939–954.

Tinto, V. (1975). Dropout from higher education: A theoretical synthesis of recent research. *Review of Educational Research, 45,* 89–125.

Toles, R., Schultz, E. M., & Rice, W. K. (1986). A study of variation in dropout rates attributable to effects of high schools. *Metropolitan Education, 1,* 30–38.

Ullmann, C. A. (1957). Teachers, peers and tests as predictors of adjustment. *Journal of Educational Psychology, 48,* 257–267.

Valverde, S. (1987). A comparative study of Hispanic high school dropouts and graduates: Why do some leave school early and some finish? *Education and Urban Society, 19,* 320–329.

Vosk, B., Forehand, R., Parker, J. B., & Rickard, K. (1982). A multimethod comparison of popular and unpopular children. *Developmental Psychology, 18,* 571–575.

Walters, H. E., & Kranzler, G. D. (1970). Early identification of the school dropout. *The School Counselor, 18,* 97–104.

Wehlage, G. G., & Rutter, R. A. (1986). Dropping out: How much do schools contribute to the problem? *Teachers College Record,* 374–392.

White, R. W. (1960). Competence and the psychosexual stages of development. In M. R. Jones (Ed.), *Nebraska Symposium on Motivation* (Vol. 8, pp. 97–141). Lincoln, Nebraska: University of Nebraska Press.

White, R. W. (1963). *Ego and reality in psychoanalytic theory.* NY: International Universities Press.

Williams, S. B. (1987). A comparative study of Black dropouts and Black high school graduates in an urban public school system. *Education and Urban Society, 19,* 311–319.

Zaslow, M. J., & Takanishi, R. (1993). Priorities for research on adolescent development. *American Psychologist, 48,* 185–192.

14 What's "emotional" about social motivation? A comment

Sandra Graham

Reading the chapters for this section of *Social motivation: Understanding children's school adjustment* reminded me of an incident that occurred about ten years ago when my older son was beginning middle school. With some apprehension, I was sitting in the audience at the parent orientation meeting, wondering whether I had made the right decision in allowing him to attend such an academically competitive private school. The headmaster approached the podium, scanned the sea of nervous-looking faces, smiled, and then said: "Relax, parents. We know that there are only two questions your son or daughter will be asking this year: "Where's my pencil and who's my best friend?"".

The insights of this headmaster reflect a common theme underlying the five chapters in this section of Juvonen and Wentzel's edited volume. That theme is that the academic outcomes of children and adolescents are integrally related to their social outcomes. Thus, the motivational psychologist concerned with individual achievement strivings also needs to examine how social relationships and affiliative concerns influence these strivings.

Although the specific outcome examined and scope of the coverage are quite disparate in the various chapters, each in some way is concerned with social influences on individual motivation. Beginning when children first enter school, Birch and Ladd (Chapter 9) describe the young child's relationship with his or her teacher as a determinant of academic adjustment. Relationships characterized by intimacy, nondependency, and the absence of conflict appear to facilitate the young child's adaptation to the academic environment, particularly during the transition from kindergarten to elementary school.

Adopting a goal theory perspective, Wentzel (Chapter 10) considers how prosocial goals (e.g., being cooperative and helpful towards others) and social responsibility goals (e.g., following rules and keeping commit-

346

ments) can be predictors of positive academic outcomes. Students who endorse being kind to others and complying with classroom norms as important pursuits appear to do better in school and to be more accepted by both teachers and peers.

Rather than peer influences in general, Berndt and Keefe (Chapter 11) focus on dyadic relationships, or close friendships, which are characterized by equality and mutual respect. Here the data suggest that students are influenced by both the attitudes of their close friends (e.g., their valuing of academic achievement) as well as the quality of the relationship (e.g., the degree to which it is mutually satisfying), and these influences can have both positive and negative effects on academic adjustment.

In the most empirical of the five chapters, Kindermann, McCollam, and Gibson (Chapter 12) consider how peer networks can be an antecedent to academic engagement of children and adolescents. Even though children's choice of workmates (networks) show much fluctuation over the course of a school year, at least one characteristic of selected group members (i.e., their motivational orientation) remains quite stable and is predictive of an individual's level of academic engagement.

Finally, Hymel, Comfort, Schonert-Reichl, and McDougall (Chapter 13) discuss the influence of peers on a more molar adjustment outcome – school dropout in adolescence. It is evident that children who are rejected by others during the elementary years are at greater risk for early school withdrawal. These same youngsters are likely to affiliate with peers who also have become academically disengaged, thus reinforcing the acceptability of early dropout. In sum, all of the chapters to some degree examine the social context of school adjustment, spanning early childhood to adolescence, including teacher, peer groups, and close friends as the social influence, and addressing motivationally-relevant outcomes ranging from grade-level academic achievement to the decision to complete or withdraw from high school.

There certainly is a precedent for relating achievement concerns to social concerns, inasmuch as the historically dominant theories and theorists of motivation implicitly recognized the importance of relationships with others as determinants of behavior. For example, Freud stated that work (achievement) and love (affiliation) are the two major motivations in life (cf. Weiner, 1992); Maslow (1968) placed the need to belong between survival needs and self-actualization in his needs hierarchy; and motive theorists include affiliative needs with achievement and power needs as the most important human motives (see McClelland, 1985). Recognizing this tradition, Baumeister and Leary (1995) recently reviewed a large body of literature supporting their hypothesis that the need to belong, or the desire for interpersonal attachments, is a fundamental human motivation.

While acknowledging social influences, however, the field of motivation has always been and continues to be dominated by the study of intrapsychic processes and individual achievement strivings. How relationships shape and are shaped by individual behavior, which is more properly the domain of social motivation, has never played a prominent role in the study of personal motivation. By highlighting broad socialization processes, that is, the influences of close friends, peer groups, and teachers on student academic adjustment, the motivation researchers who authored the present chapters have moved our field a step closer to a needed integration of the study of personal motivation and the study of social motivation in achievement settings.

In my own research on African American youth, I have only recently come to recognize the importance of this kind of integration between achievement strivings and social relationships. I began my career by studying academic motivation in African American youth from an intrapsychic perspective. I have always believed that far too many minority children perform poorly in school not because they lack intellectual competencies or even specific learning skills, but because they have low expectation, feel hopeless, deny the importance of effort, or give up in the face of failure. These are prototypical individual motivation concerns. But I now believe that far too many ethnic minority children also perform poorly in school because they have few friends, they adhere to an oppositional peer culture, or they elicit anger from teachers and peers. These also are prototypical motivational concerns, but of a social rather than individual academic nature. What I now try to do is study individual motivation, or achievement strivings, and social motivation, in this case aggression, within the context of a general theoretical framework that applies to both motivational systems.

What do I mean when I talk about social motivation and its importance for understanding individual motivation? If we take as a starting point the present authors' reviews documenting the importance of peers and teachers as socializers of individual achievement strivings, then a social motivational analysis should tell us something about process, or how these social forces influence what individuals do. For example, one might choose to study because she expects that those in her peer work group will be angry if she does not "pull her weight." In this case, the anticipated reactions of others guide the expenditure of effort. Or a popular student might invite a shy classmate for a playdate because he feels sorry for peers who have difficulty making friends. Here the emotions directed toward others influence prosocial responding. These examples intimate that one possible dimension of a social motivational analysis might be to examine whether individual behavior is a response to anticipated emotional reactions of others versus emotions that are elicited about others.

In the remainder of this commentary, I will elaborate on this and other distinctions as I attempt to describe what I see as some of the dimensions of a social motivational analysis. Of course, it is possible that how I conceptualize the "social" in social motivation will be perceived as idiosyncratic. Many of the examples I use to support my analysis are drawn from attribution theory, which reflects my own bias to view the social world through an attributional lens. This bias notwithstanding, my goal is to stimulate the reader to think more about how a social motivational analysis might uncover some common themes that link the chapters in this section of Juvonen and Wentzel's volume.

Dimensions of a social motivational analysis

The importance of affect

A first important dimension of social motivation is that it is likely to have an affective component. Students like or dislike their teachers, they feel accepted or rejected by their classmates, they are sometimes angry at their parents, proud of their teammates, embarrassed by public failure, etc. Students may also attempt to control the feelings that others have about them and to manipulate what others think by means of affective displays. Thus, emotional reactions in social contexts have motivational significance.

Interplay between self-directed and other-directed emotions. Emotions in social contexts may be distinguished as to whether they are self-directed or other-directed. For example, a pupil may feel guilty or ashamed following failure; these are feelings directed toward the self. In the same context, a teacher may experience anger or pity toward the same failing student; these are other-directed feelings. How we feel about ourselves and how others feel about us are often intertwined and may be guided by the same set of underlying principles. This interrelationship has clearly been demonstrated in numerous empirical findings based on attribution theory. Summarizing this work, Weiner (1995) recently provided a theoretical analysis of the relations between the self-directed emotions of guilt and shame and the other-directed emotions of anger and pity based on the causal construct of perceived controllability in self and others. These relations are depicted in Table 14.1.

Consider again a failing student who ascribes her poor outcome to either a controllable cause (e.g., lack of effort) or to one that is uncontrollable (e.g., low aptitude). These particular attributions have quite disparate affective consequences. As Table 14.1 shows, one feels guilty when the causes of personal failure are due to controllable factors. This includes not only lack of effort, but also any other causal ascription subject to one's own volitional influence. Shame, in contrast, is more likely to be experienced when personal failures are due to uncontrollable factors such as low aptitude.

Now consider this same outcome and causal analysis from the perspective of the teacher. Anger and pity are other-directed emotions that follow attributions about controllability and the closely associated judgments about personal responsibility. Perceiving the student's failure as caused by controllable factors leads to inferences that the person is responsible for her outcome. Responsibility implies freedom of choice; the student is free to try hard or not. Attributions to controllability and inferences of responsibility tend to evoke anger (imagine your feelings about the gifted athlete who never comes to practice). On the other hand, attributing someone else's failure to low aptitude elicits perceptions that the outcome was uncontrollable and the person was not responsible. Ascriptions to uncontrollability and inferences of nonresponsibility then often evoke feelings of pity or sympathy (think of your reaction to the retarded child who continually experiences academic difficulty).

Emotional reactions not only reflect causal thinking; they also provide guides for future action. As depicted in Table 14.1, self-directed guilt due

Table 14.1. Self- and other-directed emotions and their behavioral consequences as a function of causal controllability (adapted from Weiner, 1995, p. 265)

	Attribution for failure	
Perspective	Controllable	Uncontrollable
Self-directed		
Emotion	guilt	shame
Behavior	enhanced performance	diminished performance
Other-directed		
Emotion	anger	pity
Behavior	punishment, reprimand	help

to lack of effort often functions as a motivational enhancer; it propels the individual to work harder in the future. In contrast, self-directed shame due to perceived low aptitude may interfere with achievement strivings. Shame often leads to withdrawal or giving up in the face of failure. Other-directed pity and anger (which are the respective complements of shame and guilt – i.e., they have the same causal antecedents) are linked to prosocial versus punitive behavior. Pity instigates approach behavior and the desire to help a needy person, whereas anger begets punishment, reprimand, and the withholding of help.

These emotions and behavioral responses of both student and teacher in response to student failure are likely to be occurring simultaneously and to be mutually reinforcing. For example, anger from a teacher can be a cue to the student that he is not trying hard enough (see Graham, 1984). Assuming that this attributional message is accepted, the student feels guilty and augments her achievement strivings. By the same token, the low aptitude student who feels shame and displays achievement withdrawal is likely to elicit especially high levels of sympathy from the teacher and offers of help. Excessive sympathy and unsolicited social support then further exacerbate the student's perception that "I cannot."

In sum, affective cues from others can influence a variety of thoughts, including self-attributions. Communicated emotions therefore play an important role in self-esteem and individual achievement strivings. This kind of analysis, where emotions play a key role as mediators between causal thought and action, provides one framework for integrating personal motivation (how we feel about ourselves as a determinant of behavior) and social motivation (how others feel about us as a determinant of behavior).

Anticipated versus actual emotions of others. The above examples of emotional reactions in a social context indicate that people respond to the affective displays of others. Now imagine another situation, one that many of us have probably encountered in our role as teachers. A student fails to complete an important term paper on time. Let us further assume that the reason for this outcome was that she went skiing with friends instead of working on the paper. On the day the assignment is due, the student comes to her professor and immediately says: "I was sick over the week-end and couldn't finish my paper. Can I have an extension?" Providing an uncontrollable explanation for achievement failure, and assuming that the explanation is accepted, preempts anger from the teacher. In this case, then, the "spring" of action is the anticipated rather than actual reaction of another. Actual emotions from others are those that are communicated through facial expressions, verbal messages, and bodily or postural gestures. Anticipated emotions, in contrast, are *possible* feeling states that we expect from others based on our understanding of the norms and rules of social interaction. We may behave obediently to ward off others' potential anger, comply with their requests to insure their gratitude, show modesty so as not to arouse their jealousy, etc.

Individuals often respond to the anticipated emotions of others, and the motives underlying their actions provide important dimensions of a social motivational analysis. For example, a number of well-documented impression management strategies from social psychology research are guided by the desire to control others' emotions. That is, individuals often act to create a favorable impression of themselves and thus gain social approval by manipulating how others feel about them (see Snyder & Higgins, 1988).

In attribution research on account giving, we have been able to demonstrate how excuses, confessions (apologies), and other kinds of accounts are used by children and adults to alter perceptions of responsibility and anticipated anger (e.g., Graham, Weiner, & Benesh-Weiner, 1995; Weiner, Graham, Peter, & Zmuidinas, 1991; also see Juvonen, this volume). For example, socially-adjusted children as young as age 6 or 7 and even boys known to have conduct problems recognize that communicating an uncontrollable excuse for breaking an appointment (e.g., "I was sick" versus "I wanted to be with other friends") alters perceptions of responsibility and preempts others' anger.

Emotions, helping, and aggression. Prosocial behavior, including helping and acceptance, and antisocial behavior, including aggression and rejection, are two broad classes of behavior that are a natural context for studying social motivation. A great deal of research documents that the proximal determinants of both helping and aggression are often emotions. Recall the earlier discussion of teacher affective cues. Teachers who think student failures are caused by uncontrollable causes feel pity and want to help. Furthermore, a very reliable finding in the attribution literature on helping behavior is that emotions, more than causal beliefs, are the immediate determinant of helping (see review in Weiner, 1995). Thus, attribution theorists propose a particular set of relations between thinking, feeling, and acting whereby causal ascriptions about another determine affects directed toward those others; and affects, in turn, guide behavior. Emotions therefore provide an important link between thinking and doing.

A similar analysis can be applied to the study of peer aggression. One robust finding in the peer aggression literature is that aggressive children overattribute hostile intent to others in ambiguous situations (see Dodge, 1993). That is, in situations where they experience negative outcomes due to the actions of a peer, such as being pushed while waiting in line, and it is unclear why this outcome occurred, aggressive children are more likely to infer that the peer's actions were initiated "on purpose." Attributions to hostile intent are related to perceptions of controllability and responsibility and therefore elicit anger. Anger, in turn, is an antecedent to aggression. Just as in the study of helping behavior, we have been able to document that emotions, more than causal beliefs, are the direct determinants of aggressive responding (Graham Hudley, & Williams, 1992). Substantively we interpret our findings to mean that when aggressive children reason about the causes of their peer provocation, much of the relationship between what they think (e.g., "He did it on purpose") and the way they intend to behave (e.g., "I am going to get even") can be accounted for how they feel (e.g., "I'm really angry about this"). Our thoughts tell us how to feel and our feelings tell us what to do.

We have also found that normally adjusted children use emotions in this manner to guide their decisions about social acceptance or rejection. For example, Graham and Hoehn (1995) documented that children as young as age 5 or 6 differentially reacted to aggressive versus shy/withdrawn classmates based on perceptions of responsibility, intentionality, and feelings of pity and anger. In this study, excessively shy hypothetical classmates were perceived as not responsible for their social maladjustment, and they elicited pity. Aggressive peers, in contrast, were perceived as responsibly for their behavior, and they evoked anger. Furthermore, independent of causal beliefs, feelings of sympathy elicited (were directly predictive of) social acceptance of the shy student, whereas feelings of anger predicted rejection of the aggressive student. Thoughts guide feelings and feelings guide behavior. That is the motivational sequence that I believe to be quite prevalent in everyday social interaction at school, in the classroom and on the playground, and even among very young children.

Summary. The above sections describe how emotions play a key role in understanding how individual behavior shapes and is shaped by relationships with others (which is my working definition of social motivation). Three functions of emotion in a social motivational analysis have been highlighted. First, emotions from others are sources of information about the self (i.e, our failures are due to low aptitude or lack of effort), and these self-ascriptions then have implications for individual achievement strivings. Second, anticipated emotions of others instigate the desire to control those affective states by means of strategic impression management tactics. And third, our beliefs about the causes of others' behavior determine how we feel about them; and these feeling states, in turn, guide both prosocial (helping, acceptance) and antisocial (aggression, rejection) behavior.

Although none of the chapters in this section of Juvonen and Wentzel's volume is organized around the study of affect, most are implicitly concerned with self-, other- directed, or anticipated emotions. For example, Berndt and Keefe review research on need for social approval as an important motive that helps explain the influence of friends on academic adjustment. Some adolescents may study hard to gain the approval of others (i.e., so that their friends will like them), whereas others may avoid academic effort to achieve acceptance (i.e., so that their friends will not dislike them). I have already suggested that the need for social approval can sometimes instigate impression management tactics that allow an individual to manage the emotions of others. Similarly, Kindermann et al.'s study of the socialization effects of peer networks seems to implicitly draw on anticipated emotional reactions of others as motivational determinants. If affiliating with highly motivated peer networks has a positive effect on student engagement, while associating with disaffected networks has a negative effect, this intimates that the individual's achievement strivings are at least partly influenced by the anticipated reactions of the members of those networks (e.g., "If I don't do my share, they'll be angry at me"). Hymel et al.'s discussion of aggression and peer rejection as antecedents of school dropout fits within an analysis of the motivational significance of emotions directed toward others. The anger that is aroused when others are perceived as responsible for their undesirable behavior is known to elicit the very behaviors that Hymel et al. present as precursors of early school withdrawal. Finally, the chapters that focus on child-teacher relationships as antecedents of academic adjustment (Birch & Ladd and Wentzel) in part may reflect the child's responsiveness to the affective cues of others. Teachers are powerful sources of information that implicate the self, and much of this information is likely to be conveyed by affective displays.

The empirical findings and theoretical literatures reviewed in these chapters are quite amenable to analyses that incorporate emotions from a social motivational perspective. A systematic mapping of the function of emotions in interpersonal contexts might be a useful way to organize these vast and diverse literatures that examine social influences on academic achievement.

Although the focus of my commentary has been on emotions, I want to briefly address two other dimensions of social motivation that I believe uncover other less apparent themes common to the chapters in this section of Juvonen and Wentzel's edited volume.

The targets of social influence

A second dimension of a social motivational analysis applied to the present chapters pertains to the target of social influence. The kinds of social relationships described in this volume occur at the dyadic level, as in close friendships that are examined by Berndt and Keefe, or at the group level, as investigated by Hymel et al., and in the peer network research of Kindermann et al. Relationships may also be egalitarian (i.e., involving peers), or hierarchical, where the source of influence is one's teacher or parents (Birch & Ladd; Wentzel, both this volume).

Children may respond to the anticipated or actual reactions of close friends versus peers versus authority figures like teachers or parents. However, their goals may differ depending on the target of their reactions. This was illustrated in a recent study that my colleagues and I conducted on children and adolescents' use of excuses following a social transgression (Graham et al., 1995). In this study, third through eighth grade boys were asked to imagine that they failed to keep an appointment with a friend or their mother, and the reason for the social transgression was manipulated to be either controllable or uncontrollable. For each of these causes of social misconduct, respondents rated the likelihood that they would reveal that "true" cause. We documented that all children were less likely to disclose controllable than uncontrollable causes – that is, they were more likely to substitute an excuse rather than admit personal responsibility for their social transgression. This is consistent with attributional analyses of excuses as altering perceptions of responsibility away from the self.

More pertinent to the present discussion, other data from this study suggested that the children's goals of account giving may have been different when the target was their mother versus a friend. Before presenting the manipulated causes, we asked respondents to tell us what they would say to their mother or friend if they failed to keep their appointment because they decided to "hang out with (other) friends" (i.e., a controllable reason for social transgression). When the target of the transgression was a peer, children's free responses indicated that the goal of excuse giving was to alter peers' perceptions of responsibility in order to maintain the social bond. Children's answers referred most frequently to concerns about not hurting the other person's feelings and protecting the friendship. For mothers, however, the open ended responses made frequent reference to offering an excuse in order to minimize their parent's anger and reduce the likelihood that they would be punished for their behavior. Thus, an impression management tactic can be guided by either relationship-enhancing goals (promoting social acceptance) or self-protective goals (avoiding punishment from others) depending on who the actor is attempting to influence.

A similar analysis was reported by Juvonen and Murdock (1993) in a study of eighth graders' communications to peers, teachers, and parents about the reasons for their academic failure (also see Juvonen, this volume). Juvonen and Murdock documented that eighth grade students were more likely to tell peers that they failed because of lack of effort. This is consistent with the notion that adolescents often experience a general devaluing of effort, so that having one's peer group perceive you as not trying is likely to promote social acceptance. In contrast, these same respondents were more likely to communicate to teachers and parents that they failed because of low aptitude. Recall that in attributional analyses, perceived low aptitude in others elicits pity, help, and the absence of reprimand (see Table 14.1). Thus, adolescents prefer to tell authority figures such as parents and teachers that they were not responsible for their failure in order to avoid criticism and punishment.

In sum, relationship-enhancing goals and self-protective goals seem to be two important social goals that guide much of children's behavior, including their tactics of impression management. How these different goals interact with the targets of social influence is a relatively unexplored topic in social motivation research.

Proximal versus distal social influence

Yet a third dimension of a social motivational analysis suggested by the present chapters concerns the conditions of the social influence. One condition may be defined as that in which the actor comes in direct contact with another person or group of persons. For example, peer networks and teachers in the classroom both intimate direct contact in the here and now, where the social presence may provide specific cues to the actor about how to behave in a particular situation. If someone in my work group scribbles on my paper and I perceive his behavior as intended, I am likely to respond with hostile retaliation (see Dodge, 1993). Thus the behavior of someone else, as well as how that behavior is interpreted, is an immediate stimulus to act aggressively.

In contrast, there are conditions where others are an antecedent to an actor's behavior, but the social influence is more distal inasmuch as there is no immediate contact or specific cues. For example, if I am studying for an exam rather than going out with friends, and wondering what these friends might be thinking about me, I am responding to possible reactions of others with whom I subsequently will come into contact. Their "presence" is psychological and does not provide specific cues to guide my current actions, although the influence may still be strong and capable of initiating and/or intensifying my behavior.

I suspect that the more molar the adjustment outcome examined, the more likely the social influences will be distal rather than proximal, and the more difficult it will be to predict their effects. Thus, studying broad achievement outcomes such as school withdrawal (Hymel et al.) are probably less amenable to a social motivational analysis. This may partly explain why, as many of the authors note, it has been difficult to determine the conditions under which peer groups have positive versus negative effects on a student's general academic adjustment.

Summary

Table 14.2 summarizes the dimensions of a social motivational analysis as outlined here and a representative research topic associated with each. The underlying message of this analysis is that the study of social influences on school adjustment might benefit from greater attention to (1) the interplay between self-directed and other-directed emotions; (2) how children's strategies for navigating their social lives change with contextual (e.g., target) demands; and (3) specific classes of social and achievement behavior with predictable antecedents rather than global adjustment outcomes. Other dimensions could surely be articulated based on a reading of the chapters in this book, and the choice of these three is not independent of my own theoretical and empirical biases. Nonetheless, I do believe that they provide a common language for discussing a number of themes that permeate all five chapters in this section of Juvonen and Wentzel's volume.

The work of the authors featured here also suggests other fruitful directions for research guided by a social motivational analysis. For exam-

Table 14.2. Dimensions of a social motivational analysis and illustrative research topics

Dimension	Research topic

I. Emotions
   Self-directed vs. other-directed
   Anticipated vs. actual emotions of others
   Emotions as mediators between thoughts and actions
	How feelings of others influence feelings about the self

II. Targets of Social Influence
   Friendship dyads
   Peer groups
   Authority figures
     teachers
     parents
	Goals of impression management (e.g., maintaining the social bond vs. avoiding punishment)

III. Proximal vs distal influences
   Peers and others present in the here and now
   General social influences or those about whom
     one ruminates
	Predicting general vs. specific adjustment outcomes

ple, the study of peer influences on academic outcomes naturally implicates the study of achievement values, yet this has been a relatively neglected topic in motivation research. This may partly reflect measurement difficulty as well as the focus on cognitive (e.g., expectancy) determinants of achievement strivings. Whereas the study of cognitive expectancy variables can be carried out at the intrapsychic level and need not involve others, it is not possible to study values independent of their social context. I believe that understanding values and how they get expressed in the broader context of parent, teacher, and peer influences represents one of the most promising topics for motivation researchers.

Secondly, I talked a great deal in this commentary about the importance of affect in social motivation research, but only a relatively circumscribed set of attributionally-determined emotions was actually discussed. Affective life in the classroom entails a myriad of social emotions including, for example, pride, envy, jealousy, gratitude, embarrassment, and humiliation, to name but a few. Once emotion researchers liberated themselves from exclusive reliance on facial expressions and physiological indices to measure emotion, such feeling states became legitimate topics of study, and many now have growing empirical literatures (see Tangney & Fischer, 1995). Furthermore, when expressed in the classroom, these affects are integrally linked to social rejection and acceptance, and the time therefore seems right to explore their motivation-

al significance within the context of social influences on academic adjustment.

A final note

There was a time when the study of personal motivation, or the "why" of achievement strivings, and the study of social motivation, or the "why" of interpersonal behavior, were independent pursuits. As the chapters in this volume demonstrate, signs of rapprochement are now abundant. This signals a new vitality for the field of motivation, as new areas of inquiry are opened up and new opportunities are found for cross fertilization with other disciplines.

References

Baumeister, R., & Leary, M. (1995). The need to belong: Desire for interpersonal attachments as a fundamental human motivation. *Psychological Bulletin, 117,* 497–529.

Dodge, K. (1993). Social-cognitive mechanisms in the development of conduct disorder and depression. In L. Porter & M. Rosenzweig (Eds.), *Annual review of psychology* (vol. 44, pp. 559–584). Palo Alto, CA.: Annual reviews.

Graham, S. (1984). Communicating sympathy and anger to black and white students: The cognitive (attributional) antecedents of affective cues. *Journal of Personality and Social Psychology, 47,* 40–54.

Graham, S., & Hoehn, S. (1995). Children's understanding of aggression and withdrawal as social stigmas: An attributional analysis. *Child Development, 66,* 1143–1161.

Graham, S., Hudley, C., & Williams, E. (1992). Attributional and emotional determinants of aggression in African American and Latino early adolescents. *Developmental Psychology, 28,* 731–740.

Graham, S., Weiner, B., & Benesh-Weiner, M. (1995). An attributional analysis of the development of excuse giving in aggressive and nonaggressive African American boys. *Developmental Psychology, 31,* 374–284.

Juvonen, J., & Murdock, T. B. (1993). Hoe to promote social approval: The effect of audience and outcome on publically communicated attributions. *Journal of educational Psychology, 85,* 365–376.

McClelland, D. (1985). *Human motivation.* Glenviile, Ill.: Scott, Foresman & Co.

Maslow, A. (1943). A theory of human motivation. *Psychological Review, 50,* 370–396.

Snyder, C., & Higgins, R. (1988). Excuses: Their effective role in the negotiation of reality. *Psychological Bulletin, 104,* 23–35.

Tangney, J., & Fischer, K. (Eds.) (1995). *Self-conscious emotions: The psychology of shame, guilt, embarrassment, and pride.* New York: Guilford Press.

Weiner, B. (1992). *Human motivation: Metaphors, theories, and research.* Newbury Park, CA.: Sage.

Weiner, B. (1995). *Judgments of responsibility: A foundation for a theory of social conduct.* New York: The Guilford Press.

Weiner, B., Graham, S., Peter, O., & Zmuidinas, M. (1991). Public confession and forgiveness. *Journal of Personality, 59,* 281–312.

Author index

Subject index